Theologies in the Old Testament

Theologies in the Old Testament

ERHARD S. GERSTENBERGER

Translated by
John Bowden

FORTRESS PRESS
Minneapolis

THEOLOGIES IN THE OLD TESTAMENT

Fortress Press edition 2002

This edition published under license from T&T Clark Ltd., Edinburgh, Scotland. Authorized English translation of *Theologies im AT. Pluralität und Synkretismus alttestamentlichen Gottesglaubens.* Copyright © W. Kohlhammer GmbH, 2001. Translation copyright © John Bowden, 2002. All rights reserved. Except for brief quotations in critical articles or reviews, no part of this book may be reproduced in any manner without prior written permission from the publisher. Write: Permissions, Augsburg Fortress, Box 1209, Minneapolis, MN 55440.

The publishers gratefully acknowledge the support of Inter Nationes, Bonn, Germany

Cover design: BND
Typesetting: Waverley Typesetters, Galashiels

0-8006-3465-9

Manufactured in the U.S.A.
06 05 04 03 02 1 2 3 4 5 6 7 8 9 10

Contents

Preface

Lectures are meant to give students specialist knowledge, but also to make clear the complexity of the material, the current state of discussion and the lecturer's own position. In my view, wherever at all possible, a discussion of all these points should be part of a lecture series. From the lecturer's point of view the aim is to stimulate – even provoke – the audience to think, to discover new perspectives on the question for themselves and thus to advance the shared, ecumenical quest for a responsible theology that we need today. Thus lectures belong among the oral literary genres: in their own special way they are contextual, and unlike work done at the desk are transitory and provisional.

The study presented here grew out of lectures in Brazil and Germany. I have preserved the style of the spoken word even to the point of retaining phrases which are directly reminiscent of the lecture room. The material has been slightly expanded; bibliographical references have been enlarged, and the structure has been revised. The farewell lecture printed at the end of this volume can also be read as an introduction. Part of the manuscript has been available on the Internet in German since 1997, and many surfers have asked me for the whole text. It appeared in book form in German in 2001 and now, only a year later, appears in English. I would value comments of any kind. My e-mail address is *gersterh@mailer.uni-marburg.de*. I would like to thank those who listened to these lectures, the majority of whom also joined in discussing them when we moved on to the broad field of the Old Testament testimonies of faith, and my student assistants who helped me prepare the manuscript.

Translations of work into other idioms open up new horizons. They make possible trans-cultural dialogues and discussions so very necessary in present times. Talking about ancient theological foundations, we touch upon the ground then laid for our own convictions. The ensuing reflection from different cultural angles will help us to find authentic answers of faith in a torn-apart and confused world. My cordial thanks therefore go to my English translator, Dr John Bowden, and to my British and American publishers, represented by Dr Geoffrey Green and Dr K. C. Hanson, for making possible this opening up of horizons.

Giessen, *15 August 2000*   ERHARD S. GERSTENBERGER

1

Preliminary Remarks

The title of this work, which is based on a series of lectures given in Brazil and Germany, emphasizes the plural: 'Theologies in the Old Testament'. Usually a self-confident singular is used. The reason for my choice is relatively simple. The Old Testament, a collection of many testimonies of faith from around a thousand years of the history of ancient Israel, has no unitary theology, nor can it.[1] The unity of belief in God, which we constantly want to emphasize (or have to emphasize, because we need it in many respects), does not lie in the texts themselves, even in the collected writings or the canon, but solely in our perspective. We use what the Bible says as guidance for our faith and action. We need the biblical texts as a basis for our identity, so they must not be broken up pluralistically. But the Old Testament cannot of itself offer any unitary theological or ethical view, since it is a conglomerate of experiences of faith from very different historical and social situations. Moreover the testimonies are very fragmentary; and they have been edited and manipulated very heavily before coming down to us. More of that shortly. Here at the beginning, and time and again later, I simply want to emphasize that I in no way regard the plurality and the clearly recognizable syncretism of the Old Testament tradition as a disaster, but as an extraordinary stroke of good fortune. The diversity of the theologies opens up for us a view of other peoples, times and ideas of God; it relieves us of any pressure to look anxiously for the one, unhistorical, immutable, absolutely obligatory notion and guideline in the ups and downs of histories and theologies. It frees us for the honest, relaxed assessment of the theological achievement of our spiritual forbears that they deserve, and it makes us capable, in dialogue with them and with the religions of the world, of

---

[1] Thus also Gerhard von Rad, but with another theological aim: '. . . the Old Testament has no centre . . .' (*Old Testament Theology* 2, Edinburgh 1965, 376).

finding and formulating the 'right' faith in God, i.e. a faith to be expressed here and now, for an age which represents a turning point and perhaps an end.

Traditionally, the authors of 'Theologies of the Old Testament' use the singular in the title as if in the many layers of the texts and compositions of the Hebrew Bible with skill and patience one could in fact bring out a single doctrinal structure, a scarlet thread, a theological ground base, a hidden 'centre', etc. But because most modern theologians have been trained in historical criticism and cannot overlook the exciting diversity of the collections of writings, such unification cannot be achieved without violent means. Those who want to depict *the* theology of the Old Testament must declare that one element, one stratum, one idea of their choice is the dominant voice of the great Old Testament chorus of faith. All other elements then have to be made subordinate to it. The arbitrariness with which the theological orchestra is conducted is evident from a mere comparison of the current textbooks.[2] The basic tendency of Christian Old Testament theologies seems to me to begin from the nature of Yahweh as the eternally unchangeable God and to want to make biblical statements transparent to this absolute. In that case the true unity of the theology would be grounded in the transcendence of God. However, this is to overlook that as theologians we do our business in immanence (regardless of how the boundaries of the transcendent may be defined) and have no adequate notions or categories of the depth dimension or the universal dimension of all being. Thus theology in reality has exclusively to do with time-conditioned experiences of faith, statements and systems, in short with ideas of God and not with God in person or essence. Old Testament theology – formulated as orientation for our day – should be content with the contextual images of God in the Hebrew Bible and in a similarly provisional and time-conditioned way venture to make binding statements or statements which nevertheless have only limited validity.[3]

---

[2] Accounts of the debate on the 'theology of the Old Testament' are given e.g. by Gerhard F. Hasel, *Old Testament Theology*, Grand Rapids [2]1975; Manfred Oeming, *Gesamtbiblische Theologien der Gegenwart*, Stuttgart [2]1987; Walter Brueggemann, *Theology of the Old Testament*, Minneapolis 1997, 61–114; Otto Kaiser, *Der Gott des Alten Testaments* 2, Göttingen 1998, 9–28; Ben C. Ollenburger, 'Theology, OT', in John H. Hayes et al. (eds), *Dictionary of Biblical Interpretation* II, 562–8; Werner H. Schmidt, *VF* 43 ,1998/2, 60–75, and, most recently by James Barr, *The Concept of Biblical Theology. An Old Testament Perspective*, London and Minneapolis 1999.

[3] Cf. Erhard S. Gerstenberger, 'Der Realitätsbezug alttestamentlicher Exegese', *VT.S* 36, 1985, 132–44 (reprinted in *ZdZ* 42, 1988, 144–8); id., 'Macht und Ohnmacht Gottes', in Bernard Jendorff and Gerhard Schmalenberg (eds), *Theologische Standorte*, Giessen 1986, 33–50; id., 'Warum und wie predigen wir das Alte Testament?', in Bernard Jendorff and Gerhard Schmalenberg (eds), Giessen 1989, 33–45; id., 'Contextual Theologies in the Old Testament', in Saul M. Olyan and Robert C. Culley (eds), *A Wise and Discerning Mind*, BJSt 325, Providence 2000, 125–37.

Is the designation 'Old Testament'[4] legitimate? My answer would be that I too see this as a very well-established, *Christian* designation, which can have derogatory overtones. However, all the substitute names are equally defective: 'First Testament' can suggest that (as is customary in law) the Second Testament abrogates the First. Tanak (Torah, Neb'iim, Kethubim) gives the impression that we ourselves are Jews. 'Septuagint' leaves out the Hebrew text. Wherever we turn, in any nomenclature we betray our own standpoint and our history. And our action is even more reprehensible: we apply the Old Testament tradition directly to ourselves by reading and exegesis as if it had been made only for Christians. But it has not; we are the intruders. However, taking account of the historical realities of the mission and expansion of Christianity, we can gain access through the world-wide openness which is also characteristic of the traditions of ancient Israel, provided that we refrain from claiming to be sole representatives and acknowledge that other traditions, interpretations and theological formulations have equal rights.[5]

---

[4] Cf. Hedwig Jahnow et al., *Feministische Hermeneutik und Erstes Testament*, Stuttgart 1994, 22f.; Ernst Zenger et al., *Einleitung in das Alte Testament*, Stuttgart 1995, 14ff.

[5] This theological insight is extremely difficult for all of us. It goes strictly against our natural sense of justice. But in recent times more and more theologians have been arguing for the plurality of the theological quest for truth, cf. the writings of Paul Knitter, especially *No Other Name*, Maryknoll and London 1985, and *One Earth. Many Religions. Multifaith Dialogue and Global Response*, Maryknoll 1995; also Reinhold Bernhardt, *Christianity without Absolutes*, London 1994; Dietrich Rössler, *Grundriss der praktischen Theologie*, Berlin [2]1994.

2

Introduction

Before we turn to the diverse theological statements of the Old Testament tradition (from Chapter 4 on) we must clarify a few questions of principle and standpoint. Such self-critical reflection has been practised in Latin American liberation theology. It would benefit any theological and exegetical undertaking, regardless of the context in which it takes place.

2.1 From what context do we consider the Old Testament?

The question of the author's own position is usually criminally ignored in exegetical and theological work in our latitudes. Even experienced and shrewd academic theologians usually act as if there were only one 'objective' standpoint in theology, although they have learned to use the historical-critical method. It is no coincidence that this Archimedean point proves to be their own. Other standpoints, especially those of rival colleagues, can then easily be dismissed as time-conditioned and subject to alien influences.[1] Over against this widespread, fundamental error in theology and the church we must insist that any theological 'approach', including any exegesis of the Old Testament and any 'theology' of the Old Testament based on it, is subject to its own limited, concrete, contextual conditions and therefore cannot be absolutized. At the same time it is an integral feature of the wealth of ecumenical Christian theology and the global concert of all religion that theological truths manifest themselves in connection with specific places, times and societies and can be mutually fruitful. I

---

[1] It has been observed in the discussion that theological 'self-opinionatedness' is perhaps to be explained by the need to take firm positions in the church struggle. I suspect that the reasons lie deeper; they are already given with some biblical traditions which require a claim to absoluteness not only for God but also for the mediated word, etc. (cf. Deut 4–6; Isa 40–44).

would want to make only the following points on the question of stand-point, i.e. on the way in which our theological understanding is conditioned by our time and our society. These are by way of example (and not exhaustive).

- The process of the formation and canonization of the Old Testament tradition was intrinsically a long and difficult one: it covers around a thousand years (its counterpart, the New Testament, was completed in a hundred years at most). Since the completion of the Old Testament (around 200 BCE) again more than two thousand years have passed; in other words, not only has a great deal of water flowed down the Rhine, but all the other rivers of the world, from the Euphrates to the Nile, the Yan-tse-kiang, the Mississippi and the Amazon, have moved a great deal of earth and human beings and have undergone historical changes. We European biblical exegetes live in a specific place on this globe and have barely passed the famous end of the second millennium (which we have established by our Western Christian system of co-ordinates), whereas, e.g. the Jews are counting the year 5761 and the stricter Muslims the year 1421. We can thus say with very great certainty that today we are living in a historical context which in many spheres – cultural, religious and social – is remote from the origins of Old Testament faith.

- But it can be asserted with the same certainty and indeed demonstrated that we are bound to the biblical origins, over the millennia and the 'horrible' historical abyss by an unbroken chain of tradition and interpretation. Uniquely, the beliefs contained in the writings of the Bible have become so influential that today they can still be found in our culture and religion, and also in Jewish and Muslim culture and religion (and perhaps in other areas on the religious map).[2] As Rudolf Augstein once demanded many decades ago, we have at least to grapple with this biblical heritage which has flowed into our culture, which we cannot deny and cannot undo.[3] The Old Testament has had an

---

[2] We have often traced these consequences of the Old Testament in orientation projects for beginners in the Faculty of Protestant Theology in Marburg. The Old Testament often still unconsciously plays a significant role in basic attitudes ('one God', 'one world', definitions of 'good' and 'evil') and in particular ethical decisions (e.g. on questions of secularity, peace, ecology, law, the organization of the state and business) and in cultural and religious matters (e.g. questions of worship, ministry, prophecy, the preaching of the word, gender roles in the cult).

[3] Here of course it is a matter of the critical use of the tradition. How could it be otherwise? For example, Carl Amery argues that Old Testament faith is mainly to blame for the destruction of creation, because in Gen 1:26 human beings are said to be given unbounded dominion over the earth (Carl Amery, *Das Ende der Vorsehung. Die gnadenlosen Folgen des Christentums*, Reinbek

effect on our own system, our own flesh and blood; the original stimuli have changed in many ways, but they are still recognizable. So if we ask critically who we are, we also come upon influences from the ancient Near East, and of course also from the spheres of Persian, Greek and Roman culture. We have an obligation to pay attention to them and to examine their viability for our time. Furthermore, given our insight into human nature, we also have to reckon with anthropological constants. In some respects – despite deep social and cultural revolutions – human beings have always remained what they have been, since the Stone Age and early periods of which we no longer have detailed knowledge. The eternally human characteristics of joy in life and anxiety about life, social responsibility and religious faith, also appear here and there in Old Testament texts. But they are to be found within changed intellectual and social configurations and structures. Individual co-ordinates of the system by which we now live, from which we read, interpret and act, are needed to clarify the special situation.[4]

• The current picture of the world, with niches and folds in which many archaic remains are certainly also hidden, has shifted considerably over recent centuries as compared with that of antiquity. We may remind ourselves that in the biblical and ancient sources the earth is the centre of the universe. In some texts (cf. Ps 8), the human being is without any question the crown of creation, on which all being, all nature, is orientated (e.g. Ps 104 differs). Here, however, the human being is relatively dependent on the wider forces which stand over and beyond what is (only with the Enlightenment did 'Western man' become the absolute maker and ruler).[5] Human beings can live rightly only in harmony with the supremely powerful Being. In modern Western culture all this has been turned quite upside down. The universe has extended to infinity and no longer has any recognizable centre. It makes no difference where the Big Bang took place. Through the achievements of science and technology, human beings are the undisputed sole rulers of Planet Earth and its immediate

---

1974); cf. also Karlheinz Deschner, *Kriminalgeschichte des Christentums* (5 vols), Hamburg 1989ff.; Erhard S. Gerstenberger, '"Macht euch die Erde untertan"', in Cornelius Mayer et al. (eds), *Nach den Anfängen fragen. FS Gerhard Fautzenberg*, Giessen 1994, 235–50.

[4] Cf. similar definitions of position in Erhard S. Gerstenberger, VTSup, 36, Leiden 1985, 132–44; id., *Yahweh the Patriarch*, Minneapolis 1996, XIII-XV.

[5] Cf. Horst Eberhard Richter, *Der Gotteskomplex. Die Geburt und die Krise des Glaubens an die Allmacht des Menschen*, Reinbek 1979.

environment. They have multiplied to an extraordinary degree, and increasingly subjected all the regions of the earth, even the remotest ones, if only to exploit them for tourism. However, in the process, by sheer excess numbers and the most sophisticated intensification of consumerism and pleasure, they are destroying at a breathtaking rate all that is necessary as a basis for life: the air up to the stratosphere, the water down to the deepest depths, the icebergs and primal forests, the surface of the earth and the rivers. The world has truly become different from the world at the time of the Bible (though even then the environment was being destroyed!). So it has to be reinterpreted, and human beings have to be redefined, and in dialogue with us today the ancient texts do not say what they did fifty years ago, let alone three thousand years ago. The human beings who thought they were a floating earth, borne on a wild primal sea, under a bell-like firmament occupied or ruled by gods, inevitably thought differently from we who know ourselves to be on an unimaginably tiny speck of earth, lost in a galaxy called the Milky Way, somewhere on the edge of a universe which has extended so far that we cannot grasp it.

- The changes in science and technology also brought revolutionary transformations in all cultural and social spheres. Granted, there are structural analogies between social organization then and now. We still find family groups, though they are drastically reduced in number and functions; there are still village and suburban communities (cf. the moot halls in Hessen and in the East German Länder), but they no longer have the same significance as justice at the gate in ancient Israel. Of course we know about tribal communities, and perhaps here and there Swabians, Saxons, Friesians and Bavarians regard themselves as tribal groups. To our dismay (or is it?), in all modern forms of society power-struggles are still taking place as they were at the beginning of recorded human history. Above all we know state structures which, while they have been democratized, in their bureaucracy and totalitarian claims have not moved all that far from the absolute monarchies of the ancient Near East. Finally, there is the social formation of the religious or confessional community, which came into being in the late phase of the Old Testament and to the present day lives on in various developments and transformations. Our parochial or personal communities are very much descendants of this new creation of the exilic and post-exilic Jewish communities. So we can see social and religious links with ancient Israel. But in no circumstances can we ignore the tremendous differences. Today the majority of people in our regions live predominantly in large urban cultures, which have their own character and have hardly anything in common with the 'great' cities of antiquity.[6] Indeed it is the megalopolis of the industrial age that sets the tone, with an incredible atomizing of social structures and a pathological transformation of the ideal of autonomy ('to each his or her own centre of the world'), along with the increasing anonymity of the individual, the exclusion of the weak (the old, the young, the handicapped), ongoing discrimination against and oppression of women with a dynamic of its own (the sexist society), and the tribalization of small groups and interest groups, with the fateful exclusion of those who do not belong to them. A Brazilian film, *Raoni*, shows the life of the Xingu Indians in a village in the primal forest. Then the film-makers take the chief and some elders to São Paulo, one of the ugliest and most grandiose monster metropolises in the world. In this documentary film, commentaries are quite superfluous. One need only see the dismay in the eyes and the attitudes of the people from the primal forest to understand that human socialization can take place in diametrically opposed ways. And again we have to note that our environment is by no means irrelevant, if we are entering into the difficult work of interpreting biblical texts and making theological statements.

- Given the general situation of civilization, European men and women have an amazingly ambivalent view of life. On the one hand we enjoy the blessings of a technological and electronic world, which has relieved us of the physical burden of manual labour, has increased productivity at work and raised incomes, has heightened mobility and global consumption, has fantastically extended life-expectancy by comparison with former generations, and has endowed us richly with leisure time in which to become human. On the other hand we feel increasingly strongly the psychological stress of our competitive society, the responsibility for the state of a world that is far beyond our grasp, the exploitation and destruction of the planet which are progressing with ever-increasing rapidity, the excessive competition between peoples, the dangers of man-made catastrophes and war-induced

---

[6] Harvey Cox has discussed the theological significance of the culture of the big city; in the euphoria of the 1960s for him the city was the guarantor of liberation. Cf. Harvey Cox, *The Secular City*, London and New York 1966. Those who know the inhuman slums of today's big cities on some continents will be ashamed of present-day urban freedoms. Be this as it may, as far as I can see, most of the cities of antiquity were like big villages. Metropolises with more than 100,000 inhabitants were rare; at that time they also had the reputation of being especially inhuman (Sodom and Gomorrah; Nineveh; Babylon; Rome); cf. Gernot Wilhelm (ed.), *Die orientalische Stadt*, CDOG 1, Berlin 1997.

poverty, the disappearance of ways of life close to nature, and the dis-integration of structures of solidarity. The result is a widespread loss of orientation which is expressed in increasing apathy about questions of meaning or in an intensive search for new and sometimes exotic patterns of interpretation. Here and there drop-outs find niches in a simple life. The majority seem to be falling in with the changing currents of time and fashion and waiting for some great stroke of good fortune. But minorities are working to shape life responsibly inside and outside the academic world, and are achieving truly great things – usually out of sight – in numerous associations, working parties and action groups.

• In searching for the co-ordinates of our position and then above all for theological statements and in our current situation we must also note the importance of the fact that we live in the privileged, indus-trialized, northern hemisphere of the planet. None of us can choose our place of birth or our parents. We have been put here 'by chance' in this area of the world, and sometimes it is worth wondering: What if I had been born in a slum in Africa, Asia or Latin America? What would my theology look like then? How then would I have had to read the Old Testament and interrogate its statements? Unfortunately this extraordinarily important definition of standpoint has been almost completely suppressed in our theological activity, probably out of shame and a bad conscience. So I would emphasize that we live in an area of the world which has been unilaterally favoured by the history of colonialization and imperial conquest. As a result of the dependent relationships which have grown up in history (and with the use of every available means, even those which scorn humanity – cf. e.g. slavery), it has 'so happened' that millions of poor people in the southern hemisphere have toiled and died for the élite northerners. The economic structures (e.g. world prices for most raw materials and agricultural products) compel the people of the Third and Fourth Worlds to sacrifice themselves for a starvation wage: sugar-cane cutters and other seasonal workers in north-east Brazil; people in the copper mines of Bolivia; children who sew carpets in Pakistan or Morocco; girls who have a chance of survival only in Asian sex tourism, and so on. This is modern slavery, which is readily accepted by Europeans, for all their lip service to universal human dignity and human rights for all. They have had to listen to assured commentaries by European travellers or loan technicians in Third World countries that indifference and recriminations predominate there. Occasional sympathy for the wretched of this world is the most that can be expected. The awareness that we are also involuntary accomplices in causing the world-wide misery has hardly begun to develop anywhere. But we should remember this, since those who live on the side of the prosperous, who know no hunger, who have a doctor and school within reach, and for whom hundred and thousands of wretched people toil to provide them with their beloved tea, coffee, rice and dozens of other pleasures, along with the iron, copper, bauxite, gold and other commodities they need, necessarily read the Bible differently from those on the shadow side of life.

• Finally, in defining our own standpoint we should be aware that, as I have already indicated, we are still trapped in an androcentric and even sexist transition which in part has arisen from biblical roots. I do not believe that male sexism (and that above all is the issue, although of course there are also female counter-movements) can be derived from a patriarchal revolution, the depotentiation of mother figures and the expulsion of goddesses in a grey prehistory. The thesis of an original matriarchate, argued for by Johann Jakob Bachofen in 1861,[7] is historically no longer tenable, and its adoption by committed feminists is more to be understood as the use of antimyths against stupid male claims to priority (e.g. in Gen 2–3).[8] But on the basis of a traditional social distribution of roles (the domestic scene is the realm of women; the outside world the realm of men) and particular developments in early Judaism, i.e. the alleged monotheizing of religion, Jewish-Christian faith has come to be given a penetrating male stamp. We must note that we cannot simply take over as normative and eternal what in reality is very much conditioned by time and society. Many women theologians rightly complain that women have been largely excluded from Christian theology – to the detriment of the *whole* quest for theological truth.[9] The overall picture is dominated by male images (God as king, ruler, father, etc.), male values (battle, subordination, obedience, etc.), male prejudices (woman as sinful, seductive, gossipy, etc.) and male structures (man as

[7] Johann Jacob Bachofen, *Das Mutterrecht*, Frankfurt [5]1984.
[8] For the whole problem see Gerstenberger, *Yahweh the Patriarch* (ch. 2 n. 4); cf. Heide Göttner-Abendroth, *Das Matriarchat I. Geschichte seiner Erforschung*, Stuttgart 1988; Gerda Weiler, *Ich verwerfe im Land die Kriege. Das verborgene Matriarchat im Alten Testament*, Munich 1984; ead, *Das Matriarchat im Alten Testament*, Stuttgart 1989; Elga Sorge, *Religion und Frau*, Stuttgart 1985. The discussion of the matriarchate died down in the 1990s. The problem of the predominantly masculine perspective in the assessment of biblical conditions and present-day structures remains.
[9] Cf. Phyllis Trible, *God and the Rhetoric of Sexuality*, Philadelphia 1978; Marie-Theres Wacker (ed.), *Der Gott der Männer und die Frauen*, Düsseldorf 1987; Hedwig Jahnow et al., *Hermeneutik* (ch. 1 n. 4).

king, priest, elder, prophet). Only exceptionally are these schemes broken through. Even if one presupposes, as I do, that up to the exile women had a strong position inside the home and there set the tone in economic, cultural and religious terms, their exclusion from the public sphere, in which official religion always belonged, had a catastrophic effect. From this we have to conclude for the definition of our standpoint and interpretative work that this imprisonment in patriarchal conceptuality and thought-world must be broken through if we want to achieve a theological discussion between women and men on an equal footing.[10]

The conclusion to be drawn from this is that a critical consideration of the horizon of our own questions and our own context compels us to make certain demands on theological work from our own situation. It is no longer a matter of simply investigating the biblical texts for norms or ideas which are timeless and beyond history, and which could have immediate validity for us. The epistemological, social, economic and gender-specific conditions of our time are so different from those of antiquity that we must first relate any statement of the Bible, however good and relevant, to this reality of ours and discuss it before it can be a stimulus and criterion for our theological decisions. It is impossible, for example, to derive ethical norms from a supposedly 'objective' appearance of God on Sinai around 1200 BCE, which, it is claimed, produced statements that are immutable and valid once and for all. The Decalogue and the appearance at Sinai are late constructions: however, they tell us important things about the community of the sixth/fifth century BCE and its idea of God and ethics. Beyond doubt these notions have stamped us down to the present day, and therefore they are extremely significant for our quest for the right theology and ethics. But they are not an eternally abiding law of 'nature' The recognition that they are time-conditioned frees us to be responsible for a consciously time-conditioned theology and ethics.[11]

2.2 What is the status of the Old Testament writings?

Why do we study the biblical writings at all? That is something that has to be explained. In fact such study, and the pressure to engage in it, has declined

---

[10] Cf. Gerstenberger, *Yahweh the Patriarch* (ch. 2 n. 9).

[11] The discussion of the Decalogue as a basic document of Jewish Christian faith has also proved contextual; cf. e.g. Frank-Lothar Hossfeld, *Der Dekalog*, OBO 45, Fribourg and Göttingen 1982; Christoph Levin, 'Der Dekalog am Sinai', *VT* 35, 1985, 165–91; Paul G. Kuntz, 'Decalogue', in *Dictionary of Biblical Interepration* I, 256–62; Werner H. Schmidt, *Die Zehn Gebote im Rahmen christlicher Ethik*, EdF 281, Darmstadt 1993.

steadily over the last few decades. Even in preaching, which is the traditional core of Protestant pastoral activity, and religious education, at least at a secondary level, it is often thought that we can dispense entirely with the Bible, or at least the Old Testament.

Why do we turn to the Old Testament anyway? In short, because we have to investigate our origin, i.e. compare the influence of the Bible on us with its origin and its tradition, in order to understand ourselves. In addition there is a critical element: those who define themselves only in terms of the present will be able neither to understand nor to correct themselves, and the theological element of 'God' or 'the Unconditioned' or 'the Whole' or our 'Ultimate Concern' (to use Paul Tillich's phrase) encounters us in the biblical testimonies to faith.[12] Thus the study of biblical theology functions for us as illumination and criticism. Moreover, and above all, the Old Testament/Hebrew Bible contains such a mixture of human self-knowledge and such a critique of both society and religion, which is still not exhausted, that time and again repeated reading can only prove life-giving.[13]

What do we find in the Old Testament? First of all we come upon a very complex book which has been in this form for almost two thousand years and has been declared by our own Christian tradition to be the binding basis of faith.[14] In more recent times the number of scholarly voices which want to content themselves with this has increased: they claim that the canon of the Old Testament scriptures has been presented to us by decisions of the early church; it says what we have to believe and therefore it is the written document of our tradition. In its existing final and fixed form it is both the object of our interpretations and the subject from which we receive orientation.[15] However much some representatives of this integralist approach reject the idea, in their canonical theology they are in fact following a fundamentalist path. For they are attempting through the decision of the

---

[12] Cf. Erhard S. Gerstenberger, 'Warum und wie' (ch. 1 n. 3).

[13] Cf. Ernst Bloch, *Atheismus im Christentum*, Frankfurt 1969. Bloch reads the Bible against the grain of official theology and the church and opens one's eyes much as biblical exegesis by the marginalized of the Third World and clear-sighted feminist theologians does.

[14] The decisions were taken early in the history of the church and in the face of strong opposition (e.g. Marcion), which wanted to exclude the Old Testament as the makeshift work of a subordinate, mere creator God, but not the God of the Spirit.

[15] To mention only a selection of names and some works which represent this 'canon-critical' view of things: Brevard S. Childs, *Introduction to the Old Testament as Scripture*, London 1979; Rolf Rendtorff, *Kanon und Theologie. Vorarbeiten zu einer Theologie des Alten Testaments*, Neukirchen-Vluyn 1991; id., *Theologie des Alten Testaments* (2 vols), Neukirchen-Vluyn 1999ff.; Erich Zenger, 'Was wird anders bei kanonischer Psalmenauslegung?', in Friedrich V. Reiterer (ed.), *Ein Gott, eine Offenbarung*, Würzburg 1991, 397–413; Norbert Lohfink, 'Was wird anders bei kanonischer Schriftauslegung?', *JBTh* 3, 1988, 29–53; id., 'Der Psalter und die christliche Meditation: Die Bedeutung der Endredaktion für das Verständnis des Psalters', *BiKi* 47, 1992, 195–200.

early church to prescribe an intrinsically coherent, unitary doctrine as binding, or as a revelation given once and for all and timelessly valid. Thus the canonical approach is dictated by the need for unity and binding force. It is a very short-sighted, unhistorical and self-seeking principle, as it suppresses all that we now know about the origin of the biblical writings and wants a priori to exclude everything that does not fit into our own previously established pattern of thought and faith.

Against 'canonical' interpretation we must object, first, that there is no one uniform coherent canon, however much attempts are made to construct it. And secondly, it is impossible for us to ignore the preliminary stages prior to the completion of the book of books, i.e. individual collections and individual texts, or the thousand-year-old historical depth-dimension of the corpus of scripture that we have received as canon. Thirdly, the present with its structure and questions has to be brought into theological statements.

On the first point: scholars very much want to tie the decision on the canon to a hypothetical Jewish synod of Jamnia which is said to have taken place around 100 CE: however, this is probably a pious invention. What help would it be to establish a day and hour for the collection of the corpus of scripture if the corpus itself is quite disparate? For the Jewish canon itself is not completely undisputed: the canonical status of individual books (like the Song of Songs or Koheleth) was challenged time and again. But it is more important that the Christian churches attached themselves to a completely different corpus (which also was never wholly undisputed) with an essentially *different* internal structure (Pentateuch – Writings – Prophets) and the addition of apocryphal writings. If the formation of the canon is an internal decision on doctrine (a religious group fixes the scriptures which are to be its own criterion), then it is quite impossible to see why the church should want to base itself on the Hebrew collection and not on the Graeco-Jewish Bible exclusively used by the early Christians, the Septuagint (LXX), which existed in parallel.

Furthermore, it is impossible for a canon of writings which has grown up in history over generations to represent a coherent theological doctrinal structure. Even then, the times and situations in which people spoke and sang of God were so different that there simply cannot be any question of a uniform picture of God. And more than two hundred years of research into the Old Testament have exposed many different forms and strata in the texts, each of which needs to be evaluated as an independent testimony of faith at a particular time. It is quite clear that finally redactors of the early Jewish community went into action and brought together the collections which had been handed down, revised them by also incorporating much material of their own and creating whole new consecutive histories (e.g. the Deuteronomic and Chronistic histories), and this must also be taken into account. So certainly – and we owe this recognition to the canonical critics – there was a communal final redaction of considerable theological importance. It must be considered and discussed. But it has no special theological status over and above the earlier collections and revisions or even the later commentators.[16] For each time people are speaking and acting in a particular situation, in specific conditions. And what emerges here is always a contemporary testimony to the faith by which these people lived at this particular time.

If these reflections are right, then in looking for the theologies in the Old Testament we are not so much going behind the written testimonies from the ancient Israelites of those times as attempting as far as possible to recognize the faith that they were practising in their everyday life and social group, in order to be able to enter into conversation with such expressions of faith. We are dealing with faith and life, not the 'paper pope', a term which in some circumstances Martin Luther could apply to the Bible.[17] The faith of individuals and groups is lived out in specific historical and social situations. That is why these situations in life are so important and must be brought out with and behind the texts if we are to have better knowledge of people's beliefs.

If our concern is with the faith of ancient Israel in its contemporary environment and in everyday life, then in our interpretation we cannot want to limit ourselves to the great historical acts, as so-called 'salvation-historical' theology has often done.[18] Life as it was lived in Israel at every social level and in all realms of life is interesting and important to us. Nor is it accessible to us solely through the writings which have come down to us – in their final versions they certainly derive from particular groups and were composed by particular professional classes which of course were expressing their own interests and views. We can also openly resort to the testimony of archaeology: artefacts and inscriptions similarly tell us something about the faith and everyday life of the people of the time. Sometimes these

---

[16] Cf. Erhard S. Gerstenberger, 'Canon Criticism and the Meaning of "Sitz im Leben"', in Gene M. Tucker et al. (eds), *Canon, Theology, and Old Testament Interpretation*, Philadelphia 1988, 20–31.

[17] Luther was much more tied to this point of reality than the later orthodox Lutherans; but cf. the even more impressive attempt by Carlos Mesters to make 'life' the criterion in biblical exegesis: *Vom Leben zur Bibel, von der Bibel zur Leben*, Munich 1983.

[18] Von Rad is an example: his *Old Testament Theology* begins from the history of Yahweh with his people, i.e. it always presupposes 'all Israel' as a sociological entity. The faith of the small groups and the individual is discussed in an appendix, but still under the heading 'Israel's Response', whereas wisdom theology in fact came later in a late work of von Rad's (Gerhard von Rad, *Wisdom in the Old Testament*, London 1972).

sources serve to supplement written sources, but increasingly frequently from archaeological material we make new and independent discoveries about the people whose texts we read or about whom we read texts. Thus the cautious and appropriate interpretation of finds makes an important contribution to knowledge of the theologies of the Old Testament.[19] Moreover the counter-voices to the 'official theology' (which never existed as a uniform world-view) that can be heard in the Old Testament must also have a say.[20]

From what has been said so far it emerges that we may not read the biblical texts as a uniform norm of faith. They did not have that function when they were composed, even where there are demarcations from 'pagans', 'aliens' and the 'godless'. For these demarcations are always made in particular historical conditions and thus can be explained and understood from the situation. That means that they have no absolute claim to validity. Moreover, on closer inspection all texts without exception are deeply woven into the world of the ancient Near East, so it is no longer possible to understand them without in principle bringing in the neighbouring cultures and religions. That is even true of the core statements of the faith of ancient Israel, that 'Yahweh is one and only one' and reserved for Israel (Deut 6:4). Of course it is right that in their historical situation people in Israel should and may have worshipped the God who was exclusively real to them because he was near to them and cared for them. But we cannot conclude either from this exclamation or from the theological explanations of Deutero-Isaiah that Yahweh had an objective uniqueness which was equally clear to all other groups and which they accepted as binding. In a concrete way, the exclusiveness of Yahweh remains the hope and expectation of limited communities who are fond of transferring their claim to others. It is not an objective fact that can be verified, from which we may simply proceed in our theology. There were often monolatrous and indeed monotheistic claims in the history of the ancient Near East.[21] If my view is correct, such claims cannot conceal the fact that in principle any belief in God is limited to a

---

[19] Rightly, archaeology and extra-biblical evidence are increasingly being included in the historical and theological debate, cf. Gösta W. Ahlström, *The History of Ancient Palestine*, Minneapolis and Sheffield 1993; Niels Peter Lemche, *Die Vorgeschichte Israels*, BiE 1, Stuttgart 1996; Volkmar Fritz, *Die Entstehung Israels im 12. und 11. Jahrhundert v.Chr.*, BiE 2, Stuttgart 1996.

[20] Cf. Walter Brueggemann, *Theology* (ch. 1 n. 2), 317–403.

[21] Monolatry is the term used for preferential worship of one God while recognizing other deities for other groups and peoples; monotheism is the claim that there is exclusively one God for all human beings. Cf. Mark S. Smith, *The Early History of God*, San Francisco 1990; Herbert Niehr, *Der höchste Gott*, BZAW 190, Berlin 1990; Othmar Keel, *Monotheismus im Alten Israel und seiner Umwelt*, BiBe 14, Fribourg 1980; Bernhard Lang (ed.), *Der einzige Gott. Die Geburt des biblischen Monotheismus*, Munich 1981; Walter Dietrich and Martin Klopfenstein (eds), *Ein Gott allein?*, OBO 139, Göttingen and Fribourg 1994 (bibliography).

particular group and that equally fundamentally in many Old Testament texts there is an almost unlimited openness to the neighbouring ancient Near Eastern cultures and religions.[22]

2.3 What are our aims in interpreting the ancient traditions?

It is quite legitimate also to reflect on the direction that this work is to take. Unless we do so, unperceived hidden desires will become established and direct exegetical efforts and theological results. One can demonstrate at every turn how that happens, even among the great scholars of our discipline (cf. Julius Wellhausen, Bernhard Duhm, Hermann Gunkel, Gerhard von Rad, etc.). In retrospect it then seems a matter of course that even the great were 'children of their time'.[23] Only for the present does everyone concerned keep asserting how tremendously objective his or her own view is. Here it is significantly better for us to be clear from the start that we are not approaching the Old Testament with absolutely no intentions, but are bringing along quite specific ideas which we shall be reading into the texts.[24]

I have already indicated that we do not read the Old Testament and attempt to discover its theological statements because we are interested in them as museum pieces. The Old Testament is not to be put in a stained-glass window, so that a wondering posterity can file past it. It is not to be laid up in a mausoleum. No, the Old Testament has always been a living book and has been constantly used, read, read aloud, sung and played; it has also entered into graphic art and the literatures of the peoples in a rich and fruitful way, and also into music and drama (and into law, politics, philosophy, ethics, etc.). Be this as it may, the Old Testament is a book which is full of life and which belongs to life; as such we need to pick it up and keep it with us. It will be our dialogue partner in the most difficult questions of life and faith. From this book we hope for clarifications of what is good and evil today, of how God and human beings, world and future, nature and culture are to be defined and treated today. So after duly analysing the

---

[22] I have attempted to describe how demarcations can be constructed in an article entitled 'Andere Sitten – Andere Götter', in Ingo Kottsieper et al. (eds), '*Wer ist wie du, Herr, unter den Göttern?*' *FS Otto Kaiser*, Göttingen 1994, 127–41.

[23] Biographical research into previous generations always produces extraordinarily interesting connections between methods and results of research on the one hand and the places of socialization and socio-cultural conditions on the other; cf. e.g. Rudolf Smend, Jr, *Deutsche Alttestamentler in drei Jahrhunderten*, Göttingen 1989; Werner Klatt, *Hermann Gunkel. Zu seiner Theologie der Religionsgeschichte und zur Entstehung der formgeschichtlichen Methode*, Göttingen 1969; Burke O. Long, *Planting and Reaping Albright. Politics, Ideology and Interpreting the Bible*, University Park, Pennsylvania 1997.

[24] Few scholars see this necessary process of 'eisegesis' as clearly as J. Severino Croatto, *Hermeneutics of Freedom*, Maryknoll 1978.

conditions of faith, arrived at with all the scholarly means at our disposal, our aim is to attempt a conversation with the urgent demands of today. Only in this way, in my view, can we arrive at theological results which are viable in our apocalyptic times.

3

A Sketch of the
Social History of Israel

The five main chapters which follow (on God in the family circle, in the community in which people live, in the tribal alliance, in the monarchy, in the parochial community) all have a sociological orientation. I want to try to demonstrate the typical ideas of God and other theological configurations in each of the social contexts and to demonstrate their consequences for social ethics. Because the social formations have such central importance, I shall sketch them out quite briefly here,[1] as far as Old Testament texts and other evidence allow.

3.1 Family and clan

The long, prehistoric period of humankind was presumably an age of small groups and hordes. The people were hunters and gathers (transitions to an agricultural civilization are known in the Near East only from the tenth century BCE). The ideal size of itinerant groups looking for food must have been between ten and thirty persons. Like groups of primates, this number can easily keep in contact in a kinship horde. In the Near East, larger families with a strict genealogical and patriarchal structure will gradually have emerged from such hordes.[2] According to what we think we know, they must have been characterized by economic, legal and religious autonomy. It is not quite clear how great the authority of the head of the

---

[1] Cf. e.g. Winfried Thiel, *Die soziale Entwicklung Israels in vorstaatlicher Zeit,* Neukirchen-Vluyn 1980; Joseph Henninger, *Die Familie bei den Beduinen,* Leiden 1942; Roland de Vaux, *Ancient Israel,* London and New York 1971; Erhard S. Gerstenberger and Wolfgang Schrage, *Frau und Mann,* Stuttgart 1980. There are bibliographies in Niels Peter Lemche, BiE 1, 96–109; Volkmar Fritz, BiE 2, 121–8; Rainer Albertz, *A History of Israelite Religion* (2 vols), London and Minneapolis 1994, *passim.*

[2] Cf. Darcy Ribeiro, *O Processo civilisatório,* German *Der zivilisatorische Prozess,* ed. and trans. with a postscript by Heinz Rudolf Sonntag, Frankfurt 1983.

family was. On the one hand, in the later Old Testament period he could clearly beat a disobedient son to death with impunity (Prov 19:1); on the other, he had to fear a 'troublesome wife' (Prov 21:9). On the one hand, the herds officially belonged to him, but on the other his wife looked after the business of the household and property (Prov 31:16). Presumably the head of the family did not exercise an absolutist rule, but rather was the representative of the family in the outside world, whereas his wife looked after domestic matters (one has only to think only of the way in which both parents are usually mentioned in connection with the upbringing of children in the Wisdom writings). Archaeologists have recently claimed that the houses in Israelite towns were not particularly large. They provided room for only around five to ten people, and so could not accommodate extended families of up to thirty or fifty people, as was perhaps customary in the country.[3] Possibly, however, individual houses of groups with family links were attached to one another.[4] Be this as it may, throughout the whole of the Old Testament period we have to reckon with a close clan community. As a manageable group focused on acquiring food together, and thus a group which indubitably shared all that it found and acquired, it clearly also developed specifically theological ideas centred on its own ongoing existence and the health, happiness and procreation of its members.[5] One typical expression of this small-group piety is the individual lament to be found in the Hebrew Old Testament and in the environment of Israel.[6]

3.2 Village and small town

The place where people lived (camp, village, settlement) grew quite naturally through the division of families and additions from outside. In Israel a large part of the population always lived in small localities, walled or not, in other words outside the capital or larger administrative centres. The communities which formed locally had different tasks and duties from those predominant in the family. Economic collaboration was often needed, along with the exchange of goods and brides. A system of jurisdiction developed in law. In religion and the cult, common obligations towards the higher powers were recognized, e.g. in the celebration of rites of passage (puberty; resettlement) or the ceremonies of seasonal work in the fields and the harvest.

---

[3] Helga Weippert, *Palästina in vorhellenistischer Zeit*, Munich 1988.
[4] Carol Meyers, 'The Family in Early Israel', in Leo G. Perdue et al. (eds), *Families in Ancient Israel*, Louisville 1996, 13–21; Lawrence E. Stager, 'The Archaeology of the Family in Ancient Israel', *BASOR* 260, 1985, 1–36.
[5] Cf. Karel van der Toorn, *Family Religion in Babylonia, Syria and Israel*, Leiden 1996. The work offers a great wealth of material from the cuneiform literature and the Bible.
[6] Cf. Erhard S. Gerstenberger, *Der bittende Mensch*, Neukirchen-Vluyn 1980.

In the military sphere, protection against enemies had to be organized. A larger group of people requires more social investment and internal structuring.[7] However, as a rule the necessary co-operation was arranged through negotiations among the small groups or by their heads. Everything was still very direct and democratic. The Old Testament has handed down some scenes which show a locality or the representatives of its families in action, as in e.g. Ruth 4:1–12; Deut 21:1–9. Interests which transcended the family or arose out of an accumulation of common efforts had to be looked after by local authorities. And that still happened without any formal administration, simply by discussion among the men at the gate or in the open air, and among the women by the well. The elders of the city or the locality were given the authority to find the right solution in the common interest (cf. e.g. Ezek 14:1; 20:1). Anthropological studies from the present day confirm how a locality functions because everyone knows everyone else.[8] Accordingly the religion of the settled village community was attuned to the protective functions of the deity/ies. This applied to human foes, but also the life-threatening powers of nature, heat, storm, flood and plagues (cf. Joel 1–2; 1 Sam 9, etc.).

3.3 Tribal alliances

The clan and tribal community also developed among nomads and sedentary people by the extension of the larger family. At least fictitiously, the wider tribal alliance is grounded in blood kinship (but that does not prevent the incorporation of alien clans, which in the genealogical fiction then become relatives, e.g. the clans of Hobab or Caleb in Israel; cf. Num 10:29–32; Judg 1:12–16). The formation of clan and tribe overlap. Large clans already exercise the functions of tribes: these consist in the first place in mutual obligations for protection and vengeance, and perhaps also – as in the local community – in religious ties. Places usually had local sanctuaries in their territory; semi-nomadic tribes marked off larger areas of pasture or hunting-

---

[7] Modern group sociology can make a major contribution towards illuminating formative social forces; cf. Mysore Narasimhachar Srinivas, *Village, Caste, Gender and Method*, New Delhi 1998; Michael Hainz, *Dörfliches Sozialleben im Spannungsfeld der Individualisierung*, Bonn 1999; Theo Schiller, *Demokratie und kommunale Praxis*, Frankfurt 1999; Herbert Lindner, *Kirche am Ort*, Stuttgart 2000; Ulrich Beck et al. (eds), *Riskante Freiheiten*, Frankfurt 1994; id. et al. (eds), *Individualisierung und Integration*, Opladen 1997.

[8] A comparison could be made between studies on human settlements in antiquity and the extensive anthropological study especially of the literature of the Indians. E.g. Leo W. Simmons (ed.), *Sun-Chief. The Autobiography of a Hopi Indian*, New Haven 1942. A modern sociological study describes the internal structure of the present-day local community, which is perhaps less homogeneous than that of antiquity: René König, *Grundformen der Gesellschaft. Die Gemeinde*, Hamburg 1958.

grounds from one another. They may have taken portable symbols of deities with them; settled tribes perhaps tended also to visit certain regional sanctuaries. The individual families or clans of a tribe were connected through the exchange of wives. So it is not surprising that according to Winfried Thiel the tribe is predominantly a grouping which presents itself to the outside world, leaving the families and clans quite untouched.[9] However, the collaboration in situations of common interest (e.g. in a defensive war; aggressive wars were hardly waged to gain territory or power) also led to the interpenetration of wisdom and religious customs in all the groups involved. I have already indicated that the families themselves did not develop a completely independent ethic but tended rather to follow general custom. The partially identical descent and language also worked in this direction. By contrast, a tribal jurisdiction is conceivable at least in situations of crisis. As opposed to the locality, where people lived tightly packed together and urgently needed a functioning system of rules, the nomadic tribe, or the tribe dispersed over several localities, was looser in its structure, lighter in its demands, and more sparing in its exchange of goods and services. In the Hebrew tradition, Yahweh, the warrior God, is quite clearly initially a tribal deity; only secondarily does he become the divine supreme head of the nation and also of the family.

3.4 The monarchical state

The biblical sources indicate that the monarchy developed only late in the historical period, and its origin is no longer projected back into grey pre-history (as e.g. in the Sumerian kingship mythology). The biblical tradition mentions quite clearly the motivation for the establishment of the central authority. All the peoples round about already have a monarchical focus; this form of state and government is in fashion because it is more effective than the looser, more chaotic tribal structure. An absolutist central authority which appears as a representative of the deity can develop power more quickly and more thoroughly than any semi-democratic tribal structure. Therefore in Israel (apparently especially in the Philistine wars, but that could be a subsequent labelling) the efforts towards unification and the formation of a state, which were in any case present, were activated as a counter-reaction to strong, small neighbouring countries. Saul's kingship had some initial success; however, it then came to grief internally and externally, and David established in Jerusalem a dynasty which was to last for more than four hundred years.

[9] Winfried Thiel, *Entwicklung* (ch. 3 n. 1), 110.

The springboard, an innovation by comparison with the tribal constitution that preceded it and also the most important factor in the formation
of the religion, was without doubt the centralization of power at one point
in the system. In the local community there had been a body of elders
which looked after the limited common interests and tasks. In the wider
tribal society the system was one of elders or sheikhs, tribal leaders on an
equal footing (similarly in the tribal alliances there was probably a body of
tribal leaders as an *ad hoc* organ of leadership). External pressure from enemies
or rivals necessitated a concentration of the power of command at one
point.[10] The consequence was the building up of a central administration,
economy and army. No central authority can emerge without the strict
centralization of communication, resources and methods of production.
And to safeguard the whole of this new organization of society, the
monarchy urgently needed a central cult for the kingdom in order to
legitimize power. A monarchy can no longer be organized on a kinship
basis. That made divine support for the ruling dynasty all the more necessary,
as is evident e.g. in Judg 9 or 2 Sam 7 (Ps 89).

3.5 Confessional and parochial communities

As is well known, in Israel the age of the monarchy came to an end in
the northern kingdom very early (722 BCE), and in the southern kingdom
135 years later (587 BCE). It was a horrific end. Babylonian troops occupied
Jerusalem, perpetrated a massacre and destroyed city and temple. The
monarchy was abolished.

The socio-political structure that then came into being is remarkable,
perhaps unique. Officially Judah became a province of the Babylonian,
later the Persian, empire and was subject to the administration of the relevant
imperial metropolis. In the occupied tribal land, as in the Diaspora among
those who had been carried off or who had fled, Jewish communities must
have formed, with elders and a clerical leadership (scribes, the descendants
of priests). It is clear from the form of organization that it naturally took
over traditions related to families, clans and tribes. The structures of the
monarchy had indeed been shattered and would have offered competition
to foreign rule. On the other hand, the needs of the new religious
community must have come to the fore. People were under the strict control
of the occupying power. There was not much scope for preserving their
own identity, but the religious scope could be exploited relatively well.

---

[10] Christian Sigrist, *Regulierte Anarchie* (1967), Frankfurt ²1970, describes similar developments by
means of material on African tribes.

Thus, after the exiling of the upper class to Babylon, an organized religious community came into being in local communities which in the Persian period was apparently given its own 'constitution' (Ezra 7; Neh 8). The state of the sources is very difficult – as indeed it is for the research into the social structure of ancient Israel that has already been mentioned. We have no detailed contemporary descriptions of the social structure of society. Only from the indications scattered through the late strata of the Old Testament about individuals, offices (elders in Ezek 20:1), conflicts (cf. Neh 5), projects, religious institutions, etc. can we even approximately reconstruct the structures of the early Jewish community. Some extra-biblical texts come to our aid here, like those which have been excavated in the Jewish garrison on the island of Elephantine in the Nile. These texts attest offerings, marriages and correspondence from the Jewish mercenaries in the service of Persia. They also indicate a degree of religious pluralism. Yahweh appears in the company of deities like Bethel or Anat.

To sum up, it can be said that in our quest for the different theologies of ancient Israel we are not starting from the revealed word of God. Revelation is a category of faith which cannot be examined by a third party. Instead of this, we shall first of all investigate the social conditions in which belief in God was lived out and formulated, and attempt to understand this faith contextually and functionally. Here a priori it seems natural to assume that the different interests of the individual social groupings, often existing side by side, produced group-specific theologies which also existed side by side. This situation might be compared with the way in which a present-day church congregation lives out its faith. Modern families, too, are interested above all in the deities, or divine functions, which help to secure the existence of the family,[11] whereas larger anonymous social structures aim more at protection from enemies, the inner harmony of all members, the fertility of the fields and cattle, just conditions, etc.

---

[11] Cf. Ulrich Schwab, *Familienreligiosität,* Stuttgart 1995; Klaus Peter Jörns, *Die neuen Gesichter Gottes,* Neukirchen-Vluyn 1997.

4

The Deity in the
Circle of Family and Clan

4.1 The horizon of faith

As I remarked, the Israelite family was a community which shared life, dwelling place and belief to an extent and with an intensity that we in our atomized little remnant families can no longer imagine. This fact can best be illustrated in the economic sphere: whether we are thinking of the more semi-nomadic shepherd families or the more settled peasant families, all the members of such a basic group in antiquity formed a fixed community which shared work and possessions. The productive and protective[1] activities of wife and husband, children and elderly in the family association were directed together to the one goal, making possible the survival of the group and thus of each of its individual members from year to year – in times of crisis even from day to day. There was no legal distinction between 'mine' and 'yours', or at most this distinction was rudimentary and limited to specific functional spheres, even if to outsiders the head of the family could appear as the 'owner' of all the family possessions including land, house, women, children, male and female slaves, herds, etc. Internally (as is still the case in similar social situations to the present day), in principle everyone shared common possessions.[2] Jesus significantly says, 'Who, if his son asks for bread, will give him a stone?' (Luke 11:11f.), and in so doing takes up a proverbial rule from the internal morality of the family which was taken for

---

[1] Carol Meyers, 'Procreation, Production, and Protection: Male-Female Balance in Early Israel', *JAAR* 51, 1983, 569–93.
[2] In his classical 'On the Origin of the Family, Private Property and the State', Friedrich Engels probably paid excessive attention to the question of sharing possessions and its gradual dissolution. Be this as it may, how possessions are owned is an important element in the development of civilization alongside other factors from social psychology; cf. Darcy Ribeiro, *Prozess* (ch. 3 n. 2).

granted. The opportunities in life which were exploited together in the family alliance were shared with parents and brothers and sisters. Egotism in the family was always felt to be abnormal. Within the intimate group, in which for better or for worse all were dependent on one another, nothing was sold; there was give and take in the solidarity of kinship. In cases of conflict people normally did not turn to the legal system in society but had disputes and settled them within their own households after the custom of their fathers and mothers, with a traditional assignation of roles. Individuals did not look for a cult which they liked but remained within the framework of the family traditions that had been handed down.[3]

The religious expectations and notions which develop in a community marked by family solidarity[4] can be defined very precisely on the basis of the evidence of the Old Testament but also by analogy with family links, ancient and modern.[5] Any family faith turns and hinges on the prosperity of the small intimate association. This shared faith seeks to protect the life of the intimate group in which individuals know that they are safe, to avert dangers of all kinds, and to increase prosperity and good fortune. The fields in which the battle for survival and the increase of opportunities in life is fought vary. Attention can fall on internal social organization and roles and on the interplay of individual members; on the yield of the family, above all from land and flocks; or on the state of individual members of the family.

---

[3] Of course violations of norms occur time and again in antiquity, but precisely for that reason they are particularly notable and worth handing down: children dispute over inheritance and power (cf. Gen 27; Num 27:1–11; Judg 9:1–6; 2 Sam 13); parents bring a rebellious son before the elders (Deut 21:18–21); men complain about their wives (Num 5:11–31); there is sexual violence (2 Sam 13); draconian punishment is inflicted on a member of the family who goes to join an alien cult (Deut 13:7–12) or he is even rewarded (Judg 6). But all these special cases must be seen and judged in connection with the particular literary tradition, i.e. the social structures presupposed. In part we have pressures and interventions from social formations which take shape beyond the level of the family and change the formerly self-sufficient family association from outside.

[4] This concept rightly plays a central role in present-day social and political discussion. Atomized mass society knows as a supreme value only the independence of the individual; cf. Hans Jonas, *Solidarität in der Krise*, Frankfurt 1996; Ulrich Beck et al. (eds), *Riskante Freiheiten – Individualisierungsprozesse in der Moderne*, Frankfurt 1994. Therefore time and again in church and politics a 'solidarity' is conjured up which can really be rooted only in the family association.

[5] In our time the family is the object of numerous sociological, socio-political and socio-pychological investigations; cf. e.g. Ingeborg Weber-Kellermann, *Die deutsche Familie. Versuch einer Sozialgeschichte,* Frankfurt 1974; Horst Eberhard Richter, *Patient Familie*, Reinbek 1970; Lazlo A. Vaskovics (ed.), *Familienleitbilder und Familienrealitäten*, Opladen 1997; Tilman Allert, *Die Familie: Fallstudien zur Unverwüstlichkeit einer Lebensform*, Berlin 1998; Hansjosef Buchkremer, *Familie im Spannungsfeld globaler Mobilität*, Opladen 2000. In the sphere of the church and theology the family is noted above all from the perspectives of ethics, ecclesiology and practical theology; cf. the informative survey by Siegfried Keil, 'Familie', *TRE* 11, 1983, 1–23, and Karl-Friedrich Daiber, *Religion in Kirche und Gesellschaft*, Stuttgart 1997; Dietrich Rössler *Grundriss der praktischen Theologie*, Berlin ²1994; Henning Schröer, *Kompendium der praktischen Theologie*, Stuttgart 1988. By contrast, the family is hardly noted as an independent, theologically creative social unit.

Externally the relationships with neighbouring groups and superior forces are enormously important; but the forces of nature are also personal entities, often threatening, which are to be taken seriously: one has to grapple with them in religion. However, both inside and outside one's own group, it is always the group that is important: it is meant to exist as an integrated community with the aim of survival. Thus whenever religious expectations are articulated in the family alliance, they refer to a particular group. To put it another way: the theological horizon of the family is governed and limited by its own existence. Its own microcosm is the tranquil central system of reference; everything that exists outside it is related to it. Concerns outside the family, wider interests such as those pursued in a wider association, originally have no place in the small group. Thus even the notions of God and religious expectations in the family which are associated with such more far-reaching efforts are irrelevant. The faith of the family is aimed (really to the present day!) quite simply at prospering where one lives (cf. l^{c}ma^{c}an yīṭab l^{c}kā, Deut 5:16: the reason for the commandment about honouring parents; 4:40; 6:18; 12:25, 28; 22:7; Jer 7:23; 42:6).[6] The most basic needs of life are to be satisfied: that is the first goal of family faith, the first obligation of the family God, who – as we shall see – is fully incorporated into the family alliance.

In fact, when we speak of family religion, this is primarily a theology of the elementary needs of life. In antiquity and well into modern times the family (above all in agricultural society) was the only or the quite pre-eminent social unit which was responsible for food, clothing, dwelling, health and education with all its religious implications. There were other 'providers' only in borderline and exceptional situations. For example, when Elisha offers the Shunammite woman help ('intercession with the king or the army commander') she replies, 'I dwell securely among my people' (2 Kings 4:13) – a model of the independence and self-sufficiency of a farming family with property. Life under one's own 'vine and fig tree' (Micah 4:4; 1 Kings 5:5; Zech 3:10) is an ideal daydream. Any expectation that higher authorities could intervene to help and satisfy basic needs at that time indicates only a catastrophic disruption of the normal order in which the family is responsible for sustaining life. When the Aramaeans besiege Samaria we have this report:

---

[6] The Deuteronomic definition of the purpose of obedience to the will of Yahweh is certainly addressed to the whole religious community of 'Israel', but nevertheless it is founded on the individual family, if not on the individual. It seems to me that with this theological statement Deuteronomy has grasped the old family religion; cf. Rainer Albertz, *History of Israelite Religion* 1 (ch. 3 n. 1), esp. 25–49: 'Religious elements of early small family groups ("patriarchal religion")'.

. . . an ass's head was sold for eighty shekels of silver, and the fourth part of a kab of dove's dung for five shekels of silver. Now as the king of Israel was passing by upon the wall, a woman cried out to him, saying, 'Help, my lord, O king.' And he said, 'If Yahweh will not help you, whence shall I help you?' (2 Kings 6:25–27).

The family themselves are responsible for getting food. Anyone who is not an independent producer must manage with barter. Personal initiative is supported by the deity, theoretically also in times of need. Joseph's policy of state provisioning in Egypt, which also seems to be reflected in reports of the time of Solomon (cf. 'store-cities' , 'granaries', e.g. in 1 Kings 9:19: ʿarē hammiskᵉnōt), probably originally applied more to the provisioning of troops and/or royal preparations for war. They do not put in question the basic principle that the family looks after itself with mattock and plough, flock and garden, spinning wheel and bricks and mortar. And it is not just ancient cultures which have the insight that religious questions arise especially over the problems of satisfying elementary needs. Awareness of the need for human work ('in the sweat of your brow you will eat bread', Gen 3:19), which can bring in the desired yield only if it is not affected by other factors like storms, blight and so on which even today cannot (or cannot yet) be completely manipulated, has not died out. Indeed today this awareness is even on the increase. So for the Israelite period the basic existential question is: How can a family get the basic minimum on which it or its members can exist? Today, as a consequence of the industrial revolution, the analogous basic question in Western European society has largely shifted to the wider society. But in both cases religious components are automatically included in the basic questions and the mechanisms of action which result from them – down to our very clumsy and sometimes painful harvest festivals. Who or what gives and guarantees, encourages and hinders, those forces which make life possible and sustain it, be they the fertility of nature or human productivity and creativity?

With increasing socialization the need to secure food and survival, originally entirely a problem of the smaller family group, drives the questioning and quest for divine forces (sun, rain, wind) beyond the narrow limits of the individual farm or herd. The forces of life are not only related to one's own group. They reign in an area of pastureland or a particular region, or even permeate the whole world. One can and must tackle them – in so far as they are present – in collaboration with one's neighbours. More general problems and greater forces also open up horizons in the elemental sphere. But that does not do away with the first and principal responsibility of the family, namely to satisfy basic needs. As long as the family is the primary community which provides for its members, its cult and faith will also have priority. Thus family theology is primarily the theology of basic human needs, which in higher forms of community may be taken up sporadically or continuously when circumstances change, but can probably never completely lose its reference to the family.[7] And what I have said about ensuring that there is food also applies in other elemental spheres of life, e.g. in the question of abode: 'Unless Yahweh [here quite other designations and forms of God are conceivable in the family circles of ancient Israel] builds the house, their labour is lost who build it' (Ps 127:1; cf. Ps 128:1–4). The dwelling, the roof over one's head, is not a profane matter either. External circumstances are too changeable to be able of themselves to guarantee the ongoing existence of a building or tent (or even a cave). Therefore the friendly higher powers must be invoked to take over the protection of a building. Numerous inscriptions on the beams of old craftsmen's houses in Hessen speak the same language. Deities bless and protect a house and its family.

Neither then nor now, however, was or is a full bread basket and a full spoon, a stable house and decent clothing, enough to safeguard human life. The satisfaction of elementary needs may keep a group of animals capable of functioning. But the animal group has refined instincts which regulate the way in which it functions. Human beings, on the other hand, are deficient in instincts and must first create their own social order. That is perhaps true to a lesser degree of the family, but it is true of it as well, as is indicated by different family systems in the various cultural regions.[8] Over the millennia, particular lines of human socialization, language and customs have formed, in particular for the family sphere.[9] They are best indicated by the key words 'division of labour', 'assignation of roles', 'patriarchal or matriarchal authority', 'solidarity'. The basic principles behind these watchwords are the participation of all members of the family in accordance with their age, gender and capabilities in a shared approach to coping with life and working for commodities, and the differentiation of authority within the family in accordance with the tasks and roles

---

[7] Karel van der Toorn judges the basic situation in Israel differently: state religion and family religion were always in a clinch; finally the former overcame the latter (*Religion* [ch. 3 n. 5], 375f.).

[8] Cultural anthropology has produced many individual studies (cf. the South Sea researcher Bronislaw Malinowski, Reo F. Fortune, Margaret Mead and others) but has hardly undertaken comparative global studies; cf. *TRE* 11, 1–23. This article by Siegfried Keil, 'Familie', concentrates on the present situation of the intimate group; a sociological or anthropological account is not provided for in this mighty Protestant reference work; cf. also René König, *Die Familie der Gegenwart. Ein interkulturellen Vergleich*, Munich 1974; Claude Lévi-Strauss, *The Elementary Structures of Kinship* (1949), Boston 1971, and above, ch. 4 n. 5.

[9] Cf. Darcy Ribeiro, *Prozess* (ch. 3 n. 2).

traditionally assigned. Despite the traditional tasks ('paternal/maternal custom'), the 'should' which is called for here, 'order' within the family, is not taken for granted or endangered. They have an intrinsic religious dimension, quite apart from the concrete structures of authority. This is because for human beings the innate compulsion towards the 'should' is itself mysterious and disconcerting. Specific features of internal structure are possible in individual cases and probable in regions and ethnic groups. But by and large in the ancient Near East, at the family level similar social tendencies (from old to young, from male to female) formed; this is also a sign of the intensive adjustment of customs and usages between the smallest units within the wider society.[10]

The internal relationships and structures of the ancient Near Eastern family which developed over a long period, its social skeleton, proved to be useful and necessary for the cohesion, the co-operation and the survival of the group. Therefore from primal times they were put under the special protection of deities and surrounded with a number of taboos. In the family there is no written law and there are no authorities to which to appeal. Doubt and cases of conflict must be resolved by means of direct exchanges with all those involved. The store of paternal and maternal customs, not only collected in the family but also handed down in the wider cultural context, was the hallowed basis of all internal relationships. It was presumably available in wisdom sayings (proverbs), exemplary narratives, songs and commandments (norms of behaviour), which were inculcated from youth upwards. Their venerable age alone made the basic rules of family relationships divine norms and tasks. In addition, because all the adult members of the family were on a relatively equal footing (indeed originally, despite a differentiation of roles, they were all equally important for the survival of the group), an authority outside or above the family, that of the guardian deity, seems to have been necessary. Thus in the Old Testament the precedence of parents over children seems to be a pre-existing order with a divine sanction (cf. Prov 15:20; 17:25; 19:26; 20:20; 23:25; 28:24; 30:17; Lev 19:3). By contrast, evidence of the superiority of the husband to the wife is much weaker; this superiority seems to have formed only in the course of the more marked patriarchalization of society and the faith community in the late period.[11] The earlier traditions therefore recognize

[10]   Cf. Erich Ebeling, 'Familie', *RLA* III, 9–15; Raphael Patai, *Sex and the Family in the Bible and the Middle East*, Garden City 1959; Carol Meyers, *Discovering Eve*, Oxford 1988; Josef Henninger, *Die Familie bei den heutigen Beduinen Arabiens und seiner Randgebiete*, Leiden 1943; Winfried Thiel, *Entwicklung* (ch. 3 n. 1); Karel van der Toorn, *Religion* (ch. 3 n. 5).

[11]   Cf. Erhard S. Gerstenberger, *Yahweh the Patriarch* (ch. 2 n. 4). The statement '. . . he shall be your lord . . .' (Gen 3:16), addressed to the woman, sounds regretful or malicious, but at all events it describes the inauthentic state.

virtually a predominant place for the wife within the household; this is balanced and exceeded by the public role of the husband as a representative. At any rate the established customs were regarded as divine criterion to which every member of the family was subject. The one who was weaker at the time could appeal to it, as is shown by the examples of the first Tamar (Gen 38:24–6: Judah says of his daughter-in-law, 'She is more righteous than I', v. 26) and also the second (2 Sam 13:12ff.: the raped woman says to the man who rapes her, 'That is not done in Israel', v. 12; 'This wrong in sending me away is far greater than the other which you did to me', v. 16). Almost regretfully or ironically, Gen 3:16 declares the degradation of the woman to be a consequence of this 'fall', which was not intended by God (here male prejudice and self-interest in the status quo are obvious). But this late reflection on the roles of the sexes also shows a suspicious and real subordination of the woman on a false basis, which had a devastating effect on the Jewish-Christian tradition.[12] This should not be overlooked.

As in many cultures, the older brother (and presumably also the older sister) was justified in instructing younger siblings (cf. 1 Sam 20:29, where the reason David gives from staying away from the king's table is the family sacrificial feast in Bethlehem: 'My [older] brother has commanded me himself', i.e. to take part in it). Possibly there are reasons unknown to us in earlier family structures why conversely in the Hebrew tradition surprisingly often the deity prefers the younger or youngest son (cf. Jacob, Joseph, David) to the older children. Other members of the family community (uncles, aunts, unmarried daughters, permanent guests, slaves) took part in the power structure in accordance with their social status, the main criteria of which were kinship to the paterfamilias, age and status by birth.

However, the grades of authority in the family were only one matter which had to be legitimated by the deity. It seems to me that everything that we learn in the Old Testament about interpersonal 'loyalty to the community' (hesed) and 'trustworthiness' (^{e}mūnāh) has its original setting in this family existence, orientated on mutuality. It is the sacred duty of the children, born out of the need to ensure common survival, to fit into the family and from early youth onwards to make the best possible contribution to the prosperity of the group. The adults for their part must fulfil the duty of care.[13] The men and women of ancient Israel or the ancient Near East,

---

[12] Cf. Helen Schüngel-Straumann, *Die Frau am Anfang. Eva und die Folgen,* Freiburg 1989, Münster ²1997.

[13] Cf. Johannes Pedersen, *Israel. Its Life and Culture,* London 1959; Raphael Patai, *Sex and the Family* (ch. 4 n. 10); Roland de Vaux, *Ancient Israel* (ch. 3 n. 1); Erhard S. Gerstenberger and Wolfgang Schrage, *Frau* (ch. 3 n. 1).

each in his or her place, had to observe the commandments of the family deities, and to take on responsibilities which served the common good of the intimate group. Alienation from the family alliance was itself a dishonourable and ungodly action, although apparently masses of 'embittered and impoverished men' went off into the hill country to avoid the slavery for debt which threatened them (1 Sam 22:2). It was also the duty of the young female members of the family to be married for the benefit of their own group, and in extreme situations even to sacrifice themselves for it.[14] It was the duty of young men, for example, to take on the role of providing protection from enemies, including blood vengeance,[15] and also to engage in levirate marriage for dead brothers. In the period that we can survey, the commandment to be faithful in marriage applied in absolute terms only to the wife (a guarantee of legitimate descendants? the warding off of alien claims?), whereas the husband could with impunity make unmarried women pregnant and incorporate them into his family (Deut 22:28f.). In short, the special duties of solidarity can be explained from the existence and the structure of the family in ancient Israel. The deity himself insisted on the preservation of all traditional ordinances; cases of conflict arose in grey areas (e.g. how far does the levirate obligation extend?, cf. Gen 38; Ruth 4; Deut 25:5–10. How does one deal with sons of concubines or prostitutes?, cf. Judg 11:1f.; Deut 21:15–17). Moreover, as we all know, even in our time there are incredible examples of family solidarity and family dispute, in a changed system of social co-ordinates.

Because in the history of ancient Israel visible to us families never existed in isolation from one another but had for millennia developed in contact with other groups, the external relationships of the small group also stood under the sanction of the deities. However much each family built on its own religious ties, for obvious neighbourly reasons it had to respect the existence of other families and their deities. Furthermore, from time immemorial more or less exogamous customs[16] had formed in densely populated areas like the fertile crescent of the ancient Near East. That meant

[14] The most offensive examples, because in our social order they are completely incomprehensible and criminal, are the three narratives about the matriarchs (cf. Irmtraud Fischer, *Die Erzeltern Israels. Feministisch-theologische Studien zu Genesis 12–36*, Berlin 1994), in which even the chief wife must go into the harem of a foreign potentate to save the head of the family: Gen 12:10–20; 20:1–18; 26:7–11, and the story of the sacrifice of the levite's wife in Judg 19. From the beginning this latter narrative is depicted as a crime; not, however, of the husband but of the perverse Gibeonites, who above all violate the law of hospitality.

[15] Lamech's original boast, directed against his own wives, gives a vivid idea of this: Gen 4:23f.: 'Adah and Zillah, hear my voice; you wives of Lamech, hearken to what I say: I have slain a man for wounding me, a young man for striking me. If Cain is avenged sevenfold, truly Lamech seventy-sevenfold.'

[16] Cf. Claude Lévi-Strauss, *Structures* (ch. 4 n. 8).

that marriage to members of one's own household was taboo. That being so, the possibility of getting wives for one's own sons was restricted to the groups with which one was in friendly contact. Families of fathers' brothers living apart were regarded as the first place to look for a daughter-in-law, as father–cousin alliances were regarded as ideal (cf. the search for brides for Isaac and Jacob, Gen 24 and 29; however, the late, fundamental anti-pathy to everything Canaanite probably underlies these narratives!), perhaps because they helped to keep the grandfather's property together. In reality friendly or neutral families were also needed for the practice of exogamous marriage; useful bonds of co-operation with them and mutual support could be established through kinship.[17] The occasionally innocent references to Kenites, Midianites, Hittites, Moabites and Canaanites in the social bond of ancient Israel (they sometimes also run parallel to the condemnation of marriage to foreigners, as in Num 25; Ezra 10; Neh 13; cf. the book of Ruth) clearly indicate group contacts which also extend beyond the boundaries of peoples. Links going beyond the limits of the Israelite tribes – in connection with marriage through robbery or flight? – also seem to have been customary (cf. Judg 21: the Benjaminites, who have no wives, may get brides for themselves in Gilead and Shiloh). What applied to marriage contacts also appears in connection with the exchange of goods and ideas. Despite all the independence of families in the ancient Near East, contacts with foreigners were neither avoidable nor unwanted. They created a limited network of autonomous communities. Each family was dependent on the other groups at individual points; an attempt had to be made also to create favourable positions for one's own family in its external relationships. And in these spheres, too, which represent a certain primal form of 'public', religious concerns, expectations and norms played a role.

We should approach this question from yet another side. Both historical experiences and sociological and anthropological investigations attest sufficiently that from an internal perspective the external world of human groups was generally thought to be alien and hostile. The alien might arouse curiosity and provide opportunities for a wider experience of life and a

---

[17] Judges 14:3 mentions what is preferable to the Philistine woman whom Samson has chosen for himself: 'daughter of your brothers and in my whole people'. Text-critically the phrase is unclear at two points: the Syriac translation has 'Is there no woman in your father's house . . . ?' instead of '. . . among the daughters of your brothers'. The Septuagint reads: 'Is there no wife among your brothers' daughters and among your whole people?' Josef Henninger, *Familie* (ch. 4 n. 10), collects together all the reports of 'marriage to kinsfolk' in Arabia that he has been able to find (54–9). The paternal cousin option is largely preferred, but where it can be included in statistics it makes up only 13.3 per cent; marriage between more remote relatives makes up a further 20.4 per cent (58).

feeling of greater happiness. But basically the alien was felt to be threatening, because it put the pattern of one's own life in question. The alien does
not fit into one's own system but makes demands which end up in the
abandonment or modification of customary paradigms or even submission
to alien customs (cf. the fears of immigrants and asylum-seekers today).
Thus a remarkable prayer, Psalm 120, complains about the liars and
squabblers in Meshek and Kedar 'who hate peace' (v. 6), whereas the
psalmist himself is very peaceful (v. 7). And both patriarchal narratives
(Gen 12 – 36) and experiences of exile (cf. parts of the Deuteronomistic
history and the books of Isaiah, Jeremiah, Ezekiel, etc.) bear witness to
the particularly severe tribulations of the Israelites at that time, when they
lost their land and had to live abroad. The integration of the local alien or
even the alien accepted into the Israelite family was therefore always a
special problem, and also a religious one (cf. Ex 12:43–9; Lev 19:33f.;
25:38–49).[18]

Incalculable dangers lurked outside one's own group. Human and
demonic enemies could bring about sickness and disaster. One had to invoke
one's own guardian deity against them; there was hardly any other possibility
of deliverance. For a family cannot wage wars (contrary to Gen 14:13–16,
where Abraham defeats and drives away an Elamite–Mesopotamian army
with a family host of 318 armed men). Acts of blood vengeance are the
utmost violence that a family can inflict on outsiders (even family feuds and
gang wars at the family level still do not have the character of 'wars'). So
the function of the deity as a guardian against outsiders is an important
sector of family religion.

To sum up: it should be noted that at the family level various religious
dimensions open up – in the struggle for the elementary provision of food,
in the construction and preservation of an internal order which is capable
of functioning, in communication with and the demarcation from other
groups. Religious relations, usually with a particular deity, are very closely
connected with the pattern of life and the communal experiences of the
small group and, embedded in it, the individual member of the group.
Because at that time more than today life was played out in the small family
circle and had its deepest emotional and social roots there, we are to assume
that quite essential forces of religion, impulses for faith, also proceeded
from the family. On the other hand, it is all too clear that this smallest form
of human organization lacked important cultural and civilizing elements.
The family has no writing, no 'law' (because it does not produce any formal,
written law), no 'history' (because the 'great' events of history do not belong

[18] Cf. Erhard S. Gerstenberger, *Leviticus*, OTL, Louisville 1996 *ad loc.*

to it);[19] it has no bureaucratic administration, no taxes, no organized army, no official religion, in short no 'public'.

Such a description of the religious horizon of the family should and must run counter to the constant disparagement of the family in our larger society and the established churches. But it must not give the impression that religion is simply identical with the self-interest of the family alliance, so to speak a projection of the family's superego on to heaven. The Feuerbachian view of religion is quite justified, but completely one-sided.[20] Rather, in all the religious dimensions indicated we must recognize the feature which points beyond the group and self-interest. With its theological notions and constructions, family religion is reacting to the 'claim of the unconditional' (according to Paul Tillich). Wherever we observe religious stirrings in family life they are attempts to relate the family's own life, its own wishes, to the comprehensive realities and forces – God! However, these forces – deities, demons, life, blessing, etc. – are *per se* as impossible to grasp and define as the man/angel/god with whom Jacob fought by the Jabbok (Gen 32:25–32). Yet they keep emerging from the depth of being as it can be experienced, and in the small family group are perceived, addressed and incorporated into every-day life in a particular way. And the activity of the divine is accessible to our analytical concern only in the concrete form of a socially-defined group of people.

4.2 Cultic actions

In the ancient Israelite (ancient Near Eastern) family, how did one encounter the supernatural powers which made themselves evident in such different ways in everyday life and in the structure of the small world? What could one do to ensure the forces from which one could expect support and ward off the evil spirits which wanted to do damage? We should remember that for the people of antiquity the world was 'ensouled' through and through: it was not uniform, dead mass or matter which could be manipulated but was full of personal beings and spheres of competence. That is also the case in the Old Testament. In it there are sufficient references to 'demons', 'spirits', 'deities', personified forces of nature, etc. Human beings were

---

[19] Rainer Albertz has demonstrated that impressively by means of personal names; id., *Persönliche Frömmigkeit und offizielle Religion. Religionsinterner Pluralismus in Israel und Babylon*, Stuttgart 1978; on the other side; cf. the rediscovery of everyday life as a factor in social history in more recent historiography and sociology in e.g. Joachim Mathes et al., *Alltagswissen, Interaktion und gesellschaftliche Wirklichkeit*, Reinbek 1973.

[20] Ludwig Feuerbach, *The Essence of Christianity,* reissued New York 1957.

constantly in contact with them and under their influence; they had to grapple with them particularly in everyday life, and in the group which had to cope with everyday life.[21]

If we are to get a full picture of religious activities in the family sphere, in fact we need to go a long way back and begin with what Böcher calls the everyday 'fear of demons and the repelling of demons'. We disparagingly call such practices 'superstitious', and in our context in fact in some respects they merit this classification. As we saw, in pre-scientific antiquity (using the term without derogatory overtones) the powers had another status. In particular the evil beings caused sickness and misfortune (cf. Ps 91, which mentions as particularly dangerous demons 'the terror of the night', 'the arrows that fly by day', 'the pestilence that stalks in darkness', and 'the destruction that wastes at noonday', vv. 5f.). Amulets, spells, and exclamatory prayers to personal deities helped against such demonic dangers. Amulets are also mentioned in the Old Testament, compare the 'silver crescents' (saḥ⁴ronīm) which were worn by camels (Judg 8:21) or people (Isa 3:18), or the 'magic things' (lᵉḥāšīm) and 'boxes of life' (battē hannepeš, both talismen in Isa 3:20), and also the 'boxes of myrrh' (Song of Songs 8:6), 'little bells' and 'pomegranates' – the latter officially on the high-priestly dress (Ex 28:33f.; 39:24–6).[22] Compare also the mantic, magical, exorcistic practices mentioned in Deut 18:10f.; Ezek 13:1f.; Isa 65:3–5. In short, in ancient Israel the whole of life was permeated by defensive and precautionary measures against stronger, unfriendly powers. Present-day 'superstition' of every kind is only a small fragment of the defensive mechanisms of antiquity. (Moreover Latin American liberation theology is serious about 'popular belief' in all its shadings.)

Generally speaking, however, in the ancient Near East sacrifices and gifts were the usual means of communicating with deities, assuaging them, winning them over or regularly providing for them. As a rule the Old Testament reports which go beyond a mere mention of the actual sacrifice

---

[21] Little attention has been paid by Old Testament scholars to the everyday battle of the ancient Israelites with superhuman forces; cf. Nicolai Nicolsky, *Spuren magischer Formeln in den Psalmen*, BZAW 46, Giessen 1927; Georg Fohrer, 'Prophetie und Magie', *ZAW* 78, 1966, 25–47 (reprinted in BZAW 99, 1967, 242–64); Otto Böcher, *Dämonenfurcht und Dämonenabwehr. Ein Beitrag zur Vorgeschichte der christlichen Taufe*, Stuttgart 1970; Manfred Görg, 'Amulett', *NBL* I, 99; Silvia Schroer, *In Israel gab es Bilder*, OBO 74, Fribourg 1987, 414–19. The discovery of amulets in ancient Israelite cities clarifies the allusions in the Old Testament and can be evaluated despite 'wretched publishing and editing' (Schroer, 414).

[22] In Jerusalem, little inscribed scrolls made of silver leaf have been found 'in a tomb at Ketef Hinnom'. They contain fragments of Deut 7:9 and Num 6:24 and according to Keel and Uehlinger served as amulets for the dead. Both the use of holy scripture and the definition of purpose are new for this period of the seventh to sixth centuries BCE (Othmar Keel and Christoph Uehlinger, *Göttinnen, Götter und Gottessymbole*, Freiburg 1993, 417–22).

reflect developed sacrificial systems which are at a higher level of social organization, i.e. one which presupposes sanctuaries, temples and professional priesthoods. Therefore family cultic actions are far less well attested; they are only indicated in passing or must even be inferred. Sometimes they also appear in connection with larger sanctuaries (cf. Elkanah's annual sacrifice in Shiloh in 1 Sam 1; the family sacrifice with a meal in 1 Sam 2:12–17). But there were quite certainly independent cultic actions in the family in which the head of the family, male or female, or another member of the family, functioned as cultic servants. The announcement of the birth of Samson contains a possible example, even if the narrative is legendary, has undergone a Yahwistic revision and is said to be late. A divine being who was originally identified appears to Manoah's barren wife and announces that she will become pregnant and give birth; he tells her that she must dedicate the boy (Judg 13:2–5). The enigmatic visitor is offered a sacrifice without hesitation (vv. 15–21: a Yahwistic revision; cf. Judg 6:19). Thus the revelation of a numen, a superhuman figure, must be acknowledged and responded to with respect. If the appearances of the numen are manifestly hostile, then for those concerned the only possibility is decisive apotropaic defence, perhaps by exorcism, as happens with Zipporah. By rapidly circumcising the child (or man?) and by the mysterious, efficacious formula 'you are a bridegroom of blood to me' (Ex 4:24–6, with Yahwistic overpainting), she can ward off the deadly attack of a demon. Or there is the possibility of engaging in a direct confrontation with the hostile spirit, struggling with it and possibly forcing it into one's own service. Thus it is reported that the hero[23] Jacob with superhuman strength once wrestled until daybreak with the nocturnal demon who dwelt at a ford over the river Jabbok, but the name of the demon has either not been handed down or perhaps has been retouched. At daybreak the dark companion lost his force. Therefore he quickly ransomed himself from Jacob by giving Jacob the blessing he had asked for (Gen 32:23–33).[24] These two examples, which belong to the bedrock of ancient Israelite tradition, show sufficiently the kind of world of spirits, demons, deities and natural forces in which ancient men and women and their group lived, and how they had to be constantly on guard against malicious beings and to secure the help of beneficent beings. As in the ancient Near East, the high cosmic deities of heaven, earth and the underworld were approached less directly for help (often through

---

[23] Cf. Rüdiger Bartelmus, *Heroentum in Israel und seiner Umwelt*, Zurich 1979.

[24] The section has considerable Elohistic overpainting; the demon remains anonymous, 'a man' (v. 25), a 'God and man' (v. 29). Cf. 'Why do you ask my name?' (v. 30), 'seeing God face to face' (v. 31). Cf. Hermann Gunkel, Gerhard von Rad and Claus Westermann in their Genesis commentaries, *ad loc.*

intermediaries).[25] Endangered men and women in their small groups had first of all and directly to do with lesser numina in the sphere of whose direct realm they lived, and whose world they so to speak shared with them (field, spring, river, hedge, mountain, tree, etc., in the world in which the family lived). The phenomenon of deities related to the family being confined to a particular locality is known from many cultures and religions. That in the course of becoming family deities, the greater deities, e.g. Yahweh, El and Baal in Israel, also took on the functions of personal guardian deities is sufficiently attested by the personal names.[26] Whether there was also veneration of ancestors in ancient Israel – and how widespread it was – is disputed; because of the silence of the biblical sources and the absence so far of archaeological evidence it is impossible to discover more.[27]

Now it is a well-known fact in the study of religion that even small groups not only react *ad hoc* to appearances and dangers from the super-human world but also seek a steadier relationship to the deities who have encountered them. The Jacob story offers an admirable example of the foundation of a more permanent relationship with a deity. On his way to Mesopotamia the fugitive has an unexpected manifestation of God in a dream. The patriarchal saga gives the age-old holy place Bethel as the locality. Jacob sees divine beings ascending into the open heaven on a ladder. The place name is given an etymology: Jacob calls the place where he has spent the night 'house of God', and in this way the later Israelite sanctuary has been given its aetiology of foundation or rededication. It is uncertain how Jacob's 'vow', which now follows, is related to the Bethel story.[28] I see it as a model for the foundation of a new relationship between family and deity

---

[25] Above all the Sumerian and Akkadian literature relating to omens and conjuration offers a wealth of illustrative material for the vital defence against evil powers and the winning over of good powers; cf. Erich Ebeling, *Die akkadischen Gebetsserie 'Handerhebung', von neuem gesammelt und herausgegeben*, Berlin 1953; id., *Aus dem Tagebuch eines assyrischen Zauberpriesters* (1925), Osnabrück 1972; Richard Caplice, *The Accadian Namburbi Texts*, Los Angeles 1974; Werner R. Mayer, *Untersuchungen zur Formensprache der babylonischen 'Gebetsbeschwörungen'*, Rome 1976; Erhard S. Gerstenberger, *Mensch* (ch. 3 n. 6); Stefan M. Maul, *Zukunftsbewältigung*, Mainz 1994.

[26] Cf. Jeaneane D. Fowler, *Theophoric Personal Names in Ancient Hebrew*, JSOTSup 49, Sheffield 1988.

[27] The cult of conjuring up the dead attested in the Old Testament (cf. 1 Sam 28) relates to ancestor worship; really traces of this should have been found in tombs. Cf. Akio Tsukimoto, *Untersuchungen zur Totenpflege im alten Mesopotamien*, AOAT 216, Neukirchen-Vluyn 1985; Hedwige Rouillard and Josef Tropper, 'Vom kanaanäischen Ahnenkult zur Zauberei', *UF* 19, 1987, 235–54; Oswald Loretz, 'Vom kanaanäischen Totenkult zur jüdischen Patriarchen- und Elternehrung', *JARG* 3, 1978, 149–204; Klaas Spronk, *Beatific Afterlife in Ancient Israel and the Ancient Near East*, AOAT 219, Neukirchen-Vluyn 1986; Karel van der Toorn, *Religion* (ch. 3 n. 5), 206–35.

[28] Cf. Erhard Blum, *Die Komposition der Vätergeschichte*, WMANT 57, Neukirchen-Vluyn 1984, 88–98, 168–71; Matthias Köckert, *Vätergott und Väterverheissungen. Eine Auseinandersetzung mit Albrecht Alt und seinen Erben*, Göttingen 1988.

through the patriarch. Jacob says, and the statement takes the form of an oath, so it can be regarded as a kind of basis for a treaty:

> If God will be with me, and will keep me in this way that I go,
> and will give me bread to eat and clothing to wear,
> so that I come again to my father's house in peace,
> then Yahweh shall be my God . . . (Gen 28:20f.).

I shall not investigate here how far the Yahwistic reworking of the section extends. Evidently in its present form the oath is intended as a commitment to Yahweh. The characterization of God as a companion on the way is also strongly reminiscent of the Exodus tradition. But the basic framework of a commitment by both self and God on the first encounter with a friendly numen – after the assurance that elementary needs of life like food and clothing are guaranteed – is certainly older than belief in YHWH and is a model for the foundation of a family relationship with God.[29] In this context Yahweh is also understood as a family deity. The relationship between God and human beings rests on mutuality. The deity is to support the group in the struggle for life, and to this end it receives veneration, doubtless in cultic form. All over the ancient Near East that means working for the deity, providing food, clothing, incense, etc. and possibly exclusive worship of the deity.

The continual, preferred, indeed exclusive bond of a family to just one divine being is a widespread phenomenon in the ancient Near East. Vorländer already demonstrated that on a broad textual basis in his study,[30] especially also by prayer texts of the genre of the Old Testament lamentations. This textual genre is also in fact a prime example of family religion in the Old Testament.[31] Over and above it one can refer back to the personal names[32] and above all the iconography of the roll seals,[33] and as a general background to the archaeological discoveries of small-scale cultic objects (see below). Information about family relationships to particular deities and the 'private', cultic actions which go with them can be derived from all these sources. Scenes of sacrifice, prayer and offerings are richly

---

[29] There are apparently analogous phenomena of family religion in the Sudanese Nuer and Dinka peoples; cf. Edward E. Evans-Pritchard. 'Die Vätergötter der Nuer-Religion', and Gottfried Lienhardt, 'Clan-Gottheiten bei den Dinka', in Christian Sigrist and Rainer Neu (eds), *Ethnologische Texte zum Alten Testament* I, Neukirchen-Vluyn 1989, 173–90.

[30] Hermann Vorländer, *Mein Gott. Die Vorstellung vom persönlichen Gott im Alten Orient und im Alten Testament*, Neukirchen-Vluyn 1975; cf. the further discussion in Karel van der Toorn, *Religion* (ch. 3 n. 5).

[31] Cf. Erhard S. Gerstenberger, *Mensch* (ch. 3 n. 6), and Rainer Albertz, *Frömmigkeit* (ch. 4 n. 19).

[32] Cf. Rainer Albertz, *Frömmigkeit* (ch. 4 n. 19).

[33] Cf. Othmar Keel and Christoph Uehlinger, *Göttinnen* (ch. 4 n. 22).

attested from Egypt to Mesopotamia, Asia Minor to Persia.[34] The location for domestic religious actions is the flat roof, a cleaned space alongside the house, or a cultic niche (cf. Ex 21:6), a separate room, a domestic chapel (cf. Judg 17:5) or an altar in the open air (cf. Judg 6:25).

The classic investigation by Albrecht Alt, 'The God of the Fathers' (1939), had already led into the sphere of the family relationship with God. Alt's observations are still valid at essential points which are of interest to us, though in recent years in some respects justified criticism has also been made of his overall scheme.[35] Amazingly the Old Testament tradition has preserved the scanty reports of a 'patriarchal religion' which preceded belief in Yahweh and then understandably used them for the new cult of Yahweh which arose in the tribal period and the time of the monarchy. It simply brought the deities of Abraham, Isaac and Jacob together and identified each individual deity with the God of Israel known as Yahweh. But in the background there must be the knowledge of particular deities: this notion of individual deities from the early period was hardly invented in the later phases of the history of Israelite faith. Possibly the individual deities of the patriarchs and matriarchs were in fact worshipped under their own names: 'Fear of Isaac', 'Shield of Abraham', 'Mighty One of Jacob' were names used to address[36] the guardian deity of the clan. They could have been preserved in the tradition, but they could also have been newly invented. Generally speaking, the model of a family type of religion in which the head of the family can be the main partner of the deity is sufficiently attested by sources from the Bible and the ancient Near East. We may leave open how important is the bond to the deity ratified exclusively by the patriarch, which was postulated by Albrecht Alt, who himself thought in patriarchal terms. Behind the phrase 'God of my father' there may also be the less androcentric notion that this is the god of the patrilocal family, an idea which can be fitted in better with the forms of the household cult which I shall go on to discuss.[37]

---

[34] The enormous amount of material is at present edited by Karel van der Toorn, *Religion* (ch. 3 n. 5); cf. earlier still Bruno Meissner, *Babylonia and Assyria* (2 vols), Heidelberg 1920 and 1925; Thorkild Jacobsen, *Treasures of Darkness. A History of Mesopotamian Religion*, London 1976; William W. Hallo's articles on Sumerian prayer, hymns, divine letters, etc. in various American journals, and individual studies like Stefan Maul, *Zukunftsbewältigung* (ch. 4 n. 25).

[35] Albrecht Alt, 'The God of the Fathers', in *Essays on Old Testament History and Religion*, New York 1968, 1–100; Bernd-Jörg Diebner, 'Die Götter des Vaters', *DBAT* 9, 1975, 21–51; Matthias Köckert, *Vätergott* (ch. 4 n. 28).

[36] The critics of Alt's scheme point out among other things that it would have been impossible for the names of the 'father gods' to have been handed down over centuries. If that is correct, then the names, which sound authentic, would have to be inventions of a late period.

[37] Van der Toorn (ch. 3 n. 5) decides for a hierarchical interpretation of the family structure, which is indicated above as being 'too democratic' (78).

The pre-Yahwistic stamp of belief in the God of the fathers or the family God becomes clearest in the scene in Gen 31:48–51, which depicts the conclusion of a treaty between a Mesopotamian group and an Israelite–Gileadite group. In demarcating the spheres of interest Laban says,

'May the God of Abraham and the God of Nahor be judges between us . . .' (Gen 31:53).

Here the redactor unifies the two deities by adding a lame 'the God of their father'. By contrast, Jacob, Laban's party in the treaty, does not swear by the God of Abraham but by 'the fear of Jacob, the God of his father' (Gen 31:53b). At the same time this shows us a further specific function of the family deity. He was the external guarantor of his client group. In any breach of the treaty, if possible he had to be handed over to the injured party – presupposing that he was represented by a figure.

The most extensive accounts of cultic practice in the framework of the family centre on what can aptly be called 'household worship' or the 'domestic cult', 'private piety', etc.[38] In the Old Testament, in this connection we hear mainly of an apparently central cultic object, the *tᵉrāpīm*.[39] Rachel steals this object from her father, because she feels that she is being treated unjustly, and the man who has been robbed moves heaven and earth to get his *tᵉrāpīm* back (Gen 31:19, 30–5). Michal, Saul's daughter, treats the cultic figure disrespectfully to enable her husband, David, to escape the king's minions who are pursuing him (1 Sam 19:13). And the mother of a certain Micah in the territory of Ephraim has a 'molten image', 'ephod' and 'teraphim' made from a hoard of silver which is stolen and then cursed; it is lodged in the domestic chapel on his property (Judg 17:1–5). Thus the object of family worship is directly mentioned here and there in the Old Testament. However, we have no detailed knowledge of how worship was performed. In Ex 21:6, though, business is concluded before the 'God' (*ᵉlōhīm*) of a household: a man enslaved for debt, who may remain with his creditor for an indeterminate period, has his ear bored through at the

---

[38] The notion of religious family festivals has long been in vogue; it is kept alive by allusions in the Bible (cf. 1 Sam 20:6: the 'annual sacrificial feast' for David's family; Josh 24:15: 'But I and my house will serve Yahweh'). In his translation of the Bible Luther occasionally speaks of 'household gods' or 'household god', perhaps basing himself on Protestant household devotions (cf. Gen 31:19, 34; Judg 17:5; 18:17; 1 Sam 19:13). The 'household cult' has then consistently been introduced into the Old Testament discussion over recent decades; cf. Herman Vorländer, *Mein Gott* (ch. 4 n. 70); Erhard S. Gerstenberger, *Mensch* (ch. 3 n. 6); Helga Weippert, *Palästina* (ch. 3 n. 3).

[39] The etymology of the word is disputed; cf. the Hebrew lexicons. The derivation from the Hittite *tarpis*, demon, seems clearest to me; cf. Hedwige Rouillard and Josef Tropper, '*TRPYM*', *VT* 37, 1987, 340–61; Silvia Schroer, *Israel* (ch. 4 n. 21).

doorpost, where the statuette of the deity also seems to live.[40] We may conclude from this that figurines of gods and goddess had a special place in the house. Consequently they also had to be looked after there. From the contacts between the housewife and the cultic object, the *tᵉrāpīm*, which are attested in several texts, and the general distribution of the tasks of the family between an internal sphere and an external sphere, the first of which was assigned above all to the wife, I would venture to conclude that the household cult was women's business, at least in the early period of Israel. One could then go on to assume that the cultic figure was provided with food, for which the wife was responsible: corn, oil, fruit, vegetables, in short what was later offered in part in the 'food offering' (*minḥāh*, Lev 2). Probably the husband was responsible for the bloody sacrifice of animals from the flock or game which had been caught, because apparently it was an old taboo for women to shed animal blood.[41] Possibly bloody sacrifices were also offered to the guardian deity of the family, but some texts suggest that this took place at the local or regional sanctuaries, under the direction of the husband. Thus every year Elkanah offers a sacrifice in Shiloh, where he goes with his whole family. The families already mentioned, which were shamelessly and illegally exploited by the sons of Eli at the sacrificial meal, were similarly camped in front of the sanctuary (1 Sam 2:12–17). And at the Passover sacrifice the domestic community also continued to be decisive, even when the feast was centralized in Jerusalem (cf. Ex 12; Deut 16:1–8; Mark 14:12–16. Only in 2 Chron 35:1–15 do the temple personnel seem to be responsible for the whole orientation of the feast: however, that may be the perspective chosen by the Chronicler).

Though we learn little from Old Testament texts about rituals and the way in which the household cult was performed, it can clearly be seen to have existed even in the cities of the time of the monarchy. For there time and again a surprising number of figurines have been found, mostly of terra cotta, and other objects like little altars and incense stands. As a rule the figurines represent naked female figures; they are largely understood to be depictions of fertility goddesses.[42] The dispersion of these relatively small

---

[40]   Cf. with this the 'holy' room in the private house which Karel van der Toorn (ch. 3 n. 5) notes for the Babylonian family, 122f., 125f., 129f. Doorposts and thresholds are manifestly holy places (cf. Ex. 12:22).

[41]   Cf. Hans Wissmann, 'Blut I', and Otto Böcher, 'Blut II', *TRE* 6, 727–36.

[42]   The literature on the figurines has increased considerably in recent years. Cf. James B. Pritchard, *Palestinian Figurines in Relation to Certain Goddesses Known Through Literature*, AOS 24, New Haven 1943; Thomas A. Holland, 'A Study of Palestinian Iron Age Baked Clay Figurines', *Levant* 9, 1977, 121–55; Urs Winter, *Frau und Gattin*, OBO 53, Fribourg ²1987; Silvia Schroer, *Israel* (ch. 4 n. 21); William G. Dever, *Recent Archaeological Discoveries and Biblical Research*,

artefacts over the whole living area of a town (to put it negatively, the lack of a concentration on the holy precinct), does not allow any other interpretation than that these are 'private' cultic objects. If that is the case, then these finds of small cultic objects which for a long time have been neglected represent unmistakable proof of religious activities in households. However, because there is no written evidence to go with them or commentary on them, we still cannot make any reliable statements about the nature of ancient 'family services' and the way in which they were carried out. The seal stamps already cited, along with the theophoric personal names, also attest the private worship of God, but give no indication of cultic practice.

Here the only help offered is by texts which at first glance do not indicate their origin, or better their original usage, in the family sphere. In the present versions of the text, the lamentations of the individual in the Psalter seem to refer to the Yahweh community in the temple and are usually interpreted in those terms. However, studies of their form and social history have convincingly demonstrated that the original prayers were at any rate written for the intimate group, even if they were not composed in it.[43]

To take an example, the ceremony for healing the sick is a typical cultic action. It can be reconstructed with some degree of certainty from biblical texts and on the basis both of testimonies from the ancient Near East and of rites in tribal societies which can still be observed today. In normal cases of sickness mothers and fathers in ancient Israel certainly resorted to household means. Poultices and healing drinks against fever, the treatment of wounds with herbs (the 'fig plaster' in Isa 38:21 similarly comes from the domestic dispensary), baths and washings, diet and fasting were probably part of the repertory of every human group, and the knowledge of powerful magical formulae, talismen and small occasional sacrifices to the deities may also have been used at this level, depending on the need.

Only in more serious cases of sickness and manifest danger to life did people decide on a more purposeful involvement of the guardian deity or another superhuman authority known as a god of healing.[44] For just as for

---

Seattle and London 1990; Othmar Keel and Christoph Uehlinger, *Göttinnen* (ch. 4 n. 22); Diethelm Conrad, 'Zur Rekonstruktion Phönikischer Figurinen vom Tell Akko', in Rainer Kessler et al. (eds), '"*Ihr Völker aller, klatscht in die Hände!*"', *ExuZ* 3, Münster 1997, 33–49.

[43] The cultic use of individual lamentations in the family circle has been argued for by e.g. Sigmund Mowinckel, *The Psalms in Israel's Worship*, 2 vols, Oxford 1962; Erhard S. Gerstenberger, *Mensch* (ch. 3 n. 6); id., *Psalms* 1 and 2, FOTL 14 and 15, Grand Rapids 1988 and 2000; Rainer Albertz, *Frömmigkeit* (ch. 4 n. 19); Anneli Aejmelaeus, *The Traditional Prayer in the Psalms*, BZAW 167, Berlin 1986.

[44] Cf. Klaus Seybold, *Das Gebet des Kranken im Alten Testament. Untersuchungen zur Bestimmung und Zuordnung der Krankheits- und Heiligungspsalmen*, Stuttgart 1973; id., *Krankheit und Heilung im Alten Testament*, Stuttgart 1983.

us consulting a doctor is also a financial matter, so too in ancient Israel taking advice from an expert in healing similarly involved some expenditure. The tribal society already had experts in the special treatment of the sick. Today we call them medicine men, shamans, pajés, etc.[45] And the Old Testament evidence is clear. Whereas Zipporah still herself takes a stone knife and performs circumcision as an apotropaic blood rite when threatened by a demon (Ex 4:24–6), mothers who are concerned for the lives of their children go to or send for the professional healer, the 'man of God', *ʾîš hāʾelōhîm* (later levelled down to 'prophet' in the redactional retrospect). The narrative about Elisha and the Shunammite woman is a good example: the only son helps his father with the harvest and apparently gets sunstroke, since he complains of a severe headache. The father immediately sends him home, to his mother.

> . . . she put him on her lap until noon, and then he died. And she went up and laid him on the bed of the man of God, and shut the door upon him, and went out. Then she called to her husband, and said, 'Send me one of the servants and one of the asses, that I may quickly go to the man of God, and come back again.' And he said, 'Why will you go to him today? It is neither new moon nor sabbath.' She said, 'It will be well.' Then she saddled the ass, and she said to her servant, 'Urge the beast on; do not slacken the pace for me unless I tell you.' So she set out, and came to the man of God at Mount Carmel (2 Kings 4:20–5).

The self-confidence of the woman, who refuses to give her husband the slightest information about the state of their son, is, it may be said in passing, amazing. However, it is typical that the woman takes responsibility for the sick child and independently decides to involve the professional healer. In the narrative there follows the magical-conjurative treatment of the dead boy by Elisha and his subsequent revival. Other texts which describe similar situations (1 Kings 14:1–18; 2 Kings 1:1–2) insert a kind of diagnosis before the treatment proper in the form of an oracular question to an expert deity: Will the sick person get better? Does he still have a chance? (If the answer to this is no, all efforts are senseless!) Only if some chance of healing is promised[46] does the special healing service begin; following an Akkadian model one can also call it a 'conjuration ceremony'.[47] It essentially consists of ritual purifications, the offering of sacrifices and prayers by the patient, of a kind which the Psalter contains in large numbers (cf. e.g. Pss 38; 41; 69;

---

[45] Cf. Lawrence E. Sullivan, 'Healing', *EncRel(E)* 6, 226–34.

[46] Cf. 2 Kings 8:8, 14: Hazael falsifies Elisha's pronouncement of disaster so that it says the opposite, and tells his sick king Ben-hadad, 'You will be healed'. That is the positive diagnosis desired by sick people; cf. Isa 58:15; 2 Sam 12:22.

[47] Erhard S. Gerstenberger, *Mensch* (ch. 3 n. 6); id. and Wolfgang Schrage, *Leiden*, Stuttgart 1977.

102). Following Hermann Gunkel and Sigmund Mowinckel we call these prayers 'lamentations of the individual'. In reality they are not individual prayers which depict quite unique concrete biographical situations but prayer formulae of the 'man of God'. He offers a well-tried intercession which so to speak fits the case of sickness involved. For the prehistory of the sick person, his or her guilt or innocence, plays a major role in the treatment. These details in particular are brought out in the preceding diagnosis. Thus it is no coincidence that the petitionary psalms have the character of a formulary. This proves the long liturgical use of the prayer. These psalms had a chance of being handed down only as typical petitions for healing, which are appropriate for particular categories of sickness, cases of misfortune, evil omens, social contempt and suspicion.[48] In short, with the help of the ritual expert for such cases, who also had to be paid, the family could engage in a liturgical action against the powers of death in its own home.

Such rituals of conjuration and intercession were not a concern of major temple worship, so it is quite wrong to transfer the individual psalms simply to the temple, possibly the central temple in Jerusalem.[49] The comparable Babylonian conjuration texts say clearly that the healing of the sick takes place either by or in the home or on uncultivated land.[50] Comparable rituals in tribal societies, for example, the Navajo in Arizona/New Mexico,[51] confirm the rule.

The so-called rites of passage,[52] rites and ceremonies which accompany the transition from one phase of life to another, and which are thus primarily celebrated on the occasion of birth, puberty, marriage and death, are extremely important.[53] Though larger social organizations like

---

[48] The unique individual destiny, the quite specific symptom of the illness, must be noted by diagnosticians and healers, but cannot be transferred to other cases. The interpretation of the lamentations of the individual as prayer formularies for particular cases has now become established; cf. Henning Graf Reventlow, *Gebet im Alten Testament*, Stuttgart 1986; Ernst Würthwein, 'Bemerkungen zu Psalm 51', in Klaus Seybold and Erich Zenger (eds), *Neue Wege der Psalmenforschung*, Freiburg 1994, 380–8.

[49] Thus in extreme form Artur Weiser, *The Psalms* (1935), London and Philadelphia 1962; this opinion keeps appearing in the literature because exegetes want to get a unitary theology and praxis of faith forcibly out of the texts.

[50] Erhard S. Gerstenberger, *Mensch* (ch. 3 n. 6), 83; Stefan M. Maul, *Zukunftsbewältigung* (ch. 4 n. 25), 48f.

[51] Cf. Clyde Kluckhohn, *The Navaho*, Cambridge, Mass. 1974; Katherina Spencer, *Mythology and Values. An Analysis of Navaho Chantway Myths*, Philadelphia 1957; Gladys Reichard, *Prayer, the Compulsive Word*, MAES 7, New York 1944; Ruth Underhill, *Red Man's Religion*, Chicago 1965, 82–90; Leland C. Wyman, *Blessingway*, Tucson 1970.

[52] According to Arnold van Gennep, 1908.

[53] For the whole question cf. Erhard S. Gerstenberger and Wolfgang Schrage, *Frau* (ch. 3 n. 1), 20–52: 'The Life-Cycle'. There are almost no specialist studies on the individual rites in the Old Testament and the ancient Near East; cf. Saul M. Olyan, *Rites and Rank: Hierarchy in Biblical Representations of Cult*, Princeton 2000.

village, tribe and nation can influence the shape of individual transition ceremonies (one thinks, for example, of confirmation and the initiation of young people, which are arranged from 'above'), the occasion and content of such ceremonies is still supplied and motivated essentially by the viewpoints of individuals and families. The concern is always the safe passage from one state of life to another, in death the passing of the dead person into the world of the dead without danger (above all to those who are left behind). In the Old Testament we learn only in a sporadic and fragmentary way how the corresponding solemnities were performed and what content in terms of ideas and theology they had for those involved.

The birth of healthy children was an occasion for overwhelming joy (cf. Gen 4:1; Ruth 4:14f.; Jer 20:15). A thanksgiving sacrifice was announced (1 Sam 2:1–10) and the joyful festival will have taken place within the general framework of a private thanksgiving sacrifice, of the kind that we know from the story of Hannah and Elkanah (1 Sam 1 – 2) and the thanksgiving psalms.[54] Sacrifice, songs of praise and family festivities were among the essential elements of this festival. Relations and friends were invited (cf. Ps 22:26f.). In the exilic and post-exilic period the circumcision of male children was performed eight days after birth and there was a corresponding ceremony (Gen 17; 21:4). However, in the story of Isaac the festival accompanying circumcision was only celebrated later: 'Abraham made a great feast on the day when Isaac was weaned' (Gen 21:8). This event must have coincided roughly with the child's third birthday, and for the boy it probably meant that he left his mother's care and entered the phase of upbringing under his father's instructions. The child Samuel is also handed over to the temple after being weaned, in accordance with Hannah's vow. A thanksgiving sacrifice is explicitly mentioned in this connection (1 Sam 1:21–8). We see that birth and weaning could be important as stations on the way through life and in some circumstances could be marked off from everyday life with sacrifices and festivities.

Puberty and marriage were the next natural turning points in the life of young Israelite men and women in ancient times. For boys and girls puberty meant entry into the full responsibility of adult existence. In all tribal cultures down to the present day it is extensively accompanied by

---

[54] The individual psalms, which express lamentation, petition and thanksgiving, are particularly suitable for giving us insight into the cultic practice of the family; cf. Erhard S. Gerstenberger, *Psalms* 1 and 2, FOTL 14 and 15 (ch. 4 n. 43). Pss 30; 32; 41; 66B; 118; 138; Isa 38:10–20; Jonah 2:3–10 give examples of individual thanksgivings.

initiation rites of very different kinds and durations. Difficult trials of courage are often required of the adolescents, and heavy burdens are laid upon them before they are officially accepted into the adult world. If several families or clans live together, this wider society, village, clan or tribe takes over the organization of the ceremonies. The nature of the initiation (and in principle of all rites of transition) is for the adolescents to be separated from the preceding period of life and to be linked to that which is to come. The process can be depicted by symbolic dying and rising again.[55] The Old Testament contains few references to the popular rites, which were presumably theologically extremely important. Thus the young women celebrate apparently gender-related festivals 'in the mountains' or 'in the vineyards' (Judg 11:38–40; 21:19–23), which very probably are to be interpreted as puberty rites. We hear nothing in the Old Testament of rites for young men. Possibly Ps 8 comes from initiation festivals.[56] By contrast, weddings are occasionally described in the narrative strata of the Hebrew Bible, and from specific aspects (cf. Gen 29:22–30; Judg 14:10–16).[57] One can also gain individual pieces of information about the way in which the feast was arranged, the adornment of the bride, the significance of the rites, etc. from Ps 45, specific marriage laws (cf. Deut 22:13–21) and some prophetic texts (cf. Isa 49:18; 61:10). If the Song of Songs derives from normal marriage songs and not from a mythical or literary drama, then we have considerably more extensive statements about the function and of the festivities and the way in which they were carried out. According to this, the woman and the man meet in passionate joy, but with certain precautionary measures, which probably served to ward off demonic forces (cf. Gen 38:6–11; Tobit 2). At all events the nearest relatives, and also the wider community and clan, were involved in the ceremonies. Local customs defined the precise roles which father and mother, bride and bridegroom had to play. The cultic element presumably consisted in apotropaic rites and in the solemn statement of binding formulae like 'You are my wife', 'You are my husband', 'I take you as my wife', etc. (cf. Hos 2:4, 18, or 'Bone of my bone, flesh of my flesh', Gen 2:23; perhaps also 'Where you go I too shall go', Ruth 1:16; cf. Gen 2:24; 24:58). We do not know precisely. But probably a marriage treaty between the two families, watched over by the deities, was an essential element in the feast (cf. Gen 31:48–54).

---

[55] Cf. the survey in Peter Gerlitz, 'Initiation/Initiationsriten', *TRE* 16, 156–62; Mircea Eliade, Walter O. Kaelber and Bruce Lincoln, 'Initiation', *EncRel(E)*, 7, 224–38.

[56] Erhard S. Gerstenberger, *Psalms* 1, FOTL 14 (ch. 4 n. 43), 67–72.

[57] Cf. Hans Klein, 'Hochzeit', *NBL* 2, 173.

We do not know whether in Israel in the biography of the individual there were further stages of life marked by transitional rites. The nomadic group may have marked every seasonal departure for different pasturage with religious festivities (cf. Ex 12). The building of a new house was certainly an occasion for celebration in the circle of family and friends (cf. Ps 127). Family success, like victory in a legal dispute (cf. Ps 127:5), may have been worth a thanksgiving sacrifice. In addition, in the narrative texts of Genesis another key stage in life with cultic dimensions comes into view: the handing over of the leadership of the family to heirs. In a patrilinear society the firstborn son received the blessing from his father (possibly through the intermediary of his mother, Gen 27), and this transferred the supreme authority in the family to him. Younger sons apparently had to make do with a lesser quantity of power. According to Gen 27:23–9 the transfer of power is once for all and irrevocable. According to Gen 48:13–20 details like the use of the right or left hand in giving the blessing which in the widest sense is to bring happiness, prosperity, reputation and power are of decisive importance. Whereas to us the key word 'bless' probably usually suggests the official words and gestures of blessing by priests or other cultic officials (cf. Num 6:22–7; 1 Kings 8:13), the family blessing seems to have been an earlier, perhaps archaic, institution with a different dimension. The head of the family was the bearer of a divine power which was to benefit the whole group. It was a kind of spiritual, but also extremely effective, family treasure. This power of blessing apparently did not have anything to do directly with the guardian deity who was worshipped; a hero could even wrest it from a strange deity (Gen 32:25–9). But it was the highest good for the family community and had to be guarded carefully. We should not be surprised that at many points in the Old Testament, thus e.g. in some psalms (cf. Pss 91; 121; 127; 128; 131), the talk is fundamentally of the family blessing and not of the official blessing of a wider society.

Death and burial are the last stage in life which needs to be accompanied by ritual. Genesis 48:1 – 50:14 is the most extensive description of the preparations for dying, death and burial that we have in the Old Testament. Jacob, the patriarch of Israel, dies in Egypt and is buried in Canaan. His body must be put in the cave tomb that Abraham had bought for his wife Sarah (Gen 23). The farewell to the head of the family and the receiving of his testament are depicted at length; the sons play an important role, as was only to be expected in a patriarchal society. All kinds of other guests are present at traditional lamentations. However, only a sweeping description is given of the ceremonies. By contrast, we know examples of lamentation for the dead from other literary contexts: David celebrates his slain friend

Jonathan (2 Sam 1:19–27) and Saul's murdered general Abner (2 Sam 3:33f.) in song. Moreover in some prophets we have 'imitations' of laments for the dead which allow us to guess at the form and content of the real lamentations (cf. Amos 5:1–3; Ezek 32).[58] In principle, all rites of passages have religious references and meanings, despite many specific elements of folklore. And all these rites of transition are firmly rooted in the ancient Near Eastern family. By analogy, that also applies today to the casual practice of the churches, which in fact basically amounts to rites of transition for individuals and their small groups. Then, as now, we can get information about the theological notions of the family group from its cultic actions.

We should note that in ancient Israel there was demonstrably household worship on a broad basis and this was centred on the weal and woe of the family community. At least up to the exile, Israelite families probably had their small cultic corner in the house or near their dwelling, in which a guardian deity was worshipped. Perhaps originally the women, e.g. the chief wife, looked after the household cult. The family rites of passage – birth and circumcision, puberty, marriage, the transfer of the family blessing and burial – were among the central cultic events in the family sphere, though at the same time the wider tribal fellowship certainly took part in the festivities here and there. That also applies to wider cultic activities. The Passover ritual, at its heart a feast of harvest and transhumance, has largely also been a family festival from the beginning to present-day Jewish practice.[59] That probably also applies to parts of the Feast of Booths, namely 'living in booths'.[60] The Christian churches have also had certain 'official ceremonies' focused on the family, but sadly have seriously neglected the small group's own law and own theology. The cultic life of the small family group in ancient Israel followed laws of its own. It was lived within the limits of the communal work to be done in house and property, in the framework of the group and its external relationships; in the rhythm of the stages of life and seasons it manifestly served the sole purpose of sustaining and restoring the order of the family microcosm and guaranteeing the successful life of the group. The old family faith in a particular guardian deity had nothing whatever to do with Yahweh religion. Alongside the probably continuous worship of a divine family patron, male or female, the group certainly also grappled occasionally with other numinous beings (cf. Gen 32:25–31; Ex 4:24–6; Ps 91).

---

[58] For the forms and content of the lament for the dead cf. Hedwig Jahnow, *Das hebräische Leichenlied*, BZAW 36, Giessen 1923.

[59] Ernst Haag, *Vom alten zum neuen Pascha*, Stuttgart 1971; Eckart Otto, *ThWAT* VI, 659–82.

[60] Cf. Lev 23:33–43; to the present day Jewish families erect booths of branches even if only on the balconies of apartments, to indicate the itinerant situation.

4.3 Ideas of God

Children already learn in confirmation instruction that in Israel images of God were forbidden and taboo. Yahweh is the 'God without images' (today people talk in a learned way about the 'aniconic' God, but in the ancient Near East there are countless traces of aniconic worship of gods); he forbids not only his own representation but above all also any other image of a god or goddess. That there are to be no images of Yahweh is something that I shall discuss later. Our concern now is the presence of images of God and ideas of God('s power) at the family level. Here we are at one with the Old Testament. There were countless depictions of deities in Israel. Furthermore (and there is less agreement here), any notion of God, however spiritually sublime and however remote from a graven image, molten image or iconographic symbol of God, is a 'depiction' of God, even if it is 'only' mental and non-material.

If we are to imagine how deity and superhuman power were represented in family belief, then today we must necessarily also refer back to the archaeological discoveries in the sphere of Israel and the neighbouring peoples; we can no longer rely solely on the texts. The evidence of images and texts give us a fairly reliable overall picture of the numinous notions at the family level which were then possible in Israel.

Archaeologists provide the best illustrative material: they have contributed mainly small discoveries in this area, in the form of hundreds of figurines, most of which depict a female figure; however, there are also some male figures, horses and riders. Unfortunately these discoveries of small objects were treated very grudgingly by scholars of a former time, who were fixated on larger social structures.[61] Only in the past twenty years, after Pritchard first catalogued and discussed selected figurines,[62] has interest really been aroused and led to more extensive studies, at least of the small, usually female, representations made out of cheap materials like terra cotta or bone, less often of stone or metal, which were used on a small scale, in the private house.[63] In addition there has been a full-scale survey of the roll and stamp

---

[61] Othmar Keel, for example, remarks that research into the similarly large number of amulets that have been found has been criminally neglected; sometimes these amulets have been thrown away again immediately: 'Bildträger aus Palästina/Israel und die besondere Bedeutung der Miniaturkunst', OBO 67 (= *Studien zu den Stempelsiegeln aus Palästina/Israel* I), 9–11, 42f. This article (ibid., 7–47) is a good introduction to Israelite glyptic art.

[62] James B. Pritchard, *Figurines* (ch. 4 n. 42).

[63] Cf. above all Urs Winter, *Frau* (ch. 4 n. 42); Silvia Schroer, *Israel* (ch. 4 n. 21). A comprehensive catalogue of all the small pieces of plastic art found to the date of publication, with 2711 registered articles, is said to exist: Thomas A. Holland, *A Typological and Archaeological Study of Human and Animal Representations in the Plastic Art of Palestine during the Iron Age*, 2 vols, Oxford 1975 (according to Winter, 98 n. 9: even he could not get access to this basic collection!).

seals (also called stamp amulets, because they were apparently worn on a cord round the neck and contained 'effective signs' [Keel]) which have been found on Israelite territory.[64] So in both spheres, in the case of the small cultic objects (mainly figurines but also little altars, incense stands, amulets, etc.) and seals (these are roll seals of the kind used in Mesopotamia to seal clay tablets, and stamp seals, which derive more from the Egyptian papyrus culture), there are enough published materials and scholarly results to merit inclusion in any Old Testament theology.[65]

The variety of representations of God for which there is archaeological evidence in Israel and the changes in them are remarkable for our topic, and as all the small finds come from the more private sphere (though they – especially the seals – could have had public functions), we can first claim these images for the illustration of family faith.

From the Middle Bronze Age IIB to the end of the Persian period, or, to give dates, from 1750 BCE to around 300 BCE, depictions of goddesses of different kinds and in different attitudes, anthropomorphic and symbolically abstract, have persisted in Palestine – a remarkable continuity in the history of Canaanite–Israelite religion. Here in the case of the figurines there seems to be a even closer connection between the series of cultures than in the case of the seals. For in the more refined division of these 1450 years in Keel and Uehlinger clear variations in treatment and in the frequency of the images of goddesses can be observed. Thus in the first phase, up to 1550 BCE, the two authors note the iconographic dominance of the erotic, naked goddess. A change to the 'clothed lady' in the Late Bronze Age up to 1150 BCE follows, and then the emergence of warlike and lordly motifs in Iron Age I (up to 1000 BCE), the strong tendency towards abstraction and sublimation in divine symbols (but already the enthroned mother and child is announcing itself) in Iron Age IIA (to 925 BCE), an amazing 'solarization' of the deities in Iron Age IIB (to 700 BCE) and the even more amazing return of the goddess in Iron Age IIC (to 587 BCE).[66] It should of course be

---

[64] Keel and his colleagues in the Biblical Institute of the University of Fribourg, Switzerland, are aware of the new development that they are starting with research into Palestinian glyptics. Over the years they have collected more than 8500 seals from this region, from the second and first millennia. Cf. Othmar Keel et al., *Studien zu den Stempelsiegeln aus Palästina/Israel* 1, OBO 67, Fribourg and Göttingen 1985; 2, OBO 88, Fribourg and Göttingen 1989; 3, OBO 100, Fribourg and Göttingen 1991; 4, OBO 135, Fribourg and Göttingen 1994; Othmar Keel and Christoph Uehlinger, *Göttinnen* (ch. 4 n. 24). This last book is a non-technical provisional summary of the results.

[65] Traditional 'theologies of the Old Testament' use only the biblical texts, because the dominant view is that everything else represents less valuable 'popular religion', etc. Rainer Albertz's *History of Israelite Religion* 1 (ch. 3 n. 1) investigates the figurines on the periphery (87, 343 n. 52, etc.).

[66] Cf. Othmar Keel and Christoph Uehlinger, *Göttinnen* (ch. 4 n. 22), 458–76. The authors want only to emphasize the dominant features of a period. They strongly emphasize that goddesses and representations of God usually continue in the subsequent period.

noted that this development takes place on territory inhabited from the eleventh or tenth century by Israelites. Together with the discoveries of female figurines which are clearly to be assigned to the private sphere,[67] the general impression is that in Israelite family piety before the exile there was always also (or above all) the worship of goddesses who guaranteed fertility. The male figurines and symbols of gods (bearing arms, taming beasts, hurling thunderbolts, in the form of a bull, a sun, a star) attest the worship of male deities.

The goddesses in the form of figurines or images on seals have no names. Nor can they easily be identified by the attributes which are given them. From the early Iron Age plaquettes, Keel therefore conjectures that the focus should not be on the names of these goddesses (Anat, Astarte, Asherah) but on their functions.[68] This principle is worth taking to heart, even if in other periods and in particular depictions the goddess is clearly recognizable, say, as Ishtar or Hathor by additional signs. The functions of the deities remain overwhelmingly important, particularly in the family sphere, because from there we can hardly reckon on a tradition of theological reflection. The images offer a glimpse of various key features. The naked figures of the second millennium emphasize the sexual characteristics, and radiate eroticism and the power of life. Thus they emphasize the capacity of the goddess to give fertility and blessing, and perhaps also to help mothers-to-be in their birth pangs. Mention might be made of 'pregnancy flasks' as being of special interest: these are small clay jars in female form, which contained oil for the treatment of pregnant women and women giving birth.[69] Later depictions which show the goddess with twigs, stems of plants, tree symbols and also with animals (goats, lions, etc.), emphasize her dominion over the whole of animate nature. In the family such references are naturally interpreted in terms of one's own sphere of life. All in all, this is about giving

---

[67]   Cf. ibid., 374–6: 'The pillar figurines are a characteristic expression of *Jewish* piety particularly in Iron Age IIC . . . Apart from scattered finds, pillar figurines were primarily found in *private houses* and only secondarily also in *tombs*. On Tell Bet Mirsim and in Beersheba, terra cottas with a possible function in the household cult are attested in rather less than half of the houses that have been excavated. Not always, but very often, they are pillar figurines. As far as can be seen from the often defective account and publication of the finds, as a rule a Jewish private house would not have more than one figurine . . . The figurines represent a kind of "household icon". In a way comparable to the biblical teraphim they are part of the equipment of the house and in the private or family piety of Iron Age IIC they occupied precisely the same status as had already been given to plaquettes with depictions of the goddess in the Stone Age and in Iron Age I.'

[68]   Ibid., 118f. The whole excursus on the material mentioned, 110–22, is worth reading.

[69]   Ibid., 120f.: 'The affinity to the pregnancy jars and the emphasis on female sexuality to the point of motherhood must at all events indicate that the "Astarte labels" played a special role in the piety of *women*.'

and safeguarding the fertility of human beings, cattle and farmland. How could it be otherwise? In everyday experience female beings bring forth new life. So the power which makes earthly fertility possible, which is its ground and sustains it, must also be female. This is a completely legitimate theological conclusion which could only be given up in favour of a completely different – i.e. an asexual or metasexual – interpretation of the world. However, the men who shaped theology and faith in Judaism and Christianity were incapable of this neutral interpretation in their world-view, which sexually had a bipolar stamp.[70] The depictions of a pregnant and breast-feeding mother goddess which arise towards the end of the Old Testament period put the emphasis on 'motherly intimacy, peaceful rest, light and warmth',[71] and thus continue the series of female blessings. The motif originally comes from Egypt (*Isis lactans*: it is rooted in the royal cult) and was then disseminated in an unsuspected way in Christian theology and iconography. Where in the iconography of the goddess there are traces of warlike activity, hunting customs or astral significance (e.g. Ishtar in a garland of stars; cf. the Queen of Heaven in Jer 44:17f.),[72] with great probability we can notice the influence of society as a whole on the family. Family religion can take up the symbolism of the large organization, but it will always harmonize it with its own needs and expectations and thus bring it down to the elementary level of the small group.

I should really have mentioned a further series of iconographic motifs which seem to belong in the sphere of the family: animal symbols like the ox; the horse, battle scenes, depictions of male gods, etc. And where there are manifestly influences from the larger organization I should have investigated the use of the image of the god in the family circle. But it is impossible to do all this. Nevertheless, I shall also refer to a specific predominantly male divine being who exercised influence from Egypt, the demonic figure Bes; he sometimes has a female counterpart, Beset. Klaus Koch describes him as a 'dwarf god':

> Originally a guardian demon of the bedroom and the events of birth and child-care connected with it . . . He is depicted with a hideous face, a head covered with a lion's mane, animal's ears, often with wings and a

---

[70] Does a world-view homogenized by gender offer the opportunity for a metasexual under-standing of God? A tiny detail from the biblical world: Deut 7:13; 28:4, 18, 51, preserve in their wording the names of two goddesses who were mistresses of the cattle. The 'throw' (*š⁽ᵉ⁾gar*) of your cattle and the 'increase' (*'aštᵉrōt*) of your herd probably refer to the goddesses Shagar and Astarte (ibid., 266).

[71] Ibid., 381; cf. plates 327, 328 (= 383), thus at least the male view of pregnancy and motherhood.

[72] Cf. ibid., 332–5, and for the general background ('astralizing' under Assyrian influence), 332–69.

crown of feathers, with bandy legs, between which an animal tail or a long penis hangs down. It is trusted that his ugly face will be a particularly effective deterrent to demons.[73]

This figure of Bes, who as a subordinate guardian deity fits so rightly into the family milieu, also occurs in ancient Israel, both on stamp seals and – if we follow Keel – on the famous clay shards found in 1976 at Kuntillet ʿAjrud. The two seals which Keel depicts and discusses come from the Phoenician sphere (Atlit and Ashkelon).[74] There are also authentic amulets, above all heads of Bes from the time of the divided monarchy (925–722 BCE, found at Lachish, Tell es-Safi, etc.).[75] Kuntillet ʿAjrud lies in the Negeb of Judah on a caravan route from Gaza to Eilat, and in the second half of the eighth century was an unwalled but otherwise 'fortress-like' caravanserai. Inscriptions and drawings were found on the walls of the gate area and on clay shards in this very area. The drawings on jar A, two figures in the foreground, with crowns of feathers, hideous faces, ears sticking out, a tail between the legs and a lyre player in the background, have been interpreted by some scholars as 'Yahweh and his Asherah' (this is also the inscription above the lyre player). That is categorically disputed by others, including Keel, on the basis of comparative iconography.[76] However the question is to be decided, the purely iconographic situation in fact shows figures of Bes. As already indicated, they are to be assigned to the realm of family piety.

> Bes is not one of the great deities of the Egyptian pantheon but one of the demons who are especially popular in small-scale art and in 'personal piety'. From the Middle Bronze Age he was regarded primarily as the guardian of pregnancy, birth and childbearing, and in addition quite generally as a guardian power who wards off disaster . . .
>
> [The depictions] clearly illustrate the complex possibilities of associa-tion which the figure of Bes offered from the end of the Stone Age. The extremely wide spectrum extends from a more dangerous tamed demon to a god endowed with solar features who in small-scale art could be worshipped as 'a popular form of the sun god' . . . His special functions

---

[73]   Klaus Koch, *Geschichte der Ägyptischen Religion*, Stuttgart 1993, 550f. The hairy demon in the form of a goat which is mentioned in Lev 17:7; Isa 13:21; 34:14; 2 Chron 11:15, is probably comparable, see Silvia Schroer, *Israel* (ch. 4 n. 21), 133–5; Otto Böcher, *Dämonenfurcht* (ch. 4 n. 21).

[74]   Othmar Keel and Christoph Uehlinger, *Göttinnen* (ch. 4 n. 22), 437f.

[75]   Ibid., 248–51.

[76]   For those in favour and those against the depiction of Yahweh; cf. above all Keels' extensive argument in ibid, 244–76 (further bibliography, 246). Cf. also Othmar Keel (ed.), *Monotheismus im Alten Testament*, Fribourg 1980, 168–70; Silvia Schroer, *Israel* (ch. 4 n. 21), 30–40; Pirhiya Beck, 'The Drawings from Horvat Teiman (Kuntillet ʿAjrud)', *Tel Aviv* 9, 1982, 3–68.

include protection for pregnant women and small children and preservation from snake bites.[77]

Given the number of Bes amulets (Keel speaks of dozens which have cropped up in many places), it is impossible to interpret them all as chance finds, say as souvenirs brought back from Egypt or the property of Egyptians residing in Israel. Rather, during the time of the monarchy and the exile, belief in Bes or the religious veneration or use of this demon was known and widespread in Israel. And the areas of tasks attributed to Bes clearly relate to the intimate sphere of the small group. There were probably a large number of demons or guardian deities of this kind in ancient Israel. In the surrounding cultures and religions at any rate there is very strong testimony to clearly evil beings who bring death, and such a benevolent and helpful character is very well attested below the level of the great gods.[78] In connection with the relationship between Yahweh and Bes in Israel, we should ask: if Yahweh, like a Bes deity, could assume protective functions for Israelite families, why should not he and his Asherah then also be depicted in the form of Bes and Beset? In that case, on pithos A of Kuntillet ʿAjrud we should after all have a folk portrait of Yahweh and Asherah.

On closer inspection the biblical texts also confirm what the archaeologists unmistakably reconstruct on the basis of their finds in excavations – the domestic or household cult in Israel.[79] For the cult of Baal and Asherah, which is often condemned and which especially according to the denunciations of the exilic Deuteronomists is said to have been practised at the high places, and the measures against the 'monstrosity' of interpreting signs, conjuring up the dead and magic are only minimally focused on the official state religion in Jerusalem. Rather, also according to the view of the historians of the time, a considerable percentage of the practices attacked consist of unofficial, family-related cultic actions.[80] Behind the 'mediums and the wizards and the teraphim and the idols and all the abominations' of 2 Kings 23:24 or the 'anyone who practises divination, soothsayers, augurs or sorcerers, or charmers or mediums, or wizards or

---

[77] Othmar Keel and Christoph Uehlinger, *Göttinnen* (ch. 4 n. 22), 248, 251.
[78] Cf. Erich Ebeling, 'Dämonen', *RLA* II, 107–13; Otto Böcher, 'Dämonen', *TRE* 8, 270–4; Eduard Schweizer, 'Geister', *RAC* 9, 688–797.
[79] Cf. as a summary also Helga Weippert, *Palästina* (ch. 3 n. 3), *passim*.
[80] Cf. e.g. Josiah's reforms according to 2 Kings 23:4–14, which according to the later Deuteronomistic view were certainly said to be centred on Jerusalem but were constantly directed against the 'high places' and then also against the lesser cult; cf. Rainer Albertz, *History of Israelite Religion* 1 (ch. 3 n. 1), 'The fight against private syncretism and internal religious pluralism', 210–15. The conflicts between the state cult and the cult of the high places or the family (the two are to be distinguished) are an exilic fiction which still burdens our theological understanding.

necromancers' of Deut 18:10f. stand the demons and guardian deities who in ancient Israel were approached and worshipped, and were so important for family groups.

However, mention should be made not only of indirect references but also of more or less open descriptions of family cults and their deities. The patriarchal narratives have already been mentioned. But it is already notable that at two points it is conceded that the ancestors once worshipped 'other gods' (Ex 6:3; Josh 24:2). The reference can only be to the so-called 'patriarchal' or, better, family deities, or perhaps the village and tribal gods. And in Judg. 6 such numinous beings related to the wider family or clan are identified with Baal and Asherah (v. 25: 'The altar of Baal which belongs to your father, the image of Asherah which stands beside it'). In Isa 65 those who apostasize from Yahweh evidently withdraw to private worship (vv. 3f.: 'sacrificing in gardens', 'broth of abominable things', v. 11: 'sacrifice to Gad and Meni'), others 'burn incense on the roof tops'. Finally, in Jer 44:15–19 the cult of the 'Queen of Heaven' is described at relative length; the person addressed is probably none other than Ishtar, but now hardly in all her heavenly glory (Venus in a cosmic radiance of light); she is more related to the family. For the families perform their worship under the direction of the lady of the house, with consecrated cakes – probably in the form of Ishtar – and other domestic gifts. By this example – if it is authentic, i.e. if we do not have a later redactional 'cosmicizing' to balance the goddess with Yahweh – we see how the high goddesses of heaven can also emerge in the family cult. If that is the case, however, they were transformed in connection with the needs of the family below.[81]

Alongside these reports there is also more indirect evidence for the family deities in ancient Israel. In the ancient Near East national gods tend to be related to the people as a whole and to the ruling royal house. They usually belong to the type of remote, high deity who, like the absolute monarch in the capital, requires obedience, devotion and submission. Wherever in unintentional allusions we meet the near, the small, the family God, the small group as a background will not be far away. The God who visits Abraham or Lot at home, who walks behind Adam or meets Hagar face to face, is such a God in human form who is near to human beings. Later, theologians replace him in the old narratives with an angelic mediator being (cf. Judg 13; 2 Sam 24; Job 33:23). By contrast, the God whom one can address as 'father' and who does not listen (or no longer listens) to the majestic and warlike appellations (king of kings, lord of lords, judge, creator of heaven and earth, rider on the clouds, etc.) is basically a near God to

---

[81] Renate Jost, *Frauen, Männer und die Himmelskönigin,* Gütersloh 1995, neglects this aspect.

whom there are personal ties (cf. Isa 63:7 – 64:11).[82] The individual songs of lamentation and thanksgiving similarly use intimate designations for God. A deity who in justice, wisdom and prophecy passionately calls for solidarity with the weak and among brethren is not a cold administrator of anonymous orders, but commits himself to a small social circle. Reasons of state also introduce an equitable administrator at the divine level, rather than an angry and zealous sovereign. So in later texts, too, we may reclaim a whole series of divine properties, ideas and metaphors as the distinctive contribution of family deities. And regardless of when they were formulated, the much-vaunted characteristics of Yahweh indicating his friendliness towards human beings are largely to be regarded as a legacy of family theology.

> Yahweh is merciful and gracious,
> slow to anger and abounding in steadfast love.
> He will not always chide, nor will he keep his anger for ever.
> He does not deal with us according to our sins,
> nor requite us according to our iniquities.
> For as the heavens are high above the earth,
> so great is his steadfast love toward those who fear him;
> as far as the east is from the west,
> so far does he remove our transgressions from us.
> As a father pities his children,
> so Yahweh pities those who fear him (Ps 103:8–13).

What a difference from the bureaucratic and also 'impartial' reckoning of guilt of a large society and its theologians! The Deuteronomists attempt to give a theological interpretation of the severe fate of Judah and Jerusalem in 2 Kings 22–23. They award king Josiah, well-disposed to reform and supposedly completely loyal to Yahweh, the best possible marks (cf. 2 Kings 22). In an obituary they say that he was uniquely good:

> Before him there was no king like him, who turned to Yahweh with all his heart, and with all his soul and with all his might, according to all the laws of Moses; nor did any like him arise after him. Still Yahweh did not turn from the fierceness of his great wrath, by which his anger was kindled against Judah, because of all the provocations with which Manasseh had provoked him (2 Kings 23:25f.).

---

[82] I have explained the title 'Father' as a return to family religion after the collapse of state religion, in Erhard S. Gerstenberger, *Yahweh the Patriarch* (ch. 2 n. 4), 1–12. Cf. also Irmtraud Fischer, *Wo ist Jahwe? Das Volksklagelied Jes 63,7–64,11 als Ausdruck des Ringens um eine gebrochene Beziehung*, Stuttgart 1989.

That is the judgment of the administrators of larger social groupings. Here the collective guilt is weighed impersonally; it cannot be counter-balanced by any individual achievement, however good. In other words, secondary organizations which act by justice and law, without respect of persons, cannot practise any mercy. Forgiveness and care come to bear only in direct human relationships, as unbureaucratic promptings 'from the belly, with compassion' (Hebrew *reḥem*, womb), as must be the case in the solidarity of intimate groups. Large organizations are incapable of this. But they have the advantage of judging individual fortunes unemotionally, in a matter-of-fact and potentially just way, as is necessary at this level of society.

Certainly ideas from the wider society have found their way into Psalm 103 with its hymnic expression of trust. Moses and Israel are mentioned in v. 7; the view of heaven and earth, of the broad horizon from which morning and evening come, the plurality of the community whose voice is heard, are all indications of the higher structures of society. But the core of vv. 8–13 with its talk of fathers and children and the individual way of coping with guilt is good family tradition. We would have to go through the whole of the Old Testament tradition in this way to trace the relationships of the deity to the house and family alliance. We would discover that strong theological influences from the small group have survived and found their way above all into the exilic and post-exilic formation of communal belief in God (see below, Chapter 8).

Another approach to ideas of God in the family should at least be mentioned briefly. This involves the Israelite personal names preserved in the Bible and outside it, especially from the time of the monarchy in Israel and Judah. Each time the nomenclature follows dominant currents of fashion, then as now. It is 'in' to give the new-born child a particular name. But because in Semitic antiquity the 'theophoric' names composed of verb or noun plus designation of God were widespread,[83] one can investigate them in terms of the deity addressed. Personal names also remain relatively stable in the tradition (cf. Jacob, Ishbaal; Jerubbaal, Mephibaal, the divine element in which has been changed in the tradition: Gen 32:29; 1 Chron 8:33; 2 Sam 2:12f.; 9:6; Judg 6:32); as a rule they are not given with the awareness of instructing later hearers (programmatic names like Isaiah, Elijahu, Malachi, Obadiah, etc. could be the exception) and give so to speak innocent testimony about the contemporary world of the gods.

[83] However, the name of the god can be missing, e.g. 'Nathan' = 'he [God] has given'. Cf. Martin Noth, *Die israelitischen Personennamen im Rahmen der gemeinsemitischen Namensgebung*, Stuttgart 1928; Jeaneane D. Fowler, *Names* (ch. 4 n. 26); Johann Jakob Stamm, *Beiträge zur hebräischen und altorientalischen Namenskunde*, Göttingen 1980.

Two studies on the theological content of personal names may be mentioned as representative: Albertz devotes a chapter of his Habilitation thesis to the topic,[84] and Tigay presented to the Harvard Divinity School a comprehensive monograph which in important sections deals with personal names.[85] Albertz points out that the biblical names – as a rule expressing petitions, wishes, thanks and calls for praise for the person who bears the name – are not connected with the official larger cult, e.g. with the salvation-historical themes of exodus, wilderness wandering, settlement, royal dynasty, etc. 'The close connection of the names is . . . not to the cult generally, but quite specially to the genres of the lesser cult: to the lament of the individual, to accounts of praise and to the oracle of salvation.'[86] For example he interprets the names indicating deliverance and help (Isaiah = Yahweh has saved, or Eliezer = my God is [my] help) very attractively in terms of the deliverance and help of the god in the dangers of birth, not the experiences of deliverance relating to all Israel.[87] All along the line, according to Albertz, the personal names attest the personal relationship of the one who bears them and the group to the guardian deity, in whose blessing, support and readiness to hear they trust.[88] The designations of God in the name are varied: kinship names occur in a way which is typical of family religion: the deity is designated 'father', 'brother' or 'uncle' (*'am*), e.g. in Ahiram = my brother is exalted; Amminadab = my uncle has urged on [the process of birth?]; Abida = my father knows. Precisely the same formations occur in composites with El or Yahweh and occasionally also with other divine epithets like Melek, Baal, Adon and Gad.[89] Albertz quite rightly infers from this that the personal names come from the sphere of the family and reflect its experiences and the world in which it lives, and that the divine names can be exchanged, i.e. each time are brought within the horizon of family thought, which remains the same.[90] By contrast, Tigay's investigations

---

[84] Rainer Albertz, *Frömmigkeit* (ch. 4 n. 19), 49–77.

[85] Jeffrey H. Tigay, *You Shall Have No Other Gods. Israelite Religion in the Light of Hebrew Inscriptions*, HSS 32, Atlanta 1986; cf. id., 'Israelite Religion. The Onomastic and Epigraphic Evidence', in Patrick D. Miller et al. (eds), *Ancient Israelite Religion*, Philadelphia 1987, 157–94; Nahman Avigad, 'The Contribution of Hebrew Seals to an Understanding of Israelite Religion and Society', in ibid., 195–208.

[86] Rainer Albertz, *Frömmigkeit* (ch. 4 n. 19), 49; the author establishes by word statistics that the verbs and nouns combined with the name of a god largely recur in the liturgical texts of the lesser cult mentioned above.

[87] Ibid., 55.

[88] Cf. the individual analyses in ibid., 60–71.

[89] Cf. the table in ibid., 72.

[90] Ibid., 71–7. The personal relationship with God in terms of the family becomes very vivid, e.g. in the name Amaziah = Yahweh takes protectively into his arms; cf. Isa 46:3f.; Hos 11:3 (ibid., 75f.; Helen Schüngel-Straumann, 'Gott als Mutter in Hos 11', *ThQ* 166, 1986, 119–34). Albertz demonstrates the independence of family faith: ' "the God" in the family is

completely ignore the functional and family aspects. He is interested only in establishing the designations of God and in showing that in the pre-exilic period in the heartland of Judah the overwhelming majority of personal names which appear contain the element Yahweh. However, in order to arrive at his overwhelming result Tigay must bracket out the names containing El and those which contain no designation of God.[91] And he has great difficulties in explaining the prophetic polemic against the alien cults in the land.[92]

A difficult problem which the Israelite names both in the biblical sources and in the extra-biblical inscriptions pose to us has still to be mentioned: there are virtually no names which mention a goddess as a theophoric element. Now because we know with certainty from Hebrew traditions and from the archaeological evidence that Ashera, Anath and Ishtar had followers in ancient Israel, the lack of indications in the onomastic survey is very surprising.[93] The only reference to a goddess is the name Shamgar ben

---

characterized in a purely functional way; the important thing is that he gives the family a child, that he supports individuals when they are threatened, that he protects them and rescues them from danger, not who he is called or what kind of "properties" he has . . . Granted, people adopted the designation of God which was customary in the sphere in which the family lived, which meant for the most part the official religion, but what was expected and experienced from the "God" in question was the same as had always been expected and experienced of God in the sphere of the family' (72f.) – and the parallel nomenclature disseminated throughout the ancient Near East serves as proof.

[91] 'Of the 738 individuals, 351, or nearly half, bear names with YHWH as their theophoric element. Forty-eight others bear names with the theophoric element *ʾēl* ('God/god/the deity El'), or *ʾēlī* ('my God'). Since there is no way of telling to which deity this element refers, names with these words as their theophoric element were not included among the theophoric names in this study. Of all the remaining names, most mention no deity at all. Only twenty-seven seem clearly or very plausibly to refer to deities other than Yahweh' (Jeffrey H. Tigay, *Religion* [ch. 4 n. 85], 162f.).

[92] Ibid., 178–80: the idolatry took place among the élite at the royal court, for political reasons, and was generalized only by prophetic exaggeration: '. . . there existed some superficial, fetishistic polytheism and a limited amount of more profound polytheism in Israel, though neither can be quantified' (ibid., 179). Amazingly, Keel adopts Tigay's findings with little criticism; cf. id. and Christoph Uehlinger, *Göttinnen* (ch. 4 n. 21), 5f. ('pioneer achievement'), 230–4. As a comparison see also Alfonso Arcchi (ed.), *Eblaite Personal Names and Semitic Name-Giving*, Rome 1988 (including an article by Dennis Pardee, 'An Evaluation of the Proper Names from Ebla from a West Semitic Perspective', 119–51).

[93] Keel refers to this situation with as much amazement as Tigay had shown (cf. Othmar Keel and Christoph Uehlinger, *Göttinnen* [ch. 4 n. 22], 232). Keel then adds: 'We must be aware of the limits of onomastic documentation; we cannot conclude decisively from the absence of goddesses in the personal names of Iron Age I that they were generally unimportant in eighth-century Israel' (ibid., 233). Even the Ugaritic texts, which attach a great deal of importance to the goddesses, demonstrate hardly any female theophoric names; only the Phoenician-Punic texts contain many personal names which have Astarte as a component. Keel and Uehlinger thus conclude that the absence of similar names in Israel must 'initially be connected with particular laws of nomenclature', and they refer to Pardee, 'Evaluation' (ch. 4 n. 92) (ibid., 233).

Anath (Judg 3:31; 5:6), i.e. the mother (or the father?) of the judge is named directly after Anath, in Ugarit the consort of Baal.[94]

The ideas of God which can be recognized in the Israelite family milieu are therefore not unitary. Presumably the particular family deity – male, female or thought of as a couple – claimed the main attention in the cult and religion. But any person in antiquity knew that he or she was put in a world permeated with personal powers. Therefore other divine beings too could be observed in everyday life, possibly to ward them off, to avoid them or to propitiate them. It is important for us to recognize that at the family level in ancient Israel and in the ancient Near East this is a form of religion which already has a thousand-year-old tradition behind it. This tradition is the real stream of religious tradition from which all the later 'high' religions that arise in larger societies and cultural spheres draw. Although the ancient texts indicate that there was hardly any formal theological reflection in the family sphere, the store of religious experience in small groups represents the firm basis for all subsequent systems of faith. In our evaluation of family faith we must therefore not be led astray into applying the criteria of the later great religions. On the contrary, the creative, practical 'theology' of the families of the ancient Near East and also of all other cultures, which was utterly related to life, has to be seen as the source and inspiration of the later, wider notions of faith.

4.4 The ethic of family and clan

As I remarked, human beings must construct their own social order because regulation by instinct is not sufficient. To do this they need to be incorporated into the outside world which transcends them; they need the approval of the forces and deities of which they have become aware. How did what Peter Berger has called 'the social construction of reality' take place in the history of ancient Israel, with the acceptance or direction of the family deity? What can we know or reconstruct from the sources at our disposal? I have already mentioned the spheres of family interest (shared work, the relationship between individual members, the tendency towards authority and the distribution of roles, the relations to other groups and to society as a whole). Now we are concerned with the way in which the family ethos was shaped in detail.[95]

[94] Cf. also the Israelite place names Anathoth (Josh 21:18; Isa 10:30; Jer 1:1) and Beth-anath (Josh 19:38; Judg 1:33), and the occurrence of the goddess Anath in the Elephantine texts.
[95] I refer to Raphael Patai, Sex and the Family (ch. 4 n. 10), and my study 'Frau und Mann', which go into some of the questions discussed here in greater detail: Erhard S. Gerstenberger and Wolfgang Schrage, Frau (ch. 3 n. 1), esp. 20–31; also Erhard S. Gerstenberger, Wesen und Herkunft des 'apodiktischen Rechts', Neukirchen-Vluyn 1965.

Granted, then as now the process of the socialization of adolescents largely took place unconsciously. Children and young people learn predominantly by observation and imitation, by example and practice, how they are to fit into society and what rules prevail there (so much so that deliberate attempts at education by parents and adults are often completely useless!). Nevertheless in this process of the adaptations which from the adult perspective we call 'education', reflection also begins. And we call reflection on and the handing down of norms 'ethics', the teaching of 'good' or 'right' customs. It begins in the family sphere and has its deepest and most significant foundations there.[96] In the periods from which our sources come what Keel has called an 'osmotic communication' has always taken place between the groups of a cultural region. As early as 10,000 BCE, Syria and Palestine were intensively settled areas; for example, traces of settlement in the city of Jericho go back to the late tenth millennium BCE.[97]

The sources for our knowledge of biblical family morality are narratives, wisdom traditions and those parts of the legal tradition of Israel which with great probability can be derived from the socialization of children: the so-called prohibitives (cf. Ex 20:12–17; 23:1–9; Lev 19:13–18, etc.).[98] The negative form of these norms is in fact a first striking characteristic. 'You shall *not* do this or that', and one can almost add: 'We don't do that sort of thing!' From this it can be seen that behind the prohibitive we are to presume the knowledge of a positive norm. The forbidden behaviour damages a recognized, common good, life together, the harmony of one's own group. There is no need to discuss this basic value. And what constitutes the group, what is good for it, is more or less intuitively and directly clear to all its members because it has been long been communicated by unconscious socialization and deterrent examples from the environment. The family is the community which is necessary for life: mutual solidarity alone holds the social organism together; identification with it is completely in the interest of the individual and individuals. Thus upbringing can start from these basic data. Family self-respect, the mutual solidarity of all, an alliance to provide protection and resistance against outsiders, are the basic values. However, it is also necessary to recognize and avert everything that puts these values in question or endangers them. So the admonitions are given to young people (moreover almost all over the world) in the form of

---

[96] In accordance with the traditional patterns of thought, Eckart Otto's *Ethik des Alten Testament*, Stuttgart 1994, begins from the wider society which first lays down the law. He derives the (Yahweh!) ethic from that.

[97] Cf. Helga Weippert, *Palästina* (ch. 3 n. 3), 80–117; Ludwig Schwienhorst-Schönberger, 'Jericho', *NBL* II, 290–3; Michael Frotin (ed.), *Syrien, Wiege der Kultur*, Quebec 1999, 39–49.

[98] Cf. Erhard S. Gerstenberger, *Wesen* (ch. 4 n. 95).

prohibitions. Even the most anti-authoritarian upbringing must sometimes temporarily work with prohibitions (and of course also with enlightenment) if children are unaware of the danger of their actions.

One story which is set in the late pre-exilic period gives a good impression of the norms within the family. The narrative has been shaped from another perspective than that of the small group, but it is a good model of what happens in the patriarchal family: Jeremiah is to set an example for the Rechabites. They are totally opposed to the life of the cultivated land, and Jeremiah must tempt them with wine on the orders of Yahweh:

> But they answered, 'We will drink no wine, for Jonadab the son of Rechab, our father, commanded us, "You shall not drink wine, neither you nor your sons for ever; you shall not build a house; you shall not sow seed; you shall not plant or have a vineyard; but you shall live in tents all your days, that you may live many days in the land where you sojourn." We have obeyed the voice of Jonadab the son of Rechab, our father, in all that he commanded us . . .' (Jer 35:6–8).

The verbs used for 'command' and 'obey' (*siwwāh*; *šāmaʿ bᵉqōl*, vv. 6, 8, 10) are also used for behaviour towards the Torah, so we are to assume that this passage has been moulded by later community theology.[99] Nevertheless the pattern within the family can be recognized: a patriarch gives a binding solution to the way in which life is shaped. The family is to continue in its nomadic or semi-nomadic way of living – certainly in harmony with other groups, but quite specifically as a family. The prohibition against drinking wine belongs in the series of other prohibitions which forbid the sedentary, agricultural mode of production and way of living. For emphasis, it is put first. The group's own nomadic existence with its rules for life is the presupposition; the repudiation of agricultural customs and structures which are undesirable because they put in question the identity of the group and a right, good life, is the main thing. The fact that the nomadic ideal is still given a positive formulation is certainly connected with the unusual situation of the narrative: descendants of a family of zealots for Yahweh (Jonadab is depicted as a supporter of Jehu in the ninth century BCE, 2 Kings 10:15–17) in the besieged city of Jerusalem maintain the old ancestral norms more than two hundred years after they have been obligated to observe them by Jonadab. In itself this positive explanation of, or basis for, the prohibitives in the family sphere would be insignificant.

---

[99] Cf. Christoph Levin, 'Die Enstehung der Rechabiten', in Ingo Kottsieper et al., '*Wer is wie du, HERR, unter den Göttern?*', Göttingen 1994, 301–7 (the narrative is said to be a late fiction resting on misunderstandings and theological reflection).

However, before we investigate the main content of the family norms which are seen as prohibitions, we need to survey the sphere of wisdom, especially in the proverbial material of the Old Testament, to see the far-reaching parallels in the collections of other peoples and cultures. We also need to look a little into the narrative material. Here of course we immediately think of the 'patriarchal narratives' of Genesis and perhaps of the book of Ruth, and of the collection of family songs, though only a small and fragmentary selection of these have come down to us. All these sources certainly did not come into being in specific individual families. Rather, they betray regional and perhaps ethnically limited usage. This is the common material of many related groups. But in its spiritual horizon and in its manner of thought and argumentation it clearly presupposes the family and clan structure of society. For example, the Song of Songs may be deeply rooted in family wedding customs. Proverbs is about the minor matters of everyday life. In Israel, socialization in the context of the family was not achieved by the constant raising of a finger to emphasize the fundamental norms, by the prohibitions issued by the head of the family. As elsewhere, the child to a large degree learned correct behaviour, prescribed by ancestral custom, from exemplary stories and from proverbs which work with a 'gentle, social pressure'.[100] They praise good behaviour, appeal a great deal to reason and are concerned with experience, but usually mock action contrary to the rules or even indicate that it will incur the contempt and punishment of the community.

> The sluggard says, 'There is a lion in the road! There is a lion in the streets!' As a door turns on its hinges, so does a sluggard on his bed. The sluggard buries his hand in the dish; it wears him out to bring it back to his mouth. The sluggard is wiser in his own eyes than seven men who can answer discreetly (Prov 26:13–16).

Here we have an accumulation of proverbs which do not want to sing the praise of laziness. After this instruction, which uses both exceptional events and common incidents in everyday life as illustrations, what youth would want to be as lazy, idle and arrogant as the sluggard referred to?

> The eye that mocks a father and scorns to obey a mother will be picked out by the ravens of the valley and eaten by the vultures (Prov 30:17).

Here the vocabulary of obedience is different, more civil, than in the paraenesis of the law: *lāʿag*, 'mock'; *būz liqhāh*, 'scorns to obey'; the noun

---

[100] Arland D. Jacobsen, 'Proverbs and Social Control: A New Paradigm for Wisdom Studies', in James E. Goehring et al. (eds), *Gnosticism and the Early Christian World*, Sonoma 1990, 75–88.

yᵉqāhāh occurs only here and in Gen 49:10. Here all the wrath of the adults about potential rebels is unleashed within the small group. Although of course proverbs, like jokes, anecdotes and other minor literary genres, circulate in the wider community, we note many themes which originally communicate responsibility and purpose. No wonder that the genre of 'teachings about life', which was markedly developed in ancient Egypt, but which also left behind its traces in Old Testament wisdom,[101] basically presupposes the situation of the family. Father and mother together, or also individually,[102] instruct the son and daughter about their duties in the small group and in life generally.

The same goes for family narratives and songs which refer to the family. As we have them now, they have already been adopted and adapted by wider society – material that it is completely specific to the family is not handed on to the wider framework – but still betray their roots in and origin from the small group. That is the case with the patriarchal narratives in Genesis.[103] As a rule they function as prototypes, perhaps sometimes even critical prototypes; in other words, the narratives seek to influence the behaviour of the members of the family who listen to them. For example Abraham and Sarah do not simply appear in ideal form, but in such a way that the young generation can and should draw conclusions from the behaviour of their ancestors. Here shrewdness and a capacity for survival, good relations with the deity and reliable family relationships play the largest role, but these are all virtues from the innermost family circle.[104] Similarly,

---

[101] Cf. Hellmut Brunner, *Altägyptische Weisheit. Lehren für das Leben,* Zurich and Munich 1988; Bernhard Lang, *Die weisheiltiche Lehrrede,* Stuttgart 1972.

[102] Cf. Prov 30:1: 'The words of Agur son of Jakeh, of Massa'; Prov 31:1: 'The words of Lemuel, king of Massa, which his mother taught him.' Such superscriptions probably contain original material which the tradition itself no longer understood, as e.g. the geographical detail 'Massa'. The title king recalls the Egyptian court teachings which were current especially among scribes and officials. For the genre of 'teaching about life' in Egypt see Diethard Römheld, *Die Weisheitslehre im Alten Orient. Elemente einer Formgeschichte,* Munich 1989; Nili Shupak, *Where can Wisdom be found?,* OBO 130, Fribourg and Göttingen 1993.

[103] Hermann Gunkel had understood them as patriarchal sagas, in *Die Urgeschichte und die Patriarchen,* Göttingen 1911; Claus Westermann as patriarchal family narratives (cf. his Genesis commentary); Erhard Blum as family history which becomes popular history, in id., *Komposition* (ch. 4 n. 28); Matthias Köckert in terms of the family as the primary form of society, in id., *Vätergott* (ch. 4 n. 28), 304, 310; Irmtraud Fischer consistently as 'stories about ancestors', in ead., *Erzeltern* (ch. 4 n. 14).

[104] Each individual story must of course be examined for its evaluations and values, taking into account the standards of the time. Thus for example the threefold narrative about the betrayal of the matriarch – certainly today one of the most offensive traditions in the OT – must be seen against the background of the family ideology of the time. Certainly Fischer's discovery is in some respects correct: 'Gen 12:10–20 . . . is a narrative about surrender which becomes a narrative about rescue on the basis of Yahweh's intervention' (ibid., 136), i.e. Sarah's fate stands at the centre, not Abraham's behaviour. But if the surrender of the matriarch was unethical in the situation depicted, then a divine reaction to it had to follow.

one could speak at greater length about the songs deriving from the family. In all probability we know only a tiny fragment of the poetry from the extant tradition which was circulated at the time. According to what we have, marriage and death are the main occasions on which there was singing in the smaller group. The Song of Songs is a marvellous example of this; the funeral songs at the death of a member of the family, of which only a few fragments already transposed to the group of friends and professionals have come to us and others can be reconstructed by inference from prophetic and liturgical forms,[105] are the counterpart to the marriage songs.

Otherwise we know little, for example, about songs relating to work, going to sleep, dancing, harvest, puberty and so on, which could have played a role in the family. The same is true of magical sayings, riddles, omens, calendar sayings and similar genres of 'minor literature', which certainly existed but which have come down to us only sparsely, if at all, in the Hebrew scriptures.[106]

For our present purposes it is important also to investigate here the religious roots or direction of the minor family literature, which was originally oral (!), and its norms. From the few examples given above we may note that the wording at least of proverbs often sounds very pragmatic and profane, as if the individual were alone in the world with his like. We must probably correct the impression given by the narratives – we must imagine pre-Yahwistic original forms – for even in such a profane story as that of Ruth and her mother-in-law the mysterious guidance of the deity plays an important role, not to mention the Abraham–Sarah, Isaac–Rebecca and Jacob–Rachel–Leah narratives. Certainly the 'profanity' of some literature and thus also of some activities in antiquity must not be under-estimated. We should not construct a false picture of the religious ties of our spiritual ancestors, as if they spent the day occupied only with pious thoughts and sketches of family theology. No, the profane character which is certainly there, and is even consciously there, a profane character which

---

[105] For this see still Hedwig Jahnow, *Leichenlied* (ch. 4 n. 58).

[106] The literatures of the other peoples of the ancient Near East often give more information. However, they are not easily accessible and there seem to me to be no overall accounts of the minor literature, especially from the perspective of an origin in the family; cf. Emma Brunner-Traut, *Die alten Ägypter. Verborgenes Leben unter Pharaonen*, Stuttgart 1974; Claudia V. Camp, *Wisdom and the Feminine in the Book of Proverbs*, Sheffield 1985; Carol R. Fontaine, *Traditional Sayings in the Old Testament*, Sheffield 1982; ead., 'The Sage in Family and Tribe', in John G. Gammie (ed.), *The Sage in Israel and the Ancient Near East*, Winona Lake 1990, 155–64. Willem H. P. Römer mentions a number of popular genres for Sumerian literature, though of course these have also been listed in connection with the collections of tablets by professional scribes: letters, proverbs, fables, parables, popular narratives, riddles, jokes, instructions, cradle songs, drinking songs and work songs, etc. (id., *Die Sumeriologie*, AOAT 262, Münster, ²1999, 199–202: 219).

attributes something to human experience and might, is found under the aegis of belief in God. The motto even of Proverbs, with its experiential wisdom, is 'Man proposes, God disposes' (the wise Joseph also says words to this effect in Gen 50:20: 'You meant evil against me, but God meant it for good'). This comprehensive religious connection can be demonstrated everywhere in ancient literatures.[107] The openly profane character of some texts and genres rules it out only by questionable modern criteria. The religious consciousness of our ancient ancestors simply permeated the whole of everyday life, including profane life.

Let us return to the prohibitives, which show the work of socialization and education most clearly and should therefore serve as an example for some of the main content of the family ethic.[108] As I have already remarked, the conscious work of education in the family begins from the parents. Amazingly, both parents are specifically mentioned even in later strata of the Old Testament: father and mother, and once even mother and father (Lev 19:13), are both equally, though with slightly different intensity, described as the representatives of the deity who do his will towards the children. That means that the prohibitions handed on in the family which basically define the group identity and are meant to safeguard the existence of the group by defining the limits of what is not allowed are regarded as sanctioned by God. That is quite understandable, as the existence of the group is the supreme good for the people of the time, and what is supremely good is always given a religious explanation: it is transfigured and protected by religion. Even in the late texts, the parents are wholly bound into the Israelite system, whether this is primeval recollection of the autonomy of the family in the period before the state or a rediscovery of the family traditions at the time of the century of the exile or later, when the state no longer existed. An old (but perhaps also late) series of 'transgressions worthy of death' in Ex 21:13–17 twice contains a strict prohibition against 'striking' or 'cursing' father or mother (vv. 15, 17; cf. Deut 27:16). And the parallel prohibition against attacking 'God' or the 'oldest' in the people (with magic formulae?) (Ex 22:27) only carries out what has already been indicated in the mention of the death threat (*mōt yūmāt*, he must die). The transgressor is then handed over to God's judgment.[109] The deity is the guardian patron

---

[107]   Because we find it difficult to take seriously the lesser literature which in fact comes 'from ordinary people', for most scholars research into it is also a less attractive sphere of work.

[108]   Cf. Erhard S. Gerstenberger, *Wesen* (ch. 4 n. 95); Wolfgang Richter, *Recht und Ethos*, Munich 1966; Johannes Hempel, *Das Ethos des Alten Testaments*, Berlin 1938; Frank Crüsemann, *The Torah*, Edinburgh 1996; Eckart Otto, *Ethik* (ch. 4 n. 96), bibliography.

[109]   However, in my view the invention of a special 'death sentence' imposed by clergy (?) in Hermann Schulz, *Das Todesrecht im Alten Testament,* BZAW 114, 1969, is the dirty trick of an over-excited imagination and should not be constantly repeated, as by Eckart Otto, *Wandel*

of the family and thus the parental authority. Luther took up this theological insight from old family structure and made it a cornerstone of his ethics.[110] The family approach in this bestowal of authority is immediately recognizable, even if already in ancient Israel there were further stages of development. The appointment of parents as mediators of the divine will for members of the family is an extraordinarily far-reaching decision. According to the understanding of the Hebrew scriptures it concerns not only discipline within the family, the good behaviour of children, but all ethical spheres and dimensions and also what we would call the content of religious instruction. The parents as mediators of the will of God are the decisive authority for the family in the teaching and life of the small group. The commandment in the Decalogue – by way of exception formulated positively – invites children to 'honour' father and mother (*kabbed*, Ex 20:12; Deut 5:16); the version in Lev 19:3 speaks of 'fearing' (*yāre'*), and here uses an even more important theological term which extends beyond reverence for God. Deuteronomy prescribes that 'rebellious and disobedient sons', who are also characterized as 'gluttons and drunkards' (Deut 21:18–21), are to be brought to court by their parents and there condemned to death. How far turning away from Yahweh is also meant in the charges would have to be shown by careful analysis.[111] At all events it is within the intention of the Deuteronomists also to make the family the stronghold of belief in Yahweh; the appointment of parents or the head of the family as the guardians of faith (cf. Deut 13:7–12) confirms this picture. Such a development can only build on old rights and customs, i.e. on the fact that the family was a religious unit and that the leading figures in the small group also had responsibility for family religion. Thus the late texts also attest that the internal structure of the family is an inherited order which is acquired, comes into being and worked for, and is under divine protection.

But not only the relationship of the members of the family to the couple at its head, or (at a later time?) to the head of the family and patriarch, was regulated by a divinely sanctioned order. The members also had to observe

---

der Rechtsbegründungen in der Gesellschaftsgeschichte des antiken Israel, Studia Biblia 3, 1988; Hans Joachim Boecker, *Recht und Gesetz im Alten Testament und im Alten Orient*, Neukirchen-Vluyn ²1984; cf. Erhard S. Gerstenberger, 'Apodiktisches Recht', 'Todesrecht?', in Peter Mommer et al. (eds), *Gottes Recht as Lebensraum*, Neukirchen-Vluyn 1993, 7–20; id., '. . . He/They Shall be Put to Death', *ExAu* 11, 1995, 43–61.

[110] Martin Luther, *Great Catechism*, on the Fourth Commandment: one must regard parents 'after God as the authorities'; for 'God has established this state, indeed has put it in its place on earth'.

[111] Cf. Frank Crüsemann, *Torah* (ch. 4 n. 108), 295ff.; Elizabeth Bellefonteine, 'Deuteronomy 21, 18–21: Reviewing the Case of the Rebellious Son', *JSOT* 13, 1979, 13–31.

an ordinance to be responsible in solidarity if the family was to continue to exist. The slogan for the group in relation to outsiders was 'one for all and all for one'. As I have already mentioned, the obligation to exact blood vengeance is the most visible expression of this solidarity. The obligation to enter into a levirate marriage under the protection and ordering of the deity is another example. But family solidarity extended to the whole of life: it was maintained so to speak through thick and thin; in other words, the question of objective right had to be put in the background in the interests of internal cohesion (the right for close relatives to refuse to testify in court which is enshrined in present-day legal ordinances is a modern example of the old principle). So Jacob is dismayed by the ambush and murder of the men of Shechem by his sons, but does not distance himself publicly from them (Gen 34). Saul expects loyalty and attention to his interests from his son, even if friendship with David must be sacrificed as a result (1 Sam 20:27–34). Joseph's brothers are envious because their father loves him more than the other siblings (and shows this clearly); the conflicts intensify when Joseph deliberately tells them his dreams, according to which the family order is to be stood on its head (Gen 37:3–11).[112] A fine balance was preserved in families in ancient Israel on the basis of gender, age and assignation of role, but it was apparently disturbed often enough. At all events, order was hallowed by custom and faith and generally recognized and internalized.

Sexual relations were particularly worth protecting because they were a potential source of unrest in a community living together. One text (Lev 18:6–16) is very remarkable because, as Karl Elliger established in 1955,[113] it still quite clearly shows its origin in the family. This is not primarily a list of 'prohibited degrees of affinity' between which marriage was forbidden. Rather, it initially concerned only sexual intercourse, which had to be regulated within the wider family. If several generations lived under one roof, the temptation will have been great also to engage in sexual relations with other women than one's wedded wife (or, conversely, other men than one's wedded husband, but in fact only males are mentioned!). That would lead to disastrous confusion, and to internal quarrels which could only weaken the group. Therefore from primal times such catalogues of internal prohibitions have became customary and an important basis of family existence. The person addressed is the husband of the middle generation who lives in his parents' house but already has his own children and

---

[112] But cf. Thomas Mann's interpretation in *Joseph and His Brothers*, London 1970, 314–91.

[113] Karl Elliger, 'Das Gesetz Lev 18', *ZAW* 67, 1955, 125 (reprinted in id., *Kleine Schriften zum AT*, Munich 1966, 232–59); cf. Erhard S. Gerstenberger, *Leviticus* (ch. 4 n. 18), 246–58.

grandchildren. By analogy the rules must be transferred to the others in-volved, perhaps also to the wives. The talk is always of 'uncovering the shame'; this is to be taken literally, since the mere sight of private parts is dishonouring (cf. Gen 9:21–5; 2 Sam 10:4f. Probably the later Christian abhorrence of nakedness has a root here). On the other hand, though, the expression also clearly implies sexual intercourse. So for the person addressed here, the prohibition is of sexual contact with the wives of his parents' generation living in the house (his own mother, his father's concubine, and aunts on the paternal and maternal side, who had probably found their way into the household as spinsters, related either by blood or marriage). That in v. 7 the father also seems to be an object of sexual lust or curiosity is best explained from Gen 9:21–5. This story seems like a commentary on Lev 18:7a and gives a reason for the cursing of Ham, the Canaanite (Gen 9:25–7). The other more remote possibility would be that the prohibition against having sexual contact with the father was originally addressed to the daughters (the commentary on that would be Gen 19:30–8: Lot's daughters conceive by their father, just as execrable an act as that of Ham, who sees his father Noah naked). The absence of the second person feminine in the address could be caused by the linguistic usage – where both sexes are referred to, the masculine gender is preferred – which is inclusive. At the level of the middle generation the prohibition is of sexual contact with sisters of all kinds (full sisters, half-sisters and nominal sisters: vv. 9, 11) and with one's sister-in-law (brother's wife, v. 16). Of subsequent generations only the daughter-in-law (wife's son, v. 15) is mentioned. Remarkably, there is no mention of one's own daughter, who is occasionally specifically mentioned in ancient Near Eastern laws. Is she thought of as having already married and gone away? Was there no sexual abuse by fathers of their own daughters in ancient Israel? Is the case covered by v. 7a or v. 17?[114] There follows the generation of the grandparents: here too sexual contact with all the female grandchildren is carefully made taboo (v. 10). In short, the list is concerned to be precise and complete; it excludes the illegitimate contacts in the wider family, potentially covering four generations, which are made taboo and stand under the curse, and implicitly allows sexual activity within the household only to legitimately connected couples or polygynous partners, male and female. That in emergencies not even marriage with a half-sister was completely impossible is attested by texts like 2 Sam 13:13 (Tamar says to Amnon, 'Speak with the king, he will not withhold me from you') or the note in Gen 20:12 (Abraham on Sarah: 'She too is truly

---

[114] Cf. Elke Seifert, *Tochter und Vater im alten Testament*, Neukirchen-Vluyn 1997. The special legal relationship (the father is the guardian of the children) may have played a role in the failure to mention the daughters.

my sister, for she is my father's daughter, but not my mother's daughter; so she has become my wife'). In Israel, marriage to a female cousin (the daughter of a father's brother) was regarded as the best course. This cousin is not mentioned in Lev 18:7–17; perhaps she was deleted from the tradition when people no longer recognized the original setting of the taboo definitions. In that case people would not have wanted to obstruct this possibility of marriage in the late phase.[115]

Be this as it may, the catalogue of prohibited sexual contacts in the family seems to be a primal block of family tradition. It corresponds to the rules about incest observed in many cultures, which are meant to prohibit marriage between relatives defined in different ways.[116] The reasons given for the prohibitions also have an archaic flavour. The positive factor is blood-relationship (vv. 6, 12, 13, 17), which can also be addressed simply by the mention of the degree of relationship ('mother', 'sister', etc. vv. 7, 11, 14); the negative factor is 'shame' (*zimmah*, v. 17b), which can be caused simply by uncovering nakedness and looking at the naked body ('it is the nakedness of', vv. 8, 10, 16). Underlying both interrelated notions is also a fear of magical spheres which one cannot penetrate with impunity, above all if the community is living together in a confined space. The combination of the norms with the world of the deity or superhuman forces also came about at this point.[117] The members of the family live under the same roof as the household god, and moreover in a world loaded with forces. So everyone has to observe given norms. The Yahwehizing of the taboo is a late phenomenon which must have taken place in stages in Lev 18. Whereas the original catalogue of prohibitions is still intrinsically completely free of references to Yahweh, the framework statement in v. 6 introduces the first references to the God of Israel, and this is picked up again later (vv. 21, 30). It is the redactional supplements at the beginning and end of the chapter (vv. 1–5 and 24–30) which put the taboo regulations completely at the service of the exclusive and delimiting Yahweh religion. But this no longer has anything to do with the family faith of all times, which cannot claim to be exclusive.

The realm of everyday obligations and roles certainly also became a concern of the families and has found a record in rules about behaviour and ethical demarcations. The biting characterizations of the idle (Prov 26:13–16), already cited earlier, may be a bit of family tradition, since they relate to the core of duties within the family, work in looking after the group.

---

[115] Cf. Erhard S. Gerstenberger and Wolfgang Schrage, *Frau* (ch. 3 n. 1), 24–50.

[116] Cf. Claude Lévi-Strauss, *Structures* (ch. 4 n. 8).

[117] In the case of the sexual taboos one can perhaps speak of an anthropological constant, as most known cultures seem to know such rules about avoidance in some form.

Even now, small groups with no money or no exchange of commodities worth mentioning live on the common labour of all. Anyone who wants to evade this basic obligation towards the group is first of all called to order by mocking comments about his or her laziness. By contrast all the characterizations of the 'just', 'wicked', 'foolish', 'wise', etc. probably grew up on another ground, because they presuppose more far-reaching criteria of comparison, whether this is the local community, the religious community, the school community or simply wider society. Otherwise, though, we have few examples of norms or role-patterns from the family sphere. One exception is the so-called 'praise of the virtuous housewife' (Prov 31:10–30), which shows the household from the domestic perspective of the husband. The poem praises the prudent woman at the head of the family who has a firm grasp of the family business and works from early to late. She seems to have a great deal of scope, to the point of dealing independently in land. The husband sees himself merely as taking part in a tribal discussion (v. 23). The wife alone is responsible for order and food, clothing and charity. Amazingly, this woman does not suffer from an excess of work, but is cheerful and in good spirits and can also make wise remarks (v. 26). A concluding sentence attributes to her a fear of God which is said to make such achievement possible for others (v. 30). Granted, this is an ideal picture from a male perspective, but it indicates that in Israel at times the woman had a strong position in the domestic sphere and played a decisive part in shaping the life and the spiritual and ethical orientation of the family.[118]

Otherwise there are few explicit norms for the domestic sphere. For example, the commandment to love one's neighbour (Lev 19:18) is already focused on wider social contexts than the family. For the *rēaʿ* is the 'neighbour' who also has a relationship with the person subject to the norm because he or she lives near or is remotely related (the tribal bond!), but does not belong within the innermost circle of the family.[119] Within that circle people call themselves son, father, brother, daughter, mother, sister, and although these intimate designations can also be extended (e.g. so that they come to mean 'brother in a tribe or people'; 'father of a prophetic group', etc.), they are typical of the firmly closed family circle, in which one may not call the other *rēaʿ*. It would be extremely interesting to bring out the degree of familiarity and strangeness within these designations throughout Hebrew scripture and define them more precisely; one way of

---

[118] Cf. Frank Crüsemann and Hartwig Thyen, *Als Mann und Frau geschaffen*, Gelnhausen 1978; Carol Meyers, *Eve* (ch. 4 n. 10); Erhard S. Gerstenberger and Wolfgang Schrage, *Frau* (ch. 3 n. 1).

[119] Cf. Dieter Kellermann, *ThWAT* VII, 545ff.

doing this might be to investigate the structures and forms of dialogue in the narrative texts.

Many of the ethical norms also handed down elsewhere, which come or could come from the family sphere, relate to the external relations of the group. These also need to be regulated, because they too have decisive significance for survival. We can take the commandments in the Decalogue as an example. The compilation of this basic catalogue of norms of behaviour took place between the late exilic and the post-exilic period in the early Jewish cultic community, but some of the individual regulations are very much older. The commandments of the second table in the sphere of social ethics must in principle come from instruction in the family or clan.[120] A quick run through the Ten Commandments can clarify these questions of origin. In their present version, the first to third commandments are clearly the work of the Deuteronomic–Deuteronomistic community. The prohibition against alien gods, images and the misuse of the divine name accord with the precepts of developed Yahweh religion and the content of the corresponding liturgical preaching. Here we can presume that the substance of these prohibitions, the obligation to be loyal to the guardian deity and the basic rule to use that deity's name carefully and cautiously, not magically as though it were under one's control, also played a role in family traditions.[121] The beginnings of monolatry, indeed predominantly monolatrous relations with a god, were to be found all over the ancient Near East.[122] Family religion was not excluded from that; loyalty to the traditional deity could only be good for the ongoing existence of the group.[123]

The fourth commandment of the Decalogue is an even clearer expression of early Jewish Torah theology than the previous one. The sabbath is a creation of the confessional community, which needs marks of identity,

---

[120] Cf. Frank-Lothar Hossfeld, *Der Dekalog*, OBO 45, 1982; Frank Crüsemann, *Torah* (ch. 4 n. 108); Eckart Otto, *Ethik* (ch. 4 n. 96).

[121] For example Assyrian kings worshipped their particular deities and received positive oracles from them which also expressed a certain claim to sacrifice and obedience; cf. *TUAT* II, Karl Hecker, 56–65; Manfred Weippert, 'Assyrische Prophetien der Zeit Assarhaddons und Assurbanipals', in F. M. Fales, *Assyrian Royal Inscriptions*, Rome 1981, 71–115. The example of Akenaten, his change of religion and cult towards the sun god Aten, and the battle with the priesthood of Thebes, are a further famous example at the royal and state level (cf. Klaus Koch, *Religion* [ch. 4 n. 73], 332–52) for the deity's claim to worship and the priestly interests associated with it. The problem is more rarely attested at the family level, but cf. in wisdom contexts (the dialogue literature of Job) the charge that the sufferer has enraged his personal God and thus has brought down the suffering upon himself (Job 8; 22, etc.).

[122] Cf. Thorkild Jacobsen, *Treasures of Darkness. A History of Mesopotamian Religion*, London 1976; Bernhard Lang (ed.), *Der einzige Gott*, Munich 1981; Othmar Keel (ed.), *Monotheismus in Alten Israel und in seiner Umwelt*, BiBe 14, Fribourg 1980.

[123] Cf. Hermann Vorländer, *Mein Gott* (ch. 4 n. 30).

defining focal points in a religiously pluralistic world. The norms relating to social ethics, which by virtue of their origin have to be strictly distinguished from the previous norms, begin with the fifth commandment. Respect for parents arose completely within the sphere of family customs, though in the version in the Decalogue it is of course shown by the community, so that young people will value religious authority. The remaining five commandments all relate to the 'neighbour' in the sense mentioned above, even where this is not explicitly stated, as in the famous triad 'You shall not kill – commit adultery – steal' (Ex 20:13–15): the neighbour is not the alien, the outsider, but one's kinsman in the tribe or clan whom one can still call 'brother' in the extended sense, but who does not belong to one's close circle of relations (one has no obligation to avenge the blood of a *rēaʿ*!). But on some presuppositions a kindred feeling of 'us' binds one to him. Murder, adultery and theft are really not crimes within the innermost family circle. There one would have to speak rather of manslaughter (Cain and Abel, Gen 4), illegitimate sexual contact (Lev 18) and perhaps embezzlement (Judg 17). The measures against such transgressions of boundaries in the family are different in ancient Israel; they were presumably predominantly taken in the sphere of the family's paternal jurisdiction. The ninth prohibition, against speaking falsely, of course applies specifically in public legal proceedings, and thus clearly presupposes a wider society. In short, the five social commandments of the second table now belong in the framework of the early Jewish community and its ethos. But in substance they presumably come from family and tribal traditions, since the behaviour for which they are norms is that of the individual (who of course has his family behind him) in relations with other friendly groups. There is no question that this behaviour towards outsiders has to be learned and given norms, and as the Decalogue – like some other sets of prohibitions in the Old Testament (cf. above all Lev 19) – makes use of the family prohibitive form, it seems very probable that we should conclude that the prohibitions came into being within the family. But at this point it must also be said that the religious basis for the norms being inculcated is not obvious. Unlike the second to fifth commandments, the brief social commandments of the Decalogue contain no kind of basis or explanation, not even an indirect indication that the correct behaviour called for has long been clear to all and needs no special foundation. Nor do they contain any kind of reference to divine sanctions. In the Decalogue these derive only from the late Deuteronomistic framework, in Lev 19 from the constant refrain 'I am Yahweh, your God' (etc.).

All in all, despite the tactic of demarcation from harmful misbehaviour practised with the formulations of prohibitions – or precisely because of this – the family ethic is orientated on the supreme goal that all members of the family are to live together in harmony. For antiquity it is true to a far greater degree than for atomized industrial societies that the patrilinear family was the nucleus and foundation of all further socialization.[124] At that time, given the living conditions (collective work and bringing up children), no other basic order was imaginable. Therefore the core of the matter is family solidarity, which can flourish only in peaceful and benevolent social life in harmony with the divine powers.

> Behold, how good and pleasant it is
> when brothers dwell in unity!
> It is like the precious oil upon the head,
> running down upon the beard,
> upon the beard of Aaron,
> running down on the collar of his robes!
> It is like the dew of Hermon,
> which falls on the mountains of Zion! (Ps 133:1b–3a).

Conversely, apocalyptic times have dawned when the smallest human society no longer functions:

> Put no trust in a neighbour, have no confidence in a friend; guard the doors of your mouth from her who lies in your bosom; for the son treats the father with contempt, the daughter rises up against her mother, the daughter-in-law against her mother-in-law; a man's enemies are the men of his house (Mic 7:5f.).

Traces of a positive picture of family community can be found in many other texts. However, they are often overpainted by the orientations of the confessional community after the exile which are gained from or derived from family solidarity. In other words, the family ethos was to a considerable degree taken up into the later community ethos. That poses a basic problem: how can intimate relations and the rules of conduct which belong to them be transposed into wider societies which no longer have a family structure?

4.5 Theology from the family – theology of the individual

We need only make a *theological* evaluation of the analyses and considerations offered so far, since it is our declared aim to recognize the theological

---

[124] In modern times this saying has at most been treated as the lip service of not very clear-sighted politicians; in reality our social and ecclesiastical activity has long been based on the pre-eminence of the individual; cf. Dietrich von Oppen, *Das personale Zeitalter,* Stuttgart and Gelnhausen 1960; Elisabeth Badinter, *Ich bin Du,* Munich 1987; Horst Eberhard Richter, *Gotteskomplex* (ch. 2 n. 5); Ulrich Beck et al. (eds), *Individualisierung* (ch. 3 n. 7).

significance of the many levels of witness in the Old Testament for our time. Even matter-of-fact, detached, scholarly observation of texts and situations in life can lead to theological standpoints; why shouldn't it? In our case that must be so because we read the Old Testament with a view to our own practice or that of the church. The leading or test question for us is: can the family as the smallest social unit be a theological subject at all, i.e. make productive statements about God which are to be taken seriously?[125] In our traditional theological thought-patterns there are really only two focal points related to society: on the one hand the abstract individual as the absolute subject of grace (as if there were in fact such a person in isolation),[126] and on the other hand the anonymous wider society, usually in the form of the church but also occasionally in the form of general social organizations. In this view the individuals are the ones who make the decisions of faith: here they are supposed to accord more or less with the already given systematized doctrines of faith, the larger organization. Such an estimation of the *Sitz im Leben* of our existence in faith cannot really be called con-textual, since the formative influences of social and cultural forces on the notions of faith do not come into view. Above all, there is no evaluation of the intermediate social authorities between the individual and wider society, which is never clearly identified (is it, say, the nation state, Europe or the ecumenical world society in which people find themselves? Perhaps indeed only the amorphous society of production and consumption?).[127] The

---

[125] Albertz initially attributes theological creativity to the family, but for him that is very rapidly covered over by belief in Yahweh and quenched, cf. *History of Israelite Religion* (ch. 3 n. 1), Vol. 1, 25–39, 99–104, 186–94, 211–13; Vol. 2, 399–407, 507–23. The overall view of the development of family religion put forward by Albertz is improbable because to begin with he rightly establishes the different character of family belief (which is entirely focused on the existential necessities of the small group) and belief in Yahweh (which comes from tribal society) and then contrary to this correct insight makes the family the stronghold of Yahweh worship, which involves salvation history and is warlike, militant and exclusive. The family is thought to have preserved the correct cult down to the time of the exile. Volkmar Fritz wants to keep the 'religion of the fathers' strictly separate from 'family religion', which can be determined by sociology (cf. id., *Entstehung* [ch. 2 n. 19], 146–8).

[126] The schemes from practical theology which still have to be mentioned are strongly concentrated on the individual subject of faith; cf. Ulrich Schwab, *Familienreligiosität* (ch. 3 n. 11), 26–30. This also includes a significant quotation from Henning Luther, which signals the paradigm change from the large organization to the individual: 'Instead of the individual subjects being treated from the perspective of the whole (the church), practical theology should perceive the whole (religion, church) from the perspective of the subjects (concerned)' (Henning Luther, *Religion und Alltag. Bausteine zu einer praktischen Theologie des Subjekts*, Stuttgart 1992, 17).

[127] The basic declaration of the EKKW, 'Witnessing to the Gospel', Kassel 1997, gives the impression that life and church life take place only within the sphere of the Federal Republic. The church has 'the task of attesting the gospel in such a way that it can be understood in the world in which everyone lives (thus for us, in our world)' (ibid., 5). The main problems that are then experienced in this world in which we live are not for example hunger, injustice, war, discrimination, etc. (these world problems play no part in the preaching of *our* gospel), but 'differentiation and an increase in complexity' (ibid., 7).

theological creativity and independence of all the productive social structures which strongly govern our everyday life and thus also influence our theological thought, like professional and working groups, associations, the rest of our family, the communities in which we live, parties, social classes, gender groups and so on are ignored or treated with mistrust (and are seen as a potential danger to theology!).

Academic and church theologies boldly make universal claims without taking account of the way in which they are conditioned by their context. Here it is evident to any unprejudiced view that any newer theology and exegesis has its specific background, conditioned by time and culture, which in the social microstructures can almost always be localized in larger contemporary societies and only in small confessional groups. Typical questions in this traditional theology are: how does personal faith, received from higher worlds, work out in particular social contexts (e.g. family, political community, etc.)? The main image is that of an infusion: faith is produced and defined in indeterminable larger communities (the church?) and then flows into the real social structures. Autonomous individuals shape spiritual and perhaps also social reality by their powers of decision. Usually, no account is taken of creating ideas of faith on one's own responsibility in a variety of forms of social organization. By contrast, I am investigating in particular the specific constructions of notions of God and ethical conceptions in the different forms of community which become visible in the Old Testament.

Two fundamental difficulties emerge for us if we want to connect the Old Testament evidence with our present-day world. First, the atomization of society into independent individuals which has already been mentioned cannot easily be brought into line with the patriarchal (!) family ideology of the biblical witnesses. And secondly, the current understanding of a revelation from outside the world which moves some biblical texts and has found its way into modern dogmatics in a magical–rational form does not correspond either with the old faith of the family or with our scientific scepticism. In the case of the first, the increasing individualization of our societies in fact necessitates fundamental new reflection in theology and the church and a rejection of romantic imagery. However, conversely we must allow ourselves to be asked by the ancient pre-industrial tradition whether the unbridled emancipation of the individual must not be corrected by new forms of society which are conscious of their responsibility. In the case of the second, theological knowledge in the family sphere for the most part rests on religious experience of the forces of the environment. Over against that stands the revelation of the religions of great societies which gives legitimation and orientation. Moses and the prophets, Jesus and Paul apparently had direct access to the transcendent truth, or they were addressed and commissioned by this transcendent power. However, we should be clear that such messages and instructions from a beyond, fashioned in whatever way, are phenomena which are intrinsically time-conditioned and cannot be checked. So they have no higher theological value than the experiential wisdom of family groups. Only present-day experiences and revelations which came from the reality of the deity or life-force alive and at work in us would be of a higher status and more important for a momentary, contextual discovery of truth. But this source of insight and orientation is unknown in most Christian theologies. We want to refer explicitly to historically remote statements, allegedly given normative codification by particular holy scriptures but fundamentally limited in context.

In order to avoid misunderstandings, let me repeat briefly: a description of the theological 'contribution' of the family association and other social groups does not involve imagining social units which are sharply barricaded against one another. These virtually ceased to exist after the neolithic period, at any rate in the regions of the ancient Near East, the densely populated 'fertile crescent'. The 'interaction by osmosis' of the different groups already cited above is, however, a fact which does not rule out the possibility of describing the typically religious constructions of each grouping side by side.

First we turn to an extraordinary characteristic of the knowledge of God in the family and its relationship to God. A number of Old Testament scholars, above all the fathers of the discipline like Albrecht Alt and Martin Buber,[128] who have already been mentioned, and colleagues like Frank Crüsemann, Rainer Albertz, Hermann Vorländer, Karel van der Toorn, etc. have referred to the personal intimacy of the family relationship with God. In fact the 'I–Thou' relationship to the personal guardian deity is a fundamental human experience deriving from prehistoric times which moves the world: family cultic practice takes account of it. The deity worshipped personally adopts individuals into his group, and is ready to see to their basic needs in life. This basic constellation of individual, group, God leads to an intimate personal communication with the deity which is stamped in advance with family customs; the deity almost becomes a member of the family. Here are

---

[128] Alt emphasized the head of the family as the person to whom family religion related. Old Testament scholars of the last two centuries have time and again referred one-sidedly to the importance of the individual for Old Testament faith, but without evaluating the anchoring of the individual in the family; cf. Bernhard Duhm, *Israels Propheten*, Tübingen ²1922; Johannes Hempel, *Ethos* (ch. 4 n. 108); cf. Martin Buber's concept of the family and religion in *I and Thou*, Edinburgh 1930.

some biblical samples, in my own translation, of the extraordinarily deep language of prayer which still moves us today:[129]

> Do not hide yourself from me;
> do not reject me in anger, I am your servant.
> You can help me.
> Do not give me up, do not abandon me,
> God my helper.
> Father and mother have forsaken me, but Yahweh will take me up
>   (Ps 27:9f.).

The deity can be reached directly and addressed personally. The deity is even closer to the family than father and mother, who can neglect their duties of solidarity towards their children (the expression 'father and mother have forsaken me' is a stereotyped way of describing the extreme instance when the family structure no longer functions or has become insignificant).[130] The deity revered in the family has different names; in the end (v. 10) it is also identified with YHWH. But its function remains the same through all the changes of name. This function of protection and care arises out of the situation in which the small groups of worshippers live. It is continuity in the flux of time.

The laments and thanksgivings of the individual offer many examples of the very direct, intimately personal dealings with the family deity. As I have already said, the personal note has been amazingly preserved in this language of prayer, although these are formulae which have been used by many people. Here are two further examples which clearly betray their connection with the family milieu:

> Yes, you have brought me out of my mother's womb,
> cared for me when I was an infant.
> From the beginning I have been dependent on you,
> for already in my mother's womb you were my God (Ps 22:10f.).

If this is an eminently biographical view of security with the guardian deity of the family, then in the next text once again we hear the current situation of distress and the breakdown of the family which has taken place:

---

[129] Erhard S. Gerstenberger, Konrad Jutzler and Hans Jochen Boecker, *Zu Hilfe mein Gott! Psalmen und Klagelieder*, Neukirchen-Vluyn ⁴1989. Many prayers from the ancient Near East are intensely personal in a similar way; cf. Adam Falkenstein, Wolfgang von Soden, *Sumerische und Akkadische Hymnen und Gebete*, Zurich 1953.

[130] Cf. Erhard S. Gerstenberger, *ThWAT* 5, 1200–8, esp. 1205f.; a similar formula can already be found in Sumerian prayers: Gudea, Cylinder A, III, 6–7: 'I have no mother, you are my mother; I have no father, you are my father' – to Gatumdu (Dietz O. Edzard, *Gudea and his Dynasty*, Toronto 1997, 70).

Lord, I long for you, my groaning does not remain hidden from you.
My heart beats wildly, my strength has left me;
the light of my eyes is also quenched.
Friends and kinsfolk stand aloof from me,
neighbours cautiously keep away.
Nevertheless I wait on you, Yahweh
you will answer me, my God and Lord (Ps 38:10–12, 16).

The Psalm text no longer presupposes the narrower family as a background. It also speaks of 'friends' ('ōhᵃbay, 'who love me'), 'other relatives' (rēʿay, 'my kinsfolk') and 'neighbours' (qᵉrōbay, 'my neighbours'), who by my definition are possibly also people from the wider environment in which the suppliant is involved. For them, even if there is not complete family solidarity, there are strong bonds of affection and mutual help, and of course mutual interests which are to be derived from living together in a place and from wider relationships in the clan.

We find the high point of personal discourse about and with God and the climax of the terrifying and comforting awareness of being bound up with the God who is responsible for the individual existence of a person in Ps 139. Certainly here too there is also theological and wisdom reflection extending beyond the family horizon. But the core of these statements is grounded in the family of the God who shows care for persons. They are presented in highly poetic language. And the name Yahweh is again a sign of an advanced community theology.

Yahweh, you see through me, you know me.
You know whether I am sitting or standing,
you know my thoughts from a distance.
You determine whether I walk or lie down;
my whole life is familiar to you.
Not a word comes on my tongue
that you have not already known, Yahweh.
You surround me on all sides,
you have taken me over.
Your insight is uncanny to me,
it is too high for me; I cannot grasp it.

Where shall I go to avoid you?
Where shall I fly if I want to get away from you?
If I ascend to heaven you are there,
if I make my bed in the underworld, you are there also.
If I fly with wings of the dawn,
settle at the end of the sea:

even there you will grasp me
and lead me by your hand.
If I said, darkness shall cover me;
may the light around me become night –
the darkness would not be dark for you,
the night would shine like the day.
Yes, the darkness would be like light.

You have created my kidneys,
you have formed me in my mother's womb.
I praise you for having made me splendidly.
Yes, your works are wonderful,
I note that very well.
My body is not unknown to you
although I took shape in secret,
although I was formed in the depths of the earth.
You already saw me when I was still formless.
Everything is written in your book.
All the days were already formed
when not a single one had begun (Ps 139:1–16).

Of course – as we shall see immediately – the personal forms of language in
dealing with the family deity express the personal nature of the deity. All
the theological content which can be expressed in the family circle is
governed by this very horizon. God is described as the caring partner and
helper; of course he can also be provoked and is unpredictable, but time
and again he can be addressed. Because that is the case, I regard the theology
of the family as the fundamental, oldest, most important expression of human
faith. It grasped the nature of God in respect of the individual and his
intimate group before any theology of larger groups, and also before any
revelation on Sinai or to the prophets. Nor did family theology die out or
become superfluous, but maintained itself despite all the restructuring of
society.[131] In the sphere of the Hebrew scriptures it developed a tenacious
power of survival which in the last phase (the exile and afterwards) led to a
new strong influence in the Jewish confessional community. Thus the Bible
at its core became a book of humankind: the insights into family theology
maintained in the Hebrew scriptures extend far beyond the rise of Israel
and Judaism. Moreover the Jewish and Christian tradition of family faith
continued to be active in the face of all tendencies towards centralization

---

[131] Some more recent theological schemes take account of this fact and of the modern individualism which is ultimately based on it; cf. e.g. Dietrich Rössler, *Grundriss* (ch. 1 n. 5). Ulrich
Schwab, *Familienreligiosität* (ch. 3 n. 11), demonstrates in his case studies that family religion
resists the domination of church theology and why it does so (cf. the summary, ibid., 274–81).

and the formation of a state in the great confessional structure that was adapted to society. After the last vain rebellions against the power of the Roman state (70 and 135 CE), Judaism did not again become a state religion, but remained limited to school and community theology.[132] This fact gives it its riches, its basic democratic tendency and its fundamental openness to divergent theological truth. Certainly (depending on the nature of the family and the community) it is also prone to the formation of parties, loss of power, misuse of office,[133] but it has been spared the orthodoxies and the persecutions of heretics that have taken place in the state and the centralized church. It has also been spared the formation of exclusivist dogmas. There have been neither crusades, nor inquisitions nor the burnings of witches in the Jewish communities. Instead, in the disputes between rabbis and regional theologies, and in splinter groups, Judaism has remained more open to family influences on liturgy, prayer and ideas of God.

By contrast, in Christianity the problems piled up as a consequence of the formation of large societies, the growth of the state, an increase in the power of the churches and the unscrupulous exploitation of the power which had accrued to it to an excessive degree. Nevertheless, in the practical piety of the people and the communities traces of the old family faith could not be blotted out, even under the supervision of the most authoritarian and the most orthodox secular and church authorities. Below and sometimes within a more abstract structure of theological thought like that of Thomas

---

[132] Cf. Georg Fohrer, *Glaube und Leben im Judentum*, UTB 885, Heidelberg 1979; Michael Krupp, *Vergesse ich dein, Jerusalem,* Metzingen 1962 (the fight for the formation of a new state, the history of Zionism); Schalom ben Chorin, *Betendes Judentum*, Tübingen 1980; Louis Finkelstein (ed.), *The Jews: Their History* (1949), New York 1970; Solomon Schechter, *Aspects of Rabbinic Theology* (1909), New York 1961; Leo Baeck, *The Essence of Judaism* (²1921), London 1936. The studies indicated refer to the inner structure of Judaism in very different ways: Fohrer depicts faith, rites, the cycles of festivals; Krupp the way of Zionism. Ben Chorin explains how prayer is bound up with the study of the Torah and also towers above this (e.g. 'Tefillah is the liturgically fixed prayer which finds its full expression only in community prayer, the fellowship of ten men. Tahanunim are the free prayers above all of the indiviual. By nature the Tefilla is appropriate as Tefillath-zibbur, community prayer, Tachanumim as Tefillath-yachid, the prayer of the individual or private devotion' (ibid., 26: both forms of prayer breathe the spirit of the small group). Schechter rejects the abstract-philosophical notion of the remoteness of God in favour of his proximity and humanity; Baeck depicts God's properties in personal categories ('Thus did the conviction of the love of God find expression in human words [i.e. as attested in scripture]; for through these words alone the soul can speak. It is in its personal, in its deepest, essence that all this is experienced; only in the forms of the personal can this be revealed to it and emerge from it. Love can be understood by human beings only in the forms of human love, and they cannot think about it without poetic imagination', ibid., 110).

[133] Cf. Morton Smith, 'Religiöse Parteien bei den Israeliten vor 587', in Bernhard Lang (ed.), *Der einzige Gott*, Munich 1981; Julius Wellhausen, *Pharisäer und Sadducäer*, Göttingen ³1967; Travers Herford, *Die Pharisäer*, Leipzig 1928; Kurt Schubert, *Die jüdischen Religionsparteien in neutestamentlicher Zeit*, Stuttgart 1970.

Aquinas a personal piety asserted itself, in the Catholic Church also humanized by the host of saints who were venerated in the small world of the family and the local community, and also in the medieval religious orders for men and women and the domestic and local communities of the Reformation churches.[134] Theology was and is a function of the wider society in our spiritual landscape and is practised by outstanding individuals. The history of theology is therefore predominantly a series of doctrinal views which are usually devised by professional theologians. Little room is given in the compendia of the history of dogma and in more recent dogmatic schemes to the theology of the ordinary person in the community and the theology of the family. If they do occur at all, it is often under the condescending aspects of popular piety and heterodoxy gone astray.

In reality, however, essential foundations of Old Testament faith can be traced back to the family, even according to biblical tradition (cf. Ex 3:15, 16; Josh 24:2–4, etc.) and they have continued to be an influence to the present day – unrecognized. The much-vaunted 'personal relationship with God' in Judaism and Christianity is a fruit of family religion. In higher bureaucratic and impersonal formations a 'personal' relationship with God cannot either be thought of or experienced. As we shall see, the tribal god is predominantly a warrior who leads men into battle and helps them to defeat enemies. One cannot have a personal relationship with him any more than one can with a general or senior army commander (whose image is therefore often personified in a mythical way). The state god of a city is concerned with the increase and the protection of the royal house and the territories ruled by it. The subject has a subordinate relation to him, not a 'personal' one. However, the predominant demand made on the subject by royal courts and imperial theologies is complete submission, prostration before the ruler, lying on one's belly with one's nose in the dust.[135] A direct human relationship with the community God of the exilic and post-exilic period is, though, both conceivable and demonstrable – but it comes from the family tradition, to which we are thus referred back. Yet alongside this stands Moses, the leader of the people, who receives the commandments

---

[134] Cf. studies of 'piety' by church historians. For the Middle Ages: Klaus Schreiner (ed.), *Laienfrömmigkeit im späten Mittelalter*, Munich 1992; André Vauchez, *Gottes vergessenes Volk. Laien im Mittelalter*, Freiburg 1993; Ulrich Horst, *Evangelische Armut und Kirche. Thomas von Aquin und die Armutskontroversen des 13. und beginnenden 14. Jahrhunderts,* Berlin 1992; Alois M. Haas, *Gottleiden-Gottlieben. Zur volkssprachlichen Mystik im Mittelalter*, Frankfurt 1980. For the more recent period, Berndt Hamm, *Frömmigkeitstheologie am Anfang des 16. Jahrhunderts*, Tübingen 1993; Albrecht Peters, *Kommentar zu Luthers Katechismus*, 4 vols, Göttingen 1990–3; Philipp Jacob Spener, *Pia desideria* (1675), Werkausgabe 1, Hildesheim 1979.

[135] Old Testament texts offer examples of encounters on an equal footing, as in the family sphere (cf. Gen 4; Ruth 1; 1 Sam 18 – 20, etc.), but also for submission rituals of a religious and a profane kind (cf. 2 Sam 19:17–21; 1 Kings 1:16; Ezra 9:5f.; 10:1; Neh 9:1, etc.).

for the great mass (Ex 19 - 20) and must act impartially (Ex 18). So how far theological concepts and thought structures can be used must be examined again against each social background. That is also true in an exemplary way for the term 'love', which is used so widely in Christian theology.

The 'personal' relationship with the family deity – whatever his name may have been – follows naturally and consistently from its membership in the family alliance. As 'father', 'brother', 'uncle' (strangely, feminine forms are not attested, probably because of the patrilinear structure of the families), the deity is bound up in the small group; he is its head, leader, final authority; holding people together, receiving their veneration and their service and giving counsel, help and blessing. In this function the deity is near and can be grasped personally; one can speak with him, negotiate with him, follow him or contradict him, in exactly the same way that one can with other members of the alliance. All that matters is the personal encounter, the relationship of trust, which of course can also be disrupted by both sides. The deity can terminate the relationship, but so too can human beings, or more precisely the partners of the deity, as can still be seen from the calls for decision for Yahweh and against other deities (cf. Gen 28:20–2; Josh 24:15; Judg 6:25–32, etc.). The personal relationship to the deity is thought of as being analogous and in fact parallel to the interpersonal relationships of the group, and that is how it is experienced.

At this point mention must be made of the characteristics and actions of the deity. Textbooks on the theology of the New Testament as a whole concentrate entirely on this theme,[136] but without noting the social origins of certain notions. Here of course the anthropomorphism of Old Testament theology (as compared to the sophisticated, highly philosophical Greek images of God) has always been striking. But after all, anthropomorphisms come from the family sphere. If the deity belongs to the family, then he must also be thought of in human categories. Thus the whole scale of human nature must also be expected in the image of God: all the emotional stirrings from gentleness and patience to the most burning anger, from love and penitence to deadly hatred. Nothing human is alien to the family guardian deity. His strength and power are also measured by the criteria of the family, not by those of a higher social organization. The many problems and aporias which arise from confrontation between an abstract philosophical theology, located on a quite different social level, and family faith are therefore often intrinsically meaningless. They are comparing the incomparable.

---

[136] Cf. e.g. Horst Dietrich Preuss, *Theologie des alten Testaments* (2 vols), Stuttgart 1991, 1992; Walther Zimmerli, *Old Testament Theology in Outline*, Edinburgh 1983.

Briefly to indicate just a few fundamental theological problems which arise from the difference in social levels: the question of the justice (righteousness) of God is a constant problem in the theology of the ancient Near East and the West. It becomes more acute under the influence of abstract, Greek philosophy. How can an omnipotent, omniscient God who is wholly good allow injustices? The family deity who is responsible for individual prosperity is not omnipotent, omniscient and all-gracious. So in the debate over the theodicy question theologians often attempt to relate the problems at two completely different levels, the individual experience of suffering and injustice and the administration of the divine rule of the world, which of course cannot come about in accordance with the principles of a community which displays the same solidarity as the family.

It is the same with the God who is near and the God who is remote. The family deity is near; he belongs to the family. A state deity is remote, a universal deity dwelling far away in heaven. It would be good not to mix up the different divine authorities in advance. However, the social structures overlap, and the ideas of God make contact with one another. So we are compelled to find room for the theological 'networking' of images of God. However, the levels on which we argue can still be distinguished. In that case the network of images of God produces a provisional mosaic of limited validity. And the universal statements which we strive to make remain the unaccomplished task which in reality of course they also always are.

Among the most important personal properties of the deity in the Old Testament at the family level, faithfulness, mercy and love predominate. Certainly these qualities can also play a role in the relationship of God to his people. But in that case they have a special stamp. Loyalty to a people is something different from solidarity with an individual or a family group. Mercy on a wider society, forgiveness of its guilt, and openness to new opportunities in life for it have different dimensions from those of the acceptance of a prodigal son back into the family or reconciliation between brothers or sisters. In the end, in the ancient world as today, love is an original concept which is quite exclusively applicable to relationships between couples and an attitude within the family. So when the Old Testament speaks very often of these three properties of God, on closer inspection we immediately see that family and clan faith is in play, and that the great God of the wider society – if something like this can be said of him – has drawn on family theology.[137] Those who speak of love of the fatherland misuse an intimate concept from inter-personal relations in a highly suspect way. Gustav Heinemann, the third President of the German

---

[137] E.g. in the Mesopotamian sphere 'love' is also a political concept: in the vassal treaties the great king desires the loyalty felt in family affection. But the transplantation of the word into the political sphere already indicates the change of meaning.

Federal Republic, once aptly said in an interview, 'I love my wife, not my fatherland!'

By way of example I shall keep to the three words mentioned: faithfulness (ḥesed), mercy (ḥnn; rᵃḥāmīm), love (ᵃhābāh) are often used of God in this or a similar form of words or statement. All the investigations of recent decades are agreed that the origin of this vocabulary lies in interpersonal relations.[138] There is a summary of the expressions in the liturgical formula:

> Merciful and gracious is Yahweh, patient and of great loving-kindness.[139]

Phyllis Trible[140] has pointed out that the statements relating to mercy are really statements about motherhood,[141] which clearly have their setting in the family sphere. In the end, the love of God for human beings is certainly exclusively related to the people of Israel or its tribes,[142] but in the opposite direction love is also required of the individual in reaction to the glory of Yahweh. That is what is said in the classic passage Deut 7:7f.:

> It was not because you were more in number than any other people that Yahweh set his love upon you and chose you, for you were the fewest of all peoples; but it is because Yahweh loves you.

This love has the specific character of affection within the family for the partner, for the weak to whom one owes solidarity; so it does not correspond to an imperial ideology which can revere only the strong and can see individuals only as statistics. Accordingly the invitation to the Israelites is:

> You shall love Yahweh your God with all your heart, all your soul and all your strength (Deut 6:5).

[138] The first investigations which clearly brought out this aspect were those by Karl Hjalmar Falgren, sᵉdāqā *nahestehende und entgegengesetzte Begriffe im alten Testament,* Uppsala 1932; Nelson Glueck, *Das Wort hesed im alttestamentlichen Sprachgebrauch,* 1927, ²1961. Nothing has changed in this insight today; cf. the relevant articles in the Theological Dictionaries of the Old Testament (Hans-Jürgen Zobel, *ThWAT* III, 48–71; Hans-Joachim Stoebe, *THAT* I, 600–21; Bo Johnson, *ThWAT* VI, 903–24; Klaus Koch, *THAT* II, 507–30). Unfortunately the argument to the *Sitz im Leben* in the family is not carried through consistently enough.

[139] Cf. Ezek 34:6; Ps 86:15; 103:6. The first passage mentioned is clearly a key passage. It uses two adjectives (*rahum, hannūn*) and the noun statements: 'erek 'appayīm (patience), *rab hesed* (complete solidarity) and *'emet* (reliability). Cf. Edgar Kellenberger, *hesed we'emet als Ausdruck einer Glaubenserfahrung,* Zurich 1982; Hermann Spieckermann, *Heilsgegewart,* Göttingen 1989 (cf. id., *ZAW* 1990).

[140] Phyllis Trible, *God and the Rhetoric of Sexuality,* Philadelphia 1978.

[141] Cf. also Helen Schüngel-Straumann, 'Gott als Mutter in Hos 11', *ThQ* 166, 1986, 119–34; Marie-Theres Wacker, 'Spuren der Göttin im Hoseabuch', in Walter Dietrich and Martin Klopfenstein (eds), *Gott* (ch. 2 n. 21).

[142] In the sphere of great, anonymous social formations 'love' cannot have the intimate sense of direct interpersonal relations, precisely because the immediate sharing of life between members of a larger community is lacking. So the term must necessarily be reinterpreted in the direction of 'loyalty to a social order'.

Here too we are moving on the level of the family, for individual worshippers must show respect and obedience, and not personal affection and solidarity, to the lofty state God. So the conceptuality within the family is used metaphorically. That is possible because the community, i.e. the early Jewish community which makes such theological statements, orientates itself markedly on the example of family faith and the structure of the family.

The love of God in the Old Testament is a problem for modern exegetes. It allegedly manifests itself – especially after the marriage allegory of the prophet Hosea (Hos 1–3) and the accompanying metaphors of Yahweh's marriage with Israel (e.g. Jer 2:2; 3:1–13; Ezek 16; 23; Isa 62:1–5) – predominantly as God's affection for his people. That is correct for the texts that we have. But these ideas of the most intimate connection between God and human beings certainly come from the family's personal relations with God. The application to the community is a metaphorical one: it matches the structure of the community and the decision of faith which is ultimately expected of the individual. Sometimes the experts also detect that, as does for example Gerhard Wallis in his article *'āhab* in *TWAT* I, 105–28. He states: 'A clean distinction must be made between God's behaviour towards the individual and towards the people. The relationship between God and people probably had a different orientation in origin from his love towards individuals. Only the covenant made by God himself associates him with the people. By nature they remain distinct from one another . . . Similarly, God's relation to the individual does not seem originally to have been felt to be a bond of love . . .' (ibid., 121). Wallis is on the right track, but he does not go far enough. Above all he does not attribute any theology to the small groups in Israel. He attests that the Deuteronomist and his followers developed a theology, indeed a systematics of the divine love (ibid., 122, 126), but this relates only to Israel as a whole in its relation to Yahweh. Wallis even complains that the love of Yahweh in worship and temple could not have developed into love of brother or stranger; here, of course, he is tacitly referring to the breakthrough in the preaching of Jesus (ibid., 127; here he neglects Lev 19:18, 34 completely). In short, our present-day theology does not want to note the small, the familiar and the near in the Old Testament image of God, because we are accustomed to engaging in a theology which is in principle that of the wider society and the state with its sweet promises of power and want to keep the lower levels of the family, the laity and the people out of the business of theology. Could that be a Western characteristic? Theologians in the poorest countries have a greater sensitivity to the smallness, the impotence and the suffering of God.

Faith in the family sphere is a counter-balance to the lust for rule and omnipotence and is therefore fundamental for humankind, even if that is not recognized. In the biblical sphere we are fortunate enough to see much from the realm of the family preserved through changing times and social conditions. Many factors contributed to this situation and prevented the superstructures from getting the upper hand in antiquity. We can sum up the particular features of family faith in a few points which take account both of the abiding value and also the dangers of any family theology. I should point out that the theological significance of the social micro-structures is sometimes better known in Latin American theology than in Europe. There it is for example the base communities which actively and often do theology in opposition to the 'official' doctrine.[143]

- The relationship to God within the family alliance is marked out by its personal character. The human dependents of a guardian deity have a direct, human relationship which is mutual, despite the unequal balance of power. The rule is mutual trust, mutual solidarity. How-ever, of course a personal relationship and a personal being which enter into interpersonal communication and action also bring into play all kinds of dangers and uncertainties which are given in such a system of relations. Persons cannot be calculated like mathematical entities or manipulated like material. Despite all their ties and group pressures they are always also subjects, subjects whose anger and affection are not completely predictable. So there are rules of behaviour for dealing with one another, and because these rules are old and proven by tradition, they usually also function to the satisfaction of all concerned. Nevertheless, extreme situations cannot be ruled out in which the unpredictable happens either from the divine or from the human side. However, even the unpredictable is made possible to grasp and live with through rites of petition, purification and the forgiveness of sins or through thanks and praise.

- In the ancient family groups people lived together and close to everyday reality; in keeping with the agricultural conditions they also lived close to nature. The given conditions were usually accepted, and people felt orientated more on the past than on the future. They claimed to be content with a modest way of living and sought to preserve harmony between members of the family. At almost every point there have been considerable changes in our attitudes to fellow human beings, the world, work and happiness. The relation of the family theology of that time to reality becomes evident in very pragmatic and hardly dogmatic attitudes. The relationship with God rested on tangible experiences. Everyday life was embedded in a

---

[143] Cf. the classical theological reporting by Ernesto Cardenal, *The Gospel of the Peasants in Solentiname*, Maryknoll 1976; Equipo Saledoc (ed.), *Religiosidad popular*, Salamanca 1976; Clodivis Boff, *Teologia pé-no-chão*, Petrópolis 1984; Fernando Castillo (ed.), *Theologie aus der Praxis des Volkes*, Munich 1978.

numinous reality. For us, by contrast, the world is a neutral playground of human experiments and desires for conquest. With an enormously heightened technical ability we have learned constantly to accumulate power and capabilities and to build up ever-increasing possessions at the expense of the weaker and of nature. Our life has become far removed from the reality of existing offers of life. We live beyond our circumstances.

- Family religion knows that it is not the only religion in the world. It does not make a universal claim. There are many other groups with other deities alongside one's own. One is predominantly dealing with a deity who is well disposed but not omnipotent, who sometimes has to assert himself against other powers. This leads to modesty and a certain natural tolerance. This modesty is an extraordinarily valuable possession because it clearly demonstrates the boastful self-opinionatedness of many religions of large societies and states. On the other hand there is a certain narrowness and independence in the narrowest family circle. The world – in so far as it exists at all as 'world' – seems to revolve only around one's own group. Responsibility to outsiders is only secondary, a second stage. That can lead to encapsulation, indifference, indeed hostility towards others outside the confines of one's own family. But this danger seems to me to be greater in the more 'highly' developed forms of society and their religions and images of God than in the family, which is dependent on co-existence.

- And once again, in the past our European, and especially German, theology and biblical scholarship were overwhelmingly orientated on the state, the mainstream church and society as a whole, and therefore were also authoritarian (a theology of rule). American theology and exegesis focuses far more on individuals and what happens to them – that is also true of all the pietistic trends in Germany since the seventeenth century, which sometimes in modern times have taken on an American colouring. Individuals and their God, both fitted into a conservative, patriarchal, established social structure, are the ideal model for Western Christianity. The relationship with God is meant to be a personal one, but it must not just function according to the rules which are outlined by the leaders of society and the church. One is not allowed to have extravagant relations with a God of one's own; this is regarded as deviant and heretical. What is believed is decided by the superior bodies. In the end the function of faith is to support the state. (Anyone can test this by examining how the main churches in Germany deal with personal problems, e.g. marriage of divorced couples, homosexuality, homelessness, military service, leaving the church, etc. In decisions, what has priority is very often not solidarity with the poor, the suffering and the outcasts but how the church is affected, whether it could suffer harm.) The way in which little people and their theology are ignored is, moreover, to a considerable degree overcome or reduced in Latin American liberation theology (although after the political changes in Europe in 1989/90 there was often sharp criticism within the church's own ranks that liberation theology was self-centred and alien to reality).[144] Here people were really asking about how families work, what they want and know.[145] The base communities themselves are organized by family and there is predominantly direct interpersonal contact between all who belong to them. Therefore the theology of the base communities of Latin America is completely tailored to interpersonal interests. Certainly it raises a demand for justice for the oppressed in the wider society, since it is this society which exercises the degrading economic pressure. But the heart of liberation theology beats – quite rightly – in the small groups of the community. Therefore there are hardly any possible schemes for the structuring of the wider economy and society which go beyond general appeals for responsibility and justice.[146]

• An unresolved fundamental question that has already been touched on is the disintegration of the family today into its individual parts and the quest for a new, tolerable and sustainable living community. Another problem which is almost as pressing is the mechanization and technologization of the world, with the shift in mentality towards the greatest possible profit and far-reaching domination which follows from it. Anticipating the next chapter, I shall go into this briefly. We have already rightly established a profile of the individual for the late Old Testament period (cf. Ezek 18; Isa 56; 58). The decision for

---

[144] Cf. Hugo Assmann, *Crítica à lógica da exclusão*, São Paulo 1994; the thematic issues of the journal *Vida Pastoral*, São Paulo, 36, Vols 180, 181, Jan–April 1995: *A fraternidade e os excluídos*; Erhard S. Gerstenberger, 'Befreiungstheologien im Wandel', in Wolfram Kurz et al. (eds), *Krisen und Umbrüche in der Geschichte des Christentums*, Giessen 1994, 155–77.

[145] Cf. Carlos Mesters, *Die Botschaft des leidnedes Volkes*, Neukirchen-Vluyn 1982: an exegesis of the Suffering Servant Songs in Deutero-Isaiah against the background of suffering men and women in Brazil; id., *Sechs Tage im Keller der Menschheit*, Neukirchen-Vluyn 1983: an account of a visit lasting several days in an underdeveloped community in the interior cut off from civilization.

[146] Cf. e.g. Paul Gerhard Schoenborn, *Sehnsucht nach dem Fest des freien Menschen*, Wuppertal 1975; Ulrich Schoenborn, *Gekreuzigt im Leiden der Armen*, Mettingen 1985, etc.

faith in Yahweh was required of the individual; at least theoretically, the community became a confessing community. 'I and my house, we will serve Yahweh' (Josh 24:15), says the head of one family. The summons 'today' to hearken to Yahweh's commandments and enter into his covenant (Deut 29 – 30; Ps 95:8–11) is nominally addressed to the whole community, but this consists of individual tribal leaders, chiefs, leaders, all men, children, women, resident aliens and slave workers (cf. Deut 29:9f.). So however firm the family bond may have been in religious terms down to the end of the monarchy, from the Babylonian exile onwards a freedom of choice developed, which also time and again led to splits in the faith community (cf. Num 16; Isa 65:1–16). Thus a tendency to self-determination can be discovered in the ancient writings, but it is far removed from our theoretical and practical individualism. The question remains whether we value the autonomy of the individual and the obligation to mutual solidarity. We will have to start from the rights and dignity of the individual, regardless of gender, race and religion. Today – in contrast to biblical times – they are pre-eminent. Communal responsibilities then need to be developed again from the needs of the individual and the necessity for shared responsibility for one another and the whole creation. It is the same with the modern world-view. Certainly even in antiquity there were almost mechanistic explanations of what happened in the world (cf. Prov 10:2–5; 12:24–8, etc.). Here, too, there is a tremendous difference from today's explanation of the world by means of physical and chemical laws. How far can we still use the predominantly personalistic model of interpretation presented by the biblical witnesses? At the level of personal and family faith it still seems necessary to have a personal understanding of God, to address God in the second person. This corresponds to our life and our experience. On this level God encounters us predominantly in human activities. The personal nature of God becomes problematical in macro-contexts, which we usually approach in statistical and impersonal ways. Here God cannot be the magician who conjures up rabbits and doves out of mathematical sequences. We cannot ignore the regularities in nature and culture. But we may discover that God himself works in them and through them.

5

Deities of the Village (Small-Town) Community

5.1 The social history of Palestine

In the dark early history of humankind, over long periods of time in thinly populated regions there were possibly completely self-sufficient family or tribal groups which had no contact whatsoever with other human beings. On the other hand, it is very probable that early in the Stone Age there were already contacts between groups of people since human beings were extraordinarily mobile, travelled in search of sources of food, and dispersed over the habitable earth, no matter where we may seek the starting point of this development (East Africa? China?). Cave dwellings or meeting places capable of being used by larger groups are known from the mesolithic and palaeolithic eras. The final phase of the palaeolithic era (after 20,000 BCE) already has fixed, though temporary, dwelling places, the number of whose inhabitants exceeded the size of the family. However, the preconditions for a longer period of settled life are at least the rudimentary beginnings of agriculture and cattle-breeding, because resources of food, raw material for clothing, firewood, etc. are rapidly exhausted when hunters and gatherers spend a lengthy time in a specific region. Ribeiro rightly regards the move to the agricultural production of food, which in the fertile crescent of the Near East evidently took place around 10,000 BCE, as a revolution in human history.[1] In Syria-Palestine there are traces of human beings in the form of crude stone tools which are at least 700,000 years old, from a find at 'Ubediye, on the west bank of the Jordan around two miles south of Lake Gennesaret.[2] In the middle of the palaeolithic era (100,000 to 40,000 BCE)

---

[1] Darcy Ribeiro, *Prozess* (ch. 3 n. 2), 65–72. Whether the hunter – and – gatherer phase really was as 'centrifugal' and the settled farmer life contributed as much to 'forming communities' as he assumes needs to be examined critically.

[2] Helga Weippert, *Palästina* (ch. 3 n. 3), 75.

the finds of tools and bones increase; there are burial places, camping grounds and inhabited or used caves, above all in the last great period of the palaeolithic era, which lasted from 40,000 to 16,000 BCE. But there were probably as yet no permanent settlements, since agriculture had not yet been invented.[3] In the mesolithic (16,000 to 8500 BCE) and neolithic eras (8600 to 4000) agricultural production then became established in Palestine – and also in northern Mesopotamia; this allowed complete settlement and stronger socialization in settled communities.[4] Alongside other finds, the excavations from neolithic Jericho at Tell es-Sultan, especially by Kenyon, then produced overwhelming evidence that people in Palestine between the seventh and the fifth millennium BCE could rise to great architectural achievements.[5] The walls and towers in the layout of the city are so enormous (moreover thousands of years later they led to the formation of the legend in Joshua 6)[6] that they allow us to infer a strictly organized citizenry capable of sharing work and with capital resources.

I would like to add here that we cannot be indifferent in the history of culture and religion, and indeed in theology, to the long archaic history of humankind which by contrast with the 'modern times' (from around 3000 BCE) attested to us through written tradition seems totally to have been lost. For – as can be demonstrated by behavioural scientists – these millions of years saw the formation of many, indeed most, basic values, patterns of behaviour, notions and even images of God which we still carry around in our minds. But it is only in the momentary final phase of human development that they are consciously documented (if we take the whole period of which I am speaking of here as a day, then the historical period lasts barely a few seconds!). Now we are wrong to think that humankind

---

[3] 'Of course the offer of plants to eat and the existence in the immediate neighbourhood of animals that could be hunted and eaten also [i.e. in addition to the availability of water] determined the length of time that one could spend in a place. All in all one must assume that in a sparse environment . . . life as a gatherer and hunter necessitated a superficial exploitation of the environment and thus also a mobile lifestyle' (Helga Weippert, *Palästina* [ch. 3 n. 3], 79).

[4] Cf. Gordon V. Childe, *New Light on the Most Ancient East*, London ⁴1969; Weippert, *Palästina* (ch. 3 n. 3), 80–117. Learning agriculture and the cattle-breeding 'was not without effect on the forms of human society. The intensive and superficial use of the soil made it possible for larger groups to lead a permanent settled life together. This set in motion two contrary developments: on the one hand specialist craftsmen came into being, and on the other there was now the workforce and the means to undertake communal projects' (ibid., 99). Jacques Cauvin, *Les premiers villages de Syrie-Palestine du IXème au VIIème avant JC*, Lyon 1978; cf. id., *Réligions néolithiques de Syro-Palestine*, Paris 1972. Cf. also the summary account by Gary O. Rollefson, 'Prehistoric Time', in Gösta W. Ahlström, *History* (ch. 2 n. 19), 72–111.

[5] Kathleen M. Kenyon, *Digging up Jericho*, London 1957; ead., *Archaeology in the Holy Land*, London 1971.

[6] Cf. Volkmar Fritz, *Das Buch Josua*, HAT I/7, Tübingen 1994, 65–76.

begins to exist only with this written historical tradition. Theologically we have to draw the conclusion that the infinitely long periods of time before 3000 BCE – which we usually call the 'Stone' Age – and before which we then want to put preliminary stages of less importance, are also of great significance for understanding God and the relationship with God. Or do we want to claim in all seriousness that God has been concerned with human beings for only a few million years? Those who assume this suffer from a dangerous overestimation of themselves. We succumb even more to this delusion if we make world history begin with the origin of Israel and the collecting of the Bible, or with the invention of writing, and neglect the previous millennia with their high cultures in Egypt and Mesopotamia. By contrast, the biblical tradition knows very well that God had always been with human beings (cf. Genesis 1 – 11), and speaks openly, without raising any warning fingers, of how the forefathers 'served other gods beyond the river' (Josh 24:1). Thus the pre-Yahwistic tradition is recognized, even if belief in Yahweh represents a new beginning.

We cannot concern ourselves in detail with the history of the settlement of Palestine and its social history, even at the end of the Bronze Age and the Iron Age which follows.[7] All that can be said is that a thinning out of the population in the early Iron Age (Iron Age I, 1250–1000) and a diminution of city settlements was followed in the next period (Iron Age IIA = 1000– 925) by a phase of population growth and reurbanization. Keel puts it like this:

> In the hill country, many of the smallest settlements were abandoned again after only a few generations of permanent settlement; at the same time the population came to be concentrated in larger villages, and some of these developed into fortified towns. At the political level this process of a concentration of settlements and reurbanization went along with the origin and consolidation of the state of Israel and Judah and the appearance of the first blossoming of Israelite kingship under the so-called 'united monarchy'.[8]

---

[7] Cf. Helga Weippert, *Palästina* (ch. 3 n. 3), *passim*; Israel Finkelstein, *The Archaeology of the Israelite Settlement*, Jerusalem 1988; Volkmar Fritz, *Entstehung* (ch. 2 n. 19), 75–91.

[8] Othmar Keel and Christoph Uehlinger, *Göttinnen* (ch. 4 n. 22), 149. For the Late Bronze Age (1550–1250 BCE) and Iron Age I (1250–1000 BCE) Weippert speaks of a 'gradual deurbanization' which expresses itself in the 'foundation of villages' but cannot automatically be explained by a violent Israelite conquest (416 and n. 9). There follows the 'period of cultural unification . . . the main characteristic of which is the foundation of cities: cities now no longer just governed the picture of settlement in the coastal region; a reurbanization also began inland: villages developed into cities and cities were refounded' (ibid., 423). There is an intensive discussion of the century in question in Gösta W. Ahlström, *History* (ch. 2 n. 19), 282–370 (= ch. 6, The Twelfth Century BCE'; ch. 7, 'The Increase in Settlements').

It is only in the last few decades[9] that experts have been able to make such precise statements: they go back to careful surface investigations in Israel (preceded by some investigations in Transjordan and in the Negeb) which make it possible to define the layout of settlements and the periods during which they were inhabited simply from a systematic evaluation of potsherds found on the surface down to a level of between five and ten centimetres.[10] For the Iron Age periods mentioned above we shall attempt to discover more about the dominant formation of village society.

5.2 Village structures

Thus we can assume that in the early Israelite period (between the thirteenth and the tenth centuries BCE), in the sphere of what later became Palestine, there were predominantly villages and small towns which displayed a typical social structure. The population may as a rule have numbered between fifty and three hundred, and in rare exceptional cases may have been as large as a thousand persons. This exceeds the size of the mere family; on the other hand personal relationships are still extremely important, even if they are no longer between each individual and all the other inhabitants. They shape the world in which people live more intensively because everyone works in the same way; this resembles the pattern of life as it is today, say, in a small village or the kind of neighbourliness which works well in an urban suburb. It is highly probable that family cults persisted in kinship groups which largely continued to exist as close communities living together, working together and producing together. But alongside them (and also above them?), common cults, beliefs and norms with a religious foundation developed on the basis of shared tasks and interests. The leap from the hunter-and-gatherer community or the individual farmstead to the agricultural, multi-family local association must be regarded as a revolution

---

[9] There is a history and bibliography of the surface investigations up to 1983 in Helga Weippert, *Palästina* (ch. 3 n. 3), 39–50. She emphasizes the rise of a refined method, 'regional archaeology', which is meant to provide an overall view of the features of a region, and mentions as a significant theorist of this research Yuval Portugali, 'A Field Methodology for Regional Archaeology', *Tel Aviv* 9, 1982, 170–88; cf. Israel Finkelstein, *Archaeology* (ch. 5 n. 7).

[10] Cf. Adam Zertal, *The Israelite Settlement in the Hill Country of Manasseh*, Tel Aviv dissertation 1986 (Hebrew); Moshe Kochavi et al., *Judea, Samaria and the Golan. Archaeological Survey 1967–1968*, Jerusalem 1972 (Heb.); David C. Hopkins, *The Highlands of Canaan: Agricultural Life in the Early Iron Age*, Sheffield 1985. There is a brief account in Gösta W. Ahlström, *History* (ch. 2 n. 19), 350–3; longer discussions in Israel Finkelstein, *Archaeology* (ch. 5 n. 7), *passim*. Volkmar Fritz, *Die Stadt im Alten Israel*, Munich 1990; id., *Entstehung* (ch. 2 n. 19), 79–102. Cf. also Niels Peter Lemche, *Early Israel*, VTS 37, Leiden 1985; id., *Vorgeschichte* (ch. 2 n. 19); C. H. J. de Geus, 'Agrarian Communities in Biblical Times: 12th to 10th Centuries BCE', in *Recueils de la Société Jean Bodin* 41, Paris and Brussels 1983, 207–37.

and a creative impulse which resulted in a spiritual and religious revolution. Here I shall be limiting myself to the history of the development of this first stage. For millennia, earlier metropolises had already been founded in the environment of Israel: temple and palace cities denote urban concentrations of power.[11] They stand for a wider monarchical organization of society and will be evaluated in Chapter 7 below.

To go into more detail: from the later neolithic era onwards, family groups combined in settlements comprising several families,[12] because these were better able to carry out specific work and tasks. Real or fictitious kinship united the small groups (the 'lineage system'). Their formation in turn gave rise to new tasks and problems which had to be solved jointly.

The existence of such settlements in the form of villages or small towns, mainly living on agriculture, is presupposed at many points in the Old Testament. For narrators and poets, alongside the semi-nomadic milieu of the patriarchs they seem to have been the norm.[13] The various Hebrew terms (mainly ʿir, 'place, city'; qiryāh, 'town'; ḥaṣer, 'village'; môšab, 'settlement') say hardly anything about the size of the place but rather something about the degree of fortification. From the perspective of the Israelites, excessively large cities are designated with characteristic adjectives: 'great city' (Jonah 1:2); 'great, with walls reaching up to heaven' (Deut 1:28); city and tower, 'the top of which reaches up to heaven' (Gen 11:4). Israel consists of small and very small settlements (cf. Micah 5:1). But each human being comes from 'his' city and identifies himself with it (cf. 1 Sam 28:3; 2 Sam 17:23; 19:38; also Luke 2:3). Territories are often designated as the sum of their cities (cf. 1 Sam 18:6; 2 Sam 2:1; 1 Kings 12:17; Isa 40:9; 44:26). The cities play a decisive role in lists of districts and boundaries (cf. Josh 10; 13; 15; 1 Kings 4:7–19). Local rulers command a considerable number of cities or give them as gifts along with their hinterland (Judg 11:33; 1 Kings 9:10–14). Yahweh issues threats against the cities, i.e. all the land that belongs to them (Lev 26:31f.; Ezek 12:20; Amos 9:14). Those deported to Babylon reorganize themselves into the settlements of Tel Abib (Ezek 3:15), Tel Melah, Tel Harsha, Cherub-addan, Immer (Ezra 2:59) and Casiphia (Ezra 8:17). These and other localities are apparently referred to when late writings mentioned dispersed inhabitants (cf. Lev 23:3, 14, 17, 21, 31). Usually and down the centuries these are normally places of a manageable size, corresponding sociologically to some degree with a tribal

---

[11] Cf. Gernot Wilhelm, *Stadt* (ch. 2 n. 6); Volkmar Fritz, *Stadt* (ch. 5 n. 10).
[12] Cf. the very vivid description of the 'village culture' of that time on the basis of the results of excavation, Helga Weippert, *Palästina* (ch. 3 n. 3), 393–407.
[13] Apart from the literature already mentioned; cf. Eckart Otto, *ThWAT* VI, 56–74; Christa Schäfer-Lichtenberger, *Stadt und Eidgenossenschaft im Alten Testament*, BZAW 156, Berlin 1986.

community. Some biblical texts also seem to start from the fact that the population of a city consists largely of families related to one another, thus Gen 34, where the city of Shechem belongs to the family of Hamor/ Shechem; Gen 4:17, which cites Enoch from the clan of Cain as its founder and the patron of a city who gives it its name; Judg 1:25f., according to which an emigrant from Canaan gives the new city which he founds the name of his home town; and Judg 18:27–9, which mentions the destruction and rebuilding of a city, now named after the victors' ancestors. The naming of settlements linked to persons is thus significant. It also betrays something about the significance of the city for a particular group of people.

The main reasons for founding dwelling-places which are larger than the family are probably connected with universal human factors: better protection against rival external groups and the possibility of producing food either co-operatively or by sharing work, building houses and setting about the manufacture of consumer goods. We can also say that a concentration in one place of a larger number of people who live together in friendship and with a readiness to help considerably increases the physical and cultural power of the human species.[14] (We should recall that an indispensable presupposition of this was the invention of agriculture and the breeding of animals!) Sowing and harvesting, and where necessary irrigation, tilling the fields, protection against wild animals and marauding bands, bringing new land under cultivation, protecting flocks from wild animals and people, and possibly walling the settlement and setting up an armed troop – all these measures towards safeguarding and furthering the goals of one's own community could be tackled much better, or could only be tackled at all, with the larger number of people who lived in the village community. The settlement, which may have developed out of the temporary camps of hunters and gatherers, proved to be the beginning of a more complex form of society. It came into being on the basis of external pressures towards self-preservation and at the same time as a product of the inner capacities of the creative human spirit. Here we should not be thinking of a sudden specialization of professions in particular localities. As a rule the families continued to be self-sufficient in terms of producing food, textiles, cooking equipment, tools, dwellings, etc. But here and there one or the other would produce objects or consumer goods surplus to need, and then use them to its advantage in exchanges with interested parties near and far. Any concentration of people in a place brings with it the opportunity for

---

[14] Cf. Elisabeth Badinter, *Ich bin Du* (ch. 4 n. 124). The author regards the complementarity of the sexes, which arose far back in prehistory, as the beginning of incomparable human efficiency. It was of course further reinforced by the possibilities for exchange and co-operation in the settlements.

developing particular gifts, for trade and profit and thus for an increase in power. There is no need specially to point out that for people to live together in the same place made it easy for them to defend themselves against enemies, and thus to meet the human need for protection. The result was improved possibilities of communication and culture.

Moreover, living together and perceiving primary and possibly secondary tasks for the community led to the development of social structures in the village or town communities. The social structure of a settlement (village, small town) was based on personal action and therefore could be grasped. The families largely continued to exist as relatively autonomous communities which lived together, worked together and worshipped together.[15] Presumably they were represented in the outside world by male representatives, and domestically led by the head wife; each member found his or her place of work and tasks for the whole group in the framework of the family. The leadership of the whole community within a settlement was taken over either by a plenary assembly of all men who were of age or by a council of elders, which was evidently formed by the 'heads' of the family.[16] This body had to discuss all common concerns and projects of the settlement and possibly implement decisions. Naturally it also had to make decisions on questions of security and on problems like the provision of water and food and the use of fields and pastures; it also had to resolve internal clashes between the individual families. Although the book of Ruth is much later, an episode from it is a good example of this *ad hoc* constitution of a council of elders, here as a forum for judgment which will settle the matter of Naomi's inheritance.

> And Boaz went up to the gate and sat down; and behold, the next of kin, of whom Boaz had spoken, came by. So Boaz said, 'Turn aside, friend; sit down here'; and he turned aside and sat down. And he took ten men of the elders of the city, and said, 'Sit down here'; so they sat down. (Then the case of Naomi, Elimelech's field and Ruth is presented and discussed and a decision is made on it which is respected by all, Ruth 4:1f., 4ff.)

How wonderfully un-bureaucratic all this is! It is all in the family. Anyone who has a matter of public concern can summon the decision-making body

---

[15] Niels Peter Lemche, *Vorgeschichte* (ch. 2 n. 19), 104, reckons with quite small nuclear families (5–7 people), so that he sees the need for protection as the main motif for close collaboration.

[16] The first variant is suggested by the expression 'the men (of a city)' – cf. Judg. 6:28, 30; 8:8, etc. The 'elders' ($z^e k\bar{e}n\bar{\imath}m$) play a major role in the various literary genres and periods of Old Testament history; they also appear in evidence from Mesopotamian and Syrian culture; cf. Joachim Conrad, *ThWAT* II, 639–50; Rainer Albertz, *History of Israelite Religion* 1 (ch. 3 n. 1), 92–3ff., etc.; Winfried Thiel, *Entwicklung* (ch. 3 n. 1), 27f., etc.

of the small town. There are no written invitations, for everyone knows everyone else, and the days are not planned out with stop-watches and diaries and in committee rooms. There are no public buildings at all and no administrative office. The interested party goes in person to the city gate – NB, the only one! – and sits down and waits until the people he needs go out to work in the fields. Then he addresses them individually, probably with a ceremonial formula, which immediately gives the one addressed to understand that there is to be a session of the council of elders on a serious matter. They obey without protest and wait until the number of judges established by custom is complete; then the discussion can take place.

There are some other texts that illuminate the tasks and activities of the elders, especially in the Deuteronomistic writings, which evidently presuppose the conditions of the exile. The council of elders in a place functions as a college of judges if parents can no longer cope with their rebellious son (Deut 21:18–21), or if rites of expiation are necessary in the case of a murder committed by an unknown hand (Deut 21:2–8). Both regulations seem remarkable. In the first instance is no family justice any longer possible, to be executed by the head and the male adults? And in the second case, are there no priests in a city who would have carried out the religious ceremonies? For the clergy mentioned in v. 5 have evidently been added to the text: vv. 2–4 and 6–8 show only the elders in action (in v. 2 there are also the 'judges', perhaps also an addition to the text). Elders carry on peace negotiations for their locality in Judg 8:4–17. In Ezek 8:2; 14:1; 20:1 they sit opposite the prophet and can be consulted or give instruction on religious questions, certainly on behalf of their city. The broad spectrum of the functions of the council of elders is in fact suspicious. Perhaps it typifies the conditions in the exilic/post-exilic community, and not so much pre-exilic local constitutions.

We need not list all the spheres of responsibility of the elders in detail and discuss them. Evidently they largely governed the public life of the village community, since we hear nothing of bodies elsewhere. Possibly the religious tasks before the exile largely lay on the one hand predominantly in the family sphere and on the other with experts on ritual who were occasionally called on, like Samuel (1 Sam 9) or the Levite (Judg 17:7–13). By contrast, within the family the women will have had their say: we can read this out of the story of Abigail and David (1 Sam 25) and similar texts (cf. also Prov 31:10–31).[17] Rather, we need to recognize this new social

---

[17] For the roles of the sexes; cf. above 3.1. and Carol Meyers, *Eve* (ch. 4 n. 10); Erhard S. Gerstenberger and Wolfgang Schrage, *Frau* (ch. 3 n. 1).

structure of a manageable settlement, in principle structured by kinship, as also a theologically important structure which was born in the late Stone Age and can be found in Israel from the beginning (thirteenth to eleventh century BCE). It has persisted in different forms through all the periods of Israelite and ancient history, through the upheavals of later centuries, down to the present day. And if it has persisted, then the theology of a community that lives together face to face, which has been preserved in some form, is still effective today.[18]

5.3 Rituals and cults

A community which works together and lives together in important spheres of life will also develop a common religion, so we must ask: What about the images of God, the cultic actions and the ethos of village and town communities in the early (pre-exilic) period and sometimes also in exilic and post-exilic Israel?

It would be rewarding first of all to investigate in detail the theophoric proper names of the localities which are known from ancient Israel. We come upon various deities who are then probably, at least in phases, to be regarded as the guardian deities of the settlements concerned. Anathoth must be connected with the goddess Anath, and Jerusalem probably with the God Shalim. Penuel points to a place commemorating El and possibly a place of El worship, as does Bethel. Baalah, 'lady' (Josh 15:9f.), could point to the prominent position of the place or to a female deity, whereas the plural Baaloth (Josh 15:24; 1 Kings 4:16) evidently allows only the interpretation in terms of goddesses. Kiriath-baal, 'city of Baal' (Josh 15:60; 18:14; cf. 2 Sam 6:2) equally clearly indicates the leading role of the Canaanite god. Strangely there are hardly any place names in which the God Yahweh appears. Not much attention has yet been paid to this problem. Othmar Keel, Max Küchler and Christoph Uehlinger go into place names at very great length.[19] One could develop the theory that Yahweh does not

---

[18] Cf. the sociological literature on the political community, e.g. René König, *Grundformen der Gesellschaft: Die Gemeinde*, Hamburg 1958. The study by Ferdinand Tönnies, *Gemeinschaft und Gesellschaft* (1887), Darmstadt 1972, is a classic. It compares the characteristics of the face-to-face group with the essential features of the anonymous large society. Ali Wardack, *Social Control and Deviance: A South Asian Community in Scotland*, Aldershot 2000; Susanne Elsen, *Gemeinwesenökonomie – eine Antwort auf Arbeitslosigkeit, Armut und soziale Ausgrenzung*, Neuwied 1998; Carlos Arenas, *Social Community Psychology on the Crossroad: A New Model?*, Bielefeld dissertation 1996; Hannelore Faulstich-Wiegand, *Individuum und Gesellschaft*, Vienna and Munich 2000.

[19] Othmar Keel, Max Küchler and Christoph Uehlinger, *Orte und Landschaften der Bibel* 1, Zurich and Göttingen 1984, 294–305. They list the giving of theophoric names with El, Dagon, Baal, Anat, Horon, etc. ibid. (294ff.) and also note the custom of burning down the existing settlements after the invasion or conquest of a foreign country (ibid., 298f., 301–3); they then

appear in place names simply because he was essentially a deity at the level of the tribe, i.e. a regional and not a local form of society.[20] The local guardian deities (also in the form of 'demoted' gods of heaven'; cf. also 'Yahweh of Samaria', 'Yahweh of Teman' in the texts of Kuntillet ʿAjrud) were responsible for the whole settlement and therefore entered the place names. By contrast, Yahweh originally had a tribal area, the name of which could be identical with the name of the father of the tribe (cf. Judah, Joseph) or a region. It seems more probable that new foundations of places in the late Old Testament period, when belief in Yahweh had become established and was generally binding (say from the sixth to the third centuries BCE), were relatively rare and that because of the considerable gaps in the texts which have come down to us, by chance place names containing Yahweh have not been handed on.

The way of life in the village communities of Israel (and also of the other villages of the ancient Near East) meant that the shared religious tasks lay in the realm of warding off dangers (from nature and from other human beings) and in the sphere of the provision of food. We may therefore assume that communities of this kind sought and worshipped above all storm and fertility deities, along with such divine powers as were strong in battle and could guarantee the defence of the shared dwelling place. In addition – if we look at the problems of the internal organization of the community – there was an urgent need of legal protection and justice which could be guaranteed by deities.

The biblical writings tell us very little about the deities and cults which were in fact present in Israel before the centralization of all sacrificial worship in Jerusalem (Deut 12). The fine old story of Saul who goes to the seer Samuel to get information about his lost asses has a little peripheral motif: the sacrificial feast of the unnamed city (Ramah?) over which Samuel is

---

concern themselves explicitly with the differences between Canaanite and Israelite nomenclature (ibid., 303–5). The result is very meagre. Place names containing Yahweh are almost completely absent; no differences whatsoever can be established between Israelite and Canaanite place names in form and content. There is no problem in mentioning alien gods in place names; Yahweh is not mentioned. By contrast, there are very probably local manifestations of Yahweh: in the mentions of a 'Yahweh of Samaria' and 'Yahweh of Teman' attested in Kuntillet ʿAjrud in fact we have the 'combination of the name of a God with a place name' (ibid., 258). Here Teman is to be associated with the Edomite god Qau (Keel et al. refer to Ernst Axel Knauf, *Midian*, Wiesbaden 1988, 55ff.; John R. Bartlett, *Edom and the Edomites*, Sheffield 1989, 194–204).

20. The only scholar who focuses at all on the question of place names containing Yahweh seems to be Wilhelm Borée, *Die alten Ortsnamen Palästinas* (1930), reprinted Hildesheim 1968. 'Names of Israelite gods are hardly used at all after the settlement in the naming of new foundations' (ibid., 122f.). 'If the Israelites had used names of gods they would also have used the name of their god as an element, as in the case of personal names' (ibid., 123 n. 1).

presiding (1 Sam 9:12–14, 22–24). Apparently such occasions, which involved ceremonies and objects of worship about which unfortunately we have no detailed information, were typical of Israelite rural localities. A cleric from the region with no fixed office takes over the leadership of the ceremonies. The city has no temple and therefore also no priest, but only an open-air sanctuary. The later Deuteronomic/Deuteronomistic campaigns against these 'high places' (Hebrew *bāmōt*; cf. e.g. Deut 12:2; 1 Kings 3:2f.; 22:44; 2 Kings 17:9, 29; 23:5, 8, etc.), show at least that the exilic theologians still had an idea of the many pre-exilic settlement cults, though this was schematized and not very concrete.[21] The equipment of the open-air sanctuaries or city shrines mentioned in this polemic is stereotypically indicated as 'Asherah' and 'Mazzebah' (symbols of the goddess and the god who guarantee both fertility and warlike power). That is a cliché, but it fits the basic expectations which according to sociological analysis are cherished in a settlement – Albertz has summarized the most important pieces of equipment in the village 'open-air' sanctuary in ancient Israel and described its functions.[22] 'This primitive type of sanctuary, which managed with a minimum of cultic equipment, corresponded much more closely to the cultural and economic circumstances of the Israelite population than the massive temple buildings in the city.'[23] He himself, however, regards the original holy places, which served completely local needs, from the perspective of the higher Yahweh religion: 'The problem was that Yahweh simply entered this traditional cultic symbolism of Palestine with no prior reflection by the people on whether they could thus give appropriate expression to the special historical experiences of liberation with Yahweh.'[24] From the perspective of the locality, a Yahwehizing of the local cult was superfluous and damaging; giving the name Yahweh to the local deity[25] or 'suppressing' it by Yahweh in the last result simply produced a domestication of Yahweh the God of war, a transformation of the warrior into a guarantor of fertility, and thus an assimilation of the tribal god to the expectations and structures of the village community. This is clearly recognizable in the book of Hosea (cf. Hosea 2). Albertz in principle takes a similar view of this development, but regards it as a regrettable mistake in relation to the liberation-theological Yahwehizing that was striven

---

[21] Cf. Wolfgang Zwickel, 'Kulthöhe', *NBL* 1994, 562–4; Avraham Biran (ed.), *Temples and High Places in Biblical Times*, Jerusalem 1981; Helga Weippert, *Palästina* (ch. 3 n. 3), 281–4; 407–10 (results of excavations); Matthias Gleis, *Die Bamah*, BZAW 251, Berlin 1998.

[22] Rainer Albertz, *History of Israelite Religion* 1 (ch. 3 n. 1), 92–5.

[23] Ibid., 85.

[24] Ibid.

[25] Cf. the names 'Yahweh of Samaria', 'Yahweh of Teman', attested in inscriptions.

for.[26] My argument is different: must the liberation components find entrance into the local cult, which is concerned with rain and fertility, self-defence and tribal solidarity? Can the problem of equality before the judge within the community only be overcome by experiences of liberation? Things possibly look different when the 'stranger' appears in the community (cf. Lev 19:33f.; 25:39–55; Deut 15:1–6, etc.). Now this question arises specifically from an incursion of wider society into the (still) personal framework of the village community.

The sacrificial festival over which Samuel presides gives us a glimpse of ritual. The men of a locality meet at a holy place, sacrifice is offered and there is a meal, i.e. the sacrificial meal is a great occasion (at which Saul, as the king designated by Yahweh, is given a choice piece of meat). We hear nothing of the special occasion for the feast. It could have been a seasonal agricultural feast which had some connection with the phases of vegetation. In fact the backbone of the Israelite festal calendar consists of originally local agricultural feasts, all of which are connected with the different harvests (Ex 23:14–16; 34:18–26; Lev 23:4–44; Deut 16:1–7). And in a small land of a few hundred thousand inhabitants it is difficult to hold seasonal harvest festivals only at a central place. That the three annual festivals (Ex 23:14–17) later centralized in Jerusalem were originally celebrated at local sanctuaries would make good sense. The Psalter contains collective hymns of thanksgiving for the harvest (cf. Ps 65:10–13, which however also contains Zion theology and a theology of the nations; Ps 67, where 'nations' perhaps originally did not mean ethnic groups but groups which visited a village festival). At the village level emergencies were met with ceremonies of lamentation (cf. Isa 15:2f.; 16:12; Joel 1 – 2); communal prayer containing lamentations and petitions can also be found among the psalms (cf. Ps 83, which in its final form was coined with reference to Israel; Pss 39; 90). Possibly individual high places were also known as places where oracles were given; at all events, Solomon received promise and blessing in Gibeon, in a dream vision (1 Kings 3:5; cf. 9:2).

Outside the seasonal festivals connected with the agricultural cycles, lamentations and dream visions, certain other ritual actions were also performed communally by the inhabitants of villages. We read, for example, of puberty rites for young women (Judg 21:19–21). That can suggest that celebrations of puberty – which probably originally belonged in the sphere of the family – also began very soon to take place in settlements *en bloc*

---

[26] Ibid., 87f.: 'Syncretism is not intrinsically bad, but in view of changing social conditions and needs is normal and indeed necessary. A syncretism in the worship on the high places which unfortunately failed finished off the village type of sanctuary that in other points was so appropriate and near to the people.'

(because of their public character? For greater effectiveness or a delight in company?). With puberty boys and girls entered a phase of life in which they could also perform tasks for the community as a whole and claim rights in it. We can also vividly imagine that preparations for armed conflicts and victory feasts could be carried out in the sphere of the community (cf. 1 Sam 18:6f.: the women who celebrate the victory of David and Saul come 'from all the cities of Israel').

Thus the small, intimate local community, easy to grasp, with its needs and its joys in the everyday struggle for life, forms the second nucleus of any Old Testament theology. The small town has its own sanctuary but needs very few personnel, if any. In view of 1 Sam 9:23f., Zwickel thinks that 'at least a slaughterer or cook' will have been appointed.[27] I think it more important that the 'seer' Samuel (or his anonymous literary predecessor) plays such a central role in his environment (cf. the remarkable note in 1 Sam 7:15–17). In the narrative he seems originally to perform the role of a soothsayer and possible healer, to whom the local community also entrusted important functions at the annual festival. With the beginning of division of work in the local community the cultic and ritual roles could also slowly have been differentiated. Groups of fifty and more people living together began to appoint religious specialists, mediators between human beings and God, for the ritual purposes of the community.[28]

Though we have little information about village life among the ancient Israelites, we get the impression from it that the communities – like analogous formations all over the world and at all times – carried on their own cultic rituals, which were governed by their own interests. The horizon of religious action and thought was set by the situation in the dwelling places and at work, communication and co-operation between the families. The wider world and the high gods of heaven were remote to the farmers in the Israelite hill country, who were not interested in regional and national themes, in the condition of dynasties and centres of power. In the village cultic celebrations people were concerned with the prosperity of the community, the fertility of the land and the herds, and the behaviour of the community. Externally they presumably marked themselves off from competing neighbours (cf. Judg 19:12) and began to seek exchanges of

[27] Wolfgang Zwickel, 'Kulthöhe' (ch. 5 n. 21), 652; cf. Peter Mommer, *Samuel*, WMANT 65, Neukirchen-Vluyn 1991, 92–110.
[28] In the Indio cults of North and South America, e.g. medicine men and medicine women perform this important service for their community; cf. Leo W. Simmons (ed.), *Sun Chief. The Autobiography of a Hopi Indian*, New Haven 1942; Charles S. Brant (ed.), *The Autobiography of a Kowa Apache Indian* (1969), New York 1991; Paul Radin, *The Autobiography of a Winnebago Indian* (1920), New York 1963; John G. Neihardt (ed.), *Black Elk Speaks* (1932), New York 1972; Joseph E. Brown (ed.), *The Sacred Pipe* (1953), London 1988, etc.

goods and wives with friendly localities (cf. Judg 17:1). Up to the end of the time of the monarchy there were hardly any clashes of interest with religious practices at higher levels. Present-day assertions that religious life in the country was Yahwehized from Jerusalem, sometimes violently, rest on a false estimate of the reports of Deuteronomistic reform or some prophetic narratives in the books of Kings.[29] The retrospective polemic against cults in the high places, which can be found especially in the Deuteronomistic strata, is made from a community perspective. However, in the exilic and post-exilic confessional communities, and only there, there was a strong interest in denouncing all deviations from the cult of Yahweh (cf. Jer 2:20; Hos 4:13; Ezek 6:3–6; 16:16; Deut 12:2f., etc.).

5.4 Ethics and the administration of justice

The ethic of the small town or village is quite evidently built on the family ethic. But now not only the brothers in one's own family (as those who are to be protected and helped, and to whom one owes solidarity), but anyone who is linked to the ethical subject by bonds of neigbourliness need to be taken into account. Beyond doubt the latter is the *rea'*, the 'neighbour', who in the genealogical system is also the (more remote) blood relation, but in the sphere of the community in which one lives simply the 'fellow-citizen'. The obligation to extract blood vengeance no longer seems to extend (wholly) to him, but protection, co-operation and respect for him are taken for granted. Brothers in the family and neighbours living nearby are the groups of persons with whom one has the closest personal ties. Because of the frequent marriages between members of clans who lived together in a city, they often also fell into the category of 'in-laws', and the gradated obligation to show solidarity also applied to them. It might also sometimes include obligations to enter into a levirate marriage (cf. Ruth 4). How the inhabitants of a village or a small town related to one another can be observed from numerous objects, for example the sharing of tangible entities, in all eras of human history.[30]

---

[29] Above all 1 Kings 18 (Elijah on Carmel); 2 Kings 18:1–8 (Hezekiah's Reform); and 2 Kings 22–23 (Josiah's reform) are often regarded as authentic testimonies to exclusive, aggressive belief in Yahweh in the monarchical period. Everything that we know about the history of Israelite religion tells against such a period and social setting; cf. e.g. Hans-Detlef Hoffmann, *Reform und Reformen*, Zurich 1980, Ernst Würthwein, 'Die Josianische Reform und das Deuteronomium', *ZThK* 73, 1976, 395–423 (reprinted in BZAW 227, 188–26); Richard H. Lowery, *The Reforming Kings*, JSOT.S, Sheffield 1991; Martin Beck, *Elia und die Monolatrie*, BZAW 281, Berlin 1999.

[30] Cf. e.g. Winfried Thiel, *Entwicklung* (ch. 3 n. 1); Johannes Pedersen, *Israel* (ch. 4 n. 13); Richard F. Fortune, *The Sorcerers of Dobu*, New York 1932; Christian Sigrist, *Regulierte Anarchie*, Frankfurt am Main 1979; Edward E. Evans-Pritchard, *The Nuer*, Oxford 1968; Erich Fromm

Experiences and observations show that the small, manageable personal community has to develop its own ethic and its own way of administering justice if it is not to go under as a result of conflicts in its own ranks. Customs and usages regulate the whole of life. Orally transmitted norms and legal precepts define in concrete terms what decision must be taken in particular situations. And the community, in which all live together in close proximity, is wholly involved in supervising the common rules, whether this happens though (malicious) 'gossip', mockery, or the exclusion of deviants. Prayers in the Psalter show very clearly how strikingly the sick, those 'punished by God', or otherwise branded scapegoats, are cut off from the community (cf. Ps 41:6–10; 71:9–11; 88:9–19). It may be that they can be rehabilitated only by means of a ritual action.

In part at this point we can refer back to 4.4, 'The ethic of family and clan'. The ethical guidelines which hold in the individual families are necessarily brought together in the community which lives together. A small group in the context of a wider society will be able to demonstrate distinctive features only at points which are generally regarded as irrelevant to existence together. Even today, neighbours may not be able to do everything they want to in their own houses and gardens (say, because they would trouble those living next door with noises or smells). So we may maintain that the supreme commandment within a close community is beyond doubt the obligation to mutual solidarity (though this is not taken so far as it is within a family, e.g. at the important points of 'blood vengeance' or 'levirate marriage', cf. Deut 22:5–10). But by the very nature of the case, in the ethic of the village community there are different emphases and claims on personal behaviour which go beyond family interest. The question of authority has to be redefined. How much obedience and following does the individual owe to the elders of the village by comparison with and perhaps in conflict with family authority? The problem of property, which will hardly have played a role in the family, can cause friction. The early Israelite village community does not know the concept of collective property. Each family has its land and its movable possessions, above all cattle and slaves. Problems of property, colliding claims, have to be settled by the council of local elders. Common cultic obligations also raise questions and put pressure on norms, not to mention the obligation to provide military defence. All in all, in the spheres which go beyond the family traditions

---

and Michael Maccoby, *Social Character in a Mexican Village*, Englewood Cliffs 1970, etc. The eyewitness accounts of the functioning of village or camp communities in pre-industrial societies are important; cf. Leo W. Simmons, *Sun-Chief* (ch. 5 n. 28); Marjorie Shostak, *Nisa erzählt. Das Leben einer Nomadenfrau in Afrika* (1981), Hamburg 1982.

there is need of constant joint discussion, the establishment of norms and the implementation of decisions that have been taken.

The Book of the Covenant, which in my view in its final form certainly goes back to the exilic/post-exilic community, has preserved all kinds of precepts and regulations from the local community. The legal regulations about slavery for debt, bodily injuries, crimes against property, the law of pledges, etc. (Ex 21:2 – 22:16) indicate a commitment orientated on the community. One can recognize the society of the village or the small town as the sphere in which these precepts applied by the way in which deviant action has to be integrated in as much a *laissez-faire* attitude as possible, or the way in which retribution is to be had against transgressions. This part of the Book of the Covenant was never state law but always the sober, unpretentious law of village and town. Moreover, in the exilic and post-exilic period the family ethic and village ethic go over into the organization of the new Yahweh community (Chapter 8 below).

5.5 The theology of the settled community

As after the analysis of family religion in Chapter 4, we can also now ask: What are the characteristics of the God of the society of the village or small town? What are the particular expectations and anxieties which are bound up with this level of human socialization? Can we draw lines from the high places of Palestinian antiquity to groups and their theologies which can be identified today?

It is certain that the theological jump from family religion to village religion is not very great. The concern on both levels is with internal order, external protection and blessing. But not inconsiderable differences which influence the image of God and ritual can be noted in the world in which people live and the organization of the village community. Family solidarity does not apply in the full sense to communal life in the village. The self-interest of the small group must be fitted into the needs of the somewhat larger community. Work and welfare need to be regulated first at the level of the family and only then at the level of the village community. That means that the village organization is looser, and is no longer guided by completely 'natural' norms of kinship, but must rather be considered carefully and shaped by process of communication and decision.

Thus the image of God which fits with this assumes features which transcend the family, as was already becoming evident in the sections on ritual and ethics. The deity is no longer just a member of the family and the secret leader of the small intimate group but the court of appeal for the conglomerate of different families with their completely divergent interests.

God becomes a God of the common concern, of the fertility in field and house which all need, and of protection from disapproving neighbours and invading enemy hordes, without which the whole community cannot live. In the face of these functions for the community the name of the deity is relatively insignificant. Above all God becomes the God of the beginnings of a balanced law for the whole community. Here quite manifestly an important step is being taken from the closed sphere of the intimate group. People begin to perceive the 'other' fellow human being (though he is still related) and to discuss among themselves within the community what is to be done, e.g. with the weak neighbour, village neighbour, and possibly also the 'stranger' who wanders in. They begin to develop criteria for membership of the community and deliberately to demarcate themselves from other communities. At all events, however, for this purpose the limits of their own family must be transcended. The sphere of responsibility for the individual and the close family group is extended. The 'neighbour' who lives in the community becomes 'like a brother' but not completely a physical relation. An important step towards the extension of identity is taken, and it is sanctioned by the valid norms of shaping life and the cult on the part of the local god.

On the other hand, the rival places and their deities and the wider society and its pantheon call for various obligatory definitions. Each village will have wanted to assert a certain superiority of its own guardian deity to neighbouring deities. 'Is there no God in Israel, that you go to consult Baal-zebub, the god of Ekron?', the narrator makes Elijah ask (2 Kings 1:3). If Yahweh or Samaria were mentioned here we would have a clear example of religious rivalry between cities. Such competitions for the stronger and more effective deity also come through in 1 Kings 18 or 2 Kings 25. As a rule this competition can be said to be peaceful in the period before the exile. Localities were unwilling to engage in competition with the great deities of the higher social organizations because there was no conflict of interests. Wherever high gods and goddesses like Baal, Anath, Yahweh and Asherah were worshipped in Israel at the local level and in open-air sanctuaries, these were local, degraded forms of these powerful deities.

The problems of the community in the village, small town or urban district, which was still manageable, have essentially remained the same down to the present day. In the very different world in which we live, social formations with similar structures are also concerned with cohesion and inner order and mutual help in emergencies (e.g. looking after isolated older citizens). There is the question of accepting or excluding strangers (cf. the debate over asylum-seekers and the fights by communities against rival sacral buildings). There is the question of warding off unreasonable external influences which often enough have their origin in higher administrative authorities (cf. battles over the building of motorways and roads, traffic calming, better schools, sports facilities, etc.). The deity of the village or urban district, today embodied in predominant shared interests, is no longer simply the God of the family but the God of the rather larger, more complex community. In Israel he is worshipped at the local open-air sanctuary, and today he is conjured up in a predominantly implicit way by the articulation of distinctive common claims which are accorded the highest priority and sometimes promised exclusive validity. In argument and definition a similar opening to the nearest other is taking place in our time, as in the social structures of antiquity. That is a first important step in the human experience of faith, which must be followed by further steps in shared responsibility. But this first opening up beyond the natural limits of family has its own abiding value. The community – even though it has its theological limitations – is a creative subject of theological thought and action which must not be sacrificed to wider theological schemes or subordinated to them.

6

God and Goddess
in the Tribal Alliance

Because the Hebrew scriptures divide Israel into twelve tribes, and because the god Yahweh was originally quite certainly a tribal god, in this chapter we must discuss in more detail the Israelite tribal system and the religious rites and sanctuaries associated with it. That is all the more important since, particularly after the Second World War, Old Testament scholars have attached great importance to the specific characteristics of the tribal alliance in Israel and the distinctive, indeed unique, characteristics associated with it – this is a time-conditioned theological perspective which even today has some slight influence.

6.1 The biblical picture of the tribal system

According to the traditions of the first four books of the Pentateuch the families of eleven patriarchs (Reuben, Simeon, Levi, Judah, Issachar, Zebulon, Benjamin, Dan, Napthali, Gad and Asher) with around seventy men and their wives went to Egypt because of a famine. There they lived for several generations and then travelled back to their homeland over a period of twenty years in a compact body consisting of 603,550 men capable of bearing arms (Num 2:32; Levi is not included in this figure).[1] So the Israelite tribes are said to have developed fully in Egypt from one family, namely that of Jacob, biologically in from fifteen to twenty generations, i.e. 430 years. They thus formed the structural framework of the people which later settled in Palestine (cf. Ex 12:40: 'Now the time that the children of Israel dwelled in Egypt is 430 years').[2]

---

[1] Ex 2:1–5; Num 1:44–47; 2:32; but cf. the whole chapter on the census of the people, Num. 1.
[2] The redactor inserts this note because he obviously has to make the marked increase in the people plausible. However, such an extended stay cannot be fitted into any historical picture; cf. H. H. Rowley, 'Israel', *IDB* 2, 1962, 750–65, esp. 752; Martin Noth, *Exodus,* OTL, London 1962, 99f.; Noth refers to the otherwise dominant assumption – e.g. Gen 15:16; Ex 6:13–30 – that the stay in Egypt lasted four generations, i.e. around a hundred years.

From a historical perspective all this is extremely improbable. Israel cannot have formed itself in Egypt, nor travelled through the wilderness to Palestine as an adult nation in a popular migration of unimaginable extent. The biblical reports are depictions exaggerated by faith, which bring together the experiences of Israel's exploitation and slavery, in their own land and in foreign lands (Babylonia, perhaps also in Egypt), and seek to praise the power of the God of Israel and the experience of deliverances from hopeless situations.[3] The biblical tradition of the exodus from Egypt is virtually unusable for reconstructing the history of Israel.[4] But what is to be done if our historical sources are silent and we still need a historical basis for understanding and evaluating the texts?

Several decades ago Noth already described in a monograph what our trained eyes and brains can establish:[5] he argued that at all events the Israelite tribes came into being in the cultivated land of Palestine, not in Egypt, since some of them bear the names of the regions in which they formed. For example Ephraim was certainly first the name of a region, then the designation of the group which lived there. And what reasons can we give for such new groupings forming in Palestine at this time? If the theory of popular migration and conquest which is indicated in the Bible and which has been vehemently defended down to our time, for example by some American scholars,[6] is historically untenable, then there are only two attempts at an explanation in the literature. One – the so-called 'immigration model' – goes back to Rost and Alt, who not least on the basis of modern obser-vations noted a constant movement of population in the peripheral areas of cultivated land. In the spring, nomadic or semi-nomadic clans graze their flocks of sheep and goats on the steppes, which receive too little rainfall for

---

[3] The beginnings of this view are present in Jorge Pixley, *On Exodus. A Liberation Perspective*, Maryknoll 1987; cf. the introduction to this commentary in Ulrich Schoenborn (ed.), *Hermeneutik in der Theologie der Befreiung*, Mettingen 1994, 25–34; Volkmar Fritz, *Entstehung* (ch. 2 n. 19); Niels Peter Lemche, *Vorgeschichte* (ch. 2 n. 19).

[4] That is the result of critical investigation of the Exodus traditions; cf. Niels Peter Lemche, *Early Israel* (ch. 5 n. 10); Thomas L. Thompson, *The Origin Tradition of Ancient Israel* I, JSOTSup 55, Sheffield 1985; Gösta W. Ahlström no longer speaks of the exodus and settlement of the tribes but instead describes the changes in the settlement structure and population density of Palestine (*History* [ch. 2 n. 19], 334–70) which can be established through archaeology. The only certain indication that the later Israelites had anything to do with Egypt in the early period is the (Egyptian) name Moses, which can hardly have been invented (cf. the speculations on the originally Egyptian monotheism which is said to have been imported to Israel through Moses, e.g. Sigmund Freud, *Moses and Monotheism*, Penguin Freud Library, Harmondsworth 1990; Jan Assmann, *Moses der Ägypter* (1977), Munich and Vienna 1998).

[5] Martin Noth, *Das system der zwölf Stämme Israels*, Stuttgart 1930.

[6] To be more precise the 'Albright' and sometimes the 'Baltimore' School; cf. William F. Albright, *From the Stone Age to Christianity*, Baltimore 1946; for a critique, Burke O. Long, *Planting and Reaping Albright. Politics, Ideology and Interpreting the Bible*, University Park 1997.

growing grain or fruit. When the fields of stubble are left in the fertile cultivated land after the grain harvest and the steppes are withering under the scorching sun, then these groups of shepherds – of course by agreement with the farmers – drive their sheep and goats down to the harvested fields. Indeed they winter there in the cultivated land, and in the spring return to the green and blossoming steppe. This system of change of pasturage or transhumance then gradually led the nomadic-type groups of shepherds to settle more permanently, and in order to assert their right to live they banded together as tribes against the city states that existed in Canaan. The paradigmatic biblical text which is meant to attest the early Israel or pre-Israelite migration is Gen 26:12–33. There Isaac's clan moves in the region of the Philistine city of Gerar; time and again it is driven out by the rulers; finally it ends up far to the south, in the more unfriendly Negeb, where the camp and city of Beersheba come into being around the wells dug by Isaac's people. But the story is told in such an anachronistic way that it can hardly be claimed for the early period: Isaac gains wealth from growing grain; he has not only sheep but already also cattle (v. 14); his people keep digging new wells, which nomads do not do because they do not have the technical skill, and so on.[7] In short, our sources are not sufficient either to support or to refute the immigration theory. The patriarchal stories are probably later, after the foundation of a political entity Israel to legitimate the claim to the land of Canaan. As in the case of the Moses stories, the historical core lies merely in the names and places. The traditions are attached to the places Beersheba, Mamre, Hebron, Shechem, Penuel, etc., but from the traditional material that we now have it is no longer possible to discover precisely what happened there and which groups lived there.[8]

The second hypothesis, which leads to the 'revolt model', comes from Mendenhall and was developed further by Gottwald.[9] The basic notion is that the exodus of a people from Israel cannot have taken place in the way described: the formation of the tribes and Israel itself took place in cultivated land, where a group with the name Israel is already attested in a victory inscription from the time of the Pharaoh Merneptah, at the end of the thirteen century BCE.[10] Sociological considerations suggest that in Palestine

[7] Cf. Erhard Blum, *Komposition* (ch. 4 n. 28), 304–7; Matthias Köckert, *Vätergott* (ch. 4 n. 28).
[8] Cf. also John van Seters, *In Search of History*, New Haven 1983; Niels Peter Lemche, *Vorgeschichte* (ch. 2 n. 19).
[9] The two most important publications are George E. Mendenhall, *The Tenth Generation*, Philadelphia 1973, and Norman K. Gottwald, *The Tribes of Yahweh* (1979), Maryknoll ³1985.
[10] There is a discussion of the textual material in Gösta W. Ahlström, *History* (ch. 2 n. 19), 283–6; in more detail Erich Hornung, 'Die Israelstele des Merenptah', in Manfred Görg (ed.), *Fontes atque pontes*, Wiesbaden 1983, 224–33; Gerhard Fecht, 'Die Israelstele, Gestalt und Aussage', also in Manfred Görg (ed.), *Fontes*, 106–38.

between the fourteenth and eleventh centuries the time was ripe for a fundamental revolution which would give a new basis to world history.[11] After Egyptian domination was relaxed, the Canaanite city states had consolidated to such a degree in an unjust feudal social system that numerous exploited slaves fled from the cities into the mountain regions which had not been settled, and there formed an ever-growing potential for unrest. How do Mendenhall and Gottwald know about this? Of course the slaves who escaped from the cities are identical with the *hapiru* of the Amarna letters. The official correspondence between the Egyptian government and the city rulers of Jerusalem, Megiddo, Gezer and Lachish, from Philistia and Syria,[12] which was found in Amarna, the new capital of Pharaoh Akenaten, in fact indicates that the city states felt themselves under constant threat from the *hapiru*, apparently a socially weak stratum of the population which led a semi-nomadic life. They asked the Pharaoh who was still titular ruler for help. The supporters of the revolt theory now assume that the *hapiru* are identical with the 'Hebrews' of the Old Testament (a quite legitimate conjecture)[13] and that these social outcasts, who were not – as others conjecture – nomadic-type shepherd clans, made their way into the Israel that was now forming. However, a Moses group from Egypt which believed in Yahweh met up with the *hapiru* and gave them impetus; it took over the *hapiru* population, won them over to faith in Yahweh, and provided the real stimulus towards the formation of tribal and then state society.

> When the exodus Israelites entered Canaan they encountered this stress-torn Canaanite society, which was in still further decline a century after the Amarna Age. The population in the hill country seems to have tapered off in the Late Bronze period, and the city-state units seem to have been reduced in number and size from the preceding century's. The advocates of a revolt model for Israelite origins picture these Israelite tribes as immediate allies of the Canaanite lower classes. Both groups shared a lower-class identity. The former slaves from Egypt, now autonomous, presented an immediate appeal to the restive serfs and the peasants of Canaan. The attraction of Israelite Yahwism for these oppressed Canaanites may be readily located in the central feature of the

---

[11] What follows is according to Norman K. Gottwald, *Tribes* (ch. 6 n. 9), esp. 210–19, 'The Revolt Model'.

[12] Cf. Manfred Görg, 'Amarna', *NBL* I, 83–5; Joergen A. Knudtzon, *Die El-Amarna Tafeln,* Leipzig 1907 (reprinted Aalen 1964); Anson F. Rainey, *El Amarna Tablets 359–379*, AOAT 8, Neukirchen-Vluyn 1970, 359–79.

[13] Cf. Moshe Greenberg, *The Hab/piru*, AOS 39, 1955, esp. 32–50, 70–6, 85–96; Benno Landsberger, 'Ḥabiru und Lulaḫḫu', *KAF* 1, 1930, 321–34; Oswald Loretz, *Habiru-Hebräer*, BZAW 160, Berlin 1984.

religion of the entering tribes: Yahwism celebrated the actuality of deliverance from socio-political bondage, and it promised continuing deliverance whenever Yahweh's autonomous people were threatened. The two groups coalesced.[14]

The quotation very clearly indicates how the author is conditioned by his time and place: he worked out his hypothesis in the late 1960s and early 1970s, at the time of the student revolts, and was consciously involved in this situation. The evidence for the acceptance of essentially Canaanite elements into the Yahweh alliance is very sparse (cf. e.g. Josh 9, the stratagem of the Gibeonites; Num 21:27–30, the tradition of the allegedly Amorite Song of Heshbon) and moreover questionable. Much to his credit, Norman Gottwald then himself refers in his reflections to the way in which he is conditioned by his time; however, he comes to the conclusion that his own situation can also encourage the understanding of analogous situations.[15] Still, given the impossibility of proving the developments claimed, the great question is whether a peasant revolution in Canaan, the immigration of liberated slaves from Egypt who believed in Yahweh, and a fusion of the two heterogeneous elements of population under the banner of Yahwism, can be historically probable. In view of the knowledge that we have of that time and in view of the biblical sources, their origin and what they set out to say, in this form the question can be answered with a simple 'no'.[16]

6.2 The origin of Israel

Are we then put in a position where we can no longer make any kind of statement about the history and social structure of Israel before the state?[17]

---

[14] Norman K. Gottwald, *Tribes* (ch. 6 n. 9), 214f.

[15] Ibid., 218f.; his conclusion on p. 219 deserves to become a classic: 'Like may indeed fabricate like, but like may also discover like.' The difficulty is that history goes on and what is 'like' quickly shifts again. There is also a basic analysis and criticism of Gottwald's position in Niels Peter Lemche, *Early Israel* (ch. 5 n. 10); id., *Vorgeschichte* (ch. 2 n. 19).

[16] Proof is of course laborious. I would refer in particular to the studies by Lemche, Thompson, Ahlström and Fritz cited above, though their sketches of an early history of Israel also need to be investigated. In Gottwald above all the key role of the 'Moses group' with its missionary zeal for Yahweh seems to me to be suspicious. Behind this domineering concept of unity there is presumably a typical pressure towards homogenization, and a specifically American one at that. Gottwald's basic concern is the foundation of freedom and democracy in early Israelite history, coupled with a primary revelation of monotheism. This primal event is then to be normative to the present day. With a changing world and with new human constructions of reality under other conditions, one can reckon with such a scheme only on the surface.

[17] Cf. Niels Peter Lemche, *Ancient Israel*, Sheffield 1988; id., *The Canaanites and their Land*, Sheffield 1991; id., 'Kann von einer "israelitischen Religion" nochweiterhin die Rede sein? Perspektiven eines Historikers', in Walter Dietrich and Martin Klopfenstein (eds), *Ein Gott allein?*, OBO 138, Fribourg and Göttingen 1994, 59–75 (with bibliography); id., *Vorgeschichte* (ch. 2 n. 19).

Must the recognition that 'evidently the Old Testament is not a source of history at all in the ordinary sense of the word'[18] prevent us from wanting to take into account the period before the origin of the monarchy? I believe that the opposite is the case: the origin of the monarchy, which is also confirmed by extra-biblical evidence in its middle and later periods,[19] itself calls for clarification of the question how something like the state of Israel could form at all in the tenth century. For states do not simply drop down from heaven.

So if we take the assured phenomenon of the monarchy as a starting point, we can go back from there to investigate those pre-state groupings which in the course of time came together in a centralized association. However hesitant one may be after the 'collapse' of Noth's and von Rad's refined and exaggerated tribal theories[20] to speak too emphatically about the 'tribes' and 'tribal alliance' in Israel,[21] in reading the later writings at least in passing remarks we encounter the organizational form of the 'tribe'. This in fact is a well-known form of society not only in antiquity but down to our own time, and one which has been investigated extensively by anthropologists.[22] However, in the Hebrew tradition we must start from the division of Israel into districts, which were allegedly introduced by Solomon to improve administration and the collection of taxes in his kingdom: in 1 Kings 4:7–19 twelve 'officials' (Hebrew niṣṣābīm, 'overseers') are appointed, but for the most part the places of residence are named; here only five (or six) names of tribes appear ([Ephraim,] Naphtali, Asher, Issachar;

[18] Niels Peter Lemche, *Religion* (ch. 6 n. 17), 67.

[19] However, it is remarkable and regrettable that Saul, David and Solomon provoked no response in the environment of Israel that has been detected so far. However, for the ninth century there are a few Assyrian and Moabite references to northern Israel (cf. Kurt Galling, *Textbuch zur Geschichte Israels* = *TGI*, e.g. nos 19; 21; 23; 24; 28; etc.; Walter Beyerlin, *Near Eastern Religious Texts relating to the Old Testament*, London 1978, 237ff.; 252ff.; *TUAT* I, passim).

[20] Cf. Martin Noth, *System* (ch. 6 n. 5); id., *History of Israel*, London ²1960; Gerhard von Rad, *The Problem of the Hexateuch*, Edinburgh 1966.

[21] Gösta W. Ahlström, for example, no longer uses the term and even Rainer Albertz is restrained: he likes to talk of the 'larger group' and 'alliance of large groups' as opposed to family and clan; cf. *History of Israelite Religion* 1 (ch. 3 n. 1), 40ff., 67ff. By contrast, in his work the tribal organization plays a subordinate role; cf. 72–6, 82f.; the 'Exodus group' is only possibly organized by tribes (44). Niels Peter Lemche wants to define the terms above all sociologically and politically and exclude the nomadic element from the term 'tribe' (id., *Vorgeschichte* [ch. 2 n. 19], 104–9: 'Tribes form where people need a common all-embracing organization to provide solidarity', ibid., 106; state and tribe are alternative forms of organization and rule). Winfried Thiel, *Entwicklung* (ch. 3 n. 1), 105–10, speaks of the effect of the tribes 'externally' and their lack of significance for the 'inner life' (ibid., 110).

[22] Cultural anthropologists concern themselves more with so-called tribal cultures or the 'indigenous' peoples who still remain. Hermann Schulz, *Stammesreligionen*, Stuttgart 1993, thinks that these people still make up at least 4 per cent of the world population (9). Cf. Walter H. Capps, 'Society and Religion', *EncRel* 13, 175–85; James A. Boon, 'Anthropology, Ethnology and Religion', *EncRel* 1, 308–16.

Benjamin; Gilead, possibly according to Alt's emendation of the text also Zebulun in v. 16). If we set alongside this the list of tribal territories in Josh 15 – 19 (the section contains a list of tribal boundaries and another of places which lie in a district), we can postulate that real divisions into districts from the period of the monarchy also underlay the legendary account of the time of Joshua.[23] At all events, as an overall finding for our question about the tribal structure in ancient Israel, we can infer from the texts cited that fragments of tribal territories can be glimpsed in the administrative districts of the time of the monarchy. The systematization into a group of twelve tribes of Israel which appears in some texts is late and artificial (cf. e.g. Gen 29:31 – 30:24 + 35:16–18; 35:22–6; 49; Num 1:4–16; 2; 26; Deut 33, etc. but the lists never completely coincide: slight differences can be detected everywhere).[24]

We can only speculate on the reasons which led alliances to extend beyond tribes. However, analogous phenomena in the history of human culture give an indication. The need for protection against hostile neighbours will have played a major role. In addition there was the concern to exchange commodities and women, but this was certainly not the ultimate reason for larger but looser social alliances.[25] There were other additional motifs like the normal growth of the population, the increase in fighting strength for offensive wars, new technical achievements and so on. It should be noted that the tribal system performed varying functions in the Old Testament tradition after the formation of the state: it served as the dark background to the monarchy; as part of the basis of the division by the kings into districts and as a partial model for the organization of the army; it provided a religious symbol (the ark); it was the source of Yahwistic faith, etc. In the post-exilic period the tribal system had another essential function: every Israelite had to be listed in the 'register of generations', especially the levites and priests, who had to demonstrate their

---

[23] For the lists mentioned; cf. Albrecht Alt, 'Israels Gaue unter Salomo' (1913), in *Kleine Schriften zur Geschichte des Volkes Israel*, KS I, Munich 1953, 76–89 (on 1 Kings 4:7–19: Alt notes the 'juxtapositon of tribes and cities', in which vv. 15–19 name tribal territories; on pp. 83f. he proposes a textual emendation for v. 16); id., 'Das System der Stammesgrenzen im Buch Josua' (1927), KS I, 193–202 (Alt thinks that the list of *tribal boundaries* dates from before the state, a view which is opposed by Volkmar Fritz, *Das Buch Josua*, HAT I/7, Tübingen 1994, 154–200: lists of this kind are 'meaningful only in respect of measures for raising taxes', ibid., 158); id., 'Judah's Gaue unter Josia' (1925), KS II, Munich 1953, 276–88 (the lists of places in Josh 15; 18:19 describe conditions under Josiah at the end of the seventh century BCE).

[24] See Martin Noth, *System* (ch. 6 n. 5); Hans-Jürgen Zobel, *Stammesspruch und Geschichte*, BZAW 95, Berlin 1965; id., '*šebeṭ*', ThWAT VII, 966–74. Herbert Donner has summarized all that is worth knowing about the tribes – though in a very conservative way: *Geschichte des Volkes Israel und seiner Nachbarn in Grundzügen*, 2 vols, ²Göttingen 1995: 1, 129–43, 145–67. Niels Peter Lemche, *Vorgeschichte* (ch. 2 n. 19), 104–9; Volkmar Fritz, *Enstehung* (ch. 2 n. 19), 121–36, differ.

[25] Cf. Niels Peter Lemche, *Vorgeschichte* (ch. 2 n. 19), 98–104.

fitness for office genealogically (cf. 1 Chron 2–8; Ezra 2:62; however, the expression *yāḥaś* in the *hithpael*, 'be entered in the list of generations', applied to all Israelites; cf. 1 Chron 5:1, 7, 17; 9:1).[26]

In the biblical passages which are not affected by the later systematization we then in fact find reports of political groups existing before the state which are designated as 'tribes'; these occur above all in the Book of Judges. The people who are brought together in these social units are already leading a sedentary life and are not (semi-)nomads. Hence it is important to speak of local rulers before the state, since the so-called judges are probably not in the first instance legal authorities but - in keeping with the original significance of *šāpat* = guide, rule, reign - princelings or petty kings.[27] Thus the 'Israelites' of a region understood themselves to be at least fictitiously related by blood and lived in a tribal organization which had a specific name and was responsible for specific tasks.

This situation can be illustrated very well from the Song of Deborah, the nucleus of which is probably very old (Judg 5). The peasant tribes living in the more rural areas of Palestine (in the text already called 'Israel') are suffering under an economic crisis: hunger is dominant in the villages. Apparently they hold the dominant city kings responsible for the situation and arm themselves for a revolt. However, the text of the Song of Deborah is not at all well preserved and the situation presupposed cannot be recognized clearly:

> In the days of Shamgar, son of Anath, in the days of Jael, caravans ceased and travellers kept to the byways. The peasantry ceased in Israel, they ceased until you arose, Deborah, arose as a mother in Israel. When new gods were chosen, when war was in the gates, was shield or spear to be seen among forty thousand in Israel? (Judg 5:6–8).

These three verses alone pose many problems in terms of language, text, connotations, history and culture. What does it mean that 'the ways' are 'abandoned' (literally 'the ways cease')? Why are the people involved here designated by the term *pᵉrāzōn*, 'lowlander', which is used only here? What is the relation between the three persons mentioned: Shamgar, Jael and Deborah? What does the title 'mother in Israel' mean? Who 'chooses new gods' and what does this act mean? What lack of arms is alluded to in what group ('forty thousand')? No wonder that the attempts at translation already

---

[26] Cf. Manfred Oeming, *Das wahre Israel*, BWANT 128, Stuttgart 1990.

[27] Thus emphatically Gösta W. Ahlström (ch. 2 n. 19), 421: 'In the so-called period of the Judges several small principalties of chiefdoms came into existence . . .' Cf. also J. Alberto Soggin, *Judges*, London 1981.

diverge markedly: here, for example, is a reconstruction by Hans Wilhelm Hertzberg:[28]

> In the days of Shamgar, the son of Anath,
> in the days of Jael the 'caravans' lay still which had to go on ways,
> they had to take crooked paths.
> There was stillness among the peasants in Israel, 'all life' lay still
> – until you arose, Deborah, arose as mother in Israel.
> 'Dumb were the warriors' of God,
> 'at an end' the battle before the 'gates',
> no shield nor lance was to be seen
> among forty thousand in Israel.

Hertzberg sees the section as a depiction of alien rule and oppression which is characterized by general obstacles to peasant life. Alberto Soggin and Carlos Dreher depict the same situation.[29] Donner sums up the dominant interpretation like this: 'The song of Deborah still indicates the reasons which led to war between Israel and the Canaanites: "At the time of Shamgar ben Anath, at the time of Jael, the ways ceased and the travellers took hidden ways" (5:6). That could hardly indicate anything other than the blocking of the main routes for the Israelites by the Canaanites.'[30]

Be this as it may, there are tribal groups in the text of the ancient song which are also already in an alliance. For in the emergency Deborah turns to kindred tribal units and expects help. Six tribes react positively:

> Then down marched the remnant of the nobles; the people of the Lord marched down for him against the mighty. From Ephraim they set out thither into the valley, following you, Benjamin, with your kinsmen; from Machir marched down the commanders, and from Zebulun those who bear the marshal's staff; the princes of Issachar came with Deborah, and Issachar faithful to Barak; into the valley they rushed forth at his heels. Among the clans of Reuben, there were great searchings of heart. Why did you tarry among the sheepfolds, to hear the pipings among the flocks? Among the clans of Reuben there were great searchings of heart. Gilead stayed beyond the Jordan, and Dan, why did he abide with the ships? Asher sat still at the coast of the sea, settling down by his landings. Zebulun is a people that jeoparded their lives to the death; Naphtali too, on the heights of the field (Judg 15:13–18).

---

[28] Hans Wilhelm Hertzberg, *Die Bücher Josua, Richter, Ruth*, ATD 9, Göttingen 1953, 171.

[29] J. Alberto Soggin, *Judges* (ch. 6 n. 27); Carlos Dreher, *A Formação Social do Israel Pré-Estatal*, São Leopoldo 1992.

[30] Herbert Donner, *Geschichte* 1 (ch. 6 n. 24), 160.

Six tribes are mentioned for their commitment to the common cause, and four are censured; here two names which do not appear in the traditional lists of tribes are striking, Machir and Gilead (moreover in v. 23 the city of Meroz, which really should have come to help, is cursed). Four traditional names are missing from the list: Simeon, Levi, Judah and Gad. So it emerges from the song that neighbouring tribes, living together in peace and probably linked by cultural bonds (language or dialect, the exchange of commodities or women), have a moral obligation to help one another. There is nothing about a formalized alliance. We cannot exclude the possibility that there is a symbolic significance in the fact that the tribal groups first mentioned (excluding the 'city of Meroz') number ten.

To conclude: the quest for historical, social and political motivations for the formation of the Israelite tribes has not proved very fruitful. We have no reliable sources from Israel itself or its environment which confirm the formation of the tribes in cultivated land and the concrete reasons for it. In the end is Yahweh religion all that is left as the factor which initially sparked off the formation of tribes and was a possible binding force in a tribal alliance? Or, to be more precise, is the famous intervention of Yahweh in the decisive battle at the same time the reason for a tribal alliance (cf. Ex 15:21; Judg 5:20, 31; Ps 68:5–13, 25–8)? But in our view of things the origin of a religion needs not only experiences of God but also plausible social starting conditions![31] We can conclude that there were tribes and tribal alliances in Israel in the period before the state. The number twelve is a late systematization, as in the case of the New Testament apostles. Yahweh, the warrior, plays an important role in the few tribal traditions that have been preserved.

6.3 The structure of the tribes

Research so far has based discussion of the Israelite tribes and their alliance largely on Bedouin conditions. Stimulated by the biblical accounts of the patriarchs Abraham, Isaac and Jacob, who are constantly on the move between Mesopotamia and Egypt, who also wander around in an unsettled way and without a home in the land of the promise and must laboriously

---

[31] After demonstrating (104–55) that the 'genealogical system' (the derivation of all the tribes from the ancestor 'Israel') and the 'geographical system' (Yahweh's gift of the land as the basis for the people of Israel) are later projections (ibid., 125), Volkmar Fritz, *Entstehung* (ch. 2 n. 19), concludes: 'Against the background of the common religion, Yahweh's war was probably the only institution for common action' (126). The making of the covenant, the theophany tradition and Yahweh's claim to exclusiveness, etc. are said to have their origin in the Yahweh war.

purchase rights (cf. the story of the tomb of Machpelah near Hebron, Gen 23), and attuned also to the old narratives according to which the forefathers of Israel lived in tents, or the important confession of faith made on offering the firstfruits, 'My father was a wandering Aramaean' (Deut 26:5), we modern observers have quickly sought parallels with the Bedouins alive today and depict Israelite tribal culture and organization solely against the background of these desert-dwellers.[32] But belief in Yahweh based one-sidedly on nomadic or semi-nomadic forms of life is a modern daydream, grounded not least in a romantic predilection for savage peoples and desert places. Granted, the Old Testament texts have retained vague recollections (or projections?) of an early itinerant life of the forefathers, but at the same time they can always imagine these same forefathers only as settled farmers or as people for whom a sedentary life was more desirable than anything else. Who can say whether the notions of instability and a lack of roots were not in reality born of the experiences of the century of exile and whether the whole exodus event is not an distancing projection of the desire to return home on the part of Babylonian exiles? That would almost reverse the relationship of Deutero-Isaiah to the exodus tradition, or the two would become parallel phenomena![33] At all events, we must reflect that Israel and its tribes first came into being in cultivated land and that therefore the tribal structure was shaped by peasant families and village communities living a sedentary life, with all the consequences that an agricultural way of living has for such a social structure and the attitudes and beliefs dominant in it.[34]

---

[32] Thiel's treatment of the social development of Israel in the period before the state is typical: for him the confrontation and fusion of the two different social systems of semi-nomadic immigrants and the Canaanite sedentary population are the two main problems of the social history of Israel. 'Israel's nomadic past' is 'much harder to grasp' than 'the class society in Syria and Palestine'. For 'although settled Israel never abandoned the memory of its origin on the steppes and its semi-nomadic beginnings, it has preserved very few direct traditions from the early phase of its history'. So we must compare nomadic societies which can be observed today, which is what Thiel does in a long first chapter (quotations: Winfried Thiel, *Entwicklung* (ch. 3 n. 1), 9; ch. II, 'Nomadische Gemeinschaftsformen', 10–51). Other authors reflect less and make nomadic society and the nomadic system of values fundamental for belief in Yahweh and all biblical theology. Cf. e.g. Victor Maag, 'Der Hirte Israels', *SThU* 28, 1958, 2–28; id., 'Malkut Jahwe', VTSup 7, 1960, 129–53; Walter Dietrich, *Israel und Kanaan. Vom Ringen zweier Gesellschaftssysteme*, Stuttgart 1979; Horst Dietrich Preuss, '. . . ich will mit dir Sein', *ZAW* 80, 1968, 139–73; Martin Rose, *Der Ausschliesslichkeitsanspruch Jahwes*, BWANT 106, Stuttgart 1975, etc.

[33] Cf. Jean M. Vincent, *Studien zur literarischen Eigenart und zur geistigen Heimat von Jes.Kap 40–55*, Frankfurt am Main 1977.

[34] Thiel takes account of this situation in so far as he immediately drops insights gained from study of the nature of the tribe among the Bedouins in discussing Israelite tribal structure: among present-day Bedouins the tribe is a (fictitious) 'connection based on blood relationships', which requires a sense of togetherness and solidarity (*Entwicklung* [ch. 6 n. 33], 11), whereas

In connection with our question we are interested first in the way in which members of the tribe lived together and the common purposes that bound them together; secondly, we are interested in the order dominant in an Israelite tribe, i.e. the regulation of questions of authority and law. On both points we are only sporadically and defectively informed by the existing biblical witnesses; thus many uncertainties remain and we constantly have either to resort to comparisons with better documented tribal societies or to take refuge in conjectures.

The territories recognizable in the tribal lists mentioned above (descriptions of frontiers, localities) each cover a number of villages: for example Benjamin has twenty-six 'cities with their villages' (Josh 18:21–26), Simeon seventeen (Josh 19:6f.), Zebulun twelve (Josh 19:15), Issachar sixteen (Josh 19:22), Asher twenty-two (Josh 19:30), Naphthali nineteen (Josh 19:38). At all events these will be small localities, so that assuming that each village with its environs had around a hundred inhabitants, we can assume an average personnel of around 1800 per tribe. The number can vary, especially downwards (though present-day Bedouin, African or Indian tribes are sometimes considerably larger), but it will have only been small. The members of the tribe go about their business in their settlements, where in turn they are divided by families. For as I have already said, the family remains the real group which satisfies all basic needs. Help from neighbours and kindred is best given in the community. The obligations of a legal, educational, ritual and cultic kind involving close collaboration similarly fall within the sphere of the village community.

But in that case what tasks are left for the tribe? From our texts (cf. the example of the Song of Deborah), we get the strong impression that only the tasks of defence and war are tackled at the tribal level; of course these include the necessary religious actions and certain structures of communication and command. The individual village groups living or working together are too remote from one another (I assume at least three to six

---

the immigrant Israelites after the settlement already gave up their tribal cohesion in favour of a bond with their own soil and the local community (ibid., 101–3). The tribes which were forming could therefore no longer be kin groups, but only fluid 'communities of interest' with a territorial identity and a secondary eponym, often personified from the place names (as in the case of Judah, Ephraim, Benjamin, ibid., 105). That the tribes, 'contrary to the notion of blood kinship fixed in the genealogies, were really regarded as territorial entities is shown by some formulations in relatively ancient texts in which the tribal names are constructed as geographical designations (cf. Judg 5:14f. with 4:6; 6:35 with 7:24; 11:29), giving the impression that the tribe is identified with its territory' (ibid., 106). Moreover anthropological research shows that people who today are still organized in tribes can live a nomadic, semi-nomadic or even a settled life (cf. Niels Peter Lemche, *Vorgeschichte* [ch. 2 n. 19], 104–9).

miles) for daily communication and aid or co-operation. The exchange of goods will of course also have flourished in the tribe, though there will have been certain specializations and offers of surplus goods.[35] But experience shows that the exchange of goods also extends beyond tribal boundaries, sometimes even among groups which otherwise do not have a very peaceful relationship with one another.[36] The villages also offered appropriately responsive families for marriages in the tribal sphere, since within one's own tribe one was sure of friendly relations. But beyond the tribal sphere the dangerous 'foreign land' began, as is evident from some episodes in the Hebrew scriptures.

In Judg 12:1–6 a bloody tribal feud develops between Gilead and Ephraim for a reason which in our eyes is trivial in the extreme. Curiously enough, on this occasion a difference in dialect between the two languages ('Shibboleth' – 'Sibboleth') and an age-old point of dispute, the arrogant charge laid by the West against the East, 'You – Gileadites – are fugitives from Ephraim' (Judg 12:4b; absent from LXX), are mentioned. The gruesome story of the rape and murder of the concubine of the levite from Ephraim similarly has tribal implications (Judg 19). For on the return home the couple find no safe lodging in Judah or Benjamin. The narrator heightens the tension and the reprehensible nature of the act to the full. For when the travellers go past Jebusite Jerusalem, 'the servant said to his master, "Come now, let us turn aside to this city of the Jebusites and spend the night in it". But his master said to him, "We will not turn aside into the city of foreigners, who do not belong to the people of Israel, but we will pass on to Gibeah"' (Judg 19:11f.). In this place of the tribe of Benjamin they hope to be safe, since the woman comes from Bethlehem in Judah, which is not far away and is friendly. Things do not work out, the two are regarded as aliens and fair prey, despite the fact that they are given lodging by an immigrant Ephraimite, though apparently he had not become completely accepted in Gibeah. The consequences are the sacrificial death of the young woman, who is handed over by her husband and the host, and a tribal war against the tribe of Benjamin.

---

[35] Lemche attaches great, perhaps too great, significance to trade in the 'formation of a differentiated society'; cf. id., *Vorgeschichte* (ch. 2 n. 19), 98–103 ('Although trade really had no direct significance for ordinary people – only members of the ruling class themselves exchanged commodities, primarily to further their prestige – it did lead to the origin of the great urban societies of the Near East in antiquity' (ibid., 102).

[36] The archaeologists can often give very precise information about the trade relationships within a region and outside it by means of imported pottery; cf. Helga Weippert, *Palästina* (ch. 3 n. 3), 373–82: 'The so-called "Philistine pottery" or the Palestinian sub-Mycenaean pottery' (after 1200 BCE, pottery from workshops in the land of the Philistines was sold over wide areas of Palestine).

That means that members of different tribes are in principle alien to one another, even within an assumed alliance of Israelite partner groups.[37] In these circumstances it is clear that even in Israel every tribe formed a political community which went into action above all to preserve the rights of the families, clans and settlements which it comprised, i.e. probably above all in negotiations and armed clashes with foreign enemies or rivals. The stories in the book of Judges clearly indicate the tribal origin of the conflicts and actions, even if they have been over-painted in terms of all Israel.

What social structures, what instruments of power, were at the disposal of a tribe to perform its tasks? Wellhausen termed the Israelite tribes a 'commonwealth without superior authority',[38] and some sociologists and theologians have taken up this derogatory slogan, modelled on the imperial majesty of the turn of the century; they speak in various ways of the as yet non-existent order of primitive societies.[39] It is the typical arrogance of people of allegedly 'higher' civilizations that they look down on indigenous cultures and deny them the possibility of real culture and a capacity for politics (and secretly long in a romantic way for such an original state?). The opposite is the case. Tribal cultures, too, have their accustomed and finely balanced structures of rule, but usually they are exercised in a less anonymous and brutal way, one less obsessed with power, than they are in larger societies.[40] That is not meant to suggest that all relationships in tribal societies are ideal. But the range of functional structures of communication and authority which still predominate in tribal society seems to be preferable to authoritarian monarchical conditions. As far as possible I shall limit myself to the Old Testament evidence.

In Israel before it became a state, the dominant warlike functions of a tribe were apparently performed by both men and women, but these were given different functions. First, we find the so-called (minor) judges, who according to the majority understanding 'judged', i.e. served as the legal authority for, Israel or one tribe of the people for a certain period. Some

---

[37] One is strongly tempted to think of the nation states which have different tribal or even ethnic groups with different languages within their frontiers. Europe offers sufficient examples: not only former Yugoslavia or Spain, Belgium, Great Britain, Russia and Italy, but also Germany with its numerous tribal groups which are still recognizable, despite all the revolutions.

[38] Julius Wellhausen, *Ein Gemeinwesen ohne Obrigkeit*, Göttingen 1900.

[39] Cf. Christian Sigrist, *Anarchie* (ch. 3 n. 10) (the subtitle is 'Investigations into the lack and the origin of political rule in segmentary societies in Africa'). As well as being termed segmentary, these societies are often said to be acephalous societies, societies without a head.

[40] In his collection of material, *Stammesreligionen*, which has already been mentioned (ch. 6 n. 22), Schulz presents some horror stories of contempt for human beings and oppression which beyond question also occur in these face-to-face societies. Nevertheless, tribal structures seem to me as a rule to be more humane than large bureaucratic societies, because they can respond more flexibly to individual needs.

decades ago great importance was attached to this 'office' of judge in Israel, and the proclamation and care of the divine law in the tribal alliance was transferred to the judge.[41] That is no longer possible; instead, some experts today tend rather to refer the abbreviated description of the allegedly 'judicial' activity to the general function of the leadership of a chieftain or petty king.[42] Be this as it may, asses as mounts (Judg 5:10; 10:3f.; 12:14) and staves as insignia (Judg 5:14) are symbols of power. Moreover the episodes of Gideon, Abimelech and Jephthah, with the occasional indication that these 'judges' would very much have liked to become kings, point to a very marked affinity between the offices of judge and king.

The second way of assuming leadership tasks was by the sudden bestowal of the spirit by the tribal god at an hour of political danger. From Gideon to Saul (Judg 7 – 1 Sam 11) stories recur which make the judge an ecstatic who goes berserk; under the influence of the spirit of God he can develop sheerly superhuman powers, like Samson (Judg 14 – 16), Jephthah (Judg 11) or Saul (1 Sam 11). The image that we thus get of the 'judges' of Israel is a split one, but it is not unrelated to the broad spectrum of the phenomena of the leadership of such a social group, especially in times of war, which are known to us from tribal societies elsewhere.[43] So I would maintain that in the event of war or self-defence, which was predominantly a matter for the tribe, the Israelite tribal system, in analogy to similar precautions in many tribal societies, had to bestow the function of a (warrior) chieftain (ecstatic judges). Alongside that there was the more permanent office of the chieftain who leads in times of peace; perhaps backed up by a council of elders (cf. Judg 11:5–11, where the elders of Gilead choose Jephthah as the tribal chieftain, exclusively to wage war?), he had a certain authority in exercising rule, probably only in the sphere of 'foreign policy', since internally the tribes and localities were completely independent. What was the tribal leader called? The two most likely terms are *šōpet* ('judge') or *nāśī'* ('leader').[44] But both words are certainly also used for other positions of leadership and not exclusively for the tribal chieftain. By way of analogy, what we have already seen at the level of the local community then also applies to the elders of the tribe: in this case they represent sub-units of the

---

[41] Cf. Martin Noth, *The History of Israel*, London ²1960, 101ff.; id., 'Das Amt des "Richter Israels"' (1950), in id., *Gesammelte Studien* 2, ed., Hans Walter Wolff, Munich 1969, 71–85.

[42] The better translation of the term *špt* with 'guide, lead, rule' proves itself here, especially in the cases of longer periods of office; cf. Ludwig Köhler et al., *HAL*, 1497–501.

[43] Cf. Ioann Myrddin Lewis, *Ecstatic Religion*, Harmondsworth 1971. For the sun dance of some North American Indian tribes; cf. Joseph G. Jorgensen, *The Sun Dance Religion. Power for the Powerless*, Chicago 1972. Max Weber already demonstrated the problems of the distribution of power in pre-state society in his study *Ancient Judaism*, New York 1960.

[44] Cf. Hermann Niehr, *ThWAT* V, 647–57.

tribe and had more or less equal rights in leading the tribe alongside the 'judges'. In the absence of any executive authority and permanently available military power, decision-making processes even at tribal level could probably be made only in a palaver, i.e. by negotiation which went on until agreement was reached, in the way that is still customary today with many tribal societies.

It is natural to suppose that possibly there were priestly offices in connection with the function of the tribe in war. Did the 'judges' or 'ecstatics' themselves perform the rites necessary for preparing and waging war? We know very little about this, except that it is clear that in tribal cultures as a rule religion develops war rituals and assigns appropriate functions to the participants.[45] In his mobilization of the Israelite tribes, Saul hacks to pieces a span of oxen and sends the bloody lumps of meat in every direction (1 Sam 11:7); as a guerrilla leader and tribal king, David used to have a priest with him who was to discover the will and council of God in all military operations with the help of the ephod and the forecasting stones Urim and Thummim (cf. 1 Sam 23:9–12; 30:6–8, etc.). Gideon is said to have destroyed the cult-place of Baal and Asherah single-handed and to have built an altar to Yahweh (Judg 6:25–32). After making a vow, Jephtah offered his own daughter as a burnt offering in gratitude for a victory that he won (Judg 11:39f.). We do not have further information about ritual activities; what we have is legendary enough and has little value as historical information. Thus the question of the priestly functions of leaders must remain open; we shall see later that religious ceremonies surrounding tribal wars still glimmer through in some biblical texts. Whereas monarchs used to make permanent appointments of priests and prophets, for tribal society we have to reckon more with the *ad hoc* duties of such ritual professionals.

The troops, the levy, are an important structural element in tribal war-making. As a rule, societies with a social organization cannot manage without a professional army. David was the first king to recognize the need for police and troops permanently at his disposal and he appointed his 'Cherethite and Pelethite' mercenaries. Up to the time of Saul the principle was that of the tribal levy; this was a merely moral obligation on individual families and tribes to heed the call to battle issued by the chief and to send able-bodied men with arms and equipment to the mustering places. So the tribal war primarily involves men, with all the social and religious consequences: the battle functions according to established rituals as a bloody trial of strength between two hostile male bands. Often the actual battle is

---

[45] There is plenty of anthropological literature, some of which has already been cited; cf. also
Florestan Fernandes, *A função social da guerra na sociedade Tupinambá*, São Paulo 1970.

preceded by a duel between the two strongest men. The scene which is very vividly dramatized in the famous legend of the victory of the shepherd boy David over the armed giant Goliath (1 Sam 17) is typical.

The arming and the fearful figure of the giant Goliath is described in detail; the terror on the Israelite side is also indicated. Then slowly the youthful hero David appears on the scene and arms himself for the duel – with only a sling and a couple of pebbles. The traditional duel of words flares up; it consists of reciprocal taunts which in the present version David uses for a radiant confession of Yahweh, the God of Israel (1 Sam 17:45–47). Then the action, which has been delayed many times, proceeds: 'When the Philistine arose and came and drew near to meet David, David ran quickly toward the battle line to meet the Philistine. And David put his hand in his bag and took out a stone, and slung it, and struck the Philistine on his forehead, and he fell on his face to the ground (1 Sam 1:48–50a).

This report is exaggerated, in the style of legend or even fairy tale, and has inspired the imagination of countless generations.[46] A parallel narrative seems closer to reality, although here too certain stereotyped ideas and the aetiology of a place play a formative role. The situation is the time after the death of Saul and the failure of the first Israelite monarchy:

> Abner the son of Ner, and the servants of Ishbosheth the son of Saul, went out from Mahanaim to Gibeon. And Joab the son of Zeruiah, and the servants of David, went out and met them at the pool of Gibeon; and they sat down, the one on the one side of the pool, and the other on the other side of the pool. And Abner said to Joab, 'Let the young men arise and play before us.' And Joab said, 'Let them arise.' Then they arose and passed over by number, twelve for Benjamin and Ishbosheth the son of Saul, and twelve of the servants of David. And each caught his opponent by the head, and thrust his sword in his opponent's side; so they fell down together. Therefore that place was called Helkath-hazzurim (2 Sam 2:12–16).

The bands of troops in tribal times were not very large. The battle is ritualized, but in military terms it is unprofessional. Twelve representatives of each side fight and the rest look on. The leaders have agreed the

---

[46] The literature on this story is extensive and has been much enriched by its long influence; cf. Hans-Joachim Stoebe, 'Die Goliathpericope 1. Sam XVII 1-XVIII 5 und die Textform der Septuaginta', *VT* 6, 1956, 397–413; Dominique Barthélemy, David W. Gooding, Johan Lust and Emmanuel Tov, *The Story of David and Goliath*, OBO 73, Fribourg and Göttingen 1986; Dieter Kellermann, 'Die Geschichte von David und Goliath im Lichte der Endokrinologie', *ZAW* 102, 1990, 344–57; Manfred Görg, 'Goliat', *NBL* 1, 902, and e.g. the treatment of the story in children's worship.

scene, which is described with the Hebrew verb *śāḥaq* in the *piel*, 'play, dance' (2 Sam 2:14), a male euphemism for the bloody work (cf. also the iconography and metaphors of the dance of death). Depending on the outcome of the individual fights the defeated side declares itself beaten, as in the case of Goliath against David, or perhaps – if the outcome is inconclusive – the real battle then flares up (as in the case of Abner and Joab). Be this as it may, the tribes wage war with untrained men who are called together only for the battle itself, with no special training, and also without any leadership trained in the technique of war.[47] The question of a possible war sanctuary and of the so-called holy war is raised in the next section.

The results of the investigation into tribal structures are sparse. We find above all forms of organization corresponding to the tasks arising in war. The legal and religious ordinances which have been so strongly emphasized in the past, particularly by Noth, are hardly to be seen in the tribes of ancient Israel. That is all the more amazing, since comparable tribal societies today do show such structures. There are places for settling disputes in civil law among individual families or village communities, extensive religious rituals which are performed together and provide a basis for and strengthen the tribal spirits, events of domestic politics like the choice of a new chieftain, etc. In Israel before the state the signs of such organizations and institutions are extremely thin.

The debate sparked off by Crüsemann in 1978 is important for our theological evaluation of Israelite tribal society and its religion. In his study on 'The Resistance to Kingship' he defined the tribal constitution as being opposed to rule and segmentary, and recognized in it essential antidotes to the establishment of a centralistic state authority.[48] Crüsemann could also appeal to extra-biblical comparative material which the Münster sociologist Sigrist, who has already been quoted, had contributed from African tribal cultures.[49] Along the lines of the 1968 revolution, he and Crüsemann focused on the origin of political rule. Sigrist wanted to oppose the thesis, often presented naively, that the drive to dominate is innate in human beings and is at work in every society:

> Contrary to all attempts to hypostatize rule as an elementary structure of
> all human societies, the position advocated here is that equality, mutuality,

---

[47] Roland de Vaux, *Ancient Israel*, London 1961, ch. 4, 'Military Institutions', is still an informative account of war in the time of the tribes and the monarchy.

[48] Frank Crüsemann, *Der Widerstand gegen das Königtum*, WMANT 79, Neukirchen-Vluyn 1978; cf. also the perspective of Norman K. Gottwald in emphasizing an opposition to domination.

[49] Important literature: Edward E. Evans-Pritchard and Meyer Fortes, *African Political Systems,* London 1940; Fritz Kramer and Christian Sigrist, *Gesellschaften ohne Staat*, 2 vols, Frankfurt 1978; Christian Sigrist, *Anarchie* (ch. 3 n. 10); Christian Sigrist and Rainer Neu (eds), *Ethnologische Texte zum Alten Testament* 1, Neukirchen-Vluyn 1989.

co-operation, solidarity, opposition and normativity are to be understood as elementary forms of human socialization – but that political rule does not belong among them.[50]

Sigrist is saying that in segmentary societies built up of groups with equal rights, while order prevails, there is no political rule. Max Weber also knows of such pre-authoritarian societies.[51] In this case anarchy does not mean unlimited collaboration and opposition but is a quite neutral term, denoting the lack of central power and authority. In Sigrist's words:

> I define 'segmentary' society as an acephalous society (i.e. as one which is not organized politically by a central authority), the political organization of which is mediated through groups with several or many levels which are politically equal and subdivided equally.[52]

This definition leaves out of account the mode of life (nomadic or sedentary). It concentrates on the sociological structure and political functions, and that means above all the question of exercising power. There is no discussion of how far democratic processes also contain power factors. In this scheme of thought one can also presuppose that transitions occur both from the tribal structure to the state and, vice versa, from the state to the tribal structure. Lemche describes the neutralized model like this:

> From the beginning of the historical period, time and again there have been these two possibilities of socio-political integration, the result of which is that a particular society which lived in the one form of organization gave this up in favour of the other. Thus after the rise of the small states of Syria-Palestine in the third millennium, one or the other state could break up, to be replaced by a tribal system, and on some occasions this new (or renewed) tribal organization could in turn break up and again be replaced by a centralized state.[53]

According to this view, the tribal structure represents an alternative model of human socialization beyond the family and clan structure, which has no elevated theological meaning. This therefore supersedes the transfiguration of the allegedly original democratic ideals of the tribal associations of ancient Israel which lasted until the 1980s, their exclusive faith in Yahweh and their clear, rigorous ethic, centred on blood vengeance and hospitality.

---

[50] Christian Sigrist, *Anarchie* (ch. 3 n. 10), XII.
[51] Max Weber, *Wirtschaft und Gesellschaft* 1, Tübingen 1956, 515; Christa Schäfer-Lichtenberger, *Stadt* (ch. 5 n. 13).
[52] Christian Sigrist, *Anarchie* (ch. 3 n. 10), 30.
[53] Niels Peter Lemche, *Vorgeschichte* (ch. 2 n. 19), 106.

6.4 Cultic actions

After what was said in the previous section, we will expect the essential cultic activities of the tribes of Israel to be in the sphere of waging war. That is also quite clearly the case from the evidence of the Old Testament sources, though it has to be conceded that they are sparse.

The so-called victory songs stand out among the earliest documents of the Hebrew Bible. So our examination of the war ceremonies will begin from their conclusion, but given the state of the sources mentioned, that should be permissible. Thus success in an armed conflict leads to a victory feast, in the course of which women join in hymns of praise. The most profane example is 1 Sam 18:7:

> When David returned from slaying the Philistines, the women came out of all the cities of Israel, singing and dancing, to meet King Saul, with timbrels, with songs of joy and with instruments of music. And the women sang to one another as they made merry: 'Saul has slain his thousands, and David his ten thousands.'

The narrative indicates only a tiny extract from the events after a victory in battle, but it is typical and important. The women, who in antiquity normally did not play an active part in battle (but there are also examples of women taking part in battles, e.g. in Arabia, in Celtic England and so on), go into action when their husbands return. They sing – probably with endless repetition – spontaneous songs which flatter the leaders and the warriors. Music and dance are among the signs of the framework and fixation of religious ritual. The note in 1 Sam 18 gives only two lines of the victory song, because only this statement is important in the context of the narrative. Presumably various strophes were composed *ad hoc* and performed by soloists, and then repeated by the crowd of those celebrating. Of course religious statements will also have been made here, as in the famous song of Miriam:

> Then Miriam, the prophetess, the sister of Aaron, took a timbrel in her hand; and all the women went out after her with timbrels and dancing. And Miriam sang to them: 'Sing to the Lord, for he has triumphed gloriously; the horse and his rider he has thrown into the sea' (Ex 15:20f.).

I shall pass over the fact that here Yahweh is already mentioned as the decisive god of war (see below 6.5). The important thing here is that women express the religious thanksgiving and therefore have a leading function in the victory celebrations. That emerges from still a third text, the great song of victory in Ps 68, which can be set alongside Judg 5. There a procession takes place, apparently to a sanctuary:

They see, God, how you enter,
how you, my God and king, enter the sanctuary.
The singers in front, the minstrels last,
between them maidens playing timbrels (Ps 68:25f.).

Women[54] are also mentioned in v. 12 – the large number of 'messengers of peace'. It is also important that the victory celebrations take place in a ritual framework, after the spoil has already been divided on the battlefield.[55] The typical instruments are hand drums; the scene is probably a holy place, perhaps a prominent sanctuary in the tribal region. Praise, worship and vows are due to the deity who has given victory (cf. Jephthah in Judg 11:30, 35). That will normally be the deity who has a relation with the tribe rather than with the subordinate families, clans or locations. So success in a defensive battle or a military campaign brought the warriors and those who stayed at home together in great festal worship and sacrificial feasts in which nothing was spared.

If the end of the war is thus a striking opportunity for the tribal faith to be articulated in festivities, the same sort of thing also happened at the beginning of the war – under the pressure of the dangers that threatened. In general we cannot say much about the causes of armed conflicts. The fight for resources (pastureland, agricultural land and water) could spark off wars just as much as violations of honour, property, law, obligations, etc. on one side or the other. In turn, accepted signals and rites with a religious basis were needed to set the tribal apparatus of war in motion, and some of these appear in the Old Testament. First of all there is the choice of a chief in war. Three methods of choosing a leader have been handed down in the Hebrew scriptures, two of which at lest have marked religious features. The choice of the supreme tribal warrior in an acute emergency may still have been made in profane fashion by the elders of a tribe (Judg 11:8–12). The chiefs in Gilead ask Jephthah to be a candidate for the post (v. 8); the candidate makes conditions which are accepted (vv. 9f.); and then 'the people' (*hāʿam*)

---

[54] The participation of women in war, mostly serving, supporting, healing, but also substituting in functions otherwise exercised by males, should not be underestimated at any time; cf. women in the war economy in modern times; women in underground armies, etc. For tribal societies, victory rituals involving the participation of women are attested in large numbers; as a concrete example I might mention the Tupinamba-Indians from the Amazon region (Hans Staden, *Brasil. Wahrhaftige Geschichte von den wilden, nacketen Menschenfresser-Leuten* [1557], reprinted ed. Gustav Faber, Stuttgart 1984).

[55] Cf. Judg 5:10, from the perspective of the mother of Sisera, who has already been murdered: 'Are they not finding and dividing the spoil? A maiden or two for every man; spoil of dyed stuffs for Sisera, spoil of dyed stuffs embroidered.'

chooses him as their 'head and decision-maker' (or 'commander', 'general', Hebrew *rōš w^eqāṣīn*). It is also interesting that Jephthah, apparently contrary to the usual rules, requires his role as leader to be extended after battle has been won (v. 9). The process of election seems quite profane; only in a last clause does the narrator note in very dry words the appearance of Jephthah at a local sanctuary, either because this is what the tradition said or because he himself found the tradition intolerably areligious: 'Jephthah said all that he had to say (*kol d^ebārāw*, rather, 'the matters concerning him') before Yahweh in Mizpah' (v. 11). In this way this relatively democratic process of election subsequently takes on a religious legitimation, as was only to be expected.

The other two typical procedures have a religious determination from the beginning. The sacral election by lot of the one chosen by God is used in what is perhaps the earlier tradition about Saul:

> (Samuel said:) 'Now therefore present yourselves before the Lord by your tribes and by your thousands.' Then Samuel brought all the tribes of Israel near, and the tribe of Benjamin was taken by lot. He brought the tribe of Benjamin near by its families, and the family of the Matrites was taken by lot; finally he brought the family of the Matrites near man by man, and Saul the son of Kish was taken by lot. But when they sought him, he could not be found. So they inquired again of Yahweh 'Did the man come hither?' And Yahweh said, 'Behold, he has hidden himself among the baggage.' Then they ran and fetched him from there; and when he stood amongst the people he was taller than any of the people from his shoulders upwards. And Samuel said to all the people, 'Do you see him whom Yahweh has chosen? There is none like him among all the people.' And all the people shouted, 'Long live the king!' (1 Sam 10:19b–24).

The choosing of someone by lot, whether the guilty party in a trial or one elected for a high office of leadership, is a favourite way in the Old Testament of discovering and performing the will of God (cf. Josh 7:16–19; 1 Sam 14:41f.; 1 Chron 26:13–19; similarly 1 Sam 16:5–13, the election of David: here no lot is needed, because Samuel is instructed directly by the voice of Yahweh). This is the well-known oracle technique with the help of the ephod pouch: 'yes' and 'no' stones are shaken, and in this way the deity gives his reply.[56] 'Israel is convinced that God holds the fates

---

[56] The ephod, the oracle pouch, contains the stones Urim and Thummim, one of which jumps out first. Cf. Werner Dommershausen, *ThWAT* 1, 991–8. For manticism in Mesopotamia, cf. Bruno Meissner, *Babylonien und Assyrien* 2, Heidelberg 1925, 242–82. Cf. Niels Peter Lemche, *Vorgeschichte* (ch. 2 n. 19), 184–207.

of human beings in his hands and that the decision by lot directly and unmistakeably reveals his will.'[57] However, Israel shares this faith with the peoples of the ancient Near East as with many others, before, at the same time and afterwards: the deity reveals himself in a manipulated omen, an announcement of the future. Many other techniques are known to us, especially from Mesopotamia, of the way in which the divine will could be discovered (interpretations using oil, the liver, arrow prophecies, the interpretations of dreams, etc.).

What most interests us is the use of the technique of the lot at the beginning of a war in Israel before it became a state. The later accounts of David's guerrilla troops and his later regular troops (1 Sam 23:2, 4, 9–12; 30:7f.; 2 Sam 5:19f.), and also the very legendary and late narrative of the covenant war against Benjamin (Judg 20:18, 27f.) suggest that the use of lots was also part of the equipment used by a tribal alliance for war. And it is very possible that (as we can see in the case of David) specialists who could constantly go into action were entrusted with this task. In that case, with the 'ephod bearer' we would have the beginnings of a spiritual advisor of the troops. The ephod chest was thus presumably part of the cultic equipment of an Israelite tribal summons, like the ark of 'Yahweh of hosts' which we shall be discussing later.

The other religious way of finding a leader for the tribal contingent of warriors is for him to be endowed with the spirit. That happens spontaneously, and is a direct intervention of the deity in human situations of conflict. By bestowing the spirit, God determines who shall lead the troops. Again a tradition about Saul is an impressive example of this: here we should remember that the Saul narratives still portray a situation before the existence of professionals: the real characteristics of an absolute monarchical central authority are lacking. The way in which Saul is seized by the spirit is described for us twice. First we hear of it in connection with an ecstatic host of prophets, which Saul meets on his way home (1 Sam 10:5–12. The proverb 'Is Saul also among the prophets?' is said to come from this encounter, vv. 11f., cf. the other version in 1 Sam 19:23f.). Then we have it in 1 Sam 11, a passage which is perhaps older, the report of the conflict with the Ammonites over a city in Gilead:

The Israelite city of Jabesh in Transjordan is besieged by the Ammonites and seems to be hopelessly lost: 'When the messengers came to Gibeah of Saul they reported the matter [i.e. the ultimatum of the Ammonite king Nahash, "On this condition I will make a treaty with you, that I gouge out all your right eyes, and

---

[57]   Werner Dommershausen, *ThWAT* 1, 993f.

thus put disgrace upon all Israel", v. 2] in the ears of the people; and all the people wept aloud. Now Saul was coming from the field behind the oxen; and Saul said, "What ails the people, that they are weeping?" So they told him the tidings of the men of Jabesh. And the spirit of God came mightily upon Saul when he heard these words, and his anger was greatly kindled. He took a yoke of oxen, and cut them in pieces and sent them throughout all the territory of Israel by the hand of messengers, saying, "Whoever does not come out after Saul and Samuel, so shall it be done to his oxen!" Then the dread of Yahweh fell upon the people, and they came out as one man' (1 Sam 11:4–7).

We also hear of the spirit being bestowed on a tribal leader in war in connection with Gideon (Judg 6:34); it has the same effect as on Saul: the leader designated by God has the right and duty to summon kindred tribes (or are they only clans?) to follow him (v. 35; cf. the contrary motive: the number of participants in the battle is reduced in Judg 7:2–8). Moreover Othniel is filled with the spirit (Judg 3:10: 'And the spirit of Yahweh came upon him and he became judge in Israel and went out to battle'), as is Jephthah (Judg 11:29) and above all Samson (Judg 13:25), though the bestowal of the spirit on Samson seems to be associated with the Nazirate and not so much with the mobilization of the tribal warriors and neighbouring tribes. The other judge-figures, e.g. Ehud (cf. Judg 3:27–9: in other respects he behaves completely like the judges endowed with the spirit, summons the neighbouring tribes to support him and proclaims, 'Yahweh has given your enemies into your hands'), Shamgar (Judg 3:31), Deborah (Judg 4 – 5), Barak (Judg 5:1), Samuel (at the level of the tradition which most makes him a 'judge', 1 Sam 7:9–12), are not explicitly said in the tradition to be given the spirit in the tradition, but perhaps that is only a fortuitous feature of the process of handing down the tradition. The bestowing of a warlike spirit of God which gives authority and possibly enables people to perform superhuman acts of power thus seems to correspond well with the tribal system. Similar phenomena can also be noted in connection with the North American Indian tribes in respect of war dances, trances and sacrificial rites.[58] If the deity of a tribe has a warlike nature, then it is only consistent and opportune that this deity should put its

[58]   Cf. Joseph G. Jorgensen, *Sun Dance* (ch. 6 n. 43); Ruth M. Underhill, *Red Man's Religion* (1965), Chicago ²1972; Ake Hultkranz, *The Religions of the American Indians*, Berkeley 1979. Jorgensen describes the historical development of the warlike sun dance among the Indian tribes of the Great Plains from around 1700 CE. Prior to the white conquest (second half of the nineteenth century), the sun dance was performed before hunting or marital enterprises on the basis of a vow by an individual (blood vengeance; hunting vow): 'In brief, the men dance for three or four days, accompanied by drums and singing. The dancers often accepted tortures like ritual fasting, thirsting and mutilations to attain power, health and success in war or in hunting and to further the well-being of the group' (ibid., 17f.).

own warlike power at the disposal of the members of the tribe, its clientele, in the hour of need in the form of a warlike, berserk spirit. The deity is then evidently himself present in the leader who is endowed with the spirit and the leader can confidently succeed in defeating and eliminating the enemy. How far the gift of the spirit (and the Nazirate, cf. Num 6) were connected or brought into connection with the ideology of the 'holy war' is hard to say (see 6.7 below).

Once the leader for the battle had been appointed in some way, battle was apparently joined with the blowing of the ram's horn (cf. Judg 3:27; cf. 6:34); this signal too presumably has religious connotations.[59] The summons to battle can apparently be given by the bloody rite attested in the story of Saul – and also to our horror in the story of the tribal war against the Benjaminites (Judg 19f.). Saul hews his draught oxen in pieces and sends the chunks to the allied tribes ('Whoever does not come out after Saul and Samuel, so shall it be done to his oxen!' – an undisguised threat behind which stands the authority of the one endowed with the spirit). In Judg 19:29 it is the corpse of the raped concubine that her husband divides into twelve pieces and sends to the tribes of Israel. Apparently the tradition took up the ancient motif of the threatening demand for tribal solidarity in war and gave it a particularly grisly form.[60]

After the public summons to war, the warriors will have prepared for the conflict psychologically by analogy with the ritualized tribal battles which are also known to us elsewhere. We know nothing about such community rituals from the Old Testament.[61] The late depictions of Judg 7 and Deut 20 with their legendary or ideological colouring at most betray that it was

---

[59] The ram's horn is not any old object but as an age-old symbol of divine power is a holy instrument. Some festivals were introduced with it even in the late period of the Old Testament (cf. Lev 23:24; 25:9; Ps 81:4, etc.). For the instrument see Helmer Ringgren, *ThWAT* VII, Stuttgart 1993, 1195f. The cultic use of the ram's horn can be seen depicted in Othmar Keel, *Die Welt der altorientalischen Bildsymbolik und das Alte Testament*, Neukirchen-Vluyn 1972, 318–22.

[60] The thesis that Judg 19f. is a literary fiction does not alter the cruelty of the imagination of the tradents, which we find perverse; cf. Phyllis Trible, *God and the Rhetoric of Sexuality* (ch. 2 n. 91).

[61] By contrast, they are abundantly known from tribal societies which can be observed today; cf. e.g. Ruth M. Underhill, *Religion* (ch. 6 n. 58), 127–41 (War Ceremonials, bibliography). If we read Underhill's collection of rites, social functions and aims and think of tribal feuds in the ancient Near East, then at least specific questions arise about the ritual manipulation of war situations in antiquity. 'Ritual surrounded every act of an attacking war party (in defence there was little time for ceremony) and to understand the ceremony clearly, we can divide the expedition into three phases. The first phase was that of preparations; when the spirit power was obtained for the volunteers. The second came during the expedition itself, when there had to be supernatural means to ensure safety and success. These two necessities were provided for in almost every tribe. It was in the third phase, the return and the victory celebration, that we find the most obvious split between the individualist hunters and the organized planters' (ibid., 128: boasting and bragging among the hunters; exorcisms of the hostile powers who

customary to exclude the weak from the fighting troop. Only those who were fully behind the joint endeavour and had possibly been put in the right mood by ritual dancing were to take part in the battle. The timid, the newly married and those who lowered morale by grumbling might be a burden on the others. We have already discussed the battle actions briefly; the religious element is hidden from us unless we see in this light such episodes as Moses stretching out his hands in blessing (Ex 17:11–13: as long as he held them and the magic wand outstretched, Israel was victorious over the Amalekites), looking at a divine symbol (cf. Num 21:8), the emanation of power from the ark (cf. 1 Sam 4 – 6) and the old warlike customs from the tribal period. That the battles were fought with great brutality and under the slogan 'Take no prisoners' emerges clearly from texts like 2 Sam 8:2 and the Mesha stele, which we have still to discuss (see below, 6.5).

It is clear from the so-called 'ark sayings' (cf. Num 10:33–6) and the 'ark narratives' (cf. 1 Sam 4 – 6; 2 Sam 6) that in the tribal period there was a special war palladium, a portable symbol of the deity, who also went out to war. Its precise form and function has been eliminated in the tradition by overpainting, but it is noteworthy that the ark was carried in battle, that it 'returned' after the battle, and then tragically fell into the hands of the enemy. The 'ark sayings', which are certainly old, but have been torn erratically out of context, run:

'Yahweh, arise and let your enemies be scattered; and let those who hate you flee before you!', and, 'Return, Yahweh, to the ten thousand thousands of Israel!' (Num 10:35).

The connection with the ark may be secondary, but the warlike orientation of these sayings is obvious. In their commanding, martial tone they are comparable to the saying in Josh 10:12 ('Sun, stand still on Gibeon, and moon, in the valley of Aijalon'). Occasionally there are passages in the Hebrew Bible that sound like an echo of the age-old sayings (cf. Ps 12:6; 94:1–2, etc.). David certainly first brings the ark to the capital to link up with the old tribal traditions and to use it for his politics. In any case the ark was an independent war sanctuary; it required its own personnel to serve it and was the centre for sacral actions which unfortunately have not been handed down. In fact it represents a second religious element in the tribal waging of war.[62] We must investigate the God of the ark in more detail later. At all

---

held on to the booty among the planters). Important ritual elements of the battle among the North American Indians are visions – fasts – sexual continence – the presence of shamans – their secret rites – treatment of the plunder (heads, scalps, prisoners, utensils, weapons) – the telling of heroic actions, exhibition of the plunder, the receipt of new names.

[62] Cf. Jörg Jeremias, 'Lade und Zion', in Hans Walter Wolff (ed.), *Probleme alttestamentlicher Theologie*, Munich 1971, 183–98; Martin Metzger, *Königsthron und Gottesthron*, AOAT 15, Neukirchen-Vluyn 1985, 309–51; Klaas A. D. Smelik, 'The Ark Narrative Reconsidered', *OTS* 25, Leiden 1989, 128–44; Eleonore Reuter and Manfred Görg, 'Lade', *NBL* II, 574–8.

events critical caution is needed since, 'Outside DtrG and ChrG the ark is attested only in Jer 3:16 and Ps 132:8, which means that the ideas associated with the ark are absent from wide areas of the Old Testament. Statements about the historical origin and function of the ark are very problematical, because the theological conceptions of the authors are brought to bear on the mentions of the ark.'[63]

Apart from the war rituals, we do not have even a hint of the tribal organization. The 'judging' in the legal sense which theoreticians of our time have made into a comprehensive tradition of law and judgment in Israel before the state was probably at most a matter of settling disputes at a local level. Deborah sat under a palm tree and pronounced judgment; her clients came to her (Judg 4:5; but cf. Gen 35:8, where a 'palm' of Deborah is mentioned in another context). Otherwise we hear nothing of specific activities of a judge and arbiter; this is first evident in the cases of David (2 Sam 15:1) and Solomon (1 Kings 3), but as an appendix to the ruler's power. Against the background of a tribal horizon, the 'judge rulers' could have been secondary 'arbiters' in this sense. We can no longer speak of the proclamation and implementation of a divine law related to the tribes such as Noth postulated for the 'minor judges'.[64] It is striking that in Deuteronomy the 'judge' plays a significant role alongside the levitical priest in the process of coming to a judgment under the Torah (Deut 17:8–13). But theology is speaking here. In the tribal alliance of ancient Israel, the contours of which we can no longer define exactly, the practice of law was decentralized;[65] it took place at a local level and presumably there were more far-reaching cases and legal interests only in connection with martial undertakings. The central cultic place for a shared cult of Yahweh has similarly been seen to be a daydream of present-day exegetes. As we have seen, there may have been cultic preparations at sanctuaries in favourable locations.

From a sociological perspective, the tribal organization in Israel (after the family and local community) was a loose, higher form of society which

---

[63] Eleonore Reuter, 'Lade' (ch. 6 n. 62), 574f.

[64] More recent literature on the subject has in part already gone beyond the problem: Albertz no longer recognizes it; cf. *History of Israelite Religion* 1 (ch. 3 n. 1), 225; the ominous term 'amphictyony' occurs only between quotation marks, ibid., 75, 83. By contrast Winfried Thiel, *Entwicklung* (ch. 3 n. 1), 126–45, can still draw positive conclusions from Noth's thesis. Cf. also e.g. Frank Crüsemann, *Torah* (ch. 4 n. 108); Jörn Halbe, *Das Privilegrecht Jahwes Ex 34, 10–26*, Göttingen 1975; Eckart Otto, *Ethik* (ch. 4 n. 96); Christa Schäfer-Lichtenberger, *Stadt* (ch. 5 n. 13); Ludwig Schwienhorst-Schönberger, *Das Bundesbuch*, Berlin 1990.

[65] Albertz, *History of Israelite Religion* 1 (ch. 3 n. 1), 92–4, also has to note that, although he is looking for the indications of the 'formation of the great cult'. 'Important though the shared reference to Yahweh was for the political coherence of the tribal alliance, there was no central cultic institution to match it' (ibid., 82) – but what then? Donner's 'poly-Yahwism' (in Albertz, 83; originally in Herbert Donner, 'Hier sind deiner Götter, Israel', in *Wort und Geschichte, FS for Karl Elliger*, AOAT 18, Neukirchen-Vluyn 1973, 45–50), could be the beginnings of a solution.

developed its religious rituals beyond the personal level on the basis of a fictitious kinship (a shared ancestor). The punitive action of the tribes against Benjamin in Judg 20 is probably narrated not because of the case which gave rise to it but because of its exemplary significance ('evil' has been done and must be atoned for, Judg 20:3, 12). From the narrator's perspective the issue is one of purity within the tribe and consequently the ongoing existence of the tribes. As a rule the Israelite tribes became active when there was an outside threat; they were apparently unconcerned with internal conditions. Originally the tribes of Israel were certainly independent in religion. In the texts that have been handed down they gather round Yahweh and perform rites for the warrior God. Thus we get the picture of a specific alliance with a purpose at the regional level. In its limited radius of action it evidently served the interest of the families, clans and local communities of which it was made up.

6.5 Ideas of God

In the previous section we came very close to the question of the role that belief in Yahweh played in the tribal period of Israel. Can we already pre-suppose worship of Yahweh in the pre-state period? All the indications are that we can. For when in the tenth century BCE David brought the ark into his new capital as a symbol of Yahweh worship (2 Sam 6; Ps 132), he was not creating a new cult, nor was he adopting an unknown cultic object, but he was skilfully and very deliberately incorporating into his concept of rule a god who had been known for a long time, perhaps who had even been forgotten.[66] The conjecture that he took over an old tribal shrine and put the old militant tribal theology around the god Yahweh at the service of his national politics can hardly be dismissed out of hand. Indeed it is now also supported by the observations and reflections, testimonies and hints, that we considered above. That raises the burning question: how did the cult of Yahweh reach Israel? After all, I have observed that the tribes were potentially and in reality independent in their worship of God. And on the basis of small indications I have conjectured that the religious orientation of the tribes was not homogeneous before the formation of the state. Cautious emendation of old texts can produce a pluralistic picture of religion in the period before the state: for example the saying of Joseph in Gen 49:24d–26c apparently contains references to other deities than Yahweh,

[66] The bringing of the ark to Jerusalem was apparently an extraordinarily important event in the history of Israelite religion, even if seems to have been depicted in an exaggerated way by the tradition; cf. Herbert Donner, *Geschichte* 1 (ch. 6 n. 24), 233f.; Gösta W. Ahlström, *History* (ch. 2 n. 19), 469–72.

not least to Asherah (v. 25e: *šādayim warāḥām*, 'breasts and womb' are typical attributes of a goddess).[67] There could similarly be an allusion to Asherah in Amos 8:14 if we regard the *'ašmat šōmᵉrōn*, 'guilt of Samaria' (which does not really make sense) as a miswriting or distortion of an original *'ašrat šōmᵉrōn*, 'Asherah of Samaria'. The distinctive name 'Shamgar son of Anath' in Judg 3:31 is striking: is the judge really being called the son of the goddess Anath? In Hos 11:4, as Schüngel-Straumann demon-strates,[68] an archaic image of a goddess may in fact glimmer through. All these are small but important references to a diversity of religion within the tribal organization. However, beyond doubt belief in Yahweh most persistently stamped the existing traditions.

None of the attempts to localize belief in Yahweh outside Israel by means of archaeology have led to any decisive results. It was most recently thought that Yahu had been discovered in Eblaite texts,[69] and formerly Babylonian texts were used.[70] There are also Egyptian texts which speak of the tribe of people of the 'Shasu of Yahu' (in which case Yahu is primarily a geographical term)[71] and a personal name with the verb 'be' is also said to have appeared in Nabataean.[72] In general, from textual indications in Hebrew writings scholars opt for groups in southern Palestine, Sinai, from which Yahweh worship is said to have emerged, namely the Midianites or Kenites.[73] It is impossible to make out precise details, but the conjecture that the origin of belief in Yahweh is to be sought outside Israel is an extremely convincing one.[74] However, that does not provide any concrete information about where, when and how the Israelite groups adopted belief in Yahweh.

---

[67] Cf. Mark S. Smith, *History* (ch. 2 n. 21), 16–19. In nn. 80–7 Smith refers to numerous controversial contributions on this enigmatic text.

[68] Helen Schüngel-Straumann, 'Gott als Mutter in Hosea 11', *ThQ* 166, 1986, 119–34.

[69] Cf. Giovanni Pettinato, 'Polytheismus und Henotheismus in der Religion von Ebla', in Othmar Keel (ed.), *Monotheismus* (ch. 2 n. 21), 31–48; Hans-Peter Müller, 'Der Jahwename und seine Deutung Ex 3, 14 im Licht der Textpublikationen aus Ebla', *Bibl* 62, 1982, 305–27: the name Yahweh does not occur in Ebla but is a personal name formed with the substitute 'he is'. This would therefore confirm the type of name 'I am', 'He is (present)'. On Ebla generally see Manfred Krebernik, *NBL* 1, 1990, 456–64.

[70] E.g. by Friedrich Delitzsch, *Babel und Bibel*, Berlin 1902; cf. Tryggve N. D. Mettinger, *In Search of God*, Philadelphia 1988, 36–40: 'Was the Divine Name Known outside of Israel?'

[71] Cf. Manfred Görg, 'Jahwe', *NBL* II, 260–6.

[72] Ernst Axel Knauf, 'Eine nabatäische Parallele zum hebräischen Gottesnamen', *BN* 23, 1984, 21–8.

[73] This thesis is suggested, e.g. by the Moses stories. For Moses marries into the priestly family of the Midianite Jethro and is evidently supported in the cult, even if not initiated into it, by his father-in-law, at least in the important narrative Ex 18.

[74] Most Old Testament scholars, including some Jewish colleagues, have adopted this standpoint in the steps of Julius Wellhausen and others; cf. e.g. Rainer Albertz, *History of Israelite Religion* 1 (ch. 3 n. 1), 2.2, 'The liberation of the liberated larger group (the Exodus group)', 40–66, with a large bibliography.

Starting from the indications, we can make the following conjectures. The stories of Moses and other references in the Old Testament texts point to the mountain regions south of Israel as the place where belief in Yahweh originated. Time and again the southern mountains are mentioned as the home of belief in Yahweh: in the stories of the patriarchs and the exodus, in the historical books and in the prophets. Sinai, Horeb, the fields of Edom, the hill-country of Seir, the southern region of Teman and the hill-country of Paran appear in a colourful succession going back to complicated processes of tradition which we can no longer trace. We usually get the impression that not even the early, let alone the last, tradents could have indicated the place. A large number of passages associate the southern mountains with powerful manifestations of the god Yahweh, a theophany which takes place with powerful phenomena of clouds, lightning and thunder at which human beings and nature are terrified.[75]

> Yahweh, when you went forth from Seir; when you marched from
>   the region of Edom,
> the earth trembled and the heavens dropped, yes the clouds dropped
>   water.
> The mountains quaked before Yahweh, Sinai before Yahweh the God
>   of Israel (Judg 5:4f.).

The geographical designations pile up to such a degree without coinciding that even this old text seems to be based more on an indication of mythical distance than on precise descriptions of places. The same is true of the two comparable depictions of theophanies, though they also deviate specifically in detail:

> Moses said:
> Yahweh came from Sinai, and dawned from Seir upon us.
> He shone forth from Mount Paran and went to Meribath-Kadesh . . .
>   (Deut 33:2)

> God came from Teman, and the Holy One from Mount Paran, Selah.
> His glory covered the heavens, and the earth was full of his praise.
> His brightness was like the light, rays flashed from his hands.
> And there his power was hidden (Hab 3:3f.).

The exodus stories often use the geographically indeterminate designation 'mountain of God' for the place where Moses is granted the first vision of Yahweh particularly in connection with Moses' stepfather, the Midianite

---

[75] Cf. Jörg Jeremias, *Theophanie. Die Geschichte einer alttestamentlichen Gattung*, WMANT 10, Neukirchen-Vluyn ²1977.

priest Jethro or Reuel. Albertz is certainly right here when he attributes to the narrator the intention of wanting to designate the household mountain of the Midianites by this name. He also concludes quite plausibly that this origin of Yahweh cannot have been invented.[76] In cultivated land Israel would not have put the origin of its God far outside its own frontiers, so that Elijah had to travel forty days and forty nights before he reached the mountain of God (1 Kings 19:8).

The point should be made in passing that the name Yahweh does not help to establish his home. Exodus 3:14 is a disguised attempt at an explanation which uses the Hebrew word 'be' (*qal* or *hiphil*?), but the derivation of this verb is not convincing – although it is shared by most contemporary exegetes. Too much theological speculation seems to have crept in – since the redactor of Ex 3:14 has played on this explanation. But none of the derivations from other roots (e.g. from *hāwāh* I–II, 'blow', *hiphil* 'destroy'/ 'be', *hiphil* 'call to life'/'be passionate', 'act', etc.) are more convincing. Possibly we have an otherwise unknown name with a basic meaning which can no longer be discovered (and which was no longer accessible even to the author of Ex 3:14).[77]

The starting point of the worship of Yahweh can no longer be localized, and even later was deliberately made increasingly unrecognizable in Israelite tradition, because people wanted to delete the excessively close religious kinship with the Midianities, who were then hated; cf. Judg 6:1–6; 7:8.[78] However, it must probably be sought to the south or south-east of Jerusalem, possibly even on the eastern side of the Gulf of Aqaba. In fact semi-nomadic or nomadic tribes lived there (in the stories about Gideon mentioned above the Midianites and Amalekites are camel nomads, Judg 6:5), who could then similarly have been worshippers of Yahweh. But how belief in Yahweh the mountain and tribal god came into the land of Canaan escapes our historical knowledge. The assumption of an exodus group and actual encounter with God on Mount Sinai which even Albertz and many other colleagues vigorously defend, along with almost all Old Testament

---

[76] Rainer Albertz, *History of Israelite Religion* 1 (ch. 3 n. 1), 51: Yahweh thus '. . . comes from an area which was not part of the territory of later Israel. So this later tie can hardly be explained from Israelite worship of Yahweh either; rather, there is some evidence to suggest that Yahweh already had his home in the mountain region south of Palestine and was worshipped there before he became the god of Israel'. Is it possible that experience of exile has already been worked in here, when Yahweh comes from a distant southern land to rescue his people?

[77] There is literature on the interpretation of the name Yahweh in Tryggve N. D. Mettinger, *Search* (ch. 6 n. 70); cf. especially Martin Rose, *Zum Streit um den alttestamentlichen Gottesnamen*, ThSt 122, Zurich 1978; Werner H. Schmidt, *BKAT* II/1, 175–9.

[78] Cf. Lothar Perlitt, 'Sinai und Horeb', in Herbert Donner et al. (eds), *Alttestamentliche Beiträge zur Theologie*, Göttingen 1977, 302–22; Rainer Albertz, *History of Israelite Religion* (ch. 3 n. 1), 51f.

scholars,[79] cannot be demonstrated historically, at any rate, and has been painted over or stamped by later experiences of oppression and liberation. Moreover in principle no encounters with God of any kind can be demonstrated, so they cannot be evaluated for positivists as absolutely normative events in the theological sense. Experiences of God belong firmly in the category of time-conditioned phenomena and therefore must keep being repeated; consequently they can claim only limited validity. An unprejudiced observer would also conjecture that people who later belonged to Israel could have lived and worked in the south, on the Sinai peninsula, or further east, beyond Aqaba. This is the thesis put forward by Görg:

> Accordingly Yahweh would originally have been a deity of the 'storm god' kind, who in a mountainous area gave a guarantee which came from above to ward off dangers, to grant deliverance and to make possible the continued existence of his followers. The elementary indications which characterize the epiphany God in the Old Testament (Deut 33:2; Judg 5:4; Hab 3:3 . . .) meet up with the notion of a deity who makes himself available to his worshippers in demonstrations of natural power and at the same time in protective support; in the possibly original meaning, 'he comes down' or the like, this god corresponds to a primary experience of mountain nomads. Those who worship Yahweh could be sought within the Shasu formations, to which in particular the Kenites and Midianites seem to correspond in the Bible. The early worshippers of Yahweh will also have come into contact with Egyptian culture and

---

[79] Rainer Albertz, *History of Israelite Religion* 1 (ch. 3 n. 1), 40–66; however, he gets entangled in all kinds of contradictions. Israel was not in Egypt as a people but only with the small Moses group; however, for sociological reasons it must have been a 'larger group' (ibid., 44). The experiences of liberation are handed down especially in the vocabulary and imagery of the time of Solomon, but the forced labour in Pithom and Ramses (though the cities cannot be connected with Israelite slave labour on the basis of any archaeology) must be historically credible (ibid., 45, 46ff.). The Israelites are not nomads in the exodus accounts, but a 'socially declassed group of foreign conscripts to forced labour whose solidarity had been undermined by state measures' (ibid., 45); still, they make a pact with the nomadic Midianites. Yahweh religion has grown up in history, but step by step it is given unique, absolute features (cf. ibid., 48f. with 63). An attractive feature of Yahweh liberation is the liberation of the socially weak from their mechanisms of oppression (cf. ibid., 48–9), but the same 'bias against domination, transcending present social circumstances, which was to become established time and again in the history of Israelite religion' (ibid., 47), is also attributed to the tribal structure ('acephalous, segmentary'), which is depicted merely in sociological terms (ibid., 82f., 92f.; against any centralism in Israel). Jörn Halbe, *Das Privilegrecht Jahwes Ex 34:10–28,* FRLANT 114, Göttingen 1975; Frank Crüsemann, *Torah* (ch. 4 n. 108), 27–58, puts the emphasis elsewhere: the exodus event and the liberation on the mountain of God are the decisive data of Israelite history and theology, with which the giving of the law was connected much later. 'If Torah is attached to Sinai, it is therefore understood as an act of liberation' (Crüsemann, 37). Cf. also Erich Zenger, *Israel am Sinai*, Altenberge ²1985; Christoph Levin, 'Der Dekalog am Sinai', *VT* 35, 1985, 165–91.

religion through the acquisition and conscription of local skilled labourers by the Egyptians and others in the zone of copper mounds around Timnah. The clashes with Egyptian border controls and the practice of deportation expand the idea of the local god and show Yahweh in the process of detachment from Egypt (>Exodus) as a god independent of place who liberates and accompanies. The advent of the 'referential god' Yahweh as a god who does not allow transcendence and immanence to be understood as opposites, but is experienced as a God who smites and heals, judges and raises up, is compatible with the archaeological discovery of a 'Silence of Amun' (the so-called Amun cryptogram on scarabs from the early iron age in Southern Palestine), which may have furthered the development of an alternative 'personal piety'.[80]

Manfred Görg's basic concept can be recognized even through the scholarly language: Shasu groups which later moved to Canaan brought belief in the mountain god Yahweh there with them. But even Görg cannot say how a new type of piety could arise from the regionally limited cult of settled 'mountain nomads'. At this point we must simply remain silent and confess our ignorance.

However, we do get on to sure ground with the early Israelite evidence, some of which has already been mentioned. It all shows Yahweh as a tribal and war god who supports his adherents in difficult situations against overwhelming enemies. The short song of Miriam in Ex 15:21 – as mentioned earlier, it was sung by women – about riders and chariots by the 'Reed Sea' also belongs in a series of texts which are generally thought to be pre-exilic and sometimes are dated to before the state, even in their written form:

> Then Miriam, the prophetess, the sister of Aaron, took a timbrel in her hand; and all the women went out after her with timbrels and dancing. And Miriam sang to them: 'Sing to the Lord, for he has triumphed gloriously; the horse and his rider he has thrown into the sea' (Ex 15:20f.).

There is no mention at all of the Egyptians; only in the later elaboration of the short archaic song of victory does the Pharaoh with his army appear (Ex 15:4; in v. 9 'the enemy' is mentioned; in vv. 14–16 only the lesser neighbours of Israel appear, but cf. Ex 14). The song of Miriam seems to celebrate a victory over enemies by the sea; we cannot infer more from the earliest tradition. The songs in Judg 5 and Ps 68 emphasize similar victory

---

[80] Manfred Görg, 'Jahwe', NBL II, 1992, 265.

celebrations. Each time Yahweh is celebrated as the ruler of nature who is superior to the hostile deities; he sets in motion rain, hail, water, lightning, clouds, thunder and earthquakes, all powers which are at the disposal not just of a mountain god but of any storm god.[81] For Israel before the state – at the level of the tribal organization and only at that level – Yahweh became the chief God because his powerful help proved effective in the fight for survival against highly superior opponents (city states with a high level of culture, civilization and military technology).

The iconography of the fighting God is widespread in the ancient Near East, though of course the depictions predominantly come from societies with a state structure. But we must assume that not all that much changed in the notion of the warrior deity with the development from the tribal constitution to state or territorial monarchy. Perhaps in exploring various sources we need to note the attributes of kings: they are not easy to imagine at the tribal level. The insignia of power in the tribal society will have been limited to the symbols customary in it. But elsewhere the monarchies will have similarly accepted and developed tribal insignia like the staff and crown (of feathers). The best survey of the warrior deity is given by Othmar Keel, once in his earlier work (*Bildsymbolik*) and then in the volume *Göttinnen, Götter und Gottessymbole* cited earlier.[82] On the type of the vegetation god[83] (is he related to the mountain god or identical with him?), Keel says:

> In contrast to the Egyptian sun god, the storm and vegetation god from north Syrian Asia Minor – north Mesopotamia – does not mediate life directly, but by his influence on the storm and vegetation. From the beginning of the second millennium he is known in Mesopotamia under the name Hadad or Adad, a name which is probably to be explained by the Arabic *hadda*, 'thunder' or 'crash'. In Ugarit, Hadad is identified with the Hurrian Teshub and at the latest from the middle of the second millennium is designated almost exclusively by the

---

[81] Until the late period these attributes of Yahweh remained, over and above the depictions of theophanies already mentioned (cf. Jörg Jeremias, *Theophanie* [ch. 6 n. 75]); cf. the speeches of Yahweh in the book of Job 'from the storm' (Job 38:1; 40:6). For the type of the ancient Near Eastern 'storm god' like Baal, cf. Mark S. Smith, *History* (ch. 2 n. 21), 49–55. The storm attributes of the militant deity are predominantly concentrated on the sudden outbreaks of power.

[82] Othmar Keel, *Welt* (ch. 6 n. 59), esp. ch. IV on 'Ideas of God' (157–223); id. and Christoph Uehlinger, *Göttinnen* (ch. 4 n. 22), esp. ch. IV: 'The Late Bronze Age: Egyptian Colonialism and the Adoption of Political and Militant Deities' (55–122).

[83] In so far as a beneficent influence on the vegetation is really attributed to the war god, there can be at transfer from the level of local religion to the militant tribal deity. When the battle of the creator god with chaos is mentioned, we still have to do with the warlike aspect of the deity and not the deity who blesses in the cycle of the year.

title Baal (owner, Lord). In the earlier period his most important attribute is the thunder club. It seems likely that he makes heaven resound with it.[84]

A limestone stele from Ugarit, 1.42 m high and around 50 cm wide, shows the 'Lord' almost in human size. On his head he wears a helmet which tapers sharply at the top, with bulls' horns pointing forward: locks of hair (or earpieces from the helmet) reach almost to his loins on the right- and left-hand sides; there he is girded with a short 'working garment' (Keel) and a sword is stuck in his girdle. His legs are in a walking or fighting position, moving from left to right. In his left hand Baal is holding a mighty spear that pushes shoots and leaves upwards, in the form of lightning. His right hand is raised up and threatens with the club. Keel connects this depiction with Ps 135:7: 'He makes clouds rise from the earth, he makes lightning for the rain. He makes the storm go from his spears.' In a similar depiction from the neo-Assyrian period, around a thousand years later, the god Shamash is standing on a bull in a walking position, storming forwards; his long cape is open because of the tension of his striding legs. His hands hold bundles of lightning and with his right hand he is in the process of letting off such a bundle. The sword girded on his left side and the bow or quiver on his back are almost completely covered by his body. But the god is also busy with the lightning. On his head he wears the high Assyrian hat; his beard and long hair emphasize his dignity and power. The full disc of the sun shines over his head covering, a symbol of the sun god Shamash. The quotation from the psalms assigned to this is: 'Dark cloud is around him . . . Fire flares out from him and scorches his enemies around. His lightning flashes illuminate the earth' (Ps 97:2a, 3, 4a).[85] To give a third example: a few pages further on Keel discusses a specific war god Resheph, who is really native to north-west Mesopotamia, but is worshipped as far away as Egypt. A limestone stele from the Egyptian new kingdom, dated around 1570 BCE, shows the deity in the same striding position as in the two depictions discussed above, against the background of four bands of hieroglyphs and a door. The great god, slim with a tall cap from which bands hang down, and a short linen robe decorated with tassels, raises his right arm with the war club. The spear in his left hand is placed on the ground, with the point upwards.

It is not . . . surprising that the ancient world experienced a quite specific, divine power in war. In the north-west Semitic sphere it bears the name

---

[84] Othmar Keel, *Welt* (ch. 6 n. 59), 192.
[85] Ibid., 194.

Resheph. In contrast to Baal, who represents the noble cosmic battle of life against chaos and death, Resheph more markedly embodies the darker aspect of (historical) war. In the Old Testament Resheph represents 'burning' (Ps 76:4) and 'plague' (Ps 78:48). God is depicted as a cruel warrior. Resheph appears alongside Deber (pestilence) in the psalm of Habakkuk 3 (v. 5). This psalm depicts the god as Yahweh's follower who with threatening force sets out to deliver his people. But just as at Passover Yahweh himself has assumed the role of the destroyer – in the view of P (cf. Ex 13:13 P with 12:23 J), so at a very early stage Yahweh himself also appears as a god of war. He showed himself as a warrior for the first time at the exodus from Egypt (Ex 15:3). He is celebrated as such in Ps 24:8. The strength that is attributed to him also appears in the title 'Lord of strength under the nine' which Resheph bears in Egypt . . .

As god of war Yahweh fights for the tribes, whose centre was the ark of the covenant. The notion of the war god who fights for his people is individualized by Ps 35 in a bold way and thus is made effective for the individual believer.[86]

The stamp and roll seals of the late Bronze Age which Keel and Uehlinger discuss in their chronological-systematic investigation emphasize the significance of warrior deities especially in the phase when Palestine was under Egyptian rule or indirect Egyptian influence (1550–1150 BCE). At the beginning of the period the Egyptians drove the Hyksos out of Palestine. Entanglements in war also continued under Egyptian supremacy and even more after the withdrawal of the occupying forces (in the fourteenth century?), as did battles between individual city rulers and the ḥapiru who have already been mentioned. The pictorial depictions which have been found in Megiddo, Lachish and Beth-shean (i.e. seals, but also small objects and some ceramic depictions) overwhelmingly display many warlike motives. The god with his right hand raised on high, bearing a club, axe or javelin, and striding out to battle, is a frequent motif. The chariot is quite new and 'the most typical iconographic symbol in the spheres of battle and war'.[87] However, the deity does not always need to appear on the chariot; there can also be the Pharaoh. The more extended depictions occasionally show the return from battle:

On a further, very famous, ivory a ruler in a chariot is returning from victory in battle (pl. 65). Two naked Shasu nomads tied to the

---

[86]   Ibid., 199.
[87]   Othmar Keel and Christoph Uehlinger, *Göttinnen* (ch. 4 n. 22), 68.

horse go before the chariot . . . The left half of this ivory, separated by three plants put on top of each other, shows the victory feast. Messenger birds spread the news of victory . . . The ruler is sitting on a cherubic throne . . .'[88]

The occurrences of battle scenes are rounded off by depictions of deities fighting with animals. These pictures probably extend into the mythological realms of the battle with chaos, etc.[89]

It is amazing that only a few experts have made any attempt to investigate individual motifs of the image of God in Israel and the ancient Near East separately, i.e. from syncretistic aspects. Perhaps with such a method one could discover parallels in the history of religion and the different *Sitz im Leben*, i.e. the different social configurations. However, two studies on the warrior god from the USA go in the direction indicated. The first is by Patrick D. Miller, Jr,[90] but, like the second, which will be mentioned next, it does not get as far as social origins. Miller applies the textual evidence about warrior deities from the environment of Israel, i.e. especially from Ugarit, to explain Yahweh's warrior role. Secondly, he investigates all the allusions from the Old Testament to Yahweh's warlike action. He comes to the conclusion:

> Yahweh as warrior was indeed a very early part of Israel's understanding of deity and during that early period perhaps the primary imagery evolved . . . Even more important, the language and understanding of God as warrior dominated Israel's faith throughout its course.[91]
>
> . . . at the centre of Israel's elaborated poetic and theological statements about God the warrior was the salvation theme . . . Or, to put it in reverse form, at the centre of the salvation experience and theology of early Israel was the 'man of war', the 'divine warrior'.[92]

Examples of the dominant metaphor of battle are offered both by the old tribal sayings and war stories already cited and by later texts, like the terrible description of Yahweh as a warrior returning from the battle against Edom sprinkled with blood (Isa 63:15; cf. also Ps 18; 135, etc.). At all events they reflect times of real armed clashes or periods in which (tribal war) was regarded as a solution to problems of survival.

---

[88] Ibid., 70.
[89] Ibid., 84–90.
[90] Patrick D. Miller, Jr, *The Divine Warrior in Ancient Israel*, Cambridge 1973.
[91] Ibid., 171.
[92] Ibid., 173.

The second study is more interested in establishing the relationship between Yahweh and the other great deities in Syria-Palestine.[93] There are only peripheral comments on the functions of the deity. 'As warrior fighting on Israel's behalf, Yahweh exercises power in Judges 5 against powerful peoples and deities.'[94] Elsewhere Smith is more interested in the parallel storm deities and the unpolemical relationship between Yahweh and the god El. He concludes from this positive collaboration or fusion of the two deities that Israel – as the name also implies – initially served El, who was then taken up into the cult of Yahweh.[95]

The individual functions of God are also evaluated in any theology of the Old Testament, but hardly ever treated as a main subject.[96] Earlier, scholars tended to turn to the names and epithets and actions of the deity and attempt to construct an overall picture of Yahweh from them.[97] We must also look briefly at these attempts.

Because the warrior god also plays an equally significant role in the time of the monarchical nation state – and then later in the eschatological and apocalyptic visions – it is difficult to separate the notions of the war god of a tribe cleanly from the later pictures of God. We can use only the criterion that at the time of the tribes talk of the warrior god is related to the tribal scriptures. Nothing that points to later social formations or ideologies can be claimed for the period before the state.

The designation of Yahweh as 'man of war, warrior' (*'īš milḥāmāh*) in Ex 15:3 seems quite authentic and is also singular in the Old Testament. Do we have old tradition here, or later historical empathy? Be this as it may, we can best assign such an anthropomorphic, perhaps even democratic, designation of God to tribal faith. Indeed *'īš* is ultimately a term which clearly comes from the human sphere: 'man' as opposed to 'woman', 'wife'. Only Isa 54:5 is comparable in its anthropological boldness or naivety: Israel or Jerusalem is being comforted: '. . . he who made you is your husband – Yahweh Sabaoth is his name'. But the title of God as 'in the male image and a warrior' does not occur elsewhere. One could argue similarly for the

---

[93] Mark S. Smith, *History* (ch. 2 n. 21). Above all, El, Baal, Asherah and the sun are the deities referred to.

[94] Ibid., 147.

[95] Ibid., 7–12.

[96] Cf. e.g. Horst Dietrich Preuss, *Theologie des Alten Testaments* I.2, Stuttgart 1991, 1882. Fohrer too mentions Yahweh's warlike acts more in passing: in the period before the state 'Yahweh continues to govern the destinies of nations and individuals. It is due both to the circumstances of the period before the state and the selectivity of the tradition that this takes place primarily through war and battle, and that the warlike features of God's activity are therefore emphasized' (Georg Fohrer, *History of Israelite Religion*, London 1973, 107).

[97] Cf. Horst Dietrich Preuss, *Theologie* I (ch. 6 n. 96); Hans-Joachim Kraus, *Theologie der Psalmen*, BKAT XV/3, Neukirchen-Vluyn 1979; Tryggve N. D. Mettinger, *Search* (ch. 6 n. 73).

description of Yahweh as a 'zealous God' (*'el qannā'*, Deut 5:9), provided that one does not see it as a claim to total exclusiveness. In my view that only developed very much later, in the exile. So attempts to base Yahweh's comprehensive claim to following and loyalty on the tribal period[98] are doomed to failure simply because the tribe regulated only a small part of life, merely war and self-defence. Because they are connected with other functional fields in different forms of society, the most important spheres, namely those of the family and the village, remain completely untouched by the tribal structures and religious ceremonies of the tribe and consequently cannot be subject to any commands for exclusivenesss from the head of the tribe. Within the tribal framework the designation 'zealous God' can only mean that the deity takes the side of the client group with great, passionate concern. The God who fights for his tribe need not be 'jealous' of a rival.[99] None of the few passages which speak explicitly of a 'zealous' God or Yahweh (Ex 20:5; 34:14; Deut 4:24; 5:9; 6:15; Josh 24:19; Nahum 1:2) is to be dated early; the majority of them are Deuteronomistic.[100] However, in their simple statement 'be zealous for' they hit on what is expressed in all the texts about battle and victory. Impetuously and with devastating force Yahweh intervenes for the people of his tribe in battle – compare Ex 15:21, '. . . horse and chariot he hurled into the sea'; Judg 4:15: 'And Yahweh terrified Sisera and all his chariots'; Judg 5:20: 'From heaven the stars fought, from their courses they fought against Sisera'. Or Hab 3:5–7:

Before him went pestilence, and plague followed close behind.
He stood up and measured the earth; he looked and shook the nations.
Then the eternal mountains were scattered, the everlasting hills sank low.
His ways were as of old;
I saw the tents of Cushan in affliction, the curtains of the land of
    Midian did tremble.

The enemies are not spared. If we take these descriptions as a background, what von Rad calls Yahweh's 'zealous holiness' describes an ancient theological character which is best explained in terms of the tribal period. But that question too may be left open.

---

98 Cf. e.g. Werner H. Schmidt, *Das erste Gebot*, TEH 165, Munich 1970; id., *The Faith of the Old Testament*, Oxford 1983.

99 With Alfred Jepsen, *ZAW* 79, 1967, 288, against Karl-Heinz Bernhardt, *Gott und Bild*, Berlin 1956, 92; cf. Jörn Halbe, *Privilegrecht* (ch. 6 n. 79), 134–40.

100 Jörn Halbe, *Privilegrecht* (ch. 6 n. 79), 136ff., constructs an old two-membered liturgical formula which is used in a process of 'renunciation' (of foreign gods) (ibid., 139f.).

The third point is equally uncertain. Yahweh is often designated as leader 'of the hosts'.[101] The problems already indicated with the name Yahweh are doubled when it comes to the meaning and date of this expression. For basically no one knows what $ṣ^eḇā'ōt$ means: hosts of Israel or cosmic deity? Or is it not a name in the genitive at all, but rather a noun used as an attribute (Yahweh: the Sabaoth)?[102] Hans-Jürgen Zobel puts the problem like this. 'Today no scholars dispute that the epithet $ṣ^eḇā'ōt$ belongs in the Jerusalem cult of YHWH, in view of the instances in the Songs of Zion in the Psalms, and in Isaiah. The only question is whether it accrued to the God of Israel who enters the city with the ark, or whether it came to Jerusalem from Shiloh as a title which had already been given to the god of the ark.'[103] Zobel opts primarily for a derivation from Shiloh, and thus for the transference of old Canaanite ideas to the ark. The title 'cherubic throne', however, is said by some scholars to be closely connected with Jerusalem.[104] If the notion and theology of $ṣ^eḇā'ōt$ contains only kingly and cosmic features from the beginning, then for the moment it says nothing for our purpose. But if it goes back to earlier traditions of battle, perhaps with the support of hosts of demons or deities who possibly also have an astral character, then the title is very important evidence for the tribal situation in Israel. In that case Yahweh would be the god who appeared with a powerful following (manifestations of the storm) and fought for his group, as appears for example in the other designation 'cloud-rider' (cf. 2 Sam 22:11 = Ps 18:11; Isa 19:1; Hab 3:8), which is related to the title 'cherub rider'.[105] In short, precise descriptions of the tribal god Yahweh, his nature and his activity, are not to be expected from the time before the state.

Not only is there a way from the zealous to the jealous deity. There is also the development – and as the inscription of the Moabite king Mesha, known in the Old Testament from 2 Kings 3:4ff., has shown, it is even closer – to the so-called 'holy war' which is waged wholly in the name of and on behalf of

---

[101]   According to Zobel the 'name $ṣ^eḇā'ōt$, which is used exclusively as a divine epithet, occurs 285 times in the OT' (Hans-Jürgen Zobel, *ThWAT* VI, 876–92). Zobel adopts Eissfeldt's view that 'in Shiloh YHWH religion attained a "higher level", through the extension of the name YHWH by the title $ṣ^eḇā'ōt$, the one enthroned on the cherubim' (ibid., 884). The '. . . new stage of YHWH religion thus stated . . . differs . . . from the earlier one by a powerful extension of the wealth of the power and majesty' of God (ibid., 885, with reference to Otto Eissfeldt, *KS* III, 421f.). Unfortunately neither scholar takes note of the social conditions of the increase of power.

[102]   There is a brief list of current interpretations in Hans-Jürgen Zobel, *ThWAT* VI, 800f.

[103]   Ibid., 881f.

[104]   Ibid., 882–4.

[105]   Cf. W. Boyd Barrick and Helmer Ringgren, *ThWAT* VII, 508–11, esp. 511.

God.[106] Indeed we may ask whether tribal wars were not always or often 'holy wars' by nature. With some caution this can be affirmed. The Mesha inscription speaks volumes: 'The king of Israel had built Ataroth for himself. But I fought against the town and took it and I slew all the people of the town, an offering (?) for Chemosh and Moab. And I brought back from there the altar-hearth of David and I dragged it before Chemosh at Qeriyoth ... And Chemosh said to me, "Go take Nebo against Israel." And I went by night and fought against it from the break of dawn till noon; and I took it and slew all: seven thousand men, boys, women and [girls] and female slaves, for I had consecrated it to Ashtar Chemosh. And I took from there the vessels of Yahweh and dragged them before Chemosh.'[107] What is remarkable is the pathos of this inscription addressed to the national God of Moab, Chemosh, the typical effort for domination and subjection with a religious foundation and the policy of extermination in the conquered territories. The system of the war of Yahweh developed successively in Deuteronomy and the Deuteronomistic and Chronistic histories (cf. Deut 20; Josh 6 – 13), but at all events betrays a later, retrospective schematization and localization.

So now for the first time we meet Yahweh at a tribal level. That corresponds completely with important statements in the Old Testament. Yahweh was not always God in Israel and at every social level. Rather, initially he belongs only to the type of storm and war gods like Baal, Anath, Hadad, Resheph and Chemosh, who were worshipped in regional alliances or states in closely defined, special situations. His original homeland was the southern regions of present-day Palestine and Jordan. Thus the regional and functional, cultural and social limitations of Yahweh should be beyond all doubt. The elaboration of ideas about Yahweh, e.g. as a guarantor of fertility, personal good fortune, head of a pantheon, creator of the world, judge of the world, etc. is gradual and only fully unfolds in the exilic/post-exilic age, always in connection with social and historical changes. Transferences and adaptations of the God of war in our time are not to be assessed either positively or negatively (cf. below, 6.7).

6.6 Faith and ethics

The most important question is how in real life the members of the tribe expressed their faith in the warrior deity who helped in times of need, went out to battle, conquered the enemy and was celebrated in victory; how they articulated their faith in this deity, what experiences they had with it,

---

[106] Cf. Manfred Weippert, '"Heiliger Krieg" in Israel und Syrien', *ZAW* 84, 1972, 460–93; Sa-Moon Kang, *Divine War in the Old Testament and in the Ancient Near East*, BZAW 177, Berlin 1989; Susan Niditch, *War in the Hebrew Bible*, Oxford 1992; Andreas Ruffing, *Jahwekrieg als Weltmetapher*, SBB 24, Stuttgart 1992.

[107] Kurt Galling, *TGI* ²1968, 52f.

and in what ethical norms of conduct the relationship with the tribal deity was expressed.

Faith among the tribes before the state was influenced and shaped by the special situation of the proto-Israelites, confronted by the strong city states, and by the rivalry between many tribal formations of the same species, when the issue was on what basis they should live in the cultivated land and the adjoining steppes. We see from the traditions how often the tribal groups were in minority situations. Battles against their neighbours, above all the highly-equipped and superior rulers of cities (cf. Judg 4f.), broke out under strong economic, political and cultural pressure from the urban areas. The Israelite side waged wars of survival as inferiors. Their enemies were considerably better armed and much stronger. Therefore in times of crisis the help of the tribal god was absolutely necessary. The deity had to intervene, otherwise all labours were in vain and Israel was lost. The enemy hordes could not be resisted alone. And the more inferior they felt, the more in the course of time the intervention of Yahweh alone was requested, granted and praised. In the Chronistic history it is the inferiority of the conquered and scattered groups of Judah which shines through. Then even in this late period – probably in mournful remembrance – Yahweh the god of the tribe and nation, strong in battle, still plays an important role (cf. 2 Chron 20), or does so once again.

We can understand belief in God in the tribal system rightly only if we start from the formation of society and the expectations that it had to fulfil. Down to the present day, human beings lead their elementary life in small groups. Earlier it was almost exclusively the family which formed the external and internal framework for the survival and well-being of the individual. In the modern industrial world there are also groups in which people are professionally involved, work, live, enjoy friendship and share interests; these communicate a security which gives meaning and preserves life. But with higher forms of association, i.e. with groups that become numerically bigger (which simply arise out of the proliferation of families and clans and by increased contacts with neighbouring groups, and then also become a political necessity: latecomers must expect to be unlucky), individuals and sub-groups create themselves a home in the wider social context. They organize themselves at a new level, and the sociological scene which displays the social formations in concentric rings one above another, like the skin of an onion, carries some power of conviction. Human beings organized themselves in the wider space of the tribe, which – especially in the ancient Near East – above all offered them more protection from outside inter-ventions. In addition, the formation of the tribe may have been effective in creating culture:[108] in the sources from Syria and Palestine to which we have access the tribe seems limited to the warlike functions discussed above. In the culture of the ancient Near East, rites of initiation and fertility (rites of passage, etc.), probably took place at the village level, which in many anthropological studies is identified with the tribal level.

Thus little can be said about the faith, spirituality and ethic of the tribal alliance. The active veneration of the tribal deity in the regions of ancient Israel will have been limited to times of emergency. We have no indications of a permanent institution of worship, at any rate since Martin Noth's amphictyony has proved to be an exaggerated construction. Possibly the tribal deity, and also initially Yahweh, was initially cultivated with a degree of regularity only by men of God endowed with the spirit, who in emergencies could be summoned by means of the deity's existing insignia of power. Perhaps there could be no regular worship because of the remoteness of the mountain of God. But in case of war the members of the tribe, above all the warriors who were summoned, knew that they were protected and motivated by the tribal deity. They called on their guardian deity and put themselves at its disposal. Consequently there were ethical rules of behaviour only for males and for the limited duration of the hostilities. Adequate and appropriate preparation for battle – also connected with fasts and sexual continence (cf. 1 Sam 21:5f.; 2 Sam 11:1: Uriah refuses to go to his wife when on leave) – are clearly attested. The brutality of the tribal war could probably only be practised rightly in a collective rush of blood.

All in all, in the Israelite tribes a sense of community developed in which the strongest elements were important experiences of deliverance attributed to the tribal deity. Here the sense of togetherness in the family and tribe will have related to the larger unit of the tribe, though it was no longer possible for people to live and work together in everyday life (because of the distance separating the segmentary groups). Nevertheless the sense of affinity (which can well rest on a fiction) so strongly held together the sub-

---

[108] Cf. Hermann Schulz, *Stammesreligionen* (ch. 6 n. 22), 13: 'The tribal religions established the foundations and the structure of the whole architecture of the universal history of religion. All the fundamental forms of religious imagery and action developed from tribal cultures and have been infinitely differentiated in the wider ritual and symbolic spheres of the tribal cultures.' He then refers to the general accounts of tribal or primitive cultures by Franz Boas, *The Mind of Primitive Man*, New York 1911; Robert H. Lowie, *Primitive Religion*, New York 1924, and other anthropologists; the last in the series is Josef Franz Theil, *Religionsethnologie*, Berlin 1984. But the studies mentioned do not distinguish exactly between family, clan and tribal religion, nor even does Hermann Schulz. So their estimation of tribal religion includes what we have called 'family faith'. At the other end of the spectrum we have e.g. Joachim Wach, *Religionssoziologie*, Tübingen 1951, who leaves the 'natural groups' behind him as soon as possible in order to arrive at the higher levels of state religion.

divisions of the tribe that in case of national threat a common self-defence was possible. The tribal groups loyal to Yahweh in Israel presumably proved especially successful. However, we do not know what parts originally belonged to them: there is no Moses tribe in the sources. Probably the central Palestinian groups qualify best for early Yahweh worship: Ephraim or Joseph, perhaps Benjamin. Be this as it may, Yahweh proved the stronger, and was successful even against the mercenaries and chariots of the cities (cf. only Ex 15:21; Judg 5). That increased the glory of the groups who followed Yahweh, and perhaps led to the first formation of a state under Saul (from the tribe of Benjamin, 1 Sam 9:1, etc.), and then under David to the elevation of Yahweh to be the tribal god (2 Sam 6).

The formation of a sense of togetherness pointing beyond the family and clan was a complex process. A person identified himself with the 'thousand' which belonged to his own tribe, assumed certain responsibilities, and thus opened up his horizon, which had previously been that of the village and small town. He had to learn once again to look beyond the end of his nose. On the other hand, a heightened assessment of people 'outside', outside the reality in which the person lived, was almost of necessity associated with this. Thought in terms of 'friendship' had extended beyond the immediate bounds of a person's own tribe and village community to a tribal region. But it seemed so exhausted by this expansion of the horizon that the demarcation from other tribes probably proved harsher than before (cf. 6.4 and 6.5 above). The heightened thought in terms of enemies was thus a direct correlative of the extended thought of friendship. And of course this hostile thought also had a religious foundation and backing. It begins with the natural sense of superiority in a group to all other possible groups.[109] As a result of this, the group makes its own status and its own needs paramount, defends its own right to resources and living space, denounces as illegitimate the rights of others in important matters, is increasingly pressurized to resort to violent means which were hardly available to the family and village community, triumphs over aggressors, experiences victory in its own camp as something which is particularly effective in creating community, possibly needs war to consolidate its sense of togetherness, and then even resorts to expansionist and provocative means of seeking armed clashes. In the course of violent and bloody clashes the 'enemies' are taunted and degraded to an inhuman level, of course all in the name of God. The accusations may be so groundless that any rational reflection could recognize how hollow they are; emotions ensure that they are believed and handed on. I have already mentioned the Ephraimite

---

[109]   Cf. Peter R. Hofstätter, *Gruppendynamik*, Hamburg 1957.

mockery of the Gileadites (Judg 12:4). The taunting of the Moabites and Ammonites, who are said to be a rabble born in incest (Gen 19:36–8), or the lament about the people of Meshech and Kedar, who are all said to be liars and schemers (Ps 120), sounds harsher (in our ears). The Edomites became the arch-enemies of Israel in the late period of the Old Testament; they are harshly denounced (cf. Isa 21:11; 34:5–15; 63:1–6; Jer 49:7–22; Ezek 25:12–14; Amos 1:11f.; Obadiah). The 'tribal sayings' handed down in Gen. 49 and Deut 33 are also not clearly composed by friends, but surprisingly contain much sarcastic mockery.[110]

Belief in one's own God as representative of 'our' group is thus associated at a tribal level with a heightened exclusion of members of other tribes. In contrast to what happens at the level of family or village, war can become an almost necessary means of self-representation and a bond for one's own social grouping.[111] The deities at a tribal level accordingly have a martial tone. Tribal religion has a markedly patriarchal stamp, because the business of war concerns almost exclusively the men. From a religious perspective tribal faith thus furthers self-confidence and aggression, but internally also legalistic thinking, solidarity and a readiness to dedicate oneself to the common cause. The tribal ethos calls for a new quality of readiness to commit oneself and hardness in favour of one's own community. An episode from the book of Judges clarifies the 'male virtues' which were thought desirable in the conflict with neighbouring tribes: Gideon, the leader gifted with the spirit, has captured two Midianite tribal chiefs, Zebah and Zalmunna:

> And he said to Jether his firstborn, 'Rise, and slay them.' But the youth did not draw his sword; for he was afraid, because he was still a youth. Then Zebah and Zalmunna said, 'Rise yourself and fall upon us; for as the man is, so is his strength.' And Gideon arose and slew Zebah and Zalmunna; and he took the crescents that were on the necks of their camels (Judg 8:20f.; there is a parallel narrative in Judg 7:25).

The son whom Gideon addresses has not yet learned to kill. In the view of the one handing on the tradition he was 'still a youth' (na'ar), i.e. he had not yet come of age or was on the verge of manhood. Under the influence of their tribe's ideology of war, the young people who were perhaps eager to prove themselves in tribal war had to learn to overcome the inhibitions about killing that they had learned in their families and

---

[110] Cf. Hans-Jürgen Zobel, *Stammesspruch und Geschichte*, BZAW 95, Berlin 1965.

[111] As I have already mentioned, the 'social function of war' has been investigated in particular among Latin American tribes; cf. Florestan Fernandes, *Função* (ch. 6 n. 45); Hermann Schulz, *Stammesreligionen* (ch. 6 n. 22).

village communities. In an emergency they had even to break the rules of fair fighting, man against man, and slaughter defenceless civilians. The tribal war set new criteria for inter-personal clashes. The history of war in the Near East is an especially bloody, cruel and crazy chapter in human development. It shows excesses of a lust to murder with a religious motivation which one can only regard with horror.[112]

6.7 Ideologies of war? Liberation theology?

From our present perspective and sense of responsibility, how can we judge that past tribal tradition and theology of Israel? The modes of behaviour and attitudes to one's own community which were learned at that time in the context of the battles in the ancient Near East for the possession of stretches of land rich in water have still left their baneful legacy down to the present day. One development can already be recognized in the Old Testament: the practice of extermination in tribal feuds led to a holy war ideology which was not applied in any way in Judah during the time of the exile. It therefore influenced the later tradition all the more deeply because it seemed to be the divine legitimation for the 'ban', i.e. for a scorched-earth policy (cf. Deut 20). The merciless extermination of 'enemies' – and, as we have seen, the term largely included the civil population – in wars which were increasingly holy arose out of this: a stain on all religions which through their specific 'proclamation of salvation' have encouraged their own party's propaganda for war and hatred. God has been and still is widely misused by all hostile groups which are fighting for domination in the sacred lands. Sadness and horror at such narrow-minded theological constructions which despise humanity are more than justified.[113]

Nevertheless, we can also learn theologically and ethically from a critical discussion of the old tribal traditions of Israel. We have seen that initially the tribes of Israel were in an oppressive minority situation. They had to fight against the far superior city states and in this historical context called on their tribal god (perhaps originally also tribal goddess or tribal gods) with all the resources at their disposal. In an analogous way to this, many minorities forced to the margin of an existence with any human dignity, and occasionally also oppressed majorities in the population, are today fighting for their survival. Should we think badly of them if in extreme need they also invoke the aid of the just God to secure their survival? Have they a theologically well-founded right to organize resistance against the

---

[112] Cf. e.g. Bernard Lewis, *The Assassins,* London 1967; Amos Elon, *Jerusalem. City of Mirrors,* Boston, Toronto and London 1989, and literature on the Holy War, above (ch. 4 n. 66).

[113] Cf. Karlheinz Deschner, *Kriminalgeschichte* (ch. 2 n. 3).

supremacy of a deadly violence? Where in this case is the boundary between the legitimate and the illegitimate use of violence on the side of the oppressed? In recent decades these questions have been hotly discussed all over the world. It seems to me that by virtue of all that we can think to be theologically correct in our pluralistic world, which is everywhere struggling for its survival, the exploited groups or societies whose downfall has been brought about by the ruling powers must be accorded a legitimate right to defence and resistance – in extreme cases even extending to armed struggle. That the resistance of the oppressed often turns into a terror which has contempt for human beings is the other side of the coin. The theologically legitimate battle for liberation lies on a narrow path which runs between abysses. But there is this way.[114]

There is no lack of examples. In many countries, the countless primal populations of the earth see themselves exposed to merciless strategies of extermination. The dominant social strata, usually deriving from colonial conquerors, gladly sacrifice to their own interests people living in the 'stone age', who in the view of the 'more highly civilized' no longer have any justification for living. The 'Society for Threatened Peoples' in Göttingen and similar organizations in many countries tirelessly attack genocide and mobilize the conscience of the world – with relatively little success. Why should our prosperous society bother if somewhere on this globe an indigenous culture disappears, if tribal societies are robbed of a basis for life or people of those 'archaic' civilizations are regularly murdered? In the name of the one just God for the one world which exists today we must give these 'indigenous' peoples who are hopelessly doomed to destruction the right to resist.

The social exploitation of large parts of the population has increased at a headlong pace in the course of the globalization of the economy and the absence of any political and economic alternative. In the course of industrialization over almost two hundred years the gulf between haves and have-nots has widened vastly. In our time the unjust distribution of commodities is assuming mindless dimensions. Recently the newspapers noted that according to a UN study there are around eighteen individual billionaires who have wealth corresponding to the Gross National Product in one year of the forty-eight smallest countries on earth, with hundreds of millions of inhabitants. Such facts are hardly imaginable, and go beyond our power of comprehension. And the social misery which lies behind them is even more impossible to assess. It literally cries to heaven. Malnourishment, sickness, the eternal sighs for wasted opportunities of

---

[114] Cf. Helder Camara, *Revolution through Peace*, New York 1972.

education and unemployment mock our talk of human dignity and solidarity. In this constantly deteriorating situation the cry 'Those without rights all over the world, unite!' is more than ever theologically legitimate. For the outcast population of the world has no effective lobby in the power centres of the industrial nations. But we know that God's will is for the salvation of the whole world, an intact creation and for all human beings irrespective of race, religion, sex or income level.

In many parts of the world ethnic, cultural and religious minorities are being oppressed and their existence is threatened. It is certainly right that from the perspective of theology and social ethics every case is special and must be assessed on the basis of its historical origin. There can be no simple recipe for solutions, like the sweeping recommendation that armed war should be waged from the underground and there should be terrorist attacks on an oppressive society. Rather, on behalf of the whole of humankind we shall have to examine the possibilities of non-violent resistance and democratic procedures in each individual case. Any use of violence, even by the marginalized and oppressed, has evil consequences for those not involved, since it draws many people in. Probably there is no case in which terrorist attacks on the public can be approved. They are always to be judged irresponsible or criminal. But if no democratic means are available by which an oppressed and threatened minority could improve its situation; if long and patient protest has had no success, then acts of resistance like boycotts, strikes and campaigns extending to armed battle must be considered. Minorities have the right to call for their independence.

Despite all the differentiation in individual countries and cultures, the women of this world belong among the exploited strata who suffer violence, however much in the rich societies they also participate in possessions and power, and thus in the structures of oppression. Loud declarations of equal human rights for all have changed almost nothing in the way in which the female sex bears a disproportionate share of the burden of world society and does a disproportionate amount of the work which is important for the preservation and survival of humankind, and of course is underpaid for it. In many countries women are declared second-class citizens, and in some regions are branded unwanted beings even before they are born. Because of the irresponsible and anachronistic domination of males, the religions have played a considerable part in the degradation of the female sex. In this hopeless situation, which has also brought few fundamental improvements even in democratic societies, the right to individual and collective self-defence also applies to oppressed women. Women have to organize themselves and exert joint pressure in order to resist daily violence and disadvantage and to attain the equality which has long been promised and is indicated in some biblical texts. In this case, too, it is legitimate to call on a just, or to the one just, deity who according to the old understanding would come down with lightning and thunder and the intervention of heavenly hosts, and today fights in numerous situations for the improvement of the situation of the disadvantaged.

6.8 How were larger societies organized?

The transition from primary forms of organization with face-to-face inter-action to anonymous social formations in which communication and ethics must be reified is an extremely important step in the development of humankind. It happened in ancient Israel in the prehistoric period, in the Israel of the first millennium BCE, before and alongside the formation of the state, and is tried out time and again in the civilizations of the world when loose associations of interest arise on a regional basis. We can therefore incorporate Israel's experiences of tribes into this overall sociological context and ask the general question how significant tribal faith is theologically.

With good reason, at the tribal level theology and ethics are no longer mediated through the structures of family and clan but need a special foundation in an appearance of God and the conclusion of a treaty. This is also the case in the social organizations that we shall be discussing next. Because the textual evidence which has been handed down (e.g. Ex 3; 6; 24; Josh 24) has been adapted to the conditions of the community, above all in the exilic/post-exilic period, I shall not attempt any evalua-tion in terms of the tribal organization here. However, I do take into account the fact that tribal religions are constituted in the same way as community religion. Furthermore, we are interested here in the question what significance the experiment of 'tribal society' in Israel has gained for our tradition of faith.

Some biblical texts betray a marked awareness that the tribal organization was a rival to the later monarchy; the assessment of the two systems varies (cf. 1 Sam 7–12). Both forms of socialization serve the need of religious population groups for protection and validity, but differ quite markedly in terms of the degree of centralization. The tribal structure leaves families and clans intact and functions in a relatively 'democratic' way through the councils of elders. Monarchies rule in a hierarchical way, raise taxes, impose forced labour, conscript soldiers and as a rule are far more effective than tribes in settling disputes or offering protection. That they easily succumb to the temptation of expressing their power in pomp and glory through architecture, military might and religion can be seen in a very negative light, but it often finds the approval of subjects.[115] In the Christian tradition, for centuries in Germany (in contrast to Switzerland) state socialization has been established as the model of divinely willed organization. By contrast, we can regard the looser, decentralized tribal structure as an early alternative model which was tried out in Israel and then also in Judaism.[116] Apart from all the Romantic transformation, the attempt at a bond through tribal alliance and representation of interests which leaves the micro-organization of society untouched and thus tends to work against an excessive and oppressive development of power might also be important for our modern sense of freedom. Little information though we may have from antiquity in Israel and in the ancient Near East, and terrifying though the beginnings of a war of annihilation may be, we should note the theological possibilities of this first larger society.

---

[115] Stephan Heym has given a brilliant description of Solomon's delight in ruling as a reflection of the East German apparatus: *The King David Report*, New York 1973; German ed. 1972.

[116] Thomas Staubli calls it a complementary system, *NBL* III, 682–4.

7

Kingdom Theologies in Israel

In the tenth century, following the pattern of the smaller nation states of Moab and Ammon and the Aramaean states of Damascus and Hamath, along with the Philistine states which had been founded a little earlier, in a period of relative peace with the world power, a centralized monarchy, Israel, came into being. That same century, in 926 BCE, it divided into two rival states which sometimes co-operated, Israel and Judah.[1] The first king, Saul, probably marks the transition from tribal constitutions to the state bureaucracy: David and Solomon established the state organization which then largely followed the pattern of other ancient Near Eastern states. How belief in God in this period (say between 1000 and 587 BCE) developed in its various currents must be depicted here in a brief sketch.

7.1 The sources

We are better informed about the history, society and religion of Israel for the period when Israel was a state, which lasted roughly four centuries, than for the tribal period. That is above all because the kings very soon put court scribes in charge of keeping annals; this was also customary elsewhere in the Near East. Fragments of, or the influences of, these royal records, though very sparse, have been used in the books of Kings. They report accessions, the length of office, the death and the successor of a king, and also report in dry words special events in his reign.[2] Thus, albeit indirectly,

---

[1] All scholarly 'histories' of Israel deal with the period in question in separate chapters; cf. especially Herbert Donner, *Geschichte* 1 (ch. 6 n. 24), 169–232 (from Saul to Solomon); 2, 233–381 (the kingdoms of Israel and Judah up to the Babylonian conquest in 587 BCE). The accounts of events in the more recent, more sceptical histories largely conform with the traditional accounts in this period; cf. Gösta W. Ahlström, *History* (ch. 2 n. 19), chs 10–19 (pp. 421–803).

[2] Cf. Burke O. Long, *1 Kings*, FOTL 9, Grand Rapids 1984; id., *2 Kings*, FOTL 10, Grand Rapids 1991.

we come upon documentary material which has been worked over (not the originals deposited in the archive, as in Mesopotamia!). The second basis for our improved historical knowledge of this period is provided by the very rich results of excavations; while these have brought few inscriptions to light, they have produced abundant finds of architectural remains, tombs, tools, and household and cultic objects.[3] They are significant above all for social history, because we can make inferences from the archaeological finds to everyday life. Thirdly, in fact some references to Israel and Judah can be found in inscriptions or pieces of writing outside Israel, since the great empires of the time were very interested in Syria-Palestine and as a rule attempted to incorporate this land bridge between Mesopotamia and Egypt into their own sphere of influence.[4]

However, joy at the good state of the sources must be relative. For the information is again not as continuous and comprehensive as we would have liked. Moreover the existing evidence for the time has not lain untouched in the earth over millennia, but has come down to us in a living process of tradition and usage. That is true in particular for the time of the monarchy: the terse court reports have sometimes been worked over from quite fixed theological positions of a later period, which offer theological evaluations of individual kings that sometimes demonstrably do not correspond to the historical realities (cf. the biblical portraits of Saul, Jeroboam, Ahab, Manasseh, Josiah, Zedekiah, etc.). We call the later anonymous revisers and editors of the books of Samuel and Kings 'Deuteronomists', and they were probably active during the exile, i.e. in the sixth century BCE. The late origin and revision of the historical events by the Chronistic authors is even clearer. They were not active before the end of the fifth century BCE, and once again they revised the historical picture of the time of the monarchy. For while they took over the basic framework of the earlier account, they simply excised the history of the northern kingdom (which for them was apostate and had vanished). They put the main emphasis on the cultic development of Judah (or projected their ideas of the cult, the priesthood and the levites on to the texts), so that David was restyled as a singer of psalms who prepared for the cult, and Solomon was the temple-builder *par excellence*. Moreover they inserted into

---

[3] Again cf. Helga Weippert, *Palästina* (ch. 3 n. 3), 417–681, and archaeological journals like *AASOR, BA, JPES, PJ, MDOG*, etc. Cf. William G. Dever, *Recent Archaeological Discoveries and Archaeological Research*, Seattle 1990; Michael Avi-Yona et al. (eds), *Encyclopedia of Archaeological Excavations in the Holy Land*, 4 vols, London and Jerusalem 1975–8; Amihai Mazar, *Archaeology in the Land of the Bible*, New York 1990.

[4] The texts are in part accessible in English or German translations in *TUAT, ANET, TGI, GAT* 1; cf. e.g. the Assyrian reports of victory over Israel or Judah in *TGI* nos 24; 26–30; 39.

the text edifying or pious model stories taken from the unknown traditions or from their own creative imagination. In these circumstances, while we may claim that in the period of the Israelite monarchy we are standing on firm historical ground, the selection and illumination of reports from that time, i.e. their assessment, and especially all the theological value judgments and condemnations, needs to be treated with great caution. What I have said of ancient texts generally applies here: they are completely time-conditioned and primarily show the historical view and the faith of the late authors. Moreover, all the texts used in the Bible have also undergone a shorter or longer period of reshaping by the community, which left behind the stamp of successive generations.

7.2 Internal organization

As I have already said frequently, social structures are extraordinarily important for religion, whether this is lived out or reflected on. Consciously or unconsciously, faith relates to the institutions, roles and balances of power in society and is also shaped by them. Here I am not talking of a Feuerbachian creation of (unreal) images of God, but simply saying that faith can only articulate contextually what Paul Tillich calls our ultimate concern. Indeed it has to do so, because being human already includes a reaction in faith to the totality of the world and its formative forces. Here the issue is the words of faith which can be recognized in the time of the Israelite monarchy. At this point we need only take up, supplement and bring together what has already been said in order to describe in a brief survey the essential elements of the social structure of the monarchy.

By contrast with tribal society, the monarchical state of the ancient Near East was a bureaucratic, centralized system. All the authority emanated from the king (and court). The segmentary groups (large families, villages, cities, tribal alliances, semi-nomadic shepherds and itinerant workers) had to submit to the royal authority wherever the well-being of the state as a whole or the leading dynasty was at stake.[5] Solomon's division into districts (1 Kings 4), which has already been mentioned, and the lists of officials, ministers and army commanders handed down from the time of David and Solomon (cf. 2 Sam 8:16–18; 20:23–26; 23:8–39, etc.), along with reports about extensive building projects and the regulated forced labour involving almost all tribes and cities, speak a very clear language. The centralized state, with an anonymous bureaucratic organization organized for the glory of the king and his god, largely claimed more competences than the loose tribal society and

---

[5] As we shall see later, evidently there were spheres of life and niches for action which were not controlled by the central authority.

leadership. With the monarchy a change in power structures and thus also a reorientation of theology was really achieved: instead of constructing the wider society from below upwards, i.e. from the segmentary groups up to a merely representative head who had authority only in time of war, all the political will now emanated from the sovereign, the king by God's grace. No wonder that at the beginning of the monarchy, or perhaps even from the beginning, there was resistance to this fundamentally new kind of great society.[6] Jotham's fable is the finest example of serious objections to the absolutism of the king:

> The trees once went forth to anoint a king over them; and they said to the olive tree, 'Reign over us.' But the olive tree said to them, 'Shall I leave my fatness, by which gods and men are honoured, and go to sway over the trees?' And the trees said to the fig tree, 'Come you, and reign over us.' But the fig tree said to them, 'Shall I leave my sweetness and my good fruit, and go to sway over the trees?' And the trees said to the vine, 'Come you, and reign over us.' But the vine said to them, 'Shall I leave my wine which cheers gods and men, and go to sway over the trees?' Then all the trees said to the bramble, 'Come you and reign over us.' And the bramble said to the trees, 'If in good faith you are anointing me king over you, then come and take refuge in my shade; but if not, let fire come out of the bramble and devour the cedars of Lebanon' (Judg 9:8–15).

The three noblest groups in society firmly reject royal dignity because they know that the monarchy has no roots in the people; it 'hovers' over the subjects and has in view only the line coming vertically from above. To be king means to give up one's own nature, to manoeuvre oneself into an artificial superior position and to want to, or have to, exert arbitrary power over others. Perhaps this criticism of the centralism of the monarchy also puts in question the absolutist claim to power of the national God, for of course according to the thinking of the time the authority of the king was installed and sanctioned by God without any explicit reference. But on the other hand some Old Testament witnesses support the new concentration of power and majesty both politically and theologically. Generally speaking, very impressive cultural achievements are possible in centralized societies, of which a looser tribal society can only dream. (Chaotic, lawless conditions in Israel are sometimes characterized with the proverbial statement, 'There was as yet no king; everyone did as he pleased', cf. Judg 21:25; 1 Sam 8:22;

---

[6] In his dissertation *Widerstand gegen das Königtum* (ch. 2 n. 19), Crüsemann has convincingly demonstrated this in sociological terms in dialogue with sociologists like Sigrist, but in so doing has encountered theologically-based opposition.

9:16; 1 Kings 5 – 10.) In Israel, probably at the level of the tribal group which had formed loosely in the time of the judges, despite all opposition and despite the resistance of elders of tribe and clans who thought for themselves, in the tenth century BCE a royal central authority came into being. The tradition makes a political and military threat from outside responsible for this: because enemies oppressed or subjugated Israel, the tribes had to come together in a strictly organized political structure.[7] In the long term the Israelite tribes had no chance of survival in the face of the neighbouring powers, large and small. According to some voices of the time, the enthusiastic defensive war inspired by Yahweh and waged with volunteer tribal warriors was not a political or military solution with any future. The only solution was to rationalize and centralize existing resources. Whether the enemy states which posed a danger to the tribes came more from the east or the west, the north or the south, was relatively unimportant. Some traditions attribute to the Ammonites,[8] who had established themselves in Transjordan (capital Rabba, present-day Amman), an attack on Israelite territory which proved to be the catalyst (a siege of Jabesh in Gilead, 1 Sam 11; cf. 6.4 above). Other texts speak of the Philistines, who in the time of Saul advanced from the coastal plain to the hill-country of Ephraim and are said to have harshly oppressed the Israelite tribes living there (1 Sam 13f.). Moreover there was possibly still a danger from the Amalekites, who are similarly said to have played a role in the beginning of the monarchy (1 Sam 15). All these traditions are very legendary. They may merely have preserved the memory that Israel had to oppose not only nomadic groups and kings of individual cities – as in the time of the judges – but also neighbouring states with a better organization. So the wish and will to have 'a king like the peoples round about' (cf. 1 Sam 8:5, a later Deuteronomistic statement) may really have come about as a result of military pressure and pressure from outside. Current scholarly discussion advances further arguments for the transformation of the political structure, e.g. the growth in population at the time and new economic conditions which affected the production of commodities.[9]

---

[7] The formation of states among the German peoples on the periphery of and within the declining Roman empire are a certain parallel.

[8] Cf. Judg 11:12 – 14:28; Hans Peter Rüger, 'Ammon', *BHH* 1, 1962, 82–3; Manfred Görg, 'Ammon', *NBL* I, 1988, 88ff. A series of small Ammonite inscriptions and graffiti have been excavated over the last decades; cf. Görg, and Herbert Donner, *Geschichte* 1 (ch. 6 n. 24), 200f.; 2, 239f.

[9] Cf. Israel Finkelstein, 'The Emergence of the Monarchy in Israel', *JSOT* 44, 1989, 43–74; the author got his data from archaeological surface investigations. Cf. further Rainer Albertz, *History of Israelite Religion* 1 (ch. 3 n. 1), 105–14, esp. 108–9, where there is a brief study of the state of research.

A development which seems to have been politically and historically unavoidable took place in Israel. The tribal structures were overlaid, taken up and done away with in a monarchical constitution which has left deep traces in the spiritual and religious history of the people and its belief in God. The structure of authority had previously gone from the segmentary units up to the tribal leadership; now, however, in an absolutist way it went from the divine pinnacle of the state government downwards. This can be recognized in many texts, not all of which come from the time of the monarchy or even the time of David and Solomon, though they have their roots there.

The two parallel sections on the permanent appointment of the Davidic dynasty in Jerusalem (2 Sam 7:8–16; Ps 89:20–38) are important examples of such texts. Both texts are later revisions or even new compositions. But they indicate very well the self-understanding of absolutist kings in the ancient Near East who boast that they have been specially commissioned by God.[10]

This is what the promises to David look like in their poetic form:

Of old you spoke in a *vision* [*ḥāzōn*] to your *holy one* [*ḥasīd*] and said:
I have raised a *hero* [*gibbōr*, Veijola, 28, 'put the crown on the head of
     the hero']
who is to help; I have exalted one *chosen* [*bāḥūr*] from the people.
I have found David my *servant* [*'ebed*]; with my holy oil I have
     anointed him.
My hand shall hold him up, and my arm shall strengthen him.
His enemies shall not overcome him and the wicked shall not humble
     him;
but I shall smite his adversaries before him, hurl to the ground those
     who hate him.
My faithfulness and steadfast love shall be with him, and in my name
     shall his head be exalted.
I will set his hand on the sea and his right hand on the rivers.
He shall cry to me, 'You are my Father, my God and the rock of my
     salvation.'

---

[10] Cf. also eastern royal inscriptions from several millennia: Egyptian, Sumerian, Akkadian, Hittite and Syrian. There are summary accounts in: Klaus Seybold, '*melek*', *ThWAT* IV, 1984, 926–56 (with bibliography); Manfred Weippert and Bernd Janowski, 'Königtum', *NBL* II, 1994, 513–20 (bibliography). The prologue to the law stele of Hammurabi and the building inscriptions of Gudea of Lagash are famous as evidence of a special dynastic status. Cf. Hermann M. Niemann, *Herrschaft, Königtum und Staat*, Tübingen 1993; Werner Heimpel, 'Herrentum und Königtum in vor- und frühgeschichtlichen Alten Orient', *ZA* 82, 1992, 4–21; Piotr Steinkeller (ed.), *The Organization of Power*, SAOC 46, Chicago 1991, etc.

And I will make him the *firstborn son* (*bᵉkōr*); the highest among the
kings of the earth.

My grace I will keep for him for ever, and my *covenant* (*bᵉrīt*) will
stand firm for him.

I will give him descendants for ever, and preserve his throne as long as
heaven endures.

But if his sons forsake my *law* [*tōrāh*] and do not walk according to
my *ordinances* [*mišpat*]

if they violate my *statutes* [*ḥuqqōt*] and do not obey my *commandments*
[*miṣwōt*],

then I will punish their transgression with the rod and their iniquity
with scourges,

but I will not remove from him my steadfast love, or be false to my
faithfulness.

I will not violate my covenant, or alter the word that went forth from
my lips.

Once for all I have sworn by my holiness; I will not lie to David.

'His line shall endure for ever, and his throne as long as the sun before
me.

Like the moon it shall be established for ever; and like the true witness
in the clouds' (Ps 89:20–38).

The section reads like an extract from or a revision of 2 Sam 7: several levels
of growth can be recognized here, which possibly go back to a basic nucleus
of tradition in the form of the promise of an eternal dynasty to David:

> When your days are fulfilled and you lie down with you fathers, I will
> raise up your offspring after you, who shall come forth from his body;
> and I will establish his kingdom . . . I will be his father and he shall be
> my son (2 Sam 7:12, 14a).

Other exegetes see the earliest attainable promise to David in vv. 11b, 16:

> Yahweh declares to you that Yahweh will build you a house . . . Your
> house and your kingdom shall be made sure for ever before me; your
> throne shall be established for ever (2 Sam 7:11b, 16).[11]

---

[11] Thus above all Leonhard Rost, *Die Überlieferung der Thronnachfolge Davids,* BWANT III/6,
1926, 47ff., and Rainer Albertz, *History of Israelite Religion* 1 (ch. 3 n. 1), 118 (cf. also his survey
of the discussion of 2 Sam. 7, ibid., 117–19). E.g. Mark O'Brien, *The Deuteronomistic History
Hypothesis: A Reassessment,* OBO 92, Fribourg and Göttingen 1989, 132–9; Hans Joachim
Stoebe, *Das zweite Buch Samuelis,* KAT VIII/2, Gütersloh 1994, 207–11 (special bibliography
on 2 Sam 7:59f.); David M. Howard, Jr, 'David', ABD II, 41–9, give information about the
complicated literary-critical and historical problems of 2 Sam 7.

As the tradition now stands, the focal point of the text now lies clearly in the safeguarding of the Davidic dynasty. Interwoven with that in 2 Sam 7 is the question of the building of the temple, a theme which is prominent in the mythology of the ancient Near East (e.g. Baal builds himself a house) and in the royal inscriptions of Mesopotamia and Egypt. Nevertheless the two motifs can be kept separate. Leaving aside the building of the temple, the divine choice and appointment of the king and the burning question of the right to succession stand at the centre. Who will reign when the monarch dies? In view of the countless unrest and rebellions when thrones change, this concern also seemed justified in the world empires of the time. But in Israel hereditary succession was a tricky new theme. For the tribal organization did not recognize any ancestral right on the part of the family of the senior sheikh or leader. We saw how much everything depended there on the agreement of the head of the family and clan, and in emergencies on the bestowal of the spirit by the deity. Here in Ps 89 we have all the vocabulary which sets the king apart from the mass of the population: holy one (v. 20b: but the Hebrew text has referred the plural 'your holy ones' to the community!) – hero – elect – servant (i.e. 'first servant') – anointed – firstborn – (Ps 89:20f., 28) are powerful titles which indicate a unique and special relationship between the monarch and his God, for example with legal and mythical implications. The references to the Torah which then follow betray Deuteronomistic, i.e. late, theology (vv. 31–5); they will also be present in the designations of David. That means that despite a notable critique of the king (cf. Deut 17:14–20), especially in the exile, in the theology of David (and also later in its messianic developments; cf. Ezek 34; Isa 9; 11) a model of the state became established which saw society as the sphere of activity of the king with a divine legitimation, as is often attested in the ancient Near East. Key statements in this ideology in the Old Testament are sayings of Yahweh like 'You are my son, today I have begotten you' (Ps 2:7) or the human address to the king 'You divine one' ($^{\prime e}l\bar{o}h\bar{\imath}m$, Ps 45:7). This fundamentally hierarchical view is completely unacceptable to our present 'democratic' sensibility.

At this point we cannot go into the complicated literary-critical, historical and theological questions posed to us by Nathan's promise to David (2 Sam 7) and its relation to Ps 89.[12] It is enough to establish for the moment that there was a tradition in Old Testament times which elevated the king of Judah far – and in the course of time further and further! – in the direction of the divine sphere. The king has confirmation from the deity (of the

---

[12] Cf. Timo Veijola, *Verheissung in der Krise*, Helsinki 1982; Erhard S. Gerstenberger, *Psalms 2*, FOTL 15 (ch. 4 n. 43), on Ps 89.

kingdom). That is also expressed in the coronation ceremonial:[13] the monarch who is designated by the retiring king and then anointed, or the Israelite ruler who is nominated directly by Yahweh through the prophetic word, receives permanent divine legitimation all his life. In the promise of Nathan it is extended to the successor or successors of his own dynasty. That establishes a social hierarchy according to which Yahweh in principle intervenes in state matters from his sphere of power. As far as the interests and functions of the nation are concerned, the king is the first recipient and mediator of the grace, the blessing, and sometimes also the wrath, of God.

Moreover the Old Testament writings contain clear traces of ancient Near Eastern court etiquette in which the king is treated as divine or semi-divine, completely in line with the mythologies of the ancient Near East (or these characteristics are subsequently projected on to them). Certainly the court prophets Nathan and Gad (cf. 2 Sam 12:1–15; 24:11–25) seem to have a direct access to the king that is not burdened by ceremonial. But frequently enough there is mention of audiences in which the protocol prescribes full proskynesis, prostrating oneself on the belly, nose in the dust (the complete expression is *qdd 'appayīm 'arṣāh wᵉhištaḥāweh*, cf. 1 Kings 1:16, 31 [Bathsheba]; 1 Sam 24:9 [David before King Saul]; 1 Sam 28:14 [Saul before the spirit of Samuel]; usually the abbreviated expression *hištaḥāweh*, lie reverently on the ground, possibly with *npl*, 'fall down' is used; cf. 2 Sam 1:2; 9:6, 8; 14:4, 22, 33; 15:5; 16:4; 18:21, 28; 24:20; 1 Kings 23:53. Otherwise the verb, likewise in the *hithpael*, is used of the worship of a deity). The vocabulary used in the proskynesis before the king serves to glorify his figure: it is an expression of almost divine worship and the diminution of the person of the petitioner. That becomes quite blatant in the encounter between David and Mephibosheth, the son of his bosom friend Jonathan, who fell from favour at an early stage.

> And Mephibosheth the son of Jonathan, son of Saul, came to David, and fell on his face and did obeisance. And David said, 'Mephibosheth!' And he answered, 'Behold, your servant.' And David said to him, 'Do not fear; for I will show you kindness for the sake of your father Jonathan, and I will restore to you all the land of Saul your father; and you shall eat at my table always.' And he did obeisance, and said, 'What is your servant, that you should look upon a dead dog such as I?' (2 Sam 9:6–8).

[13] Cf. Gerhard von Rad, 'The Royal Ritual in Judah', in *The Problem of the Hexateuch and Other Essays*, London 1984, 222–31; Siegfried Herrmann, *Die Königsnovelle in Ägypten und Israel*, WZLGS 1953/54, 33.

When a prince allows a petitioner to do away with etiquette, this is a sign of brotherhood: in this way the prince ingratiates himself with the person concerned in the battle for the royal throne. It is said of Absalom, the son of David, who is forging a plot:

> And whenever a man came near to do obeisance to him, he would put out his hand, and take hold of him, and kiss him (2 Sam 15:5).

Of course we must not imagine the hierarchical structure of ancient Israel as having been too schematic, on the model of modern dictatorships. Individual and historical modifications of the system are always possible, or rather unavoidable. And in ancient Israel many spheres of life were removed from the royal grasp (cf. also the judicial murder of Naboth in 1 Kings 21, which is clearly presented as going too far). Nevertheless, the basic pattern of royal rule in the ancient Near East is clear: the monarch is the supreme authority in matters of state. Certainly he has a ministerial council,[14] and he also maintains counsellors and prophets, along with the priests of his domestic temple, which is at the same time the temple of the kingdom; however, all are subordinate to him and none has a real right to speak or to veto. He alone makes the decisions. Therefore his subordinates increasingly seek possibilities of gaining the favour of the king and doing him service. Court intrigues – the best known of these in the Old Testament is the appointment of Solomon as successor to David, 1 Kings 1f.[15] – are the logical consequence. But nominally the king has the responsibility and is the sole decision-maker in all matters of state. The state religion serves to safeguard the kingdom and ensure its prosperity. That also means that not all the structures and institutions which provide direct support for the state remain intact and unsupervised. The temple of the capital could exist for the state and the royal house, whereas regional, local and domestic cults continued to hold undisturbed their own ceremonies for fertility, health and expiation. They probably also served their own deities, as long as these did not rebel against

---

[14] Cf. Tryggve N. D. Mettinger, *Solomonic State Officials*, CBOT 5, Lund 1971; Udo Rüterswörden, *Die Beamten der israelitischen Königszeit*, BWANT VI/17, Stuttgart 1985; Tomoo Ishida, *The Royal Dynasties in Ancient Israel*, BZAW 142, Berlin 1977.

[15] Some narratives from the time of David seem to be close to historical reality, if one can trust their natural character, their originality, the freedom of the theological or historical global visions, and so on. The court intrigue in favour of Solomon, in which Bathsheba the queen mother and Nathan the prophet, Zadok the minister for state religion and Benaiah the head of the secret police, take the side of Solomon, while on the other side Joab the chief commander of the army and Abiathar the priest support the older son Adonijah, belongs at least among the more open narratives which presumably convey a high degree of reliable historical recollection. However, that cannot be proved. We have no possibilities of checking them by extra-biblical texts.

the central authority. As a rule the level of interest of family and village cults was orientated on their own problems and was not revolutionary. However, the tribal sheikhs, robbed of their power, might find themselves on a collision course with the central government – also in the name of the deities to whom they were obligated.

Of course how far the monarch in the northern and southern kingdoms (here we are to assume differences) could intervene in the interest of the communities and private life is another question. The answer largely depends on how highly royal competence, e.g. in legal matters is to be rated. The Old Testament sources give a very unclear and partly contradictory picture. And scholars are not agreed on how to assess the situation.[16] On the one hand texts like 2 Sam 15:1–6 (Absalom makes himself out to be a better judge and arbiter than his father) and 1 Kings 3:16–28 (Solomon's wise verdict as a judge) seem at least to prove competence in law in matters of appeal. On the other hand, the judgment at the gate in the period before the state also continues in the monarchy, as is shown for example by the affair of Ahab in 1 Kings 21 (Naboth's vineyard), and also by the way in which this legal authority, near to the people, is taken for granted in the later period (Ruth 4). The Babylonian and Assyrian kings, above all Hammurabi on his famous legal stele, boast that they are responsible for justice and righteousness, because they are appointed by their deity as judges and arbiters (part of their 'pastoral office'). Letters like those of King Hammurabi prove how far the central authority in Mesopotamia could intervene in legal administration.[17] We have no evidence of this kind for ancient Israel. The report on the institution of administrative officials by Solomon (1 Kings 4) is silent about their duties and competences. But an appeal to King David in the case of the threat of a death sentence as in 2 Sam 14:1–17 (the woman of Tekoa begs for the life of her son, who has struck his brother) at least shows that the later tradents could not imagine the king without certain legal functions. A psalm (72) which is probably later depicts the comprehensive responsibility of the king at least for pronouncing judgment for the members of the population who were less well off.[18] However, we know nothing of any legislative activity on the part of the Israelite kings.

[16] Cf. Herbert Niehr, *Rechtsprechung in Israel*, Stuttgart 1987; Georg Christian Macholz, 'Die Stellung des Königs in der israelitischen Gerichtsverfassung', *ZAW* 84, 1972, 157–82; Hans Joachim Boecker, *Recht* (ch. 4 n. 109).

[17] Cf. Hammurabi's letters in Fritz R. Kraus (ed.), *Altbabylonische Briefe*, Vol. 2, London 1966; Vol. 4, 1968.

[18] Cf. Ps 72:4 and on it Erhard S. Gerstenberger, *Psalms* 2, FOTL 15 (ch. 4 n. 43); Frank-Lothar Hossfeld and Erich Zenger, *Psalmen*, Würzburg 1995 (s.v. Armenpsalter); id., HThKAT 307ff., 320ff.

The self-understanding which the tradition puts on David's lips in the so-called 'last words', his testament before his death, is very much along the lines of an exalted grace of God.

Now these are the last words or David: The oracle of David, the son of Jesse, the oracle of the man who was raised on high, the anointed of the God of Jacob, the sweet psalmist of Israel: 'The spirit of the Lord speaks by me, his word is upon my tongue. The God of Israel has spoken, the Rock of Israel has said to me: When one rules justly over men, ruling in the fear of God, he dawns on them like the morning light, like the sun shining forth upon a cloudless morning, like rain that makes grass to sprout from the earth. Yea, does not my house stand so with God? For he has made with me an everlasting covenant, ordered in all things and secure. For will he not cause to prosper all my help and my desire? But godless men are like thorns that are thrown away; for they cannot be taken with the hand; but the man who touches them arms himself with iron and the shaft of a spear, and they are utterly consumed with fire' (2 Sam 23:1–7).

The exclusive concentration on his own relationship with God and his own allegedly divine legitimation stand over against the condemnation of the 'worthless', and that could be the political opposition (or are only religious deviants meant?). Verses 6f., the devastating judgment on opponents, could be counteracting Jotham's fable, mentioned earlier, which conversely speaks of the royal clan as a useless thorn bush that knows only its own arrogance. In vocabulary and theological orientation the whole section shows a breath of Torah piety which could also be explained from the situation in early Judaism.

In the kingdom of Israel and in the neighbouring peoples the hierarchy of divine authority which flows from above downwards had matching military, economic and social structures. I have already hinted at the military organization. It comprised a professional army sub-divided by types of troops (infantry, troops of chariots), which was barracked in fortified cities. Solomon's almost proverbial building activity (which, however, some archaeologists put in question today) is mentioned, e.g. in 1 Kings 10:26 ('And Solomon gathered together chariots and horsemen: he had fourteen hundred chariots and twelve thousand horsemen, whom he stationed in the chariot cities'; the number seem very high). We hear of King Ahab from the northern kingdom, who, contrary to the vilifications in 1 Kings 16:29 – 22:40, must have been a successful politician, in an inscription of the Assyrian king Shalmaneser III. He is said to have sent a substantial contingent of 10,000 soldiers to join in the anti-Assyrian coalition of

853 BCE at the battle at Qarqar on the Orontes.[19] Such military expenditure has consequences for the social climate and the religion of an era; moreover it swallows up a great deal of money. Consequently the kings of Israel and Judah constantly had to look out for sources of finance which could be used for their military apparatus and also the other sectors in which they were active, like building and the state cult. The necessary means could be acquired only from a limited number of sources – here ancient and modern states are identical. The king could resort to campaigns of war and plunder, but such plundering forays destroyed the cattle which were needed for milking. In the long run, for organized states only very subtle plundering was successful. The king could rely on the financial power of his own citizens, and thus transfer the burdens of central apparatus to the population. In other words, he had to raise taxes and duties, which again called for a high degree of state organization. Finally, the king could build up his own commercial enterprises. That is apparently what Solomon did successfully, since according to 1 Kings 9:26–28 he even took part in the gold trade as far as Africa with his own ships (cf. 1 Kings 10:22). Moreover he carried on a booming trade in horses (1 Kings 10:28f.), and worked copper mines in the Jordan valley near Timnah,[20] where the Egyptians had already dug and processed ore. Possibly the export of agricultural products was also engaged in by royal trading organizations. The raising of taxes and duties – in addition to the forced labour (1 Kings 5:27–32; 9:15–32) which was conscripted – was presumably the main source of income. The provinces also had to pay directly, for example, for maintaining the royal court, which swallowed up vast amounts of provisions (cf. e.g. 1 Kings 10:14f.). Solomon's total income is given as '666 tithes of gold' a year, quite apart from the profit from trade and tributes and gifts from abroad (1 Kings 10:14f.), so that this 'king of peace' could develop a splendour which was previously unknown in Israel; he could erect many stately buildings in Jerusalem (including the temple and the royal palace), if the tradition is reliable. The legendary 'queen of Sheba' who travelled on a state visit is also said to have been rendered speechless at all the king's wealth and wisdom. Of course the picture is rose-tinted in retrospect and perhaps excessively overdrawn. From a historical perspective Solomon's building of the temple perhaps amounted only to the rebuilding or

---

[19] Kurt Galling, *TGI*, no. 19, p. 50: in the text there is a distinction between 'soldiers' and 'chariots', but Ahab contributed only the former. Shalmaneser then boasts of a doubtful victory – also in the name of his God: 'With the great power which my Lord Assur gave me, and with the mighty weapons which the God Nergal, who goes before me, granted me, I fought with them' (ibid., 50, lines 96f.).

[20] Volkmar Fritz, 'Bergbau', *NBL* I, 272.

renovation of a long-existing building. But the reports that have been preserved indicate the problems of economic and financial policy which necessarily arise in the monarchy.

Scholars dispute how we are to assess the social and economic structure of the time of the monarchy generally. Since Albrecht Alt investigated the social significance of the monarchy in an article,[21] there have been constant attempts to comprehend the social structure of the royal eras of the time by means of the concepts and notions of our social and economic theories.[22] These attempts are necessary, because we have no other criteria, but they also necessarily remain limited. Whether they start with Alt from a feudal order in which the king distributes more and more estates to the ministers and high officials in fief to provide them with a livelihood and an appropriate level of subsistence, or speak of 'early' or 'rent capitalism',[23] as a result of which the rich got ever richer and the poor ever poorer, i.e. lost their land and sank to the level of day-labourers or slaves, efforts are being made to classify the social reality of the time at least on the basis of a few authentic texts and pieces of information and with the help of firm theories. They may be partially successful, but we have to remember the incompleteness of the picture that they produce and the possible errors in the sources. Whether the socio-economic label 'tributarism'[24] which is usual in Latin America is a better term for the situation at the time may be left aside. This term too stems from a Marxist theory of the 'Asian model of production'[25] which is not derived from conditions in the ancient Near East. At any rate it must be clear that the economic, administrative and military changes which began with the introduction of the monarchy affected the whole social structure of the state and had decisive effects on the tribal structures and the ideas dominant in them.

---

[21] Albrecht Alt, 'Der Anteil des Königtums an der sozialen Entwicklung in den Reichen Israel und Juda' (1955), in *KS* III, Munich 1959, 348–72.

[22] Cf. the critical review of these attempts by Rainer Kessler, 'Frühkapitalismus, Rentenkapitalismus, Tributarismus, antike Klassengesellschaft', *EvTh* 54, 1994, 413–27.

[23] Cf. Herbert Donner, 'Die soziale Botschaft der Propheten im Lichte der Gesellschaftsordnung in Israel', in Peter H. A. Neumann (ed.), *Das Prophetenverständnis in der deutschsprachigen Forschung seit Heinrich Ewald*, WdF 307, Darmstadt 1979, 493–514; Oswald Loretz, 'Die prophetische Kritik des Rentenkapitalismus', *UF* 7, 1975, 171–8.

[24] Cf. François Houtart, *Religion et modes de production précapitalistes*, Brussels 1980; Milton Schwantes, *Das Land kann sein Worte nicht ertragen. Meditationen zu Amos*, KT 105, Munich 1991; Haroldo Reimer, *Richtet auf das Recht!*, Stuttgart 1992; Renatus Porrath, *Die Sozialkritik im Jesajabuch*, Frankfurt 1994; Carlos A. Freher, 'Das tributäre Königtum in Israel unter Salomo', *EvTh* 51, 1991, 49–60.

[25] Cf. Hans G. Kippenberg, 'Die Typik antiker Entwicklung', in id. (ed.), *Seminar: Die Entstehung der antiken Klassengesellschaft*, stw 1340, Frankfurt 1977; Christa Schäfer-Lichtenberger, *Stadt* (n. 199); Rainer Kessler, *Staat und Gesellschaft im vorexilischen Judentum vom 8. Jh bis zum Exil*, VTSup 47, Leiden 1992.

Already at this point I want to refer to the different developments in the northern and southern kingdoms of Israel, which will be discussed at greater length later. Generally speaking (but only on the basis of Judahite and pro-Jerusalem historiography, which of course was not unprejudiced), after the division of the kingdom in the year 926 BCE, in the north one can recognize a more unstable kingdom which first laboriously had to find a firm capital (under King Omri – he ruled from 882 to 871 BCE – Samaria became a permanent seat of government, probably from 876 BCE) and a dynastic continuity. There were numerous revolts in which kings were overthrown and royal families exterminated (cf. the overthrow of Jehu in 2 Kings 9f., which is attested at the greatest length, and immediately afterwards the story of the overthrow of Athaliah, 2 Kings 11).[26] Prophets and the prophetic designation of the new king play a decisive role in the diverse confusions over the throne. From this we can conclude that the tribal structures had not yet been forgotten in northern Israel. Just as formerly in the tribal constitution, on the basis of his gift of the spirit, a charismatic could assume leadership in times when the existence of the tribe was threatened, so in the monarchy of the northern kingdom the pretender was designated by a prophet, but during his lifetime. However, this divine act of election did not automatically support a claim to the dynasty. Moreover, we can point to the institution of two national sanctuaries in Bethel and Dan by Jeroboam I (926–707 BCE), if we want to reinforce the thesis of a stronger Yahwistic tribal tradition. For the formula with which Jeroboam presents his image of a golden bull to the people recalls the old exodus traditions: 'Behold your God, Israel, who brought you out of the land of Egypt' (1 Kings 12:28). Whereas apparently the exodus tradition was not specially fostered in Jerusalem, but rather the worship was predominantly of the God on Zion, in the northern kingdom people possibly held far more firmly to those traditions of the homeland of Yahweh and his advent from the regions of the south. But the presupposition for the reconstruction is the authenticity of the interpretation of the Yahweh bull in Bethel and Dan mentioned above. The story is indeed written from the perspective of the south, according to which in the North all belief in Yahweh was at least suspect of heresy – a quite dubious theological judgment. And this suspicion can really only have emerged in the post-exilic period, when people began to assess the commonwealth, states and individuals exclusively in terms of their faith in Yahweh.[27]

---

[26] Cf. Christoph Levin, *Der Sturz der Königin Atalja*, Stuttgart 1982.

[27] Cf. the parallel narrative of Ex 32, which quite clearly betrays the confessional aspect. It is a question of orthodoxy versus heresy. It is at least doubtful whether this viewpoint stood in the foreground as early as the tenth century.

The kind of urban and dynastic way of living and thinking that we also know elsewhere from centralized state structures in the ancient Near East possibly prevailed far more markedly in the southern state. We need not discuss here whether this culture and attitude to life should be given the label 'Canaanite'.[28] Perhaps it can be called 'urban', 'big city' or even 'metropolitan'. It is a widespread assumption that by occupying (capturing) Jerusalem and centring his kingdom on it David laid the foundation stone for this development. In that case there is also possibly some truth in the conjecture that the primeval Jebusite city persistently influenced the people of Judah with its know-how in administrative matters and monarchical style,[29] in religious ideas and sacral rites.[30] Anyone who so wishes can see in this fact the great apostasy from and falsification of the originally pure nomadic religion of Israel. But those who do this are only showing the insatiable Western longing for an unchanging timeless foundation for belief in God which removes us from historical relativity and today spares us our own theological quest and attitude. At any rate from olden times great economic, military, political and religious organizations have developed a tendency to concentrate power, and theology must grapple with this. We cannot close our eyes to these phenomena of great societies any more than we can ignore the doubtful features of social micro-organizations. A flight into the lower social spheres of pure solidarity and brotherly and sisterly love is no help here.

7.3 Foreign policy

As is well known, the internal condition of a commonwealth is also always dependent on external facts and relationships. In bad times that means that no one can remain peaceful if he displeases his hostile neighbour. And in good times one could say that noble and co-operative neighbours further prosperity and happiness. Both tensions and exchanges with neighbours inevitably have religious dimensions and theological consequences. Especially in the Near East, throughout human memory the neighbourly relationships

---

[28] In Old Testament scholarship it is still customary to note a strict opposition between genuine Israelite faith and the Israelite social order and the Canaanites, in the interest of a Yahweh religion which is as pure and as unmixed as possible; cf. e.g. Walter Dietrich, *Israel und Kanaan,* Stuttgart 1979.

[29] There are six letters from the vassal ruler Abdi-hepa of Jerusalem to the Egyptian Pharaoh in which he urgently asks for help against the *hapiru*; cf. Joergen A. Kundtzon, *Die El-Amarna-Tafeln,* Leipzig 1915, nos 285–90; cf. *TUAT* I (Manfred Dietrich and Oswald Loretz), 512–16 (two letters) or William F. Albright, *ANET,* 483–90 (EA 286–90 = five letters are translated).

[30] Cf. e.g. Fritz Stolz, *Strukturen und Figuren im Kult von Jerusalem,* BZAW 118, Berlin 1970; Eckart Otto, *Jerusalem,* Stuttgart 1980, 57–60.

between peoples have been burdened with far-reaching conflicts. The confrontations between the peoples who live there today sometimes sound like the echoes of former latent and bloody conflicts. The density of the population and the supply of water and food, which is generally very sparse, but over-abundant in some places, plays its part in exacerbating clashes of interest. From ancient times, religious convictions have helped to absolutize these clashes. At all events peace processes are extraordinarily difficult to set in motion and maintain on the land bridge between the great powers and in the zones bordering on the wilderness, as most recent history teaches us. Prime Minister Rabin and President Arafat were rightly awarded the Nobel Peace Prize for their persistence in the politics of peace. At the end of 1995 Prime Minister Rabin paid for peace with his life. And even now negotiations between the two groups are still in crisis.

Here, quite briefly, are some characteristics of Israelite foreign relations at the time of the monarchy. The united kingdom of David and Solomon was so powerful that it could annex small neighbouring states or hold them in a vassal relationship. In this phase Israel became the hub of international movements and economic exchanges. Caravan routes ran through the land and connected the states by the Nile with Mesopotamia and Asia Minor. Trade and political treaties were made on all sides: Solomon's trade relations with Hiram of Tyre are well known. Solomon also drew his temple builders from the Phoenician port (1 Kings 5:15–26). Thus the type of temple widespread in Syria – a nave with a holy of holies[31] – came to Jerusalem. And the architectural form also influenced theology.

The glory of the great kingdom did not last long; at most half a century. Then the state of greater Israel split and two small states came into being. These very quickly came to be dependent on the great powers, especially those in Mesopotamia. Relations with lesser neighbours then depended essentially on the political climate. There were times when the domination and military presence of the neighbouring empires – in that phase the main power was Assyria, though the Egyptians also occasionally appeared on the scene as rivals of the Assyrians or Babylonians – was so oppressive that the small states of Syria and Palestine had no alternative but to submit as simply and rapidly as possible. But sometimes the great powers underwent periods of weakness. Then, given sufficient resolve, there could be revolts in the vassal regions. They even had a chance of success if there was a sufficient

---

[31] There is a good deal of literature on the Jerusalem temple; cf. T. A. Busink, *Der Tempel von Jerusalem I. Der Tempel Salomos*, Leiden 1970; Othmar Keel, *Welt* (ch. 6 n. 59), 133–44. 'However, the Jerusalem temple not only displays a certain tendency to length like the Late Bronze Age temples of Hazor and Lachish, but is explicitly a nave' (ibid., 138). Cf. Volkmar Fritz, *Tempel und Zelt*, WMANT 47, Neukirchen-Vluyn 1977.

concentration of power, in other words a well-grounded and well-led alliance of the petty monarchies: the example of Ahab as a participant in such an alliance against Shalmaneser III has already been mentioned. The events surrounding the so-called 'Syro-Ephraimite war' in 734–732 BCE – King Ahaz of Judah asked the Assyrians for help against the anti-Assyrian coalition which wanted to force Judah to join them (1 Kings 16) by paying tribute to them – similarly take place against the background of a vassal rebellion against Tiglath-Pileser III.[32] A further example in the other direction is the dangerous and ultimately inconclusive policy of an alliance between the court of Judah and the Egyptians against the Assyrians (cf. 1 Kings 3:1; 2 Kings 18:21, 24; Isa 20, etc.)

By means of a variety of biblical stories which have been often over-painted, are legendary, and have theological connotations,[33] together with the historical experience of all peoples and times, we can elaborate what the two main types of involvement in foreign politics looked like at that time. Israel was rarely respected and feared as an independent power, whether at an imperial level or as an important member of a coalition of conspirators. The relevant moments of national euphoria also tend to find expression in theological images and claims. In the role of a dependent vassal state Israel has had to accept countless humiliations and alienations which could have brought on psycho-social depressions. These in turn are also theologically important, as is the mood of national pride. In Israel, as in all other peoples,

---

[32] Cf. the summary in Herbert Donner, *Geschichte* 2 (ch. 6 n. 24), 303–13. Michael E. W. Thompson, *Situation and Theology. OT Interpretations of the Syro-Ephraimitic War*, Sheffield 1982; Gösta W. Ahlström, *History* (ch. 2 n. 19), 632–6, are more sceptical about the historicity of the biblical accounts.

[33] A survey of the books of Kings shows that the tradition has introduced heroic, nationalistic and theological emphases, mostly from the perspective of later exilic or post-exilic experiences. Important blocks of text relevant to foreign policy (I am excluding economic relations) are: 1 Kings 10 (the visit of the queen of Sheba; glorification of a super-king: 'Thus king Solomon was greater in wealth and wisdom than all the kings on earth'); 1 Kings 11:1–13 (Solomon's foreign wives lead him astray to idolatry, a tendentious Deuteronomistic report); 1 Kings 11:14–25 (Hadad of Edom and Rezon of Damascus as Solomon's main opponents; a relatively neutral report from annals); 1 Kings 20 (Ahab's war with Benhadad of Aram/Damascus; very legendary, with theological colouring but with different strata); 1 Kings 22 (Ahab and Micaiah ben Imlah in the war against Aram, prophetic legend); 2 Kings 3 (Joram, Jehoshaphat and the Edomite king fight against Moab: prophetic legend); 2 Kings 5 (the Syrian general Naaman is healed: prophetic legend); 2 Kings 6:8 – 7.16; 8:7–15 (Elisha in the Aramaean wars: prophetic legends); 2 Kings 15:29 (notice from the annals: Tiglath-pileser occupies parts of Israel; cf. v. 37); 2 Kings 16 (Ahaz as a vassal of Assyria; the building of an altar, priestly?); 2 Kings 17 (the end of northern Israel, Deuteronomistic); 2 Kings 18 – 20 (Hezekiah international; with the help of Yahweh he asserts himself against Assyrians, Babylonians and Egyptians; predominantly Deuteronomistic fiction, e.g. the great speech by the Rabshakeh, the Assyrian chief spokesman, in terms of the theology of history, about the defeat of Judah willed by Yahweh, 2 Kings 18:19–35); 2 Kings 23:29f. (Josiah at Megiddo killed by Pharaoh Necho, annalistic note); 2 Kings 24f. (the end of the state of Judah, the Babylonian captivity, predominantly annalistic stories).

the task of the state deity (the god of the kingdom or the main god worshipped by the king) is to protect the nation from enemies, to legitimate the rule of the dynasty and the people, and possibly to comfort and support the people in times of distress and defeat. In the time of the monarchy, an opposition motivated by religion and politics opposed this theology which supported the kingdom (see 7.5 below).

I now want to examine two special areas of foreign relations more closely; they can also serve as examples for other spheres of life in which external contacts were made. The first is the broad sphere of economic and trade relations. Israel was never a very rich land (despite the promises of a land 'flowing with milk and honey', cf. Ex 3:8; Num 13:27; Deut 8:7–9, etc.); there was hardly any agricultural surplus and there were few other natural resources.[34] No wonder that Solomon simply had no means of building, neither materials nor the relevant know-how. He therefore had to ask his friend Hiram of Tyre for both. In the rich coastal cities (cf. Ezek 27f.) the technical standard was also high. So the ambitious ruler from Jerusalem obtained all he needed to build the temple and the palace, and apart from the wages for the immigrant workers and technicians he also made a personal payment to Hiram: 'twenty thousand cors of wheat as food for his household, and twenty thousand cors of beaten oil' (1 Kings 5:1–11: quotation v. 10). I have already mentioned other trading activities of Solomon which stemmed from the favourable central position of Israel (trading in gold, horses and chariots: 1 Kings 9:26–28; 10:26–29). Yet another example is the 'academic' exchange with the great cultural lands, above all Egypt. Solomon is similarly praised for having been extremely well educated. According to the later tradition, Yahweh says to him: 'I give you a wise and discerning mind, so that none like you has been before you and none like you shall arise after you' (1 Kings 3:12). And this wisdom is utterly international, as is indicated by 1 Kings 5:9–14[35] and the fact that ancient Israelite proverbial material in part corresponds, say, with collections of Egyptian wisdom.

---

[34] Making fields and gardens in the hill country was laborious; only in the river valleys and the coastal plains around Jezreel and Megiddo was there an above-average yield. At that time the raw material exported was salt, copper, earthenware, exotic oils and olives (cf. Willy Schottroff, 'Handel', NBL II, 1991, 28–31). The need to import all kinds of materials and foods was incomparably greater than the export possibilities; cf. Schottroff, 29: Israel had 'no significant deposits of iron or other minerals and exportable raw materials in its territory. The exportable surpluses of the land were essentially limited to agricultural produce (grain, oil, wine, honey, fruits, perfumes . . .).'

[35] 'And God gave Solomon wisdom and understanding beyond measure, and largeness of mind like the sand on the seashore, so that Solomon's wisdom surpassed the wisdom of all the people of the east, and all the wisdom of Egypt . . . And men came from all peoples to hear the wisdom of Solomon, and from all the kings of the earth, who had heard of his wisdom' (1 Kings 5:9f., 14: ET 4:29f.; 34).

In view of the political, economic and 'ideological' contacts with neighbouring peoples we are justified in speaking of a wide openness to other cultures at the time of the monarchy. But much discussion is needed as to how far it was an 'openness'[36] rather than the former closed situation, and whether we may always take belief in Yahweh as the main criterion for external relations. In my view we cannot in any way begin from tendencies towards segregation which were on the agenda later, in the exilic and post-exilic period. Certainly at the time of the monarchy there was a state god, Yahweh of the north and the south, but it was by no means sweepingly claimed that this God alone had to be worshipped in all spheres of life, or that a personal decision had to be made for this god. The so-called 'official syncretism' of the royal house and especially the Jewish capital and politics cannot therefore be taken over directly from the Deuteronomistic sources. However, the Deuteronomistic history measures all the kings by their religious behaviour and their religious policy, the model for which is presented in Deuteronomy. But that is only the criterion of a later time. We would be fairer if we did not measure the kings by it.[37] Therefore historically speaking the 'reforms' of the 'good' kings (especially Hezekiah and Isaiah), as already mentioned, were at most the concomitant phenomena of political revolts and not religious 'Yahweh alone' movements.

7.4 Theology of king and state

Given the state of the sources, it is clearly impossible to make very many precise, i.e. authentically attestable, statements about the Israelite monarchy and its religious functions. But the texts offer points of connection, and the comparative material from the ancient Near East can help us also to mark out the framework of royal theology for the Israel of the monarchical period.

In the Old Testament reports we certainly hear in rather more detail about the coronations of kings in Judah (Jerusalem), e.g. 2 Sam 5:1–5 (David); 1 Kings 1:32–40 (Solomon) and 2 Kings 11:4–12 (Joash). In all cases the religious aura which surrounds the ceremonial is tangible. The coronation of a king is not a purely profane matter, even when it is archaically initiated by the people (cf. 1 Sam 11:15: Saul). The deity is always present – as also with the short-term consecration of tribal chieftains as leaders in war. The god enters into a close relation with the one who is to crown or

---

[36] Rainer Albertz, *History of Israelite Religion* (ch. 3 n. 1), 112.

[37] Cf. e.g. J. Alberto Soggin, *Der Beitrag des Königtums zur israelitischen Religion*, VTSup 23, 1972, 9–26; Jimmy J. M. Roberts, 'In Defense of the Monarchy: The Contribution of Israelite Kingship to Biblical Theology', in Patrick D. Miller et al. (eds), *Ancient Israelite Religion* (ch. 4 n. 85), 377–96.

be crowned. The decisive religious rites of consecration are anointings (Hebrew *māšaḥ*, 'anoint', from which is derived *mašiaḥ*, 'anointed', the Messiah),[38] but religious significance is also attached to riding on a mule (1 Kings 1:39; cf. Judg 10:4, etc.) and drinking from the holy spring of Gihon (1 Kings 1:3; cf. Ps 110:7). In Israel, too, the coronation rites are performed by priests or men sent by God. Through the 'holy' personnel and the 'holy' place at which the ceremony is performed, these rites take on an extraordinary character. And the result is comparable to what we have already found with the gift of the spirit to charismatic leaders. Like the one seized by the spirit, the person anointed becomes 'another man' (1 Sam 10:6). However, the 'transformation' there relates to the momentary ecstasy which indicates a temporary commission from God and a gift of power, whereas the anointing bestows something like an indelible character, a permanent commission and authorization.

The new social structure, which was permanently centralized and hierarchical, could not cope with a short-term gift of power. Therefore the monarch is consecrated for life. In all matters of state he becomes the intermediary between people and God (and the later 'interpretation of the covenant – cf. e.g. 2 Sam 5:3; 1 Kings 11:17 – has a sound insight here); the necessary gifts of blessing – fertility, military strength; inner harmony and justice – flow through the king into the social system with its hierarchical order. Thus in affairs of state the king becomes the key religious figure in the truest sense of the word. However, that in no way means that the state religion became the exclusive and sole legitimate religious institution. We get this wrong impression only from the later, Deuteronomistic, redaction of the text. The Deuteronomists postulate the Yahweh-alone movement at all social levels and constantly measure the king by his loyalty to Yahweh, the God of Israel, and his Torah. The biblical texts themselves prove that the reality of the time of the monarchy was different; in particular in the Deuteronomistic denunciations they constantly allow glimpses of alien cults, and indicate that during the time of the monarchy Israel insatiably and

---

[38] Cf. Klaus Seybold, '*māšaḥ*', *ThWAT* V, 1986, 46–59. At least in later texts 'anointing is . . . a cultic symbolic act of divine sending and commission. . . Anointing represents the manifestation of the transmission of the spirit. *māšaḥ* becomes the theologoumenon and takes on the dignity and burden of a theological term with more or less fixed implications, evidently already beginning with the age of Solomon' (ibid., 51). Cf. also Tryggve N. D. Mettinger, *King and Messiah*, Lund 1976, esp. 185–232. However, *pace* Mettinger, the magical-mythical significance of anointing, which is also attested in other peoples, must be recognized (the purely 'contractual significance', ibid., 231, etc. is an intellectual and rationalistic reinterpretation); cf. Ernst Kutsch, *Salbung als Rechtsakt im Alten Testament*, BZAW 87, Berlin 1963; Gerald A. Klingbeil, *A Comparative Study of the Ritual of Ordination as Found in Leviticus 8 and Emar 369*, Lewiston 1998; Helmer Ringgren et al., 'Messianism', *EncRel* 8, 469–81. For the biblical images of kingship; cf. Walter Dietrich, *Die frühe Königszeit in Israel*, BiEnz 3, Stuttgart 1997, 43–93.

uninterruptedly sacrificed 'on the high places'.[39] The many village shrines thus remained, and we are to assume the same of the domestic cults, as the archaeological finds discussed above also show. However, in the capital and in the imperial temple the sacrificial worship of the national and royal god Yahweh, with an official priesthood and under the direct supervision of the monarchs, was ordered and intensified.

The formal and deeply religious coronation has also left traces in the psalms. Especially in some of the so-called 'royal psalms', clear indications are evident of a festival which, while it may be far removed in time from the reality of the pre-exilic monarchy, is nevertheless to be derived from the old royal tradition and the background in the ancient Near East. These are above all Psalms 2; 45; 89; 110; 132.[40] They add to the elements of the ceremonial that we know from the historical accounts above all verbal liturgical fragments which are very important as interpretations of the event. That e.g. the king is designated 'son of God' (Ps 2:7; 89:28; 110:3; 2 Sam 7:14) cannot be seen from mere ritual descriptions. By contrast, this notion is clearly expressed in the Psalms, and that strongly influenced the earlier discussion about the kingship of God.[41] The background to the Israelite ideas in the ancient Near East must not be excluded. We cannot – as happened time and again in German scholarship – require fundamental special conditions for Old Testament ideas which are incompatible with 'Canaanite belief' and seek to do away with the manifest analogies. It is certain that by his institution to office, by God or staged with God as an element, the king is elevated above the mass of his subjects and set on a throne by the grace of God in the interest of the state.[42]

---

[39] Cf. 1 Sam 8:12; 1 Kings 11:7; 2 Chron 33:17; Jer 48:35 – around eighty times; Klaus-Dietrich Schunck, 'bāmāh', ThWAT I, 662–7.

[40] Cf. Erhard S. Gerstenberger, Psalms 1 and 2, 14 and 15 (ch. 4 n. 43), on the texts mentioned and generally the studies by Gerhard von Rad, 'Royal Ritual', and Siegfried Herrmann, Königsnovelle (ch. 7 n. 13).

[41] Cf. Henry Frankfort, Kingship and the Gods, Chicago 1948; Martin Noth, 'Gott, König, Volk im Alten Testament' (1950), in Gesammelte Studien zum Alten Testament, Munich 1963, 334–45; Karl-Heinz Bernhardt, Das Problem der altorientalischen Königsideologie im Alten Testament, VT.S 9, Leiden 1961; Bernhard Lang, 'Der vergöttlichte König im polytheistischen Israel', in Dieter Zeller (ed.), Menschwerdung Gottes – Vergöttlichung von Menschen, Fribourg and Göttingen 1988, 37–59.

[42] Cf. Heinz-Josef Fabry, 'kissē', ThWAT IV, 1984, 247–72: 'Throne and enthronement were symbols of power', says Fabry with reference to the Assyrian kings Sennacherib and Sargon, who had their thrones erected in front of the city, ibid., 250. The book by Othmar Keel, Welt (ch. 6 n. 59), which has already been mentioned, presents many depictions of enthroned deities of the ancient Near East (cf. ibid., 223, 233, etc.) and a whole richly illustration section on the 'enthronement' of the king (ibid., 233–47), in which the human representative of the deity experiences every possible kind of purification and consecration, and then takes his place on God's throne. In the beautiful drawing (ibid., 240 no. 353), Pharaoh Horemhab sits beside the falcon god Horus. The king's throne is thus truly the throne of God. Martin Metzger in particular has investigated these connections in a monograph: id., Königsthron (ch. 6 n. 62).

So texts and images from the ancient Near East show abundantly that the king participates in the power of God, and in part also exercises it for him. That is the fundamental theological situation of any royal ideology of the ancient Near East. We have already encountered it in various texts like 2 Sam 2:7 or 2 Sam 23. Now the royal psalms show over and above the enthronement poetry already mentioned how the king was thought to participate in the power of Yahweh and in what monarchical functions this was expressed.

The king is depicted as God's partner and representative by also making him look quite different from the mass of his subjects. Saul towered by a head above his contemporaries (1 Sam 10:24); David was an extremely handsome young man (1 Sam 16:12). In the royal wedding song (Ps 45) the external beauty also extends to being in the image of God (cf. Ezek 27:3f.):

> You are the fairest among men;
> grace is poured upon your lips;
> therefore Yahweh has blessed you for ever.
> Gird your sword upon your thigh, O hero.
> Ride in radiant splendour[43] (Ps 45:4f.: literally: 'your glory and your
>   splendour', v. 5: 'your radiance shines out', the text is corrupt).

A handsome physical form radiates the glory which surrounds God. That can be seen in particular from the last sentence, which mentions the divine dignity and majesty three times: v. 4b (*hōd^ekā wah^adār^ekā*; the divine aura of power is also described in this way, e.g. in Ps 8:2; 21:6; 96:6; 104:1; 111:3; 145:5; 148:13, etc.; v. 5a: *wah^adār^ekā s^elah*: 'and may your radiance succeed').[44] The praise for the earthly ruler as an authorized representative of God culminates in this form of address:

> Your throne, divine one, stands for ever, your government takes
>   straight paths (Ps 45:7).

As Ex 4:16 shows (Yahweh to Moses about Aaron: '. . . you shall be God for him'), the designation *^elōhīm* for a human being is not all that extraordinary. But in Ps 45 it really does raise the ruler to the divine sphere. And that is also clearly expressed in verses which have not yet been quoted:

---

[43] The following translations of psalms are based on Erhard S. Gerstenberger and Konrad Jutzler, *Zu Hilfe, mein Gott. Psalmen und Klagelieder*, Neukirchen-Vluyn ⁴1989.

[44] For the text-critical problems; cf. the commentaries, especially Hermann Gunkel, *Die Psalmen*, Göttingen ⁵1968; Erich Zenger and Frank-Lothar Hossfeld, *Die Psalmen 1–50*, Würzburg 1993; Klaus Seybold, *Die Psalmen*, Tübingen 1996; for *hadar* and *hōd* see Georg Warmuth, *ThWAT* II, 1977, 357–63, 375–9.

the newly married leader is told in a toast at the wedding feast that he has a strong obligation to establish justice and righteousness for Yahweh:

> May your dignity grant you rich success, fight for truth, humility and
>   right . . .
> You honour justice and fight injustice, therefore Yahweh, your God,
>   has appointed you (Ps 45:5, 8).

The duties of the king to himself and others, which are well known from ancient Near Eastern royal texts, e.g. the prologue to the legal collection of Hammurabi or the great decree of Ammi-Saduqa,[45] namely to preserve law in his land and to help the wretched and the marginalized to secure justice, are developed more widely in Ps 72:

> God, give the king understanding of your law, give the heir to the
>   throne a sense of your righteousness.
> May he rule the people rightly, and secure justice for the wretched.
> The mountains shall give salvation to the people, the hills proclaim
>   righteousness.
> He shall defend those who need help, he shall bring help to the
>   disadvantaged, and crush the oppressor (Ps 72:1–4).

The theme touched on here is also familiar to us from the last words of David in 2 Sam 23. In large societies which need closer collaboration, there is apparently a need for divinely sanctioned norms and authorities which hold people together. The preservation of law is a divine business; this also emerges from Ps 82, in which Yahweh, the supreme god of a pantheon, rebukes the subordinate deities for neglecting to practise the law – or is the reference to the kings as those appointed by God to execute the law? 'How long will you judge unjustly and show partiality to the wicked? Give justice to the weak and the fatherless; maintain the right of the afflicted and the destitute. Rescue the weak and the needy; deliver them from the hand of the wicked' (Ps 82:2–4). The basic features of the ethic are familiar from the ethic of the village community. There already the weak are protected and the solidarity of the group is commended. In the states of the ancient Near East, this feature of care is also incorporated into the ideology of kingship, certainly for political and religious reasons. We can see that the wider society, too, does not just function on the basis of stereotypes which bring equality, though the group of the poor and the weak is of course perceived as a totality and not in its individual, personal components.

---

[45] There are translations of the text in e.g. *TUAT* 1 (Rykle Borger), 40–4, 75–80, and Fritz R.
Kraus, *Ein Edikt des Königs Ammi-Saduqa von Babylon,* Leiden 1958.

As is clearly indicated in the last sentence of the quotation from Ps 72, and as is implicit in Ps 82, the other side of the coin is the forcible exclusion of the unjust and guilty. These include both the troublemakers and those who transgress the commandments within (inner security), including those who doubt or attack the divine authority of the king, just like external enemies. And in this sector the royal psalms are even more emphatic than they are in connection with the theme of 'justice and righteousness for the weak in the land'. The king is the eternal protection given by God against the neighbouring peoples and their ambitions for the money, crops and land of the people of Israel. Thus the king of Israel says in a song of thanksgiving:

> I pursue my enemies and overtake them; and do not turn back until
>   they are consumed.
> I thrust them through so that they are not able to rise; they fall under
>   my feet.
> For you gird me with strength for the battle; you make my assailant
>   sink under me.
> You make my enemies turn their backs to me, and those who hate me
>   I destroy.
> They cry for help, but there is none to save, they cry to Yahweh but
>   he does not answer them.
> I beat them fine as dust before the wind; I cast them out like the mire
>   of the streets (Ps 18:38–43).

In some psalms this demonstration of power against the enemy which calls for execution is expanded so that it takes on a universal dimension, and thus assumes completely utopian or eschatological features. This expansion of horizons is a sign of a post–monarchical community, waiting for future redemption:

> The kings of the earth arm for war, and the rulers take counsel
>   together,
> how to overthrow Yahweh and his anointed . . .
> I will repeat the decree of Yahweh:
> He said to me, 'You are my son, today I have begotten you.
> Ask of me, and 1 will make the nations your heritage,
> and the ends of the earth your possession.
> You shall break them with a rod of iron,
> and dash them in pieces like a potter's vessel.
> Now therefore, kings, be wise, be warned, O rulers of the earth.
> Serve the Lord with fear, with trembling kiss his feet.

Offer homage to the son, lest he be angry and you perish in the way.
For his wrath is quickly kindled.
Blessed are all who take refuge in him (Ps 2:2, 7–12).

No matter when the universal, ultimate demand of rule for the Davidic
king may have arisen, it contains at its core a claim which is probably latent
in any absolute monarchy: anyone who feels that he is God's representative
on earth will also one day want to claim the rule of the world for himself.
And how far the task of establishing justice and administering it in favour of
the weak is also combined with the notion of rule needs to be investigated
far more carefully. In present circumstances we can probably say that the
establishment of a just order for the people is a divine task which remained
important all down the ages. By contrast, the lordly gestures made by petty
kings and would-be great kings must fill us with deep scepticism and horror.
There is another point if we are speaking of the main religious duties of the
king in Israel. In the Psalms there are at least hints that he is also the mediator
of all blessings that flow from God to human beings in addition to
righteousness and peace, security and human dignity. There is the fertility
of nature, rain and the flourishing of fields and flocks, and the restraint of
destructive forces like storms, floods, showers of hail; finally there is also
human health and fertility, for example in epidemics (cf. 2 Sam 24). The
king seems to have taken over earlier functions of medicine men, rainmakers
and prophets (compare Elijah in 1 Kings 18). So we hear metaphorically in
Ps 72:6:

May the king be like the rain that falls on the mown grass;
like the showers that water the earth.

The metaphorical language may indicate that the king is responsible on the
human side for favourable rain. The universal activity of the king in blessing
is expressed like this in Ps 21, a so-called 'intercession' for his majesty:

His glory (*kābōd*) is great through your help; you bestow splendour
    and majesty (*hōd wᵉhādōr*) upon him.
You have blessed his works for ever (literally: 'you have made him for
    blessings for ever', *tᵉšītēhū bᵉrākōt lāʿad*), you have made him glad
    with your presence (Ps 21:6f.).

The strengths and weaknesses, the one-sidednesses and the possibilities
of theological thought in a system which is so stamped by the central figure
of the king need to be carefully investigated. It is not enough to see the
features which are allegedly 'opposed to domination' in an allegedly fixed
and unchangeable, original Yahweh religion over against the new structure

of society with its consciousness of power, and for example to regard the formation of the monarchy as the great sin of Israel.[46] Rather, the social factors which stamped contemporary theology then and now need to be recognized and seen as a background. The key question is: how did Israelite society (and that of the ancient Near East), with its centralized government, perceive the claim and promise of the unconditional, the ground of being? To what extent, despite all the formation of classes, was the model of a divinely willed justice for all recognized and implemented? So far we have perceived an evidently gaping split between the struggle for power and the concern for justice for the poor. We need to investigate this question a little further.

I shall do so by looking briefly at the images of God in the time of the monarchy and at justice and ethics. It already emerges from the psalm passages quoted above, which are about the king and his divine glory, that the national God is the supreme authority: he is enthroned and rules in an almost unlimited abundance of power. What a difference from the expectations of the deities of family and village! The titles of the deity primarily move in the sphere of the majestic: God is king, great king, supreme king (cf. Pss 47:3; 48:23; 24:7ff.; 29:10; 145:13, etc.), who sits on a sacred throne and rules the world from heaven.[47] Of course Yahweh now is even more (by comparison with the tribal period) the 'Lord of hosts', the supreme God in the pantheon (*'ēl 'elyōn*), who like a real king on earth has to command a whole court, as e.g. in 1 Kings 22:19. Micaiah ben Imlah had a vision: 'I saw Yahweh sitting on a throne and the whole host of heaven standing beside him on his right hand and on his left.'[48] Under the impact of the earthly kingdom, Yahweh's nature, etiquette and modes of behaviour come close to the notions of the court and current customs. As well as the majestic aura this also includes the expectation that the supreme national God will ensure internal order, for the weak and those without rights. We have already seen that this is a function of the earthly king. This

---

[46] This is what the Deuteronomistic theologians did, probably out of frustration at the downfall of the kingdom; cf. Timo Veijola, *Die ewige Dynastie*, Helsinki 1975. That does not justify our simply taking over their judgments, as often happens, even with Rainer Albertz, *History of Israelite Religion* (ch. 3 n. 1), *passim*. With such denunciations they were simply attempting to establish a particular form of society (e.g. the 'nomadic') or a particular class or group ('slaves', 'liberated larger group', etc.) as timeless and normative.

[47] Cf. Hans-Joachim Kraus, *Theologie der Psalmen*, BKAT XV, 3, 28–30; Horst Dietrich Preuss, *Theologie* (ch. 4 n. 136), *passim*.

[48] Cf. Isa 6; Ps 82, etc. texts. The projection of the earthly court into heaven is also common in the Ugaritic texts and other texts from the ancient Near East. It often perplexes present-day exegetes, who maintain an unchangeable revelation of the knowledge of God; cf. Georg Fohrer, *History* (ch. 6 n. 96), 173–6; 'In Yahwism none of these heavenly beings had any independent significance; they were accepted as a kind of ancillary notion' (ibid., 175).

function is most clearly expressed in the title 'just judge'.[49] Such a ruler, who is responsible for the state as a whole and possibly for the population of the world, must ensure justice without respect of persons; he can no longer practise solidarity with the individual and the small group, seeing to all personal needs, in the way that happens in the family.

The internationalization of scholarship also acquainted Israel with an extraordinarily tolerant anthropology in the form of early wisdom teaching, which had nothing whatever to do with nationalistic tendencies.[50] It speaks in a very relaxed way of a universal human world order in which God's compensatory justice applies to all and does not absolutize the particular experiences of Israel; indeed these are not even mentioned. So we can assume that in the time of the kings the Yahweh-orientated ethic that most scholars presuppose had not even developed.[51] Rather, faith and ethic – as far as they are related to the monarchy – revolve around the deity of the kingdom, the person of the king and his dynasty, and the internal and external stability of the wider state organization. In principle, life in monarchical Israel took place on precisely the same level as in the rest of ancient Near Eastern society.

7.5 The opposition from peripheral groups (prophecy)

A central state apparatus which seeks to fulfil its tasks and goals will in any case come up against interests of the associations, groups and corporations that it has 'subjected' or 'unified'. These interests have another orientation. The interests – in our case – of families, local communities and tribes cannot all have taken the same direction as the interests (and also the desire for power) of the powerful élite in the central alliance. There were points of contact and sore points. This phenomenon of clashes or conflicts of interests within society can be studied in complex societies throughout human history. The biblical texts themselves similarly offer sufficient vivid material for this very human state of affairs. And because any social tension of this kind in antiquity very easily provoked religious reactions (or stemmed from them), we must also take it very seriously in the history of Israelite theology.

---

[49] Cf. Arnold Gamper, *Gott als Richter in Mesopotamien und im Alten Testament*, Innsbruck 1966.

[50] The image of human beings in earlier proverbial wisdom does not fit with salvation-historical theology, which in my view was exclusively valid; it has been described with amazement by Gerhard von Rad, *Wisdom* (ch. 2 n. 18). Cf. more recent investigations like that of Diethard Römheld, *Wege der Weisheit*, Berlin 1989; Nili Shupak, *Where can Wisdom be found?* OBO 130, Fribourg and Göttingen 1993.

[51] Cf. especially Eckart Otto, *Ethik* (ch. 4 n. 96); but also Rainer Albertz, *History of Israelite Religion* (ch. 3 n. 1), *passim*.

Of course clashes with a political and economic motivation between the central authority and subordinate social units remain unnoticed or are minimal provided that they do not break out in open confrontations; as long as the central authority performs its overarching tasks (protection outside, blessing and order within) well, so that all segmentary units, or at least the majority of them, profit, and as long as the measures aimed at equalization or economic pressure from the government do not become too great. This principle can be tested on all the modern nation states made up of different tribes, nationalities or confessions. The precarious equilibrium between satisfaction and desire is destroyed time and again when expectations are not fulfilled or when real pressure from the central authority can be detected. Such points at which the counter-pressure breaks out from below can occasionally be noted in the very fragmentary Old Testament tradition. Jeroboam, originally Solomon's minister in charge of forced labour, puts himself at the head of the discontented northern tribes, whose elders are rejected and intimidated by an assertive and politically unwise Rehoboam. The ten northern tribes secede from the Davidic dynasty and form their own kingdom (1 Kings 12). Already under David, Jeroboam's rebellion was preceded both by Absalom's rebellion, a dispute within the dynasty, but one which mobilized the feelings of subjects who had allegedly been robbed of their rights (2 Sam 15:1–16), and Sheba's rebellion. The background to the latter was possibly Benjaminite, but the narrative in 2 Sam 20 mixes up the private feud between Joab and Amasa and the local saga of the place Abel-beth-maachah which involves Sheba's severed head. We can confidently suppose that the events depicted were not the only political revolts against the central authority. The monarchy lasted more than two hundred years for the northern kingdom and more than five hundred years for the southern kingdom – time enough to try out rebellion against the kingdom, with or without bloodshed.[52]

But we are far more interested in the theological resistance not only to the monarchy but also to the whole of society at the time of the monarchy. In the tradition it looks as if from the ninth century onwards a purely spiritual opposition group arose, in the form of prophets who were continually active and time and again were sent out and commissioned by Yahweh. Solely in the light of belief in Yahweh and the notion of election

[52] Cf. Frank Crüsemann, *Widerstand* (ch. 6 n. 48); Rainer Albertz, *History of Israelite Religion* (ch. 3 n. 1), 122–4. With the best will in the world I cannot recognize that the rebellions were engaged in predominantly in the name of Yahweh and a faith in the liberator God opposed to domination. In the foreground are political and economic questions which possibly received a secondary religious legitimation. In citing Judg 8:22f.; 1 Sam 8:7; 12:12 as fundamental theological criticism, Albertz (ibid., 123) is relying on purely Deuteronomistic statements which emerged from the retrospective, theological reflection of the exilic period.

(Israel = Yahweh's covenant people), in the northern and southern kingdoms the prophets urgently and unanimously attacked the unbelief, the cultic hypocrisy and the anti-social behaviour of the kings and the court élite, indeed of the whole people, and threatened them with the punishment of the insulted and angry God. These punishments were then also promptly inflicted in Assyrian, Babylonian and Egyptian campaigns and partial conquests, and later massively in the deportation to Babylon. The prophets were proved right. Yahweh could not be trifled with; he punished the godlessness of his followers 'to the third and fourth generation'. He was a zealous and jealous God, though despite everything he did not abandon his salvation-historical plans for his people, but willed to lead them again through judgment to salvation and to hearing his word.

This basic image of the monarchy and pre-exilic prophecy has also been maintained in the scholarly theology of our day. In itself it is an imposing theological and historical structure, but in my view this model of prophecy belongs completely in the exilic and post-exilic period, and can in no way be used for the period before the exile.[53] What theological 'counter-positions' at all can we establish for the time of the monarchy? We have to limit ourselves to a few cautious reconstructions of prophetic figures and activities and much comparative material from the ancient Near East and modern times. A study by Robert Wilson which has remained almost unknown in Germany has done pioneer work here.[54]

Wilson first investigates the phenomenon of prophecy in modern societies. There are plenty of studies of this topic, by anthropologists and sociologists, but most Old Testament scholars in Germany do not think that they are reliable comparative material. In order to get material which is at all compatible, Wilson chooses the more neutral and comprehensive term 'mediator' in place of the word 'prophet', which is burdened with biblical and ecclesiastical interpretations. So he wants to investigate the functions of the religious 'mediator' in society, which are often at the same time critical functions. And all kinds of analogies to the Old Testament

---

[53] I can only point out briefly here that in my view the sum of more recent investigations into prophecy tell against the pre-exilic origin of the traditional picture of the prophets and salvation history. Literary, comparative anthropological and historical analyses, and analyses investigating the theological interest of the biblical traditions, allow only one conclusion: the closed notion of a continuous series of prophetic tradents of the word who basically already presuppose the understanding of the Torah in the exilic period, and the constant movement from obedience to apostasy (in the time of the wilderness and the judges this is still depicted without a 'prophetic movement') are late, unifying constructions by those who worked on the tradition from the exile on and created links. Cf. Joseph Blenkinsopp, *History of Prophecy in Israel*, Louisville 1998; Ferdinand Deist, 'The Prophets: Are We Heading for a Paradigm Switch?', BZAW 185, 1–18.

[54] Robert R. Wilson, *Prophecy and Society in Ancient Israel*, Philadelphia 1980.

situation arise in a survey of types existing today (shamans, soothsayers, magicians, mediums, priests and mystics).[55] The general precondition is for society to be programmed for a mediation of its concerns in the direction of the deities; it must have an attitude of expectation directed towards mediator figures with particular competences for such functionaries to be able to appear at all. Secondly, the mediation between deity and human beings must take place in specific, conventional forms and modes of behaviour (e.g. the indwelling of the deity = possession; the migration of souls = seeking the deity through shamans, etc.). Thirdly, a mediator attains the socially respected position which enables him to perform his function by a mixture of spontaneous encounter with God and a long period as a pupil.

> The supernatural choice of an intermediary usually takes place in one of two ways. The first, and most common, way begins when the person involved experiences symptoms which are recognized by the society as signs of illness or as indicators of spirit possession. These symptoms vary, but they may include fits, sensitivity to trance, fainting, uncontrollable behaviour, loss of appetite, allergies, and general malaise. At first, the person experiencing such symptoms is usually assumed to be ill, and steps are taken to cure him by using normal medical procedures. If this approach does not work, then spirit activity is assumed to be involved, and the patient is taken to a diviner, medium, or shaman. The practitioner performs various rituals designed to make the possessing spirit identify itself, and if the rituals are successful, the spirit possesses either the practitioner or the patient, gives its name, and announces its demands. Frequently the demands include a requirement that the patient become the spirit's intermediary. If this is the case, then the patient is initiated into the spirit's cult and after suitable instruction becomes an intermediary . . .
>
> The second way in which spirits choose their intermediaries is to act initially through an established medium, diviner, or shaman. In this case no preliminary symptoms appear. Rather, the spirit simply announces its choice through an intermediary, and the person selected is then inducted into the spirit's cult and trained in his new occupation. [56]

The main point here is that mediators are not isolated individuals who communicate only with their deity. Thus with all divine spontaneity and arbitrary intervention they undergo precise processes which are social

---

[55] The following after ibid., 21–88 (= ch. 2: 'Prophecy in Modern Societies').
[56] Ibid., 50f.

conventions before they themselves become recognized spokesmen/women and mediators of the deity. Fourthly, the same thing is true of the possible appearances and modes of behaviour of approved persons: they must fall within the given wavelength of the behaviour which is possible for their condition. And fifthly, Wilson distinguishes emphatically between 'peripheral' and 'central' mediation. A different type of mediator from the type at the centre of power usually forms in the marginal groups of society. In the marginal groups, the dissatisfaction nourished by injustice, discrimination and inferiority complexes is blatant: it often expresses itself in revolutionary demands to the central society. By contrast, the mediator figures at the centre of power usually attempt to support the apparatus in which they work.[57]

For our purpose it is important that there were certainly a number of mediator types in Israel in the time of the monarchy, some of which we can still identify from the tradition: men of God (*'anše 'elōhīm*), seers (*rō'īm*), dreamers and the interpreters of dreams (*hōl'mīm*), necromancers (*ba'alē 'ob* or *ba'alōt 'ōb*) and many others.[58] It is extremely probable that they all originally worshipped their own or special deities and made them 'usable' for their activities. However, whether there were 'Yahweh prophets' as conceived of later, i.e. as opponents of the kingdom representing all Israel, as the advocates of the national deity superior to the state, who kept a sharp eye on the people and its leaders and denounced their neglect in worshipping the chief deity, is an open question. Using the models of the prophet proposed by Wilson, we could perhaps say that occasional messages and actions are to be expected in the name of oppressed minorities of a social or ethical kind, forced to and beyond the periphery, and their deities or their marginal theology. (The Yahwizing of these groups may be secondary, or it may go back to the earlier pre-state Yahwism rooted in the tribal system, my addition.) When for example Micah opposes the arrogance and the oppression originating in the capital and directed against the people of the land (Micah 3), his words could be characteristic of a rebellion against the central authority led by an inspired man of God. The climax of the statements

---

[57] After this fundamental chapter, Wilson goes on to test his results by ancient Near Eastern and Israelite prophecy (chs 3–5: 'Prophecy in the Ancient Near East', 'Prophecy in Israel: The Ephraimite Tradition', 'Prophecy in Israel: The Judaean Traditions'). Here he falls into a quite traditional pattern of interpretation. But his approach allows a completely new assessment of Old Testament prophecy.

[58] There is no thorough treatment of all reports on the pre-exilic mediator types: the calls mentioned above are usually treated only as aspects of prophetism, but cf. the individual Hebrew designations in the Theological Dictionaries. The term *nābī'* then seems to have been used after the time of the exile (cf. 1 Sam 9:9) for the mediator of the word of Yahweh and as an umbrella term for all types of mediator.

is serious enough and was apparently handed down in the tradition over a long period:

> 'Therefore because of you Zion shall be ploughed as a field; Jerusalem shall become a heap of ruins and the mountain of the temple a wooded height' (Micah 3:12; cf. Jer 26:18, where Micah is quoted directly – that is quite unique in the prophetic tradition – albeit in a form corresponding to a more orthodox picture of the prophet, the later one: 'Micah of Moresheth prophesied in the days of Hezekiah, the king of Judah, and said to all the people of Judah, "Thus says Yahweh Sabaoth: Zion shall be ploughed as a field; Jerusalem shall become a heap of ruins and the mountain of the temple a wooded height"').

One could collect from the book of Amos similar sayings against the injustice and brutality of the rulers, which may have been formulated from the perspective of peripheral groups (cf. 2:6–8; 4:1–3; 5:10–13; 8:4–6; more later about the message). In Isaiah and Jeremiah we find isolated comparable tones of social criticism. If the biographical reports about the two writing prophets are reliable, they belonged to the Jerusalem upper class and so can hardly have been prophets from marginal groups. In that case they must have so to speak taken up the desires of the oppressed at the centre of power and made them their own. But it is equally possible that the denunciations of the abuse of power and greed for profit on the part of the rich and powerful have been added by later revisers (cf. Isa 5:8–22; 10:1–4a; Jer 22:3–19; the latter text has also clearly been theologically revised, cf. e.g. v. 9 ['Because they have forsaken the covenant of Yahweh their God and worshipped other gods and served them']). Such 'social criticism' must of course have had a critical effect on the cult and religion. Minorities which felt exploited and discriminated against from the centre may also have measured those responsible in the capital by their own principles and claims: royally guaranteed justice for all in the name of Yahweh, the God of the kingdom! (cf. Ps 72). It is only one step to a vigorous attack on the élite in the name of the God Yahweh who has been conjured up, and a discovery of the hypocritical practice which turns the promises from the throne into the opposite. And in the same breath, a prophet from the lower class, basing himself on the old clan ideal of solidarity among equals, could denounce the whole national cult as hollow and helpless and a perversion of original goals. At any rate, at the time social and cultural criticism went hand in hand.

By contrast, the perspective of complete apostasy from the only true God which is presented at many points in the prophetic canon, especially in the books of Jeremiah and Ezekiel, but also largely in the Isaiah scroll,[59] hardly corresponds to the theological and social conditions before the exile. Certainly in the ancient Near East, too, there are occasional (prophetic) charges that the king has neglected the worship and care of the national God or another important deity.[60] But in principle this concern is to be distinguished from the other, which has a certain dominance in the prophetic canon of Israel: the implementation of the Yahweh-alone claim throughout the people, in all its social strata, and among all nations. The theological demand for exclusiveness ('There is only one God and he is Yahweh, the God of Israel') was presumably woven into the prophetic canon at a secondary stage (cf. e.g. Isa 1; Jer 10 and as a model 1 Kings 18); or better, the prophetic canon was compiled from this theological perspective. That also applies to the early so-called pre-classical prophecy, above all the narrative cycles of Elijah and Elisha. What is contained in this tradition, which appears in a particular block of the books of Kings, namely 1 Kings 17 – 2 Kings 9 (with an appendix in 2 Kings 13:14–21) may as a whole be a late Deuteronomistic product, but earlier partial traditions have been worked into it.[61] Here apparently the popular, often miraculous, stories of men of God gifted with power and superhuman strength represent the earlier, completely unspecified strata, whereas the legends about the battle

---

[59]   Each prophetic book has its own tradition history. The Isaiah scroll is a gigantic conglomerate made up of sayings, narratives and poetic passages predominantly from the exilic period; cf. Otto Kaiser, *Isaiah 1–12*, OTL, London and Philadelphia 1983; id., *Einleitung in das Alte Testament*, Gütersloh and Munich [5]1994. In the case of Jeremiah it is rightly assumed that three-quarters of the text is made up of communal exilic, post-exilic preaching (cf. Joseph Blenkinsopp, *History* (ch. 7 n. 53), 135–53; Robert P. Carroll, *Jeremiah*, OTL, London and Philadelphia 1986; Ernest W. Nicholson, *Preaching to the Exiles*, Oxford 1970).

[60]   Cf. the oracles to some Assyrian kings (Robert D. Biggs and Robert H. Pfeiffer, *ANET*, 449–52, 604–7; *TUAT* II (Karl Hecker), 56–74; to the kings of Mari, e.g. Zimrilim; Friedrich Ellermeier, *Prophetie in Mari und Israel*, Herzberg 1968; Abraham Malamat, *Mari and the Early Israelite Experience*, Oxford 1989, 70–121; Walter Beyerlin, *Near Eastern Religious Texts* (ch. 6 n. 19), 122–8. However the Mari oracles have no social-critical point of reference, so we must also be careful with the above-mentioned marginal group criticism: these could be late constructions from the Diaspora situation. W. Beyerlin sums up the content of the prophetic Mari texts as follows: the 'content covers a wide range: greater reverence to the deity who makes himself known, better adornment of his sanctuary, reminders of sacrifices which are due, political advice and warnings, and clear predictions of success for military undertakings of the king. Thus the prophecies of Mari are certainly parallel to the proclamations of official Israelite *nᵉbî'îm* (which are not very well known to us), though at the same time they also recall Isaiah's words of comfort to his people, to which he struggled through in the great distress of his land, and the numerous secondary prophecies of salvation which have been inserted into the texts of the prophets and the announcements of consolation and salvation in Ezekiel and Deutero-Isaiah' (Beyerlin, ibid., 123; interestingly, among the three designations for the Babylonian 'prophets' cited, *apilum/apiltum*, 'answerer'; *muhhum/muhhutum*, 'ecstatic'; *qabbatum,* 'speaker', there is none that corresponds etymologically to the Hebrew *nābî'* (ibid., 123 n.s.).

[61]   For a summary see Peter Weimar, 'Elija', *NBL* 1, 1990, 516–20; Hermann-Josef Stipp, *Elischa*, *NBL* I, 1990, 522–3; id., *Elischa-Propheten-Gottesmänner*, St Ottilien 1987.

for exclusive worship of Yahweh obviously belong in the late community theology and the time of developed monolatry.

The conclusion to be drawn is that a theology of classic, i.e. pre-exilic, prophecy would have to be worked out all over again. It could not start from the closed picture of history and the prophets which came into being retrospectively in the exile, but only from individual figures, specific mediator types, each of which had its own distinct support group behind it. At any rate, the abstract individual prophets who mainly since the nineteenth century have been depicted as highly spiritual heroes, completely alienated from their time and completely without a social background,[62] cannot have functioned as authors of a coherent theology based on the 'word of God'. And even these figures, who became so pale, who could only be spokespersons and had to retreat behind their message, but in so doing were more capable of being adapted to the picture of a modern dialectical theology,[63] have disappeared as historical figures. It would be best to subdivide the theology of the time of the monarchy into 'official religion', i.e. court, kingdom, royal theology, of the kind practised in the ruling stratum, and popular belief. The latter would embrace all that was legendary, and was derived from wisdom and the prophetic opposition; we could to some degree date it to the centuries between Saul and Josiah.

Positively, that means that the prophetic opposition during the time of the monarchy came predominantly from marginalized social peripheral groups or represented their interests. The critics accuse the ruling groups in the name of Yahweh of flagrant violation of their duty to care for the weak and the poor. For example, we hear words of Amos like:

Thus says Yahweh: 'For three transgressions of Israel and for four, I will not revoke the punishment; because they sell the righteous for silver,

---

[62] Bernhard Duhm, *Israels Propheten*, ²1922, is a summary which still strongly influences scholarship. For more recent research into prophecy; cf. Klaus Koch, 'Propheten/Prophetie', *TRE* 27, 477–99; Bernhard Lang, 'Prophet, Prophetenbücher', *NBL* III, 172–92; Joseph Blenkinsopp, *History* (ch. 7 n. 53).

[63] The influential theology of the prophets written by Gerhard von Rad in a very sensitive and committed way (*Old Testament Theology*, 2, *Theology of the Prophetic Traditions of Israel* [ch. 1 n. 1]) no longer corresponds to the state of our literary, historical and anthropological knowledge. For the same reason Horst Dietrich Preuss, *Theologie* (ch. 4 n. 136), 2, *Israels Weg mit JHWH*, is also unsatisfying. More recent research into the prophets has been covered programmatically, for example by Ferdinand E. Deist ('Prophets', BZAW 185, 1989, 1–18). Cf. also A. Graeme Auld, 'Word of God and Word of Man: Prophets and Canon', in Lyle Eslinger et al. (eds), *Ascribe to the Lord*, Sheffield 1988, 237–51; Karl-Friedrich Pohlmann, 'Erwägungen zu Problemen alttestamentlicher Prophetenexegese', in Ingo Kottsieper et al., *'Wer ist wie du, Herr, unter den Göttern?'*, Göttingen 1994, 325–41; Ernst Axel Knauf, 'Die Mitte de Alten Testaments', in Manfred Weippert et al. (eds), *Meilenstein*, Wiesbaden 1995, 79–86; Philip R. Davies, 'The Audiences of Prophetic Scrolls', in Stephen B. Reid et al., *Prophets and Paradigms*, JSOTSup 229, Sheffield 1996, 48–52; Joseph Blenkinsopp, *History* (ch. 7 n. 53).

and the needy for a pair of shoes – they that trample the head of the poor into the dust of the earth, and turn aside the way of the afflicted; a man and his father go in to the same maiden, so that my holy name is profaned; they lay themselves down beside every altar upon garments taken in pledge; and in the house of their God they drink the wine of those who have been fined' (Amos 2:6–8).

The focus of the accusation is evident: those in power abuse the socially weak for their own selfish purposes and are not afraid to use their religion as backing. There is no mention of specific belief in Yahweh:

They hate him who reproves in the gate, and they abhor him who speaks the truth. Therefore because you trample upon the poor and take from him exactions of wheat, you have built houses of hewn stone, but you shall not dwell in them; you have planted pleasant vineyards, but you shall not drink their wine. For I know how many are your transgressions, and how great are your sins – you who afflict the righteous, who take a bribe, and turn aside the needy in the gate. Therefore he who is prudent will keep silent at such a time, for it is an evil time (Amos 5:10–13).

The ethic that underlies the accusations is none other than the principle of solidarity which is customary in clan and village communities. Concern for the weak is imposed on the community by virtue of God's command and the very natural will of the group for self-preservation. Mediators of marginal groups call for this duty of mutual care, which in manageable communities is taken for granted even by the state authorities. Indeed in the figure of the king there is an official guarantor of divine justice and human dignity who has subscribed to the principle of solidarity. In the royal predicates the élite also expresses its social responsibility. However, reality – as in our own societies – did not correspond to the ideals. The recognition and proclamation of rights for the poor, in keeping with the clan ethic, may have been necessary for reasons of state. But that did not guarantee their implementation. Compare for example Jer 34:8–22: Zedekiah is said to have decreed the remission of slavery for debt – called for by ancient laws – at a time of the utmost danger. After the withdrawal of the Babylonians this liberation was immediately reversed. Even if (as is probable) this is a later legend, the text very clearly indicates social conditions which occur time and again in human history in similar circumstances.

So we must distinguish between the pre-exilic mediator figures who are full of nuances and the Yahweh prophets who were constructed later. The latter are described above all in the Deuteronomistic writings, in accordance with a particular understanding of history and theology, as a chain of warning messengers. Their mission was in vain, but the fact that Yahweh sent them makes his decision of judgment on Israel and Judah understandable (cf. 2 Kings 17:13f.; Zech 7:7). They are placed sparsely in the historical narratives themselves, above all by the headings of the books in the prophetic canon projected into particular critical times like the second half of the eighth century (cf. Hos 1:1; Amos 1:1; Isa 1:1; Micah 1:1, etc.). Apart from small survivals (e.g. Isaiah as healer, Isa 38:21) they are all receivers and mediators of the word, basically modelled on Moses (cf. Deut 18:15). Such an overall view of widely scattered individual phenomena is always possible only in retrospect, like any historiography *per se*, and already in the Old Testament the cohesion achieved in the view of the prophets is meant to help the exilic communities to cope with the past and find identity. The picture of prophecy, or better of mediation, in the pre-exilic period that we can obtain on the basis of our biblical and extra-biblical historical sources[64] cannot demonstrate this uniformity. It is fatal that the traditional interpretation of the prophetic books relies on the exilic/post-exilic construct of the prophetic and builds its own consolidated theology of the prophets on that. It can be said to be the present-day premise for the understanding of the so-called 'classical' (i.e. pre-exilic) prophets that they represented a coherent prophetic movement in a course of history which is theologically clear (the obedience and apostasy of Israel from belief in Yahweh). This movement was characterized by lifelong calls of individual prophets whose biographies can sometimes be reconstructed; a unitary Yahweh word theology – a proclamation predominantly of disaster, focusing on the exile; and – last but not least and typically Protestant – the priority of the prophetic proclamation of the word over the (Catholic) high esteem for the office of priest and the (Jewish) preference for the scribe. All these presuppositions are highly time-conditioned and contextual; we need only think of the decisive role of dialectical theology in post-war Europe. They need to be examined critically. To all appearances, what remains of the pre-exilic prophetic movement is, first, a diversity of mediator activities in the sphere of manticism and healing and, secondly, the sporadic opposition of marginal group mediators to the growing injustices and violations of clan solidarity in a bureaucratic and centralized society.[65]

---

[64] Cf. Manfred Weippert, 'Prophetie im Alten Orient', *NBL* III, 196–200. Even Weippert limits the term to Old Testament examples, unlike Wilson et al.: he regards a revelation of the deity and the commission to hand on the word as constitutive.

[65] Cf. Erhard S. Gerstenberger, '"Gemeindebildung" in Prophetenbüchern?', BZAW 185, 1989, 44–58; id., 'Ausblick', in Joseph Blenkinsopp, *Geschichte der Prophetie in Israel*, Stuttgart 1998, 266–90.

7.6 Were there special features in the northern kingdom of Israel?

I have already pointed out that the religious development did not take the same course in each of the divided kingdoms. The north pursued different ways from the south, and not just in shaping society. But it is difficult to identify its theological peculiarities given that the tradition has been predominantly shaped by the southern state of Judah and later by the Diaspora communities. The biblical traditions tell of the kingdom's sanctuaries of Bethel and Dan, which were erected by Jeroboam soon after the splitting of Solomon's empire and which are said to have had statues of bulls as a sign of Yahweh's presence. But all over Israel smaller representations of bulls (up to 18 by 12cm) have been found in large numbers; this leads Silvia Schroer to suppose that 'YHWH was worshipped in Israel in the image of the bull, or, to put it another way, one of the manifestations of YHWH was the bull.'[66] Archaeologically no distinction can be made between the northern and southern kingdoms, since a considerable number of bull figures come from Jerusalem.[67] None of the efforts of scholars to reconstruct a genuine theology of the northern kingdom by means of the E source of the Pentateuch, Deuteronomy and the prophets Amos and Hosea have proved successful, because the material cannot be identified and dated with any certainty. So we could put forward the well-founded conjecture that because of its specific situation, structure and history the northern kingdom produced its own theological positions, but today these are extant at best in a polemical revision from the south, so that they are hardly recognizable. According to the traditions mentioned above about the greater proximity of the northern kingdom to charismatic and tribal traditions and the relatively greater distance from dynastic thinking and a hierarchical divine kingship, the religious and cultic development there was perhaps more archaic, less 'modern' than in the south, in other words – contrary to the polemic of the theologians from Judah and the exile – closer to the Yahwistic faith of the tribal traditions. However, none of that is in itself to be rated a theological plus, for there was never a transcendent, pure Yahweh religion, and the official theology of the Jerusalem state may have been a quite correct and responsible syncretism. Still, the religion of the northern kingdom was apparently always thought to be false and traitorous by the south: this was a natural consequence of the political rivalry. The situation was accentuated by the resettling of

---

[66] Silvia Schroer, *Israel* (ch. 4 n. 21), 95f.; the account of the 'bull images of Israel' is on 81–104 (with bibliography). Othmar Keel and Christoph Uehlinger, *Göttinnen* (ch. 4 n. 22), 215–20, etc. Cf. the bull images of Ashkelon: Lawrence E. Stager, *Ashkelon Discovered*, Washington 1991, 3, 6f.

[67] Silvia Schroer, *Israel* (ch. 4 n. 21), 94.

elements of alien peoples after 722 BCE by the Assyrian rulers (there is a later Deuteronomistic account in 2 Kings 17) and by the Samaritan schism – the split in the community of Gerizim, some time in the late-Persian or Hellenistic period.

7.7 The theology of the southern kingdom after David (Jerusalem theology)

Beyond doubt we have far more evidence from the southern kingdom, especially from Jerusalem, than from the northern kingdom, which disappeared much earlier. Probably large parts of the Pentateuch, prophetic books, wisdom writings and psalms come from the cultic community of Jerusalem or Judah after 587 BCE, and a smaller part (perhaps pieces of the Priestly Writing, Ezekiel, Esther and Koheleth) from the Babylonian Diaspora. In individual cases scholars argue over the location of writings and collections. At all events Judah, which was a Babylonian, Persian and then a Greek province, played a major part in setting the Hebrew canon down in writing, commenting on it and editing it.

It would take us too far afield to bring together all the traditions of Judah that have been preserved from the time of the monarchy and help us to form a picture of the characteristics of Jerusalem theology.[68] The experts usually (in somewhat contradictory fashion) begin by assuming that with the occupation of Jerusalem by David and the establishing of his civil, military and religious central administration in the Jebusite city a great deal of Canaanite thinking and religion infiltrated Israel and belief in Yahweh, but at the same time this alien material was completely assimilated and benefited belief in Yahweh.[69] Moreover the Canaanite environment is often denounced even by scholars today as syncretistic, idolatrous, or simply misguided. That seems to be an imperialistic attitude. We take what we

---

[68] Cf. Christoph Hardmeier, *Das Königreich Juda im 7. und 6. Jahrhundert*, BiE 6, Stuttgart 2000.

[69] Georg Fohrer speaks, for example, of the monarchy as the 'second influence' after Mosaic Yahwism (*History* [ch. 6 n. 96], 123–222). Werner H. Schmidt, *The Faith of the Old Testament*, Oxford 1983, 133–206, similarly attaches great importance to the time of the monarchy: 'The new relationship of Yahweh to dynastic monarchy on the one hand and to Zion on the other profoundly altered and enriched Israel's beliefs about God; but Canaanite ideas about God also had a profound influence. The Yahwistic faith, quite apart from the borrowing of cultic usages, made borrowings directly or with alterations from the neighbouring religion, which must now be discussed. In this way it developed and in the course of the relationship evolved something new' (ibid., 135). Rainer Albertz argues in a similar way: the kingdom is indeed sharply opposed to the authentic Yahweh tradition, but in the reform movements inspired by the prophets it moves to a new variant of the authentic Yahweh religion (cf. id., *History of Israelite Religion* 1 (ch. 3 n. 1), 156–86; the prophetic 'total opposition'; 163–75: Hezekiah's reform; 180–5: the Deuteronomic reform movement).

need from an alien culture and religion because we are in the right and on the side of the only God, and condemn everything that does not seem to accord with our criteria.

So after the time of David, the kingship and Zion theology which I have already occasionally touched on developed in the south.[70] It was a theology which served the state of Judah and its ideology, but it also provoked resistance from the impoverished and marginalized parts of the population. Moreover the exaggerated certainty with which people relied on God's presence in the temple and on the side of the house of David[71] proved counter-productive. Just as in imperial Germany or in the time of Hitler, myths of superiority and invincibility flourished and then collapsed to nothing as a result of the devastating defeats of 1918 and 1945, so the supporters of the king and the priests in Jerusalem time and again suffered contemptuous humiliations at the hands of more powerful foes, whose gods must therefore also have been stronger. That went on until the final collapse in 587 BCE. Then in the course of the centuries the question was sometimes put even in the innermost circle. What have we done to deserve this? Is our God still reliable at all or has he secretly gone away? Are we right in our boundless trust in temple, Zion, city and king? The theology of absolute certainty about God has itself been painfully tested in the history of the faith of both Jews and Christians, and has been reforged time and again in pain and despair.[72] That has found moving expression in other books than the book of Job.[73] We see that precisely on the ground of a national faith we must guard against false securities and absolutist statements about God and seek an authentic certainty in faith which knows that it is secure despite the recognition of catastrophe (cf. Dietrich Bonhoeffer).

---

[70] Cf. e.g. Fritz Stolz, *Strukturen* (ch. 7 n. 30); Walter Dietrich, *Königszeit* (ch. 7 n. 38), 274–302.

[71] One example: Ps 46, the model for 'A Safe Stronghold our God is Still', seems to stand with other Zion songs (Pss 48; 76; 84; 122) at the centre of a trust in blessedness: 'God gives us security and power; he is a strong helper in need. Therefore we have no anxiety even if the world begins to totter, even if the mountains were to fall into the midst of the sea . . . A river with many arms makes the city of God happy, there is the holy dwelling of the most high. God is in its walls, nothing can shake it. He brings help when morning approaches' (Ps 46:2f., 5f.).

[72] It would make sense to follow the battle over belief in Zion in the Old Testament. The sharp attacks by the marginalized prophet Micah have already been mentioned. But there are many other relevant witnesses, for example the narrative in 2 Kings 18f. (also mentioned above), of Sennacherib's siege of the city and his miraculous departure; the book of Nahum, which is probably the basis of a prophecy against Jerusalem which is then reinterpreted in terms of Nineveh (cf. Jörg Jeremias, *Kultprophetie und Gerichtsverkündigung in der späten Königszeit Israels*, WMANT 35, Neukirchen-Vluyn 1970); the celebration of the eschatological city of God in Isa 60 – 22 (and in other passages in Isaiah, etc.).

[73] As one example of the utterly unimaginable shock which the Holocaust perpetrated by Germans had on theological thinkers see Hans Jonas, *Der Gottesbegriff nach Ausschwitz*, Frankfurt 1987.

But on the other hand the national theology in Judah must also be taken seriously (see 7.9 below). It represents a variant of the attempts undertaken for millennia, closely following models from the ancient Near East, to shape an anonymous larger society the order of which is not simply present 'naturally', i.e. on the basis of long custom. But the temptation to abuse is strong. Perhaps it is in principle possible (and some far-sighted and modest monarchies have shown in history that it is possible) to incorporate self-corrections into hierarchical systems so that the rights of other nations and groups with divergent views in a territory are preserved. In that case even a monarchical principle would be responsible under certain conditions, at any rate to its time. How does Micah 4:5 put it? 'For all the peoples walk each in the name of its God, but we shall walk in the name of Yahweh our God for ever and ever.'

7.8 Popular belief

The sources also allow us to say something about the 'unofficial' religion of the time of the monarchy. We must reconstruct what was possible at the level of village and family in the time of the (semi-)absolutist central state in Israel and what statements can really be made about religion and faith. Here we can begin from the insight already quoted that if at all, pre-exilic Israel knew belief in Yahweh only at the state level, in other words that the regions and localities, families and clans remained with their traditional deities, and worshipped them at 'high places' and on 'domestic altars'. Here of course we are to assume that there were numerous influences from central Yahwism at the lower social levels. But a 'poly-Yahwism' (to use Donner's term) of whatever nature is also polytheism. Moreover we know that at the lower social levels faith is concerned with the questions which have to be coped with there, of sickness and fertility, love and happiness, safety and solidarity in the correspondingly smaller circles.

The narratives in Genesis and the books of Kings, the laments and thanks-givings of the Psalms, and the popular wisdom collections can very easily convey to us the mood of people at that time, depict their expectations and anxieties, and indicate the convictions that upheld them. Like men and women of all times they toiled for daily survival, suffered and rejoiced, complained, sang, prayed, met one another in mistrust or in friendship, worked, loved and dreamed. For example, Joseph is the youngest of twelve and has ambitions, like many born last; he is chastened and purges himself. David, the smallest of eight brothers, looks after the sheep and plays the lyre, and has to bring food to his brothers in Saul's army. Saul as a private individual seeks his father's asses. Always within the framework of national events there are reports of all kinds of relationships of love, friendship and hatred, of rape, murder and blood vengeance, but also of generosity and sacrifice for one another. And what religious form is given to this private life orientated on family and settlement? One thing is certain: the temple cult in Jerusalem or Bethel and Dan hardly played any role for the normal citizen (perhaps on the occasional pilgrimage?, 1 Sam 1f.). The sacrificial feast of the tribe is more important than presence at the royal court (1 Sam 20:6, 29). The groups of ascetics lead their own local life into which even the king is drawn; his more rational state cult is powerless against the dervishes (1 Sam 19:18–24). Even the small temples in the land assert their own life alongside the numerous open-air sanctuaries (the temple of Nob, 1 Sam 21; the temple of Shiloh, 1 Sam 1–3). Necromancy is very freely practised (1 Sam 28: the story certainly reflects a standard experience and the prohibition of the mantic cult in vv. 3, 9 betrays a later view). In private emergencies people apparently turned to all kinds of men of God and soothsayers, healers and exorcists. Elijah and Elisha are such medicine men, who are reported even to have raised the dead (cf. 1 Kings 14:1–3; 2 Kings 1:1f.; 20:7, etc.). They do not all act in the name of Yahweh, although the present context suggests this. The image of the popular religion practised, which is free of claims to absolute dogma and rule can significantly be completed by the use of the Psalms and some wisdom literature. We must agree with Albertz:

> The numerous religious and political controversies which were carried on during the monarchy related only to the official religion and official cult of the wider group. For most of the time . . . the piety of the small family group remained largely untouched. That means that while personal piety was probably adapted to the wider religious climate, its nucleus was not affected by it.[74]

But for Albertz then to make family religion at the end of the monarchy the scene of the battle between Yahweh and Moloch is pure hypothesis, prompted by an all too literal interpretation of Deuteronomy.[75] If the references to a cult of the queen of heaven widespread in Jerusalem (!) (Jer 7; 44:15–19) have any historical value, they only prove how little down to the sixth-century people at the lower social levels were concerned about worshipping Yahweh alone.[76] Family, clan and village religion is incredibly

---

[74] Rainer Albertz, *History of Israelite Religion* 1 (ch. 3 n. 1), 187.
[75] Ibid., 188–94.
[76] Renate Jost, *Frauen, Männer und die Himmelskönigin. Studien zu Jer 7.17–18 und 44, 1–25,* Gütersloh 1976, differs: she emphasizes the official character of the cult in question.

tenacious and often survives even persistent 'official' strategies of suppression.[77] And in fact it is only the – exilic! – Deuteronomic and Deuteronomistic Yahweh-alone regulations which speak of such oppression (cf. Deut 18:9–13). We cannot paint too colourful a picture of religious life in the time of the monarchy. The countless testimonies to 'popular faith' that we have from the environs of Israel can additionally give us an idea of what religious notions, rites, practices, etc. were possible in the ancient Near East.[78]

7.9 National religion?

The history of nation states since antiquity has had its vicissitudes. It swings between the very complex great kingdoms and ethnically uniform types of organization. But without doubt the idea of the nation experienced a high point (and nadir) in Europe in the nineteenth century and the first half of the twentieth, and our experiences are stamped by this most recent period. By comparison with tribally governed society one can generally note a repression of the ecstatic and personal element, a strict hierarchical division from the head of government downwards, and consequently the abolition of an original democracy. (Here I am not referring to modern declarations of human rights and state constitutions but to the possibility of face-to-face interactions within small manageable communities.) The nation states of the European tradition in the time indicated (the USA was different) have a centralized structure and a religious foundation. The German constitutions of Weimar and Bonn may indeed externally have superseded the monarchical structure, but the reference to the religious foundation of society and state has so far been preserved despite all objections from the side of liberalism and atheism.[79] And the concentration of power in urban and industrial centres which is based on the exploitation and degradation of the environment is also the rule under democratic orders – as it was in antiquity (the phenomenon of the centre and the periphery!).

What is to be our theological verdict on the nation state today? What can be regarded as a worthwhile legacy of this form of the larger

---

[77] Even in Christianity old 'pagan' customs, but above all the basic interests of the faith of small groups, have persisted almost everywhere to the present day; for the Lutheran church in Brazil see André Droogers, *Popular Religion*, São Leopoldo 1985.

[78] Cf. Bruno Meissner, *Babylonien* 2 (ch. 4 n. 34); Thorkild Jacobsen, *Treasures* (ch. 4 n. 34); Emma Brunner-Traut, *Ägypter* (ch. 4 n. 106); Jan Assmann, *Ägypten. Theologie und Frömmigkeit einer frühen Hochkultur*, Stuttgart ²1991; Karel van der Toorn et al., *Dictionary of Deities and Demons in the Bible*, Leiden 1995.

[79] The discussions about the constitution before 1949 and after 1989 temporarily brought the problem to public awareness; cf. Peter Römer, *Im Namen der Grundgesetzes*, Hamburg 1989; Hagen Schulze, *Staat und Nation in der europäischen Geschichte*, Munich 1994.

human organization which has been functioning for millennia? One cannot simply condemn this level of human socialization, despite the mistrust of the caprice of the monarchy which is recognizable from the beginning. As a rule, social structures cannot be judged in black-and-white terms.

The essential perspectives in theological evaluation are really the questions of the use or misuse of the power at the disposal of the state. If need be, we can still see from our present-day perspective that all power should come from God. But that it should be channelled to ordinary people by king and government is simply incompatible with our democratic understanding. 'All power comes from the people' – this principle is fundamental to our constitution and it has direct theological implications. In accepting its validity we must become accustomed to thinking of God in a democratic state. That has not come easily to the Christian churches in the past because the accustomed traditions of the exercise of rule sanctioned by the Bible are extraordinary influential.[80]

But if the state, ruled by the authorities and operating by the grace of God, respects human rights, protects the weak, renounces self-glorification and expansion, and internally and internationally strives for law and justice, then it too may further God's will and serve life rightly understood. With these provisos, which were already expressed in ancient Israel in a diversity of biblical voices, there are also, however, indications of the great dangers which threaten the state, ancient or modern. The accumulation of power in the hands of a few people is a recipe for arrogance. Power intoxicates the powerful. According to ancient traditions, the human thirst for ever broader and greater domination made even God afraid and thus expressed the ambivalence of the anonymous wider societies. The story about the building of the tower in Gen 11 urgently tells of the power of a humankind which is still organized as a unity:

> Yahweh said, 'Behold, they are one people, and they have all one language; and this is only the beginning of what they will do; and nothing that they propose to do will now be impossible for them. Come, let us go down, and there confuse their language, that they may not understand one another's speech' (Gen 11:6f.).

---

[80] Cf. the definition which Rudolf von Thadden attempted in a lecture at the 1993 Munich Kirchentag (reprinted in *Frankfurter Rundschau* 139, of 19 June 1993, 14): as valid tasks of the state today he mentions, among others: encouraging people of different origins to live together; working for the peace of the world; venturing on more democracy; creating more openness in politics; guaranteeing social security; encouraging the right of women to equal opportunities.

Uniform language indicates the alliance of humankind in a world empire which is thoroughly organized.[81] This empire is so powerful that it can storm heaven and depose God. From this perspective the Babylonian empire has tremendous, godlike power. Perhaps the same notion, coined more on the capacity to recognize the whole of humanity, lies behind the seductive sentence which precedes the step of Eve and Adam to full autonomy. 'You will not die. For God knows that when you eat of it your eyes will be opened, and you will be like God, knowing good and evil' (Gen 3:4f.). Thus the temptations to misuse power are tremendous in state organizations. They extend even as far as the individual human couple. So in antiquity as today there was and is a need for critical guardians, let us call them prophets, wise men, political opposition, journalists, bodies which produce church memoranda, which stand in the way of the boundless striving for power, corruption and self-deification.

It is interesting how strongly people can identify with the greater organization of a state. In the course of this book I have indicated how human existence, especially in the small groups of family, clan, village community and the like, today is lived in professional groups and groups at work, leisure associations and the most varied coherent and personal communities. Where we get to know one another, where we take on mutual obligations, and thus live in relationships, we are all really at home. We feel that the higher social formations in which anonymity and bureaucracy are the dominant features are cold and soulless. Nevertheless, the state, above all the modern nation state, has known how to bind people together in a completely irrational way and to become enthusiastic about a cause, to the point when they surrender themselves completely to the goals of the state. This phenomenon can only be explained in terms of psychology and social psychology by saying that, left alone, individuals want to fulfil themselves by identification with the great state which promises power and dreamed-of, intensified fulfilment.[82] The enthusiasm in a tribal system, for example in waging holy war against evil enemies, seems to have been limited in time and to have disappeared quickly after the battle. The modern state as an organized institution which seems eternal kindles in sensitive citizens a lasting fanatical dedication which can only be described as idolatry. On the other hand I must indicate the great possibilities of a just way of shaping life, which are given to the state to a quite different degree from larger societies with looser organizations. So justice and human dignity can have a chance even in the state.

---

81 Cf. Christoph Uehlinger, *Weltreich und eine Rede*, OBO 101, Fribourg and Göttingen 1992.
82 Cf. Horst Eberhard Richter, *Der Gotteskomplex*, Hamburg 1981.

8

The Faith Community of 'Israel' after the Deportations

We are entering the all-decisive phase for Old Testament theology: only in the exile were the traditions of ancient Israel collected, set down in writing and worked on as the fundamental documents of faith. Whatever theological insights there were, were now brought together, reinterpreted and above all largely recreated. For only from the sixth century BCE in Israel was the exclusive faith in the one God Yahweh established firmly for all parts of the population and all social groupings. And this belief in the zealous, exclusive God who tolerates no deity alongside himself became so overwhelmingly powerful that it not only stamped the early Jewish community down to its last phase, but still fundamentally governs Western thought to the present day. It goes so far that most people in our cultural environment, above all theologians with an academic training, regard the one God with his claim to exclusiveness as the absolutely unchangeable foundation of all religion and every reality that can be experienced.[1] But because in our deeply pluralistic world claims to absoluteness of any kind which seek to impose themselves on others have simply no chance of survival, and are also impossible for scholarly discussion, we must learn to think again.

8.1 The political and social situation: internal structures

The downfall of the state of Judah with the end of the monarchy and the destruction of the temple in Jerusalem left behind a social torso which one could hardly still call Israel. Several thousand members of the upper class were deported to Babylon in several stages (above all in 597 and 587 BCE). Jeremiah 52:28–30 gives realistic figures of those carried off: 3023 in the seventh year of Nebuchadnezzar, 832 in the eighteenth year, 745 in the

---

[1] Cf. e.g. Werner H. Schmidt, *Das erste Gebot*, Munich 1969; almost all systematic theologies.

twenty-third year, 'all together 4600'. 2 Kings 25:15–16 (10,000 plus craftsmen, 'and left some of the poorest of the land', v. 14; 7000 plus craftsmen, v. 16) and later sources presuppose a resettlement of all Israel ('all who had been spared by the sword'; the land 'had sabbath', i.e. was empty, 2 Chron 36:20f.). The lists of those returning in Ezra 2 and Neh 7 number around 40,000 who find their way to their old homeland after the accession of Cyrus (after seventy years?). Other groups fled to Egypt (cf. 2 Kings 25:26; Jer 7; 44), possibly also into other lands. By human standards this dispersed people 'without a shepherd, i.e. without a king' could really only go under and lose itself in the giant empire of the Babylonians, as those settled by the Assyrians in their empire after the conquest of Samaria had also got lost.[2]

Remarkably, that did not happen. The dispersed people of Judah preserved their identity, at least in part. They were settled by their new masters in closed settlements in the country (Tel Abib = Hill of Ears, Ezek 3:15; Tel Harsa = Plough Hill; Tel Melah = Salt Hill, Ezra 2:29, etc.). Perhaps this fact of living together was decisive, since experience shows that emigrants and those who are forcibly deported like to maintain protected groups which, when they exceed a certain critical mass, have chances of preserving their culture over a long period (examples of this are not only the Pennsylvania Dutch but also some German emigrant villages and towns in South America, in the Balkans, in Russia, etc.). The emigrant and settler mentality apparently took very deep roots among the deported people of Judah. It replaced the cohesion formerly offered by the state, which no longer existed – though this lived on as a hope increasingly projected on the future, and also in the form of Davidic messianism – with the reality experienced through the shared belief in Yahweh which was now made binding by strong symbols, worship and confession.

But first of all the external living conditions. The reports about the Jewish settlements are very sparse. Presumably the inhabitants had to feed themselves by their own agriculture. We have no information about forced labour imposed by the Babylonians; that is improbable, because the compact nature of the settlements tells against this (at any rate in Egypt, slaves were housed in working camps alongside great projects). Since in Ezekiel the

---

[2] For the exilic period; cf. Herbert Donner, *Geschichte* 2 (ch. 6 n. 24), 381–90; Peter R. Ackroyd, *Exile and Restoration*, London 1968; id., *Israel under Babylon and Persia*, Oxford 1970; Enno Jannsen, *Juda in der Exilszeit*, Göttingen 1956; Ernest W. Nicholson, *Preaching*; Heleen Sancisi-Weerdenburg et al., *Achaemenid History*, 5 vols, Leiden 1987–1990; Rudolf Schmid, *TRE* 10, 707–10; Bernd-Jörg Diebner, *NBL* 1, 625–31; James D. Newsome, *By the Waters of Babylon*, Atlanta 1979; Ran Zadok, *The Jews in Babylonia in the Chaldaean and Achaemenian Periods in the Light of Babylonian Sources*, Haifa 1979.

'elders' specifically appear as leaders of the groups of exiles (e.g. Ezek 14:1; 20:1, etc.), we can conclude that the old village self-administration which was customary in Palestine continued, but now limited from above by the Babylonian imperial administration. Alongside the civil authority of the elders or the tribal heads a spiritual leadership soon formed, composed of men of priestly origin and the guild of scribes. This élite stratum in particular succeeded in gathering together and developing in written form the traditions of the people which hitherto had been predominantly oral! As the spiritual leadership, this new communal authority increasingly occupied the most important position.

So we must imagine that in Palestine and in Babylonia, in Egypt and perhaps in some other neighbouring countries, religious communities of people from Judah formed which were increasingly focused on their God Yahweh and kept at a distance from their environment. As a rule they may have spent their lives quite fruitfully. Business documents of a Murashu bank which also contain Jewish names are known from Nippur in Babylon.[3] Obviously Jewish families were credit-worthy in Babylon; that may also indicate a certain process of adaptation and absorption (cf. Jer 29:5–7: 'Build houses . . . , plant gardens . . . , take wives . . .'). In fact we must assume a 100 per cent preservation of identity. Only the more resolute and strong-minded people in the Diaspora and at home in Palestine will have held firmly to traditional teaching and the correct customs; for the most part they will have developed them first when grappling with the new circumstances. But the basic attitude of emigrant communities is conservative.

So the social structure of the Jewish communities in Palestine was village-like and parochial. But at the same time a kind of ecumenical Jewish community developed which extended from Babylonia to Egypt and perhaps beyond. Between these two poles, local and universal socialization, the life of the followers of Yahweh developed in the sixth and fifth centuries BCE. The opportunities and disadvantages arose in this specific contextualization of the religious community.

8.2 The origin of the holy scriptures

Some preliminary questions are: How does it come about that a defeated and dispersed people begins to deal with its own tradition in such a concentrated way and to bring it together in holy scriptures? Why did the religious community which was coming into being not content itself with

---

[3] Herbert Donner, *Geschichte* 2 (ch. 6 n. 24), 416–18; Ran Zadok, *Jews* (ch. 8 n. 2); id., *On West Semites in Babylonia*, Haifa 1977; Michael D. Coogan, *Life in the Diaspora*, HSM 7, Cambridge 1976.

rites, festivals and customs like so many others? Why did the Jews compose writings predominantly to give individuals orientation in life and make them the supreme guarantors of the presence of God? As I have already said, a new community élite collected traditions which quickly became the supreme authority in the individual communities. From the beginning, the revelation on Sinai was apparently the focal point. There, according to ancient traditions, Moses the man of God is said to have come into direct contact with Yahweh and received the fundamental rules of life and faith from this mountain god. There do not seem to have been other traditions of comparable importance: the tradition of the wilderness oasis of Kadesh, for example (cf. Num 20:14–16; Deut 1:19–23; 32:51; 33:8–11), which is regarded by some scholars as the real place of revelation,[4] is not very well attested. The early victory songs of and for Yahweh (e.g. the songs of Miriam and Deborah, Ex 15:21 and Judg 5) contain no elements to provide a general orientation on life; they might have been important for the later community as signals of hope for liberation, but in themselves they had no primary significance for shaping the Diaspora situation.[5] If we look at the canonical Hebrew writings, we can hardly avoid the impression that they have been shaped by the early Jewish community. The will and way of the one God Yahweh have stamped themselves so firmly not only on the Torah but also on the prophetic canon and the Psalms that historical events like the liberation from Egypt and the victories over the superior armies of the Canaanite states play a subordinate role. Of the five books of Moses, the Torah, only the first is predominantly devoted to narrative material. With the exception of Ex 1 – 15, the Exodus pericope, the other four books contain almost exclusively rules for life and worship. Expressed in terms of the number of chapters, that means that in this part of the Pentateuch (Exodus to Deuteronomy) the fifteen chapters of the liberation from Egypt (Ex 1 – 15) contrast with 121 chapters of cultic and ethical instruction (Exodus–Deuteronomy). Only in particular tribulations, as temporarily in the Babylonian exile or previously under Solomon's forced labour, does liberation from slavery seem to have been a prime theological theme (cf. 1 Kings 5; 12; Isa 40 – 55). However, that does not mean that from today's perspective and in special situations we may not make it a main theme. But

---

[4] Julius Wellhausen, *Prolegomena to the History of Ancient Israel* (1883), Cleveland 1957; Hans Gressmann, *Mose und seine Zeit*, Göttingen 1913, 186–92, 431–48; Andreas Reichert, 'Kadesch', *NBL* II, 421f.

[5] Christian theology tends to put Israel's historical experiences in the foreground; Jewish exegesis has always maintained the precedence of the revelation of Yahweh's will for the structuring of the community; cf. e.g. the theologies of Gerhard von Rad and Horst Dietrich Preuss with Jewish theological outlines: Leo Baeck, *The Essence of Judaism*, London 1936; P. Navé Levinson, *Einführung in die rabbinische Theologie*, Darmstadt ³1993.

we cannot twist what the ancient texts set out to say by overpainting them with our wishes.[6]

The early Jewish communities which formed in the time of the Babylonian captivity in Palestine and in Mesopotamia and flourished after the Persian period apparently created the first and most important scriptural work, the Torah. The *Sitz im Leben* for this collection of stories and rules for behaviour was in all probability the divine assemblies and the lessons for the growing (male?) youth. The main purpose was to build up and stabilize the community internally under the conditions of foreign rule. The collection and shaping of the Hebrew canon was carried out by spiritual leaders who are described with various terms such as 'scribe', 'wise man', 'levite', 'priest', and later 'scribal scholar'.[7] They collected the divine commandments, discourses and precepts and summed them up in the tremendous Sinai pericope (Ex 19 – Num 10). Because that was not enough, they inserted the 'repetition of the law' in the book of Deuteronomy. Possibly Deuteronomy was also the first basic collection, but the stricter organization of this text is more suggestive of a systematic new edition. The much looser Sinai pericope seems far more exposed to the vicissitudes of the earlier tradition. Be this as it may, in the Torah a colourful collection of rules for life and worship came into being which offered sufficient material for further discussion and interpretation and an extraordinarily large number of beginnings, albeit contradictory, for shaping community life under the eyes of the one God. The narrative passages already mentioned, especially in the books of Genesis and Exodus, do not so much have historical and documentary value as give examples of right behaviour, the practice of faith and courage to confess the faith. In other words, throughout they are

---

[6] The number of scholars who assess the situation in precisely this way is growing, e.g. Frank Crüsemann, *Torah* (ch. 4 n. 108); Antonius H. J. Gunneweg, *Understanding the Old Testament*, London 1978.

[7] For the structure of the community after the exile see Hans Zucker, *Studien zur jüdische Selbstverwaltung im Altertum*, Berlin 1936; Salo W. Baron, *A Social and Religious History of the Jews*, New York, Vol. 1, [2]1952, chs IV and V. The development of the clerical state and the formation and tradition of the holy scriptures are described by Julius Wellhausen, *Die Pharisäer und die Sadduzäer*, Göttingen [2]1967; Travers Herford, *The Pharisees* (1924), Boston [3]1962; Joseph Blenkinsopp, *Sage, Priest, Prophet*, Louisville 1995; Philip R. Davies, *Scribes and Schools*, Louisville 1998. There is a dispute as to how uniform we may imagine the spiritual élite of the time to have been. However, the wide range of theological opinions in the Pentateuch can hardly be reduced to two or three 'parties' or 'currents'. Cf. e.g. Rainer Albertz, *History of Israelite Religion* 2 (ch. 3 n. 1): the Law came into being because certain strata in Israel were collaborating with the Persians, for the law is 'anti-nationalistic' (ibid., 468). 'With a touch of imagination one could suppose that these majority parties in the council of elders and the priestly college each appointed a commission of professional theologians and entrusted it with working out a foundation document for Israel on the basis of existing traditions which could command an internal majority and at the same time was a suitable model for the central Persian authorities' (ibid., 468; with a good deal of imagination, one might say!).

catechetical material which with great probability was used in the religious education of the youth and possibly also in the parts of worship in which instruction was given. For example, the standard priestly formula 'Yahweh spoke to Moses and said, Say to the people of Israel . . .' (cf. Ex 25:1f.; 30:11, 17, 22, 34; 31:1, 12f.; 35:1, 3, 30; 40:1; Lev 1:1f., etc.)[8] is a clear sign of how people thought that the word of God was communicated. Moses is the embodiment of the divine spokesman, just as in reality those who led the worship in the exilic community were. We can say that the figure of Moses was revised and idealized by the later community leaders in their own image. Whenever they proclaimed the will of Yahweh to the community, they appealed to Moses, their ancestor. Initially they put the words that they themselves had to proclaim into his ear and mouth. Subsequently the word of God was cited as having been delivered in the time of Moses; from there it derived its legitimation, but it constantly needed further explanation and application (cf. Lev 24:12; Num 15:34). Thus these spiritual spokesmen established themselves as the legitimate successors and authorities who gave correct instruction. The time of Moses and the exilic/post-exilic period reflect each other as in a mirror.

However, the tradition is even richer in symbolic figures, which are given great influence in the sacralization of the Torah. Ezra was a 'scribe, skilful in the Torah of Moses' (Ezra 7:6). From the perspective of the Persian court he bore the title 'priest and scribe of the law of the God of heaven' (Ezra 7:12). This delegate of the central Persian government is said to have brought the law to the Jews beyond the Euphrates and thus restored the civil order (Ezra 7f.; Neh 8). Later apocryphal traditions claim that the Torah was lost when the temple was burned in 587 BCE and was rewritten precisely by Ezra from memory. Be that as it may, in some traditions Ezra has almost come to stand alongside Moses as a teacher of the law. (Moreover Jer 36 offers a legendary narrative about the composition of the prophetic canon. However, the narratives about the beginning of the written Torah are far more ambitious: Ex 24:2, 12; 32:15f.; 34:1, 28; Deut 5:22, etc. Yahweh himself is the writer in some of these texts.)

How the other collections of sacred writings relate to the Torah is a difficult and largely unresolved question. We are used to speaking of the Deuteronomistic and Chronistic histories. According to Noth's definition the former embraces the books Deuteronomy to 2 Kings, and thus overlaps with the Torah. The latter consists of the books of Chronicles, Ezra and Nehemiah. One could imagine that the former monumental work in reality is not the work of an author in our sense (any more than the Pentateuch is),

---

[8]   Cf. Erhard S. Gerstenberger, *Leviticus* (ch. 4 n. 18), 3f., 24f.

but a collection of edifying and useful stories which were narrated, read and empathized with.[9] The whole would be shaped as a loosely connected collection of stories about the way of Israel from Sinai to the exile. And the collection of norms in Deuteronomy (Deut 12 – 26) would be a codex used as a preface, by which Israel, and also especially the community of the exilic period, was constantly to be measured. However, we can no longer reconstruct how the two corpora of the Pentateuch (or Tetrateuch) and the Deuteronomistic history (which might perhaps better be called the collection of the Deuteronomistic view) grew up after or alongside each other and were then interwoven. By contrast, the Jewish tradition does not rate the books of Joshua to 2 Kings as historical accounts but as testimonies to the early activity of prophets sent by God. Time and again in the course of the monarchy Yahweh sent his messengers who were to urge people to observe the will of God as set down in the Torah (cf. 2 Kings 17:13; Zech 7:7–10). Thus it came about that in the Jewish tradition the prophetic canon (Joshua, Judges, Samuel, Kings plus the three great [Isaiah, Jeremiah, Ezekiel] and twelve minor writing prophets) took up a good deal of space; this was probably conceived of as an appendix commenting on the Torah.

The further interweaving of a collection of norms and exemplary stories with the canon of the writing prophets is just as enigmatic for Christian scholars. It is certain that the final redaction, which can be recognized above all in historicizing titles of books, extensive comments on earlier prophetic sayings, hymnic and liturgical material for worship, and eschatologizing or messianizing accretions, regarded the appearance of the prophets from a quite specific perspective: they were sent by Yahweh and continually admonished people to be faithful to Yahweh and to trust in him; they accompanied Israel's history, but could not totally prevent the apostasy of Israel from its God. Therefore in the view of the theologians of the exile God's punitive judgment had befallen both the northern kingdom (cf. 2 Kings 17) and the southern kingdom (cf. 2 Kings 24f.: 'And Yahweh

[9] The discussion of the Deuteronomistic history is endless and frustrating. When Martin Noth's very compact account of this magnum opus (*Überlieferungsgeschichtliche Studien*, Halle 1943) seemed no longer tenable, an attempt was made to divide the work into two or three strata: a basic historical account was said to have undergone successive revisions and new editions. At one time newly-revived prophetic and then priestly-legalistic interest was noted (cf. above all the 'Göttingen school': Rudolf Smend, *Die Entstehung des Alten Testaments*, Stuttgart [4]1989; Timo Veijola, *Das Königtum in der Beurteilung der Deuteronomistischen Historiographie*, Helsinki 1977; Walter Dietrich, *David, Saul und die Propheten*, BWANT 122, [2]1992). This and other attempts to reconstruct a great literary work remain grey theory and do not help our understanding of the theological statements. Cf. the summaries of the discussion by Mark O'Brien, *The Deuteronomic History Hypothesis*, OBO 92, Fribourg and Göttingen 1989; Rainer Albertz, *History of Israelite Religion* 2 (ch. 3 n. 1), 387–99; Helga Weippert, 'Das deuteronomistische Geschichtswerk', *ThR* 50, 1985, 213–49; Wolfgang Roth, 'Deuteronomistisches Geschichtswerk/Deuteronomistische Schule', *TRE* 8, 1981, 543–52.

sent against him [Jehoiakim] bands of the Chaldaeans, and bands of the Syrians, and bands of the Moabites, and bands of the Ammonites, and sent them against Judah to destroy it, according to the word of Yahweh which he spoke by his servants the prophets', 2 Kings 24:2). At the end of the Hebrew prophetic canon there is an accumulation of programmatic declarations which make the prophets simply preachers of the law and conversion, guarantors of the Torah and the right service of God:

> When Jerusalem was inhabited and in prosperity, with her cities around about her, and the South and the lowlands were inhabited, were not these the words which Yahweh proclaimed by the former prophets? . . . 'Thus says Yahweh Sabaoth, Render true judgments, show kindness and mercy each to his brother, do not oppress the widow, the fatherless, the sojourner, or the poor, and let none of you devise evil against his brother in your heart.' But they refused to hearken, and turned a stubborn shoulder, and stopped their ears that they might not hear. They made their hearts like adamant lest they should hear the law and the words which Yahweh Sabaoth had sent by his Spirit through the former prophets. Therefore great wrath came from Yahweh Sabaoth. 'As I called and they would not hear, so they called and I would not hear,' says Yahweh Sabaoth, 'and I scattered them with a whirlwind among all the nations which they had not known.' Thus the land they left was desolate, so that no one went to and fro, and the pleasant land was made desolate (Zech 7:7–14).

Here is the whole theologically through-constructed picture of the history and prophecy of Israel. The prophets were to proclaim the Torah: vv. 9f. apparently sum up Deuteronomic (cf. 'widow, orphan, stranger, poor' in Deut 10:18; 14:29; 16:11, 14; 24:17–24; 26:12f.; 27:19) and partially also 'priestly' (cf. Lev 19:17f.) ethical notions (cf. prophetic 'sermons' with similar content: Jer. 7:5–7). In the retrospect the messengers of God did not reach the 'hearts' of those they addressed (cf. vv. 11f.; and Isa 48:4; Ezek 36:26). Rather, the Israelites closed themselves to the 'former prophets' (vv. 7, 12: *hannᵉbī'īm hārīšōnīm*) and the catastrophe had to come (vv. 12b, 14). For after he had been rejected, Yahweh, too, was unwilling to hear (v. 13; cf. Jer 7:13, 25f.; 11:14; 14:12; 35:17). The scheme 'speak, address' = 'not want to hear' is fundamentally a Deuteronomistic one which explains the continuation of the history of the elect people through times of splendour and suffering (cf. Josh 23:15f.; Judg 2:6–23; 2 Kings 17:7–23: whereas in the Deuteronomic discourse of the book of Judges the 'judges' are still the leaders guided by God, in the history of the kings this role is taken by the prophets; cf. 2 Kings 17:23; but also already Judg 6:8).

The conclusion of the prophetic canon is as illuminating as the programmatic account in Zech 7. The last verses of Malachi are evidently a
later redactional addition; they apparently go back to the beginning of the
Hebrew prophetic canon, the 'former prophets'. For we find a general
admonition to observe the law as in Josh 1:7f. and also in Deut 4:1ff., etc.
and the promise that Elijah, the prototype of a Deuteronomistic prophet,
will return soon:

> Remember the law of my servant Moses, the statutes and ordinances
> that I commanded him at Horeb for all Israel. Behold I will send you
> Elijah the prophet before the great and terrible day of the Lord comes.
> And he will turn the hearts of fathers to their children and the heart of
> children to their fathers, lest I come and smite the land with a curse (Mal
> 4:4–6).

In short, in the collection of Pentateuchal material under the name of
the great Moses obviously normative material for community life stood in
the foreground or background. The sayings of the prophets were then
brought together for the sake of the Torah; the collection obviously also
absorbed what we call the 'historical books', which possibly at some point
set out to give an independent picture of the fate of Israel in its obedience
towards Yahweh.

The other collections in the Old Testament probably go back to later
phases of the development of the community. The Chronicler's work is
usually put in the fourth/third centuries BCE, i.e. in the late period of the
Persian empire. The 'writings' (kᵉtūbīm), above all the Psalms, may also
have come together in their final form in the centuries after 587 BCE. No
matter when we date them, all the 'writings' indicate their origin in the
early Jewish community. Of course this community of the sixth to second
centuries BCE was not a uniform entity, so that we are to expect even less
uniformity of theology, politics and world-view in these collections than in
the tribal sagas or royal texts.

8.3 Yahweh, the only God

How are we to explain the fact that after the collapse of 587 BCE and the
deportation of the upper class to Babylon (national!) worship of Yahweh
with a claim to total exclusiveness became established in the newly formed
religious community of Judah? To shed a little light on the darkness we
must take into account the living conditions of the defeated, humiliated
and dispersed people. Even then plenty of questions may remain. The
theology of the Old Testament which can be brought out in connection

with the contemporary documents is the theology of the early Jewish community – diverse and also contradictory. At this point, too, we must not abandon the historical insight that the writings that we have arose in long processes of growth and usage. And all recognizable phases, stages and groupings of this growth have their independent significance. They are witnesses to a faith which in each case is contextual, of which no form became final. So however much the theological concern of the final revisers and collectors of the holy scriptures must be noted and taken seriously, they are not – and this has to be said against some kinds of integral or holistic exegesis – the only spokesmen, who set the standards for all times. But the greatness of the final stages of the collection and formation of the canon, which is often misunderstood, is that they reflect community theology from the sixth or fifth centuries BCE. And the writings from that phase which have been left to us came into being under the special conditions of Israel and the peoples and cultural world of the ancient Near East which predominated in the late Babylonian and Persian empire. (One has only to compare the legendary or historical collaboration with the Persian imperial government over the introduction of the Jewish law, Ezra 7; Neh 8.) According to the principles which guide us, none of the theological state-ments of that time are absolutely and unchangeably valid so that they could easily be transferred to our time. But everything that people then thought, knew and experienced is extraordinarily significant. That is because, first of all through the written tradition, such great importance has come to be attached to the decisions of the early Jewish theologians and communities that today we are still living by them and to some degree suffering under them. All the basic theological concepts, e.g. the notion of God, the doctrine of salvation and redemption, the basic ethical norms (cf. the Decalogue), the understanding of history (which begins and ends at a particular point), the religious and liturgical forms (e.g. Psalms, ideas of holiness, etc.), numerous social and political concepts, etc. – like the written collections of Torah and Prophets – come from that time and from these roots. The formation of the exilic and post-exilic Yahweh community briefly sketched out above (8.1) is thus an integral element – the main factor, as it were the backbone, of this theology. Even now it is not a matter of presenting some abstract belief in Yahweh as the primal model of all later faith which is unchanging because it is suprahistorical. Rather, the belief of that time and that society is an important elaboration of the tradition of faith in which we and also the New Testament Jesus community, like all later forms of the Christian community, stand, and through which in fact we are first involved. By contrast, no power in the world can take from us the notions and decisions of faith that are expected of us. They have to be ventured afresh in the light of the tradition and in dialogue with it, and also in dialogue with the other religions and our present-day reality.

Thus the social structures of the conquered Judahites at home and in the Diaspora come from the clan and village association. Those who had been subjected and integrated into the Babylonian or Persian empire no longer had to assume any responsibility at the level of wider society, even if insulted national pride sees Jehoiachin and Zerubbabel, Ezra and Nehemiah at the centre of imperial power, and in literary fiction crowns Queen Esther empress of Persia. The communities which were forming were small-scale, and found an appropriate expression of their identity and their cohesion beyond a particular region only in the tribal and national cult of Yahweh. The emigrant mentality, e.g. of German emigrants to the two Americas, is sociologically comparable. In the New World, the new settlers clung to their Germanhood because they were politically helpless and dispersed as micro-societies in an alien environment. This 'virtual' identity with the homeland and its political ideologies gave such 'foreign' communities a framework of identity in which everyday life with its demands could be led.[10] So we should not be surprised that the state religion of Judah became the basic foundation of the new reality after the dissolution of the state and its far-reaching transformation and adaptation to the conditions of small societies. The pluralistic traditions of family, clan and village were unable to produce a common denominator both for those who had been deported and those who had remained behind. And the figures in the new order predominantly came from the national élites of the shattered monarchical society.

The question still remains why after the loss of the war another deity known in Israel but less compromised, like e.g. Asherah or the Queen of Heaven, did not take on integrating and protective functions for the community. In fact women in Jer 33:16–18 argue in precisely this direction (since 'we have omitted to sacrifice to the queen of heaven . . . we have suffered all want and have perished through the sword and hunger'). I can only repeat the hypothesis that the traditional ideas of the male élites became established in the communities (in Elephantine manifestly with the retention of Yahweh) because the new community of faith was organized as a public corporation. In the public sphere men had the say. For them the old state god Yahweh was the most natural religious choice. The exclusiveness of his worship corresponded to the need to protect the new communities resolutely against all tendencies towards integration.

---

[10] As an example, mention might be made of Martin N. Dreher, *Kirche und Deutschtum in der Entwicklung der Evangelischen Kirche Lutherischen Bekenntnisses in Brasilien*, Göttingen 1978; cf. also Hans-Jürgen Piren, *Die Geschichte des Christentums in Lateinamerika*, Göttingen 1978, 742–843.

The name and exclusiveness of Yahweh

So after the collapse of the monarchy, on the urging of the upper class, which had been stripped of political power but internally continued to set the tone, the community of the people of Judah clung to the god Yahweh whom they had worshipped since tribal times and also under the monarchy.[11] Many people were haunted by the idea that in the foreseeable future Yahweh would restore the dynasty of David and the state of Judah in more splendour than before – dreams of an impotent minority:

> In that day I will raise up the booth of David that is fallen, and repair its breaches, and raise up its ruins, and rebuild it as in the days of old; that they may possess the remnant of Edom and all the nations who are called by my name, says Yahweh who does this (Amos 9:11f.).

> And I will set up over them one shepherd, my servant David, and he shall feed them; he shall feed them and be their shepherd. And I, Yahweh, will be their God, and my servant David shall be prince among them; I, Yahweh, have spoken (Ezek 34:23f.).

> Behold the days are coming, says Yahweh, when I shall raise up for David a righteous branch, and he shall reign as king and deal wisely, and shall execute justice and righteousness in the land. In his days Judah will be saved, and Israel will dwell securely. And this is the name by which he will be called, 'Yahweh our righteousness' (Jer 23:5f.).

With the delay over this restoration, hope for the new kingdom under a descendant of David then assumed increasingly more utopian and more eschatological features (cf. Isa 9:5f.; 11.1–9),[12] whereas presumably at the same time belief in Yahweh also liberated itself from the thought-patterns of the state and was transformed in the direction of the new community structures. The belief in Yahweh which arose anew after the collapse of power was orientated on the parochial community and the dispersed religious community of the Judahites, who had been relieved of all responsibility for wider society.

Thus the catastrophe of 587 BCE had not totally destroyed belief in the God who united the people and safeguarded its political existence. Or to

---

[11] Even under the monarchy it seems to have been customary to worship Yahweh as a family god. At any rate the clear increase in personal names containing Yahweh in the late period of the monarchy would seem to point to that. These names have either been handed down in biblical texts or are attested by contemporary inscriptions. Naturally both sources predominantly mention representatives of the ruling élite. Cf. Jeffrey H. Tigay, *You Shall Have No Other Gods*, Atlanta 1986.

[12] For the whole complex of expectations of king and Messiah; cf. Sigmund Mowinckel, *He That Cometh*, Oxford and New York 1954; Bernard Lang and Dieter Zeller, 'Messias/Christus', *NBL* II, 781–6.

put it the other way round, despite all the disappointments, in the exile the hard-hit officials, priests and other functionaries of the monarchy maintained their orientation on Yahweh or the faith which created identity in the upheaval of turbulent times. Compare Ps 89; Isa 40:27: 'Why do you say, O Jacob, and speak, O Israel, "My way is hid from Yahweh, and my right is disregarded by my God?"' Ps 44:12f. is even sharper: 'You have made us like sheep for the slaughter, and have scattered us among the nations. You have sold your people for a trifle, demanding no high price for them.' But the national, monarchical level of society had collapsed and under the supervision of the world empires could not be regained. For the newly-arising communities, which sociologically were more like family clans, belief in Yahweh took on a fundamental significance and provided meaning.

However, as has been said, a fixation on belief in Yahweh did not come about without clashes with other levels of faith. The text Jer 44:15–19, which has already been mentioned, is testimony to the opposition to Yahweh-alone worship from the sphere of family religion. But the élite stratum, which had really been discredited, won through. The time came when Judahites no longer identified themselves by people, fatherland, dynasty or even abode, but by Yahweh. When the sailors ask Jonah the quite normal question, 'From what land are you and from what people are you?', the fugitive replies: 'I am a Hebrew ('ibrī) and fear Yahweh the God of heaven, who has made the sea and the dry land' (Jonah 1:8f.). Here a man is (almost) exclusively defining himself by faith and confession, which, as far as we can ascertain, is something new in the history of ancient Near Eastern religion. That such a confession of Yahweh made in Israel down to the exile was at the same time strongly transformed, in other words that the notion of God fundamentally changed, can already be seen from the formula used by Jonah (and later in many different attributes of God). The expression 'I fear Yahweh' echoes a stereotyped formula, 'those who fear Yahweh', which is used especially in the Psalms of the totality of the members of the early Jewish community.[13] Psalms 15:3; 22:24, 26; 31:20; 60:6; 61:6; 66:16; 85:10 may be mentioned as examples of this:

> In whose eyes a reprobate is despised, but who honours those who fear God,
> who swears to his own hurt . . . He who does these things will never be moved (Ps 15:4f.).

---

[13] Cf. Hans Ferdinand Fuhs, *ThWAT* III, 869–93, esp. 885–93. 'Thus belonging to YHWH will be expressed in this phrase (i.e. *yir'ē yhwh*). "Those who fear YHWH" always denotes the community of YHWH worshippers' (ibid., 887).

Surely his salvation is at hand for those who fear him, that glory may
dwell in our land (Ps 85:10).

Yahweh is the God of those who are loyal to Yahweh, who are united
in the early Jewish community. Here it is presupposed that every member
has made a personal decision for the God of Israel. Presumably in 'fear' of
Yahweh there is also an allusion to the bond to the Torah, so that only the
chosen self-designation represents a clear reference to belonging to the
Torah community under the God Yahweh. The Deuteronomistic writings
also use the verb yārē', 'fear', in stereotypical fashion to express the sole
orientation of believers on Yahweh (cf. Deut 4:10; 5:29; 6:2, 13, 24; 8:6;
10:12, 20, etc.).

The exclusive bond with Yahweh which applied to community and
individual members then found its classic form in the 'Shema Yisrael' of
Deut 6:5–8, which has been influential down to present-day Judaism and
in Christianity through the New Testament:

Hear, O Israel: The Lord our God is one Lord; and you shall love the
Lord your God with all your heart, and with all your soul and with all
your might. And these words which I command you this day shall be
upon your heart; and you shall teach them diligently to your children,
and shall talk of them when you sit in your house, and when you walk
by the way, and when you lie down, and when you rise. You shall bind
them as a sign upon your hand, and they shall be as frontlets between
your eyes. And you shall write them on the doorposts of your house and
on your gates.

The sole claim of Yahweh to his people was the means of holding
together the defeated and dispersed people, giving it new self-confidence
and hope for the future. Every individual is addressed and at the same time
referred to the community. In the course of history, both ancient and
modern, many Jews have not observed the religious commandment to be
united and have been integrated into other societies and faith communities.
By contrast, the loyal Yahweh community preserved itself as an independent
cultural and religious entity at the cost of encapsulating itself from its
environment (cf. the dissolution of mixed marriages in Ezra 10 and Neh
13, also in Num 25) and separating from divergent groupings (like the
Samaritans or the Qumran community) as an independent cultural and
religious entity. Minorities and emigrant groups, including the German
emigrants mentioned above, have at all times produced similar phenomena
in asserting their identity; one might think of the Amish or the Dutch
people in Pennsylvania, indigenous peoples in industrial societies, Celtic

groups in Great Britain, Indians in South Africa, Chinese in the Western industrial states, Malays in Indonesia or in the Philippines, and so on. The special feature of the community of Judah in antiquity was that for the first time belief in God, mediated through the possession of sacred scriptures and their continuous exegesis, proved to be the dominant motif of self-assertion.

The legacy of family and village religion

Strictly speaking, from our perspective the tribal and national faith in Yahweh the warrior who sustains dynasties would have been completely inappropriate for the newly rising faith community of the Judahites, which was unmilitary and unpolitical. Theoretically that is correct. But nationalist ideology fades very rapidly after a collapse, and in any case in part gives place to the needs of minority existence. The new community structures – settlements in villages and small towns in both Palestine and Babylonia; a regime of occupation by an alien world power; the depoliticizing and 'privatizing' of life for the people of Judah; a civil constitution as a tribal system, i.e. the legal authorities which are councils of elders; the formation of social classes and religious schools; the distribution of land to those without possessions, and so on – became very noticeable and required an adaptation in beliefs. A warrior and state God could at least be used in dreams of a restoration of power and a final victory against the enemy. Everyday life required ethical and cultic orientation for politically impotent citizens who wanted to order their personal and communal affairs. The shared God Yahweh thus had to become a personal helper, counsellor and judge in a different sense from that which formerly applied in family religion. This development can in fact be read off the later strata of the Pentateuch (the Deuteronomic–Deuteronomistic work and the so-called Priestly Writing). Almost everything in the Pentateuch with an admonitory, didactic and legislative style comes specifically from this extremely creative phase of the exilic/post-exilic community under the pressure of circumstances, and also bears its stamp. Furthermore, as we have seen, large parts of the prophetic canon and the kᵉthūbīm manifestly came into existence at that time; they betray the efforts of the stateless communities to find firm ground in the multinational tumult of the world powers. Yahweh was the focal point for the whole life of his faithful. Faith and ethic refer to him. The reality of everyday life was under his supervision.

The traditions which were saved from the past in the early Jewish communities, which were gathered and put to use in connection with life in the new faith community, in part came from the old family and village tradition. In all matters pertaining to everyday life it was easier to begin there than with the tribal and state traditions.[14] So it is only natural for us to find in the sphere of social ethics that the central problems of the ethic of the time were the care of the weak and poor; the humanitarian protection of women, slaves and foreigners (though in some respects this was only rudimentary); incorruptible justice and honest trade; and an attempt at compensation in civil disputes (bodily injury, killing, crimes against property and so on). All the texts are far removed from any kind of state ethic. One might compare the legal collections in the Book of the Covenant (Ex 21 – 3), Deuteronomy (Deut 12 – 25) and the so-called Holiness Code (Lev 16 – 26). The latest version of all these literary compositions comes from the exilic/post-exilic period and not from the time of the monarchy. For nowhere do they make reference to monarchical structures. Rather, they reflect the ethic of family, village and community both in form (which is often homiletic and didactic) and content (rules about conflict for middle groups).[15]

Cultic problems are also increasingly discussed in the three collections which I have mentioned. At all events, life before and with Yahweh, the God of those who remained at home and the exiles, called for cultic and ceremonial rules, whether or not one had holy places and temples. It is a fundamental error to believe that cultic practice was limited to visiting a temple or some other place of sacrifice. We can easily establish from the food regulations in Lev 11 and Deut 14 or some sexual taboos (cf. Lev 15; 18; 20, etc.) that at least in ancient Judah the sphere of holiness extended deep into everyday life. That will already have been the case in the pre-exilic period and also among the nations who preceded Israel. Therefore as a matter of course in the exile the old precepts, religious customs often handed down orally, were collected and developed by increasingly professional scribes and scholars. The descendants of old priestly families may have been particularly prominent in looking after material from the cultic tradition during the time when there was no temple (587–515 BCE). The literary collection which we call the Priestly Writing contains a diversity of cultic material. If appearances are not deceiving, the collection and treatment of these rules, e.g. in the book of Leviticus, indicates that it was intended for community catechesis. The rules for sacrifices, cleanness and

---

[14] Thus also Rainer Albertz, *History of Israelite Religion* 2 (ch. 3 n. 1), e.g. 370–4, 399–410. However, Albertz wrongly regards the family as the bulwark of faith in Yahweh, through which it is to be 'saved'.

[15] Cf. e.g. the investigation by Ludwig Schwienhorst-Schönberger, *Das Bundesbuch (Ex 20, 22– 23, 33)*, BZAW 188, Berlin 1990. By contrast the (Protestant?, German?) predilection for state authority and structures persists, e.g. in Eckart Otto, *Ethik* (ch. 4 n. 96), 89–92, 193–7; id., *Krieg und Frieden in der Hebräischen Bibel und im Alten Orient*, Stuttgart 1999, 76–107.

other matters pertaining to the cult are not notes for the cultic official, but instructions for the regular member of the community. That can be seen as clearly from the 'priestly rules' of Lev 21 as from the 'sacrificial Torah' of Lev 1 – 7 or the laws about food and cleanness in Lev 11 – 15.[16]

So we could say that under the influence of the new community structures in the exilic and post-exilic periods belief in Yahweh took on very personal features, in contrast to theologies of tribe and state. For the individual member of the community, in analogy to the age-old family deities, Yahweh was encountered personally. Prayers of the sick and prayers for healing with an ancient stamp which had been used in the intercession of individuals needed little adaptation to the new situation. In some lamentations deriving from before the exile, only the name Yahweh had to be substituted for the earlier family deity, and the text could continue to be used.[17] The personal structure of the early Jewish local communities – in which everyone could know everyone else – made it possible to take over old experiences and texts directly from the family and clan sphere. A further development in the direction of the special features of a confessional community could easily take place. The social ethic of the community which was commended to the individual stems from the brotherhood (or sisterhood) of all the faithful. Yahweh wants all to be 'brothers' (cf. Deut 15; Lev 25). That is definitely a notion from the family and clan alliance, which also predominated in a changed form in the village community.[18] Now it was taken over in the confessing community, where it has remained to the present day. If all are brothers and sisters, then Yahweh can consistently be addressed as the 'Father' of all. This title, too, reflects the personal, intimate community of those who are related to one another.[19]

As for the cultic regulations relating to the people and the professional priesthood, we can be amazed at the degree to which scribes with a priestly inclination and community leaders allowed age-old, even pre-Israelite norms to be adopted and maintained. The different prehistoric blood taboos (cf. Ex 4:25; 12:22f.; Lev 12; 15:17) lived on undiminished. Similarly, taboos about mixtures bear witness to a fear of demons (cf. Deut 22:5, 9–11). Notions of the atoning sacrifice (Lev 16) and of Yahweh who loves the smell of burning (cf. Lev 1:9, 13, 17, etc.) are probably archaic and popular.

---

[16] Cf. Erhard S. Gerstenberger, *Leviticus* (ch. 14 n. 18), *passim*.

[17] Id., *Psalms* 1 and 2, FOTL 14 and 15 (ch. 4 n. 43). In Ps 12 we can observe very well a development of the individual lament into a lament of the community; cf. Erhard S. Gerstenberger, 'Gott hilft den Gerechten!', in Bernhard Jendorff and Gerhard Schmalenberg (eds), *Theologische Standorte*, Giessen 1983, 83–104.

[18] Cf. Lothar Perlitt, 'Ein einzig Volk von Brüdern', in Dieter Lührmann et al. (eds), *Kirche*, Tübingen 1980, 27–52.

[19] Cf. Erhard S. Gerstenberger, *Yahweh the Patriarch* (ch. 2 n. 4), 1–12.

Moreover the regulations about the cult predominantly served to orientate the members of the community; they are part of the 'community catechism'. In that phase the sacrificial cult seems to have retreated and given place to the Torah assembly.

The power and impotence of God

The exilic and post-exilic community of Israel shaped its situation-conditioned theology in the light of the depressing political changes, the new social structures and an ambivalent experience of history. Yahweh became not only the personal God but the exclusive Lord of the whole world, and this view did not develop out of philosophical considerations.[20] Behind the assertions of the superiority and the uniqueness of Yahweh stand tangible experiences and theological reflections orientated on reality. So this is the 'proof of the spirit and power' (to use Lessing's words). Because in the view of the early Jewish community or its theological spokesmen Yahweh has shown himself to be the most powerful god in the contemporary world of nations of the Babylonian and then the Persian empire (e.g. with the rise of the liberator Cyrus: Jer 45:1–7; 46:1–11), he is exuberantly given honorific titles which celebrate this power. Whether here the uniqueness and oneness of Yahweh in the world is 'proved' in a logically convincing way does not interest those handing on the tradition. At all events, this way of celebrating one's own god is amazing – it has many models in the world empires (!) of the Near East[21] – since the contradiction with reality as it could be experienced was sometimes terrifyingly great. Judah had been conquered and the elite deported to Babylon. Nevertheless, in many parts and strata of the Old Testament there are statements about the majesty of Yahweh which go on the offensive in supporting the God of Israel against the deities and peoples of the region and attributing supremacy to him. Behind such statements we are to conjecture liberating experiences, theologically positive interpretations of contemporary events. Here are just a few examples. In Moses' address, 'beyond the Jordan in the land of Moab' (Deut 1:5), he says:

> Circumcise therefore the foreskin of your heart, and be no longer stubborn. For Yahweh your God is God of gods (*'elōhē hā'ᵉlōhīm*) and Lord of lords (*wā'ᵃdōnay hā'ᵃdōnīm*), the great God (*hā'ēl haggādōl*), the mighty one (*haggibōr*) and the terrible one (*hannora'*), who is not partial and takes no bribe. He executes justice for the fatherless and the widow, and loves the sojourner, giving him food and clothing (Deut 10:16–18).

---

[20] The philosophical and inferential interest probably first comes into play with the Greek (Hellenistic) tradition; cf. Otto Kaiser, *Theologie des AT* I, Göttingen 1993.

[21] Cf. Othmar Keel (ed.), *Monotheismus* (ch. 2 n. 21); Christoph Uehlinger, *Weltreich* (ch. 7 n. 81).

Those are divine attributes in the style of the court etiquette and theology of the ancient Near East,[22] which are then used in the same breath, not of world rule (there are also such texts, cf. Ps 2; Isa 49:22f.; 60:1–22, etc.), but translated into the small currency of brotherhood and harmony within Israel.[23] That is typical of Deuteronomy. The pride of its authors is the law, which is given to the community as a guideline and backbone, and has no equal:

> Behold, I have taught you status and ordinances, as Yahweh my God commanded me, that you should do them in the land which you are entering to take possession of it. Keep them and do them; for that will be your wisdom and your understanding in the sight of the people, who, when they hear all these statutes, will say, 'Surely this great nation is a wise and understanding people' (*'am ḥākām w'nābōn haggōy haggādōl hazzeh*). For what great nation is there that has a God so near to it as Yahweh our God is to us, whenever we call upon him? And what great nation is there that has statutes and ordinances so righteous as all this law which I set before you this day? (Deut 4:5–8).

From the Deuteronomic texts we can get a rough idea of how a sense of superiority developed among the conquered Israelites. The exiles, brought close together in their communities, and those left behind in Palestine under foreign rule, cultivated a cultural and religious life of their own, as emigrants and the subjugated often do. They consolidated around belief in Yahweh and the sacred scriptures (Torah) which were coming into being and soon noted how they were respected and perhaps also hated for their religion and strict community organization. They also derived a sense of superiority to their environment from their possession of the Torah. This again was rooted in an increasingly strong awareness that they were different and unique in an alien world dominated by other deities.

> And beware lest you lift up your eyes to heaven, and when you see the sun and the moon and the stars, all the host of heaven, you be drawn away and worship them and serve them, things which Yahweh your God has allotted to all the people under the whole heaven. But Yahweh

---

[22] Cf. Assyrian, Babylonian, Hittite and Egyptian titles for God and king in the corresponding inscriptions, e.g. in James Pritchard, *ANET*, 227–319, or Otto Kaiser (ed.), *TUAT* I (Willem H. P. Römer and Rykle Borger), 289–410; Horst Steible, *Die altsumerischen Bau- und Weihinschriften*, FAOS 5, Wiesbaden 1982; id., *Die neusumerischen Bau- und Weihinschriften*, FAOS 9, I/2, Stuttgart 1991; Adam Falkenstein, *Die Inschriften Gudeas von Lagasch*, 4 vols, Rome 1966ff.; William W. Hallo, *Early Mesopotamian Royal Titles*, AOS 43, 1957, 49–56; id., 'Royal Inscriptions of the Early Old Babylonian Period. A Bibliography', *BiOr* 18, 1961, 4–14.

[23] Cf. Lothar Perlitt, 'Volk', in Dieter Lührmann et al. (eds), *Kirche*, Tübingen 1980, 27–52.

has taken you, and brought you forth out of the iron furnace, out of Egypt, to be a people of his own possession, as at this day (Deut 4:19f.).

With an intrinsic logic, a claim to election follows from the experience and preservation of otherness and a special character; this is the case time and again in the history of groups and peoples.[24] But along with election must be mentioned the conviction of the superiority of one's own God, his power and his will to rule, and that is at the same time its presupposition.

Some strata and collections from the time of the exile go much further than Deuteronomy. We note in them the euphoria of people who see themselves free or almost free from the constraints of foreign rule and who experience in this – quite rightly – the action of their own God, who has made the impossible possible. Isaiah 40 – 55, which is attributed to the so-called Deutero–Isaiah, is full of powerful statements about the exalted status and lordship of Yahweh. They have to do with the turning point which came about with the Persian advance westwards (the capture of Babylon by Cyrus in 539 BCE):

> Speak tenderly to Jerusalem and cry to her that her servitude is ended, that her guilt is forgiven . . . (Isa 40:2). Get you up to a high mountain, O Zion, herald of good tidings; lift up your voice with strength, O Jerusalem, herald of good tidings; lift it up, fear not; say to the cities of Judah, 'Behold your God! Behold the God Yahweh! He comes with might and his arm rules for him' (Isa 40:9f.).

> Remember the former things of old; for I am God, and there is no other; I am God and there is none like me (Isa 46:9).

> Hearken to me, O Jacob, and Israel whom I called. I am He, I am the first, and I am the last. My hand laid the foundation of the earth, and my right hand spread out the heavens; when I call to them, they stand forth together (Isa 48:12f.).

> Turn to me and be saved, all the ends of the earth! For I am God, and there is no other . . . To me every knee shall bow, every tongue shall swear. Only in Yahweh, it shall be said of me, are righteousness and strength; to him shall come and be ashamed all who were incensed against him (Isa 45:22–24).

---

[24] As far as I can see there is virtually no anthropological, sociological and psychological literature on the sense of election, but cf. the theological treatment of the theme: Paul D. Hanson, *The People Called*, San Francisco 1986; Horst Seebass, 'Erwählung I', *TRE* 10, 1982, 182–9; Georg Braulik, 'Erwählung', *NBL* I, 1990, 582–4: 'Generally speaking the theology of the election of the people of God must have been developed first in the crisis of the Babylonian exile, when Israel's identity and its position in the world of the nations was radically put in question, but any triumphalistic misunderstanding was excluded' (ibid., 583).

These triumphant statements in the texts could be multiplied. To an increasing degree Israel emphasized the pre-eminence of its God, especially in the midst of an environment which professed another faith. An ever more victorious confidence runs through the testimonies of the book of Isaiah. Israel is rehabilitated and may return to its homeland. The temple will be built; the Persian king is commissioned by Yahweh himself to help the people of God towards a new opportunity (Isa 44:26 – 45:7); the peoples will all have to come to Jerusalem and serve Israel (Isa 2:1–5; 45:14–17; 60).

> Thus says Yahweh, 'The wealth of Egypt and the merchandise of Ethiopia, and the Sabaeans, men of stature, shall come over to you and be yours, they shall follow you; they shall come over in chains and bow down to you. They will make supplication to you, saying: "God is with you only, and there is no other, no god besides him." Truly you are a God who hides yourself, O God of Israel, the Saviour. All of them are put to shame and confounded, the makers of idols go in confusion together' (Isa 45:14–16).

The authors and compilers of the book of Isaiah even sink to ungracious mockery of all who make idols for themselves and thus fail to see the one true God (cf. Isa 40:12–31; 44:6–10; 45:20, etc.).[25] Finally there is also talk of merciless judgment on enemies and unbelievers (cf. Isa 63:1–6; Zech 13f.). All that must be seen in connection with the changing, probably deteriorating, situation in the Yahweh community. For in fixed communities, growing pressure from outside can awaken the longing for a breakthrough and a complete change, to the point that it boils over.[26]

I want to mention one further source of statements about majesty and power, namely the psalms used in the cult (in the widest sense), which in their community genres (hymns, lamentations of the people, wisdom psalms) often go on to the superiority of Yahweh, praise it and derive consolation

---

[25] Also the extensive and alarming work by Horst Dietrich Preuss, *Die Verspottung fremder Religionen im Alten Testament*, BWANT 92, Stuttgart 1971, which apparently regards any form of humiliation of the opponent as unthinkable: may we present the conditions in the Bible as normative? Mockery as a weapon of the oppressed (e.g. jokes in totalitarian societies) is costly. Mockery of those of other faiths from the position of the rulers is criminal; cf. Erhard S. Gerstenberger, 'Andere Sitten – anderer Götter', in Ingo Kottsieper et al. (eds), *'Wer ist wie du, HERR, unter den Göttern?'*, Göttingen 1994, 127–41.

[26] The messianic movements in Brazil around the beginning of the twentieth century are a good parallel. They have been recognized by sociologists of religion as reactions to economic impoverishment and social pressure; cf. Florestan Fernandes, *Os errantes do novo século*, Petrópolis 1970.

and courage from it. Here there are very different emphases on the demarcation from other gods and peoples, groups and trends. Psalm 145 is a single joyful song of praise to the mighty God of succour who seems to be quite open to all the people who need his help. Only in the penultimate verse is there a demarcation: 'Yahweh protects all who loves him and will wipe out all the godless' (Ps 145:20). Similarly, Ps 139 is an unbelievably impressive hymn to the omnipresence of the powerful lord of heaven and the underworld (v. 8: 'If I go up to heaven you are there; if I make my bed with the dead, behold, you are there also'), completely without polemic and demarcations. But vv. 19–22 seem to be an alien insertion taken from an ardent song of lament. This begins, 'O God, when will you slay the godless?' Thus one could compare psalm by psalm the statements about Yahweh's exalted status with accusations against the enemy, etc. It would prove that each is played off against the other liturgically and perhaps also that each is dependent on the other.

Quite one-sided claims to power emerge from the hymns which proclaim that Yahweh is king (Pss 47; 93; 96 – 9). Perhaps they belong to the genre, as the lament from the abyss belongs to the petition. Thus praise of the God who is superior to all is dominant. He is the creator of the world (Ps 93:1–4; 96:5f.), who rules nature and the peoples (Ps 96:7–13; 97:1–6; 98:1–9), i.e. who executes just judgment (Ps 96:13; 98:9). The song of praise seems to be so unassailable that only a few polemical thrusts are needed: 'All the gods of the peoples are idols (*'elīlīm*)' (Ps 96:5). 'All worshippers of images (*peśel*) are put to shame, who make their boasts in worthless idols (*'elīlīm*). Worship him, all gods' (Ps 97:7, regarded by some exegetes as an insertion). Only Ps 47:4f. displays a manifest chauvinism: 'He subdues peoples under us, and nations under our feet.' So this is almost pure, exuberant praise, which relatively unselfishly seems to go over into worship.

> Ascribe to Yahweh, O families of the peoples,
> ascribe to Yahweh glory and strength!
> Ascribe to Yahweh the glory due his name; bring an offering, and
>   come into his courts.
> Worship Yahweh in holy array; tremble before him all the earth.
> Say among the nations, 'Yahweh reigns! Yes, the world is established,
>   it shall never be moved;
> he will judge the people with equity.'
>
> Let the heavens be glad, and let the earth rejoice,
> let the sea roar and all that fills it,
> let the field exult and everything in it!

Then shall all the trees of the wood sing for joy
before Yahweh, for he comes, for he comes to judge the earth.
He will judge the world with righteousness, and the peoples with his
truth (Ps 96:7–13).

These psalms are also called enthronement psalms. They culminate in the
exclamation 'Yahweh is (has become) king'. And that reminds us of the
Ugaritic texts in which after hard battles Baal accedes to royal dignity in the
world of the gods, or of the victory of Marduk in the Babylonian epic of
the creation of the world (cf. also Deut 32; Ps 82).

The statements about majesty and rule stand abruptly over against the
experiences of suffering in the early Jewish community. The majesty of the
one God who is superior to all the world is attacked, and we encounter the
helpless God; that is perhaps the decisive theological recognition of the
exilic/post-exilic community. At the level of family and village religion it
was not extraordinary also to experience God in his weakness. Whenever
his help failed, death, destruction, social upheaval gained the upper hand
and the powerlessness of the deity of the family or the place was evident.
One had to accept this and wait for a change. At the level of tribe or state
the victory of the enemy often meant the end of the defeated people and its
deity. Thanks to the different stages of Yahweh religion down to the level
of clan and village, the defeated and dispersed people of Judah could survive
the loss of the existence of the state and its cult and also compensate for it
for a while or partially by universalizing Yahweh's claim to lordship.
However, it is important that Yahweh was understood not only as a majestic
but also as an impotent God.

In the book of 'Second Isaiah' in particular, with its exuberant statements
about power and incomparability, there are also descriptions of suffering,
doubt and lowliness. Granted, there is a marked wish to put an end to all
slavery and punishment (Isa 40:1–2) and regain a dominant position (Isa
49:18–23). The signs of a political shift with the rise of Persian domination
are also clearly recognizable (Isa 45:1). The Babylonian priests who felt
betrayed by their own king Nabonidus pinned the same hopes for liberation
on Cyrus. By introducing the northern Mesopotamian moon goddess Sin
into the capital, Nabonidus had wanted to strip them of their power.[27] But
what for some was the desperate situation of the impotence of Israel lasted
beyond the catastrophe of 587 BCE, so that a number of contemporaries
asked whether Yahweh had not forgotten his people (Isa 40:27). On closer

---

[27] Cf. the taunt poems directed against Nabonidus and the texts composed by Cyrus himself:
A. Leo Oppenheim, *ANET* 308–16; 560–3, or *TUAT* I (Rykle Borger), 406–10; Kurt Galling,
TGI, 79–84.

inspection, the statements about the exalted status of Yahweh often prove to be embedded in disputations.[28] The authors or tradents are fighting over the plausibility of Yahweh's pre-eminence, which is not at all evident to some. Occasionally the wretchedness of Israel in the exile glimmers through: Isa 41:17 (wretchedness and poverty); 42:18–25 (a robbed and plundered people); 49:18–21 (Jerusalem; desolate, destroyed, solitary, driven out, outcast); 51:17–20 (desolation, damage, hunger, sword), and so on. But above all mention should be made of the four texts about the suffering servant (Isa 42:1–4; 19:1–6; 50:4–9; 52:13 – 53:12).[29] Here is a concentration of lasting experiences of oppression which are resolved only by the death of the ominous 'servant of Yahweh'.

> A bruised reed he will not break, and a dimly burning wick he will
>   not quench.
> He will faithfully bring forth justice. He will not fail or be discouraged
>   till he has established justice in the earth; and the coastlands wait for
>   his law (Isa 42:3f.).

> I gave my back to the smiters, and my cheeks to those who pulled out
>   the beard;
> I hid not my face from shame and spitting (Isa 50:6).

There are similar metaphors of maltreatment and violence in Ps 129:3 ('The ploughers ploughed upon my back; they made long their furrows') and Ps 66:11f. ('You laid affliction on our loins, you let men ride over our heads; we went through fire and water . . .').

> He was despised and rejected by men; a man of sorrows and
>   acquainted with grief;
> and as one from whom men hide their faces he was despised, and we
>   esteemed him not.
> Surely he has borne our griefs and carried our sorrows;
> yet we esteemed him stricken, smitten by God, and afflicted.
> But he was wounded for our transgressions, he was bruised for our
>   iniquities,

---

[28] From the beginning, form-critical analyses of Second Isaiah have indicated this remarkable genre; cf. Ludwig Köhler, *Deuterojesaja formkritisch untersucht*, BZAW 37, Giessen 1923; Hans Eberhard von Waldow, *Anlass und Hintergrund der Verkündigung Deuterojesajas*, Bonn dissertation 1953; Anton Schoors, *I am God your Saviour*, VTSup 24, Leiden 1973; Jean M. Vincent, *Studien zur literarischen Eigenart und zur geistigen Heimat von Jesaja Kap. 40–55*, Frankfurt 1977; Claus Westermann, *Isaiah 40–66*, OTL, London 1969.

[29] The literature on these texts is immense; cf. the short survey by Diethelm Michel, 'Gottesknecht', *NBL* I, 1991, 932–4; Herbert Haag, *Der Gottesknecht bei Deuterojesaja*, EdF 233, Darmstadt 1985.

upon him was the chastisement that made us whole, and with his
wounds we are healed (Isa 53:3–5).

In my view the servant songs can only be read in the context of the
descriptions of Israel in Second Isaiah, and of course they also refer to the
statements about glory in the hymnic sections. The theology of the exilic/
post-exilic community has these two poles: the exalted status and majesty
of Yahweh and the lowliness and pitifulness of the people of Yahweh, and
thus also of Yahweh himself.

That becomes clear in some passages of the book of Jeremiah, in which
Yahweh himself is depicted as the one who suffers. God's suffering and
human suffering reflect each other:

> Is Ephraim my dear son? Is he my darling child? For as often as I speak
> against him, I do remember him still. Therefore my heart yearns for
> him; I will surely have mercy on him, says Yahweh (Jer 31:20).

> My anguish, my anguish! I writhe in pain! Oh, the walls of my heart!
> My heart is beating wildly; I cannot keep silent; for I hear the sound of
> the trumpet, the alarm of war. Disaster follows hard on disaster, the
> whole land is laid waste. Suddenly my tents are destroyed, my curtains
> in a moment. How long must I see the standard, and hear the sound of
> the trumpet? 'For my people are foolish, they know me not; they are
> stupid children, they have no understanding. They are skilled in doing
> evil, but how to do good they know not' (Jer 4:19–22).

Whether or not this is the voice of a prophet or priest, according to the
views of the theologians of the time Yahweh is involved in the downfall of
his people. On the basis of this and similar statements in the book of
Jeremiah, and remembering his own suffering in war, a Japanese theologian
developed a 'theology of the pain of God'.[30] That is the right way. A
theologia gloriae cannot be put forward on the basis of the testimony of the
exilic/post-exilic community. It seems to me that this other basic datum –
Yahweh's compassion and impotence – as a result of the experience of
suffering in the early Jewish communities is often overlooked in the usual
theologies of the Old Testament.[31]

---

[30] Kazoh Kitamori, *Theology of the Pain of God*, London and Richmond 1965.

[31] Cf. e.g. Hans-Joachim Kraus, *Theologie der Psalmen*, BKAT XV, 3, 1979, 26–36: the 'epithets
of YHWH' offer no kind of grasp for a 'theology of suffering', and the gaze of the modern
scholar is directed only towards 'Yahweh's revelation and hiddenness' (ibid., 36–49), 'The
perfections of Yahweh' (ibid., 49–55), etc. Cf. also Hermann Spieckermann, *Heilsgegenwart*
(ch. 4 n. 139); Horst Dietrich Preuss, *Theologie* I (ch. 4 n. 136); Otto Kaiser, *Der Gott des Alten
Testaments* II, Göttingen 1998.

I should mention at least in passing the poetic texts of Mesopotamia.
Here (from Sumeriian times) laments of city deities are articulated which
are tuned to the loss and destruction of their settlements. Thus the great
lamentation over the destruction of Ur[32] also quotes the lament of Ningal,
the consort of the moon god Sin:

> O city of (a great) name – now you are destroyed, city of high walls –
> your land has perished. . . . O Ur, my exalted chamber – my house in
> ravaged city which has been destroyed, which has been torn down like a
> shepherd's cot, and my treasures which towered on high in the city,
> have been scattered (to all the winds).

Such lamentations by gods seem above all to mark the end of city states
and only to touch peripherally on the question of survival. They show the
local deity in his or her weakness; they are a fixed genre in the Mesopotamian
tradition. The Israelite example in all probability belongs to this general
current of tradition. The so-called Lamentations of Jeremiah (1 – 5) and the
lamentations of the people or the community are further important examples
of the Israelite theology of impotence. Everywhere behind the laments
there is the acute awareness of forsakenness, i.e. God's justified or unjustified
turning away from his people, experienced in particular historical situations.
'Yahweh has become like an enemy, he has destroyed Israel; he has destroyed
all its palaces, laid in ruins its strongholds; he has multiplied in the daughter
of Judah mourning and lamentation' (Lam 2:5). Along the lines of the
Deuteronomistic revision of the past, the lament can then give way to self-
accusation and confessions of guilt.[33] Psalms 78 and 106 or the great
penitential prayers of Ezra 9; Neh 9 and Dan 9 are examples of such texts.
But as I have said earlier, there is also the other possibility, namely the
accusation that God has forgotten his obligations. A correct assessment of
the theology of the early Jewish community cannot leave aside this theological attitude, which discloses God's weaknesses and imperfections:

> Yet you have cast us off and abased us, and have not gone out with
>   our armies.
> You have made us turn back from the foe, and our enemies have
>   gained spoil.

---

[32] Translated by Samuel N. Kramer, *Lamentation over the Destruction of Ur*, AS 12, Chicago 1940.
Cf. Mark E. Cohen, *The Canonical Lamentations of Ancient Mesopotamia*, 2 vols, Potomac 1998;
Piotr Michalowski, *The Lamentation over the Destruction of Sumer and Ur*, Winona Lake 1989.
For the text quoted here see Walter Beyerlin, *Near Eastern Texts relating to the Old Testament*
(ch. 6 n. 19), 117.

[33] Cf. Rainer Kessler, 'Das kollektive Schuldbekenntnis im Alten Testament', *EvTh* 56, 1996,
29–43.

You have made us like sheep for slaughter, and have scattered us in
many directions.
You have sold your people for a trifle, demanding no high prices for
them.
You have made us the taunt of our neighbours, the derision and scorn
of those about us.
You have made us a byword among the nations, a laughing-stock
among the peoples.
All day long my disgrace is before me, and shame has covered my face,
at the words of the taunters and revilers, at the sight of the enemy
and the avenger.
All this has come upon us, though we have not forgotten you, or been
false to your covenant.
Our heart has not turned back, nor have our steps departed from your
way,
that you should have broken us in the place of jackals, and covered us
with deep darkness.
If we had forgotten the name of our God, or spread forth our hands to
a strange god,
would not God discover this? For he knows the secrets of the heart.
Lo, for your sake we are slain all the day long, and accounted as sheep
for the slaughter (Ps 44:10–23).

Historical experiences from the sixth century BCE evidently play the
main role in this psalm; one might compare other laments of the people in
the Psalter which are apparently also set against the defeat by the Babylonians
and the destruction of the temple (Pss 74; 79; 80; 89). Yahweh is not (or is
no longer) the always powerful and caring God of the intact or invincible
sanctuary of Zion. He does not sit eternally on his throne in heaven and
make nature and human beings tremble at his power.[34] Rather, in the
theology of the community Yahweh is the near and personal God who
displays the features of a family deity (cf. 4.3). The theologians of Israel
experience the God around whom they gather as impulsive and vulnerable,
angry and driven by deep compassion, in solidarity with Israel and then
again incomprehensibly neglectful and forgetful of his duties. We could
even say that the community experiences in its own body the deep division
between the near family God and the remote God behind the state.
Statements about majesty and glory are turned into the opposite. The local
community of the defeated and dispersed also recognizes in its own fate the

---

[34] Cf. Hans Jonas, *Gottesbegriff* (ch. 7 n. 73).

impotence of its God. However, there remains the dream of the past happiness of national independence and there are the visions of future glory, the contours of which are sometimes taken from the Babylonian and Persian rulers of Israel. For the honorific statements made by Israel at that time came into being under the conditions of the world empires. In particular the theological question of the power of God, which still constantly arises over the problem of justice, is very closely connected with the social structure in which believers find themselves.

Justice and peace

Just as important as the notions of God's power are the views of God's action and functions, the determination of his being as it relates to the shaping of human life. Here for the moment I am pushing into the background the questions relating to the being of the Absolute, on which excessive stress is put in the Christian tradition. For while the statements about the omniscience, eternity and omnipresence of God, like those about a purely abstract omnipotence, are not uninteresting, they are relatively unimportant for a practical theology of the Old Testament.[35] The ideas and recognitions which emerged from the exilic/post-exilic community embrace a broad spectrum and because of the group interests which soon emerged are not uniform.

The nature of the God of the community of Israel can be seen and understood only in connection with this community. An internal structure necessarily developed in the exilic/post-exilic community which went back to family and clan traditions, and also – at least in the sphere of future expectations – to ideological constructs of the state. Here not only the experiences of the downfall of their own monarchy but also the general structures of the empire in which the community found itself provided the framework of reference. So we cannot expect any smooth identifications with earlier images of God from Israelite tribal and state society or from family religion. The community understands itself in a way as a family, but it is not a family in the sociological sense. It feels that it is part of a greater social whole, but it can only represent that whole imperfectly. Community theology is an enlarged family theology against the background of popular, ecclesial or state ambitions and pressures on the whole of society which come from outside.

We can start by noting that in the exilic/post-exilic community, to a degree previously unknown, the individual, and above all the person of the

---

[35] They are also discussed rarely in Old Testament theologies but often in community discussions. The questions often asked are: 'Is there a God?', 'What properties does God have?', 'Is God just?'

head of the family, has come of age in religion. The pious individual (in his or her community) becomes the model of the righteousness of Yahweh. One example of this is the discussion in Ezek 18 of the tricky question whether sons had to pay for the misbehaviour of their fathers. Apparently this was discussed vigorously in the exile.[36]

> If a man is righteous and does what is lawful and right – if he does not eat upon the mountains or lift up his eyes to the idols of the house of Israel, does not defile his neighbour's wife or approach a woman in her time of impurity, does not oppress any one but restores to the debtors his pledge, commits no robbery, gives his bread to the hungry and covers the naked with a garment, does not lend at interest or take any increase, withholds his hand from iniquity, executes true justice between man and man, walks in my statutes, and is careful to observe my ordinances – he is righteous, he shall surely live, says the Lord God.
>
> If he begets a son who is a robber, a shedder of blood, who does none of these duties, but eats upon the mountains, defiles his neighbour's wife, oppresses the poor and needy, commits robbery, does not restore the pledge, lifts up his eyes to the idols, commits abomination, lends at interest and takes interest; shall he then live? He shall not live. He has done all these abominable things; he shall surely die; his blood shall be upon himself (Ezek 18:5–13).

The author of this argument, which is carried on in a very legalistic way, decides clearly and harshly that each generation and each Yahweh worshipper is responsible for itself. Behind this lies the other fundamental decision which had to be taken at that time: did the Judahites at home or in exile want to belong to the ancestral people and faith community or not (cf. Josh 24:15)? This decision was personal and had to be made in the family group. Many Jews at that time made the same decision as Joshua ('But I and my house, we will serve Yahweh'). So for born Judahites it was a matter of staying in the alliance of the people. Those who joined the group, married into it or were interested in it had to be accepted into the Jewish community. A personal decision also had to be made on this question, and where possible the decision had to be endorsed in a public rite (cf. Josh 24:14–24; Deut 29:9–28; 30:11–20; Ps 50). There are various occasions and situations in which a decision for Yahweh has become a theme. Ruth 1:16b, 'Your people is my people and your God is my God', is probably a typical form of incorporation; Ex 12:48 is another:

---

[36] The discussion is of a popular proverb (v. 2): 'The fathers have eaten sour grapes, but the children's teeth have been set on edge'; cf. Jer 31:29.

'And when a stranger shall sojourn with you and would keep the Passover to the Lord, let his males be circumcised, then he may come near and keep it; he shall be as a native of the land.' Jonah 1:9, 'I am a Hebrew and fear Yahweh' (cf. also Deut 23:1ff.; Isa 56:5, 6: the condition is observance of the sabbath).

In a relationship with God which is so dependent on personal decisions and is no longer simply attuned to membership of the family, the faithfulness and concern of God and his care and righteousness for all adherents must be a main expectation of believers. Such personal concern is not unknown in the religions surrounding Israel.[37] In the Jewish community that was coming into being, under the above-mentioned conditions of subjection to foreign rule, political dependence in a world empire and the relatively democratic self-administration of a village body, it developed specifically out of family faith. Justice for every man (and to a certain degree for every woman, cf. Ruth) first of all means sufficient opportunities in life, blessing for one's profession and everyday life, health and prosperity, of the kind that we know from family religion. Secondly, it means solidarity with the weak – seen from the perspective of a village ethic. Now these concerns are taken into the sphere of the community. As I have already said, the old individual lamentations are reinterpreted. God cares not only for a single family group but for all the families brought together in the community. As we can see in a model way in Ps 12, now petitions for several sufferers can also be recited in worship. The petitioners and those who receive help appear in the plural.[38] The community accepts them, and the faith of the community expects help from Yahweh. Moreover the experience of fellowship in the suffering of the individual leads the psalm literature to progress to communal lament and petition which, alongside the acute occasions of sickness and persecution (here the experts in ritual had many traditional texts of lamentations which could well be used), increasingly took as its theme the universal fortunes of human beings: their mortality, the barrenness of life (cf. Pss 39; 90; Koheleth, etc.), and finally also the injustice of God (Job).

---

[37] Cf. Hermann Vorländer, *Mein Gott* (ch. 4 n. 30); Karel van der Toorn, *Religion* (ch. 3 n. 5). After a separation, members of a family in ancient Babylonia had for example to cleanse themselves and pray for one another in a ceremony to Shamash and Marduk like this: 'I am your servant, who because of the wrath of my god and my goddess constantly entered into my solitude, then my years declined into oppression and lament. On this day come to me. What happened to the one taken away (into captivity), plundered, exploited, forgotten and remote, who approached me, at your exalted command, cannot be changed. But with your firm Yes, which is unshakeable, obliterate the tribulation of our heart, grant that our days may be long, give us years of our life to a distant time, then I will glorify your great deeds (and) praise you before the people everywhere' (Stefan M. Maul, *Zukunftsbewältigung* [ch. 4 n. 25], 414).

[38] Cf. Erhard S. Gerstenberger, 'Psalm 12: Gott hilft den Unterdrücktem', in Bernard Jendorff and Gerhard Schmalenberg (eds), *Anwalt des Menschen*, Giessen 1983, 83–104.

God's justice for individual believers was now spoken of and expected in the context of the life of the community before God:

> Yahweh, let me know my end, and what is the measure of my days;
> let me know how fleeting my life is.
> Behold, you have made my days a few handbreadths, and my lifetime
>   is as nothing in your sight.
> Surely every man stands as a mere breath. Selah.
> His life is only a shadow.
> Surely for naught they are in turmoil;
> man heaps up and knows not who will gather (Ps 39:5–7).

And as an example of the existential frustration of believers to whom the ordering of the world has become suspect:

> Again I saw that under the sun the race is not to the swift, nor the battle to the strong, nor bread to the wise, nor riches to the intelligent, nor favour to the men of skill; but time and chance happen to them all. For man does not know his time. Like fish which are taken in an evil net, and like birds which are caught in a snare, so the sons of men are snared at an evil time, when it suddenly falls upon them (Eccles 9:11f.).

In the internal structure and arrangement of the communities this justice is linked at the level of the individual and community to the idea of the God who imposes demands on the community. The fellowship of several families leads to a certain principle of benefit: *do ut des*, 'I give to get something in return.' Economic exchange begins. Village communities function according to this new principle of mutuality and so too – in a way which is increasingly formalized and moulded in legalistic forms – do the more highly developed social organizations. Although the early Jewish community was at a pre-state stage of socialization, it is no exception here. It lives by a certain solidarity, but also by exchange between members. Receiving and giving are thus also customary at the spiritual level. Our debate about the 'free grace' of God and the necessary human 'works' is thus pointless, because it ignores the two levels at which one or the other is 'right'. So it is no wonder that in the community which draws on two different traditions, while help in solidarity is expected from Yahweh, so too are demands, as in a treaty.

Now if the higher level of social exchange applies, it is not surprising that in his faithfulness and correctness Yahweh also makes comparisons between individual followers and is forced to conclude that some believers pay more respect to the divine controller of history and others less. Already in ancient texts there was a 'greater' or 'lesser' degree of obedience towards customs and traditions (cf. Gen 38:26). Sensitivity to socially balanced actions which were for the common good and pleasing to the gods had been part of ancient Near Eastern cultures for millennia. But now this was made into a system, a sometimes exclusive relationship. It was also important to mark out on the human side the justice which was to be shown in accordance with divine providence and impartiality. The high respect for the Torah, the source of life, the constant study of it and meditation on it, were regarded as the closest approximations to the will of God (cf. Pss 1; 119).

> Blessed is the man who walks not in the counsel of the wicked,
> nor stands in the way of sinners, nor sits in the seat of the scoffers.
> But his delight is in the law of Yahweh, and on his law he meditates
>   day and night (Ps 1:1f.)

Now in the course of such devotion to the God of Israel – here too taking up earlier hostile stereotypes and the excluding disturbing elements from the community – there came into being the image of the 'godless' which permeates the Psalms and can also be noted elsewhere.[39] In this way the spirituality of the community arrived at a personal God, but one who was to be experienced by way of the Torah. Now in the community the Torah was mediated through leaders who soon took on the special colouring of scribal specialists. All this needs to be taken into account in a description of the God's justice for the individual.

But 'justice' also relates to the wider faith community which had succeeded the tribe and the state. Dispersed to every corner of the globe and often enough divided into feuding factions, members of the Jewish community nevertheless saw themselves as a religious and ethnic unit. And in respect of this people now – even more, but perhaps also for the first time – the firm, fundamental 'doctrine' of the elect people, the people which is Yahweh's possession, was developed. The exile is the real background for the 'doctrine' of Yahweh's covenant with Israel, as Lothar Perlitt perceptively demonstrated as long ago as 1969.[40] Certainly the discussion in Old Testament scholarship has gone on since then as though nothing had happened. Nevertheless, Perlitt's investigation has set down an immovable marker which we cannot go back on. And we must see the community's expectation of Yahweh's justice for his people in the light of

---

[39] Cf. Othmar Keel, *Feinde und Gottesleugner*, Stuttgart 1969; R. B. Y. Scott, 'Wise and Foolish, Righteous and Wicked', VT.S 23, 1972, 146–65; Helmer Ringgren and Bo Johnson, *ThWAT* VI, 898–924; Helmer Ringgren, *ThWAT* VII, 675–84; Moshe Weinfeld, *Social Justice in Ancient Israel and in the Ancient Near East*, Minneapolis 1995.

[40] Lothar Perlitt, *Bundestheologie im Alten Testament*, WMANT 36, Neukirchen-Vluyn 1969.

the idea of the reciprocal covenant of Yahweh with Israel developed after the exile.

Here once again Israel is no longer a nation in the traditional sense, nor a state in accordance with the rules of either antiquity or modernity. It is a faith community grounded in the people but also theoretically open to outsiders, whose members and communities are dispersed over the then known world. We know of contacts between the 'communities abroad' and the homeland, both in Babylonia (cf. Jer 29) and also in Egypt (cf. the Elephantine correspondence). We know of controversies in the spheres of theology and politics, and between family dynasties and particular classes (e.g. 'priests' v. 'levites' in the Chronistic work). Nevertheless a bond remained between the groups and the communities in the realm of the spirit, in the life of the people and in domestic politics and laws. The one God and the one Torah held everything together, though the Torah was ambiguous and was often interpreted differently in individual centres of learning.

This colourful fabric of a faith community was articulated in the canonical writings (and in addition in apocryphal and pseudepigraphical books); it called for justice on the basis of a special treaty with Yahweh, the Lord of the world. The community developed the complex image of the just God Yahweh who had promised to give the community satisfaction, and who at the same time, as a partner in the treaty, insisted that the regulations should be observed. Already at that time the right to exist was the criterion for justice, and the right to exist was bound up with a piece of land from which one could feed oneself and on which one could confess one's faith. Above all in the Deuteronomistic writings, the problem of the land is a centre of the theology of justice. The Israel that depends on Yahweh expects the free gift of its land. That can be heard in the promises of the land in Genesis and also in some psalms: 'How could we sing Yahweh's song in a strange land?' (Ps 137:4). The jewel which first makes the land Yahweh's land is Jerusalem, and in it the temple, allegedly first built by Solomon and then rebuilt under Darius, the king of the Persians. It is towards Jerusalem that the ardent longing of believing Jews is increasingly directed. 'If I forget you, O Jerusalem, let my right hand wither! Let my tongue cleave to the roof of my mouth, if I do not set Jerusalem above my highest joy' (Ps 137:5f.). On the other hand, the observance of the revelations of Yahweh's will was the great theme of later redactors and theologians. With different emphases, the Deuteronomistic work (including Deuteronomy), the Priestly and Chronistic strata make the observance of the Torah and maintaining the right cultic place and worship the main criterion of life with Yahweh.

According to the standards of the time, protection from external hostility and oppression is also part of justice for the spiritual people of Yahweh. And because hostility and oppression recurred time and again, and threats, defeats, dependent relationships seriously damaged self-confidence and often enough also brought physical misery and death, the just God was obliged to defend and avenge the community in the same way as a tribal and national deity.

> Remember, Yahweh, against the Edomites the day of Jerusalem,
> how they said 'Rase it, rase it! Down to its foundations!'
> O daughter of Babylon, you devastator! Happy shall he be who
> requites you with what you have done to us!
> Happy shall he be who takes your little ones and dashes them against
> the rock! (Ps 137:7–9).

As we already saw at another point, on the negative side this attitude can intensify to the point of undisguised chauvinism. Such misinterpretations of the principle of justice are always possible. Justice for one's own group then becomes unconcealed self-righteousness and contempt for others. Of course that was and is theologically illegitimate, both then and now. For in the grandiose ideas of the one God for the one undivided world there is necessarily a recognition of other peoples and doctrines. We have noted traces of this recognition in the Old Testament. With no illusions we should concede that these traces are amazing, that they are far ahead of their time, and even now have never been displaced, even in the lauded Christian world. But the question of justice for individual groups, communities and certainly also states remains. It really has to be put from a position of strict monotheism; indeed perhaps it can only be put at all from there. For if an unrestrained polytheism prevails, then the survival of a community depends completely on chance or good fortune. Those with the weaker or more impotent god must go under; that is also the way in capitalist systems! Strangely the monotheistic empires act as if they believed in many gods. They make no serious efforts to help the threatened ethnic groups (cf. the Indians in Brazil, the Aborigines in Australia, etc.)

So in the ancient community justice means a fair distribution of the opportunities in life within one's own faith group. The weak, foreigners, the excluded are to get their possibilities of survival. That means having a special covenant relationship with Yahweh which involves firm obligations. And it means with Yahweh's help having a strong position over against enemy nations and neighbours, which one can call on.

Now because the conquered Judahites' belief in God had taken on an ecumenical and universal orientation, 'justice and peace' also extended over the other peoples. In the understanding of the exilic/post-exilic community, Yahweh is the one God over the one world. Thus the orientations on justice and peace also apply to the 'other' societies known at the time. That is expressed not only in the prophetic books as an 'eschatological' perspective on the development of the world or the participation of peoples in the final pacification of the word, but also in the book of Psalms in the exuberant praise of Yahweh's universal 'works', 'acts', 'wonders', etc. (cf. also Ps 148).

> O sing to Yahweh a new song, for he has done marvellous things.
> His right hand and his holy arm have won him victory.
> Yahweh has made known his victory, he has revealed his vindication
>   in the sight of the nations.
> He has remembered his steadfast love and faithfulness to the house of
>   Israel.
> All the ends of the earth have seen the victory of our God.
> Make a joyful noise to Yahweh, all the earth; break forth into joyous
>   song and sing praises!
> Sing praises to Yahweh with the lyre, with the lyre and the sound of
>   melody.
> With trumpets and the sound of the horn make a joyful noise before
>   Yahweh the king.
> Let the sea roar and all that fills it, the world and those who dwell in
>   it.
> Let the floods clap their hands; let the hills sing for joy together
>   before Yahweh, for he comes to judge the earth.
> He will judge the world with righteousness and the peoples with
>   equity (Ps 98).

In the hymns to Yahweh as king, which are also called enthronement hymns (Pss 47; 93; 95 – 9), there is the expression of belief in a universal justice. It has cosmopolitan dimensions and is only a little constrained by particular interests (cf. Ps 97:3 'All those who serve images shall be ashamed ...'). Community theologians venture into a truly global arena and their leading concept is 'law and justice for the peoples'.

We see that for the exilic/post-exilic community the justice of Yahweh permeates the whole of reality, i.e. within the horizon which this same community experiences as a boundary. Internally Yahweh sees that there is a balance between the social groupings. Externally, after the loss of its independence as a state, the community develops a seismographic sense of the dimensions of the empire, the pulse of history, as it is governed by Babylonians and Persians and rival peoples. Prosperity and peace are bound up with the justice that Yahweh, God of the word, wills to introduce. *Shālōm*, 'salvation, prosperity', can arise only where human interests are in balance. The framework given to the community is expressed in some self-designations. For example the terms *qāhal* and *'ēdāh* point to the liturgical 'assembly' of the community,[41] whereas designations from the political sphere – like *'am*, 'people', and *gōy*, 'nation', and also the name 'Israel' – express the ecumenical dimension of following Yahweh and also the dream of national and universal responsibility.[42]

Creation and history

In Babylonia the exiled Judahites experienced an empire with its own ideologies and mythologies. The creation faith handed down in Gen 1 and 2 demonstrates the lively clashes between the dispersed believers in Yahweh and the doctrines of the world around. In the exile the God of Israel becomes a universal God of the worlds, and therefore the creation of the world is also attributed to him. Probably there were no explicit myths about the creation of the world in ancient Israel.[43] For how long this was the case is a matter of dispute: did the non-universalist phase extend to the beginning or the end of the period of the state? But the answer to this question is not decisive for our purposes. It is enough to say that the narratives about the creation of the world that we have in Gen 1 – 2 quite certainly developed only at a late stage from the Mesopotamian sphere or were brought from there. Similarities with the Babylonian myths (above all Enuma Elish and Atrahasis) down to terminology can be established.[44] That also applies to the existing versions of the creation narratives in Genesis, which strongly reduce the mythical features and possibly introduce the idea that Yahweh calls the world to life by his word alone.[45] At the beginning, like Marduk, the Babylonian ruler of the world, Yahweh has to conquer chaos: Tiamat, the horrible primal mother, lives on in the Hebrew word *t°hōm*. Moreover the features of the struggle with chaos are elaborated in some Psalms more broadly than in Gen. 1 (cf. Ps 18; 77; 104; 114). Yahweh becomes the

---

[41] Cf. Heinz-Josef Fabry, *ThWAT* VI, 1204–22; Frank-Lothar Hossfeld, *Volk Gottes als 'Versammlung'*, WD 110, Freiburg 1987, 123–42.

[42] Cf. Paul D. Hanson, *People* (ch. 8 n. 24); Ralph W. Klein, *Israel in Exile*, Philadelphia 1979; Milton Schwantes, *Sofrimento e esperança no exilio*, São Leopoldo 1987.

[43] In his dissertation *Weltschöpfung und Menschenschöpfung*, Stuttgart 1969, following Claus Westermann, Rainer Albertz traced the fundamentally different narratives about the creation of the world and human beings and worked out their different genres. The creation of the world belongs to the wider society.

[44] Cf. Hans-Peter Müller (ed.), *Babylonien und Israel*, Darmstadt 1992; William G. Lambert, *TUAT* III, 565–602 (Enuma Elish).

[45] Cf. Ps 34:6–9; but there are also such models of creation by the word in Egypt: Klaus Koch, *Geschichte der ägyptischen Religion*, Stuttgart 1993, 377–82.

creator of the whole visible world with the earth, the sea and the firmament of heaven. He himself is enthroned above everything in his castle, which is located in the heavenly ocean. He has the powers of chaos under full control; only in respect of the underworld is Yahweh's rule not so clearly attested. Some psalms lament that the dead are remote from God (Pss 6; 88); others also speak of the rule of Yahweh which extends to the deepest depths (Ps 139; Jonah 2). We can see from these different descriptions and convictions of faith how fluid theological insights were.

As well as the physical environment, Yahweh has of course created all living beings including human beings, and that means human beings generally, not just the Israelites. For all the peoples on this earth stem from the first human couple (Gen 5; 10). All the wisdom writings thus have a universal human background and perspective. The traditions of election and history play no role in them. Yahweh (or simply ʾᵉlōhīm or šadday) is responsible for the creation and human beings. This universalism and the remoteness of the supreme God of the worlds is brought out particularly impressively in the great speeches by God in the book of Job:

> Where were you [Man] when I laid the foundations of the earth? Tell
>   me if you have understanding.
> Who determined its measurements – surely you know, or who
>   stretched the line upon it?
> On what were its bases sunk, or who laid its cornerstone,
> while the morning stars sang together and all the sons of
>   God shouted for joy?
> Or who shut in the sea with doors when it burst forth from the
>   womb;
> when I made clouds its garment, and thick darkness its swaddling
>   band,
> and prescribed bounds for it, and set bars and doors,
> and said, 'Thus far shall you come, and no farther, and here shall your
>   proud waves be stayed'? (Job 38:4–11).

At that time this wisdom theology was international, or, better, it was disseminated over an empire consisting of many peoples; that must not be forgotten in the concert of theologies in the early Jewish community.

History is really also a universal field, only no one has yet been able to compose impartially a universal history of humankind. Self-interests are too influential and distort the ideal 'objective' judgment. That is also always the case in Israelite historiography where interests of Israel are touched on. Consequently we must also read these documents as particular testimonies.

Even the biblical tables of nations[46] which contain the genealogy of humankind serve to demonstrate the descent of Israel. Genesis 10:1–31 initially seems only to contain primeval information about the descendants of Noah. But then the genealogy of Shem continues down to Tara and his three sons Abraham, Nahor and Haran (Gen 11:10–26). The prophetic sayings about foreign nations show predominantly a devaluation of the others from a internal perspective. We have suffered, the others must be punished (cf. Isa 13 – 23: the prophecies or taunt songs on Babylonia open the collection; Jer 46 – 51: the speeches against Babylonia conclude the collection; Ezek 2 – 32: predominantly speeches against the Phoenician coastal cities and Egypt, with some positive reference to the Babylonian Nebuchadnezzar). Only the sayings against foreign nations in Amos 1:3 – 2:12 give Israel the same weight as the neighbouring peoples or even give that people a worse position. In the great apocalyptic visions of world history Israel can then easily go under: only the world empires are significant, but they will be destroyed by Yahweh for the sake of the future of his people (Dan 2; 7). All in all, the Israelites of the exilic/post-exilic period were human beings like those in most other eras of history. They saw their own group (religious community) at the centre of world history (Gottwald recognizes that very well in his sociological introduction to the Old Testament).[47] In this way the universal history of humankind easily becomes the history of the election and salvation of Israel. We can constantly ask the accounts in the Old Testament: how did the other peoples, nations or religious communities mentioned in these narratives, legends, didactic examples, experience the same state of affairs? Kolakowski asks sarcastically what the Egyptians would have thought of Ex 14:30: 'And they saw the Egyptians lying dead on the sea shore.' Such critical questions need to be put to the biblical tradition, because they arise out of the time-conditioned nature of the texts. We all have to ask the question *cuius bonum?*, for whose good?, when we examine our own theological statements.

Guilt and atonement

More than almost any other community, the exilic/post-exilic community raised the question of its own entanglement in the course of events. Certainly the recognition that it was partly to blame for its own fate was age-old, reaching back into the prehistoric period. From the beginning of written

---

[46] Cf. Robert R. Wilson, *Genealogy and History in the Biblical World*, New Haven 1977; Manfred Oeming, *Das wahre Israel*, BWANT 128, Stuttgart 1990; Josef Schreiner, *ThWAT* VIII, 571–7.

[47] Norman K. Gottwald, *The Hebrew Bible – A Socio-Literary Introduction*, Philadelphia 1985.

traditions the question of guilt is formulated with increasing intensity at the different levels of human and cultic organization and in the course of time. The collapse of Judah in 587 BCE deeply stirred up those who believed in Yahweh. To different degrees communities blamed themselves for the collapse. Again they chose different ways of atoning for their guilt. All these differences indicate different contexts and ideas of God.

In the Israelite priesthood, which was also partly responsible for building up the communities and the assemblies and festivals orientated on the word of God, the theology of the temple and sacrifice was predominant.[48] Private and collective guilt was atoned for by precisely defined sacrificial rites (Lev 1 – 7; 16, etc.). 'in the symbolic rite of blood on the day of atonement, Israel, which had incurred guilt, came into contact with the God who revealed himself on the *kappōret* [the special place of the presence of Yahweh over the ark, Janowski, ibid., 346], who condescended here . . . Thus to Israel, entangled in the deepest guilt, the reality of God's opening of himself to human beings which was inaugurated with the event on Sinai is opened up again in the cultic atonement of the annual Day of Atonement'.[49] Cultic atonement certainly also had adherents in the communities, and was thus not a matter exclusively for priests (cf. the 'holy people' and 'kingdom of priests' in Ex 19:6; Lev 2; Isa 61:6). But alongside this stood the non-sacrificial worship of Yahweh which issued in the synagogue, based on the Torah and the observance of the Torah (cf. Pss 50; 119; Neh 8; Deut 4 – 6; Micah 6:6–7, etc.).[50] Yahweh, the God of Israel, was the exclusive deity for both theological trends, and alongside him no one else could be addressed in cultic worship. As the authoritative supreme head of his community, this God required strict loyalty. The demands on believers, which had meanwhile been fixed in writing, contained rules for both sacrifice and obedience. Failure to observe these rules, or transgressions of them, had to be neutralized by repentance, penitence, intercessory ceremonies and atonement sacrifices: a continuous process of purification and reconciliation. At that time the great feast of atonement, the rules of which are given in Lev 16, became an important element of the course of the liturgical year.

Summary

Community structure and insights of faith. While the early Jewish community from the sixth century BCE on was divided by families and clans (cf. e.g. the

---

[48] Cf. Bernd Janowski, *Sühne als Heilsgeschehen*, WMANT 5, Neukirchen-Vluyn 1982; Israel Knohl, *The Sanctuary of Silence*, Minneapolis 1995; Erhard S. Gerstenberger, *Leviticus* (ch. 4 n. 18).

[49] Bernd Janowski, *Sühne* (ch. 8 n. 48), 349.

[50] Cf. Menahem Haran, *Temple and Temple-Service in Ancient Israel*, Oxford 1978; Erhard S. Gerstenberger, *Psalms* 1 and 2, FOTL 14 and 15 (ch. 4 n. 43), on Pss 50; 51; 119; 132.

lists of those returning home in Ezra 2 and Neh 7), because of its principle of individuality and the way in which its organization for worship and instruction extended beyond the family, it became a specific ecclesial entity. That is already expressed in the lists of those returning home, with their constant mention of the totals of individual professions and the calculation of all members of the community: 'The whole community numbered 41,360 in all, excluding their servants and maidservants; these were 7,337; also 200 singers' (Ezra 2:64). It is almost impossible to reconstruct the domestic life of the families. But the relevant texts speak a clear language about the institutions and customs of the community. Early Jewish men and women gathered at festivals, perhaps already also at sabbath worship; they formed a legal community and with their special religious life felt embedded in the wider political structures of the world governments. Above all each was personally responsible for himself (and herself?).

Theological insights were stamped by the background of the village and small town and the empire. The social scope for the formation of Yahweh theology was thus very great. For the members of the community, through the Torah Yahweh was the guiding authority on all questions of life. He was a guarantor of internal order and by virtue of being a partner in the covenant the undisputed leader of his elect people. Thus God is understood both as personal protector (guardian deity) and preserver of a sense of community and law. Yahweh provides help in threatening situations, gives blessing, intervenes for the weak, fights for his people against enemies, and increasingly establishes himself as supreme ruler of the worlds. This span of theological existence can only be found in the Judahite communities which formed again after the exile. To them we owe the many dimensions and the special unity of the belief in Yahweh which now came into existence. It represents a qualitative difference from the pre-exilic situation.

Particular and universal God. Election and isolation. In its theology, the early Jewish community experienced a dangerous split which betrays a typical ambivalence in human thought. On the one hand, in Yahweh it worshipped the supreme God, the Lord of creation and the world of the nations, who was responsible for the whole of humankind. On the other, it claimed this supreme deity for itself. Deuteronomy 7 gives a basic theoretical foundation for such conflicting statements: Yahweh wants to set an example for the whole world. In accordance with a literary scheme which is used frequently he does not choose for himself the most powerful and greatest people but a small, insignificant people, in order through this 'people of disciples' to communicate his message of salvation to the world. Other texts give no reason at all for the election of the people of Judah. It has simply been made by Yahweh in his unfathomable knowledge. Acts of demarcation and isolation from the neighbouring people and the original inhabitants of Palestine correspond to the belief in election. DtrG keeps referring to the fact that Israel should have purged its land of 'unbelievers' (cf. Ex 34:10–16; Lev 18:24–29; Deut 11:8–25; 20:10–18; Josh 9, etc.). In this stratum and among the thinkers who stand behind it, co-existence is an alien word. Israel is the sole legitimate possessor of the land sought out from Yahweh. 'Foreigners', even women from other peoples (Ezra 10; Neh 13; Num 25), must be excluded. Cultic institutions for other deities are absolutely intolerable and are subject to the highest penalties. For some theologians of the time, protection from outside influences becomes a main concern.

Openness towards outsiders. Alongside nationalist encapsulation there is sometimes an amazing openness to the outside world, which corresponds completely to the monotheistic universalism of Deutero-Isaiah. God's power may no longer be commandeered by one group. Here are some examples. Eunuchs and foreigners, who formerly – if at all – were allowed only very limited entry into the assembly of Yahweh (cf. Deut 23) may now become full members of the community (Isa 56). The terrible curses on foreign nations, according to age-old tradition a powerful weapon in the battle for national existence, here and there give way to the thought of a common salvation: 'At that time Israel will become the third with Egypt and Assyria, a blessing in the midst of the earth' (Isa 29:24). Nineveh, the embodiment of the most brutal foreign rule, is promised grace, contrary to the obstinate orthodoxy of the prophet (!?) Jonah, and this grace is in fact given (Jonah 4). The pilgrim hordes made up of all the peoples which go up to Jerusalem inspire the Psalmist to offer all foreigners citizenship in the holy city (Ps 87). In short, in the deepest humiliation the scales fall from the eyes of some theological thinkers and communities. All men and women live from one and the same divine source of power. Equal rights for the peoples is the only possible consequence. Anyone who lives in the power of the one God and creator must learn to renounce the exercise of imperial or spiritual power on others. There is one and the same undivided peace for all.[51]

Future expectations. In some eschatological and apocalyptic texts, the hopes of Israel for a restoration of national independence live on. But alongside them, and increasingly clearly, the power of the peoples is set over against

---

[51] Of course the notion of peace for Jerusalem (later the heavenly Jerusalem) still has something particular about it; cf. Odil H. Steck, *Friedensvorstellungen im alten Jerusalem*, Zurich 1972.

the rule of the one God. Occasionally anthropological and cosmological notions come before the salvation history of Israel. All in all, the power of human beings and the nations is nothing. The individual and humankind become the playthings of ungodly powers until the God of the world establishes a new state of salvation by his judgment. The decisive initiative lies with the universal God, who is not bound to Israel. Where a messianic component comes into play in the final drama, the Messiah is originally the divine vicegerent, as once was the king of Judah by God's grace. But remarkably there is also the variant of the poor and humble Messiah: 'Behold [Zion] your king comes to you; triumphant and victorious is he, humble and riding on an ass, on a colt the foal of an ass. I will cut off the chariot from Ephraim . . . and the battle bow shall be cut off, and he shall command peace to the nations . . .' (Zech 9:9).

The impotence of God. In the exile the suffering and impotence of Israel – and thus of its God – become transparent to a renewal which is hidden in them. As I have already said, the experiences of impotence emerge most clearly in the servant songs, and these also speak of hope. Suffering is no longer simply a lamentable evil. Right beyond mystical or masochistic exaggeration the experience of powerlessness and the taunting and torturing to death which is provoked by it appear as the fertile ground which bears within itself the buds of new life. The divine power is not with the executioners but is to be found where one offers one's forehead impotently to violence. How is that possible? God is capable of changing roles. He leaves the pyramidal social structures of power and settles 'down below' among the sufferers and those with no rights.[52] Probably recollections of the solidarity of the clan deity or even of the obligation and responsibility of the tribal and national god to give support are taken up here. In the Pentateuch the 'slave existence' in Egypt and the liberation from Egypt are often conjured up as a paradigm. Hence the revaluation in the exilic/post-exilic community: power is not negated, trivialized or diabolized. It is shifted and given a new function. As the power of the weak and for the weak it becomes the basis of salvation. Those who, like the servant of Yahweh, withstand torture commit their whole being and resources for the others

---

[52] Modern journalistic investigations can document the reversal of fortune of the powerful so that they become the subjugated, the reality of seeing 'from below' and from the perspective of 'the other': Günther Wallraff's different reporting of the 'other side' (for example, he assumed the role of a Turkish immigrant worker in Germany); Yoram Binur, *Mein Bruder, mein Feind. Ein Israeli als Palestinenser*, Zurich 1990; Carlos Mesters, *Sechs Tage in den Kellern der Menschheit*, Neukirchen-Vluyn 1982. It seems that Emmanuel Levinas' philosophical scheme (cf. e.g. *La trace de l'autre*, Paris 1963; id., *L'humanisme de l'autre homme*, Paris 1987), goes back directly to Yahweh's change of role in the Old Testament.

and in this way overcome the fatal egocentricity of the power that is recognized by society. 'Power' has taken on a new quality.

Theology from below. Of course all the other texts of the Hebrew canon must be looked at and investigated from the endpoint of the theology of the exilic/post-exilic community, in and for which they were in fact collected and reinterpreted. If we do this, we note with amazement at how many points God's power for the weak and the sufferers appears. The legislators attempt to support the poor and helpless. The regulations of e.g. Deut 15 and Lev 25 are well known. Is it pure utopia when Deut 15:4 requires 'There shall be no poor among you' and immediately afterwards (v. 11) describes a brutal reality? Or when Lev. 25 wants every fiftieth year to restore property to a condition which is socially tolerable?[53] The prophetic writings vehemently champion those who are the victims of economic or political violence (cf. Amos; Micah 3). Proverbs reflect the problem of poverty and injustice (cf. Prov 19:1, 4, 7; 21:13; 31:5–9: 'Open your mouth for the dumb, for the rights of all who are left desolate. Open your mouth, judge righteously; maintain the rights of the poor and needy' (vv. 8f.). Some psalms indicate that there were whole communities of the wretched and poor, presumably in the exploited provinces, on the flat land, or in poor districts of the cities (Neh 5; Ps 9/10; 37; 73). Ideas of God, worship and community structure were thus probably opposed to the balance of power in competitive societies, as we can reconstruct it from the statements about domination mentioned earlier.

Experiences of power. It is hard to imagine how the early Jewish community came to make its statements about the exalted status of Yahweh and his rise to be the sole ruler of the world, which was diametrically opposed to its experience. The defeat by the Babylonians, the humiliations and deportations were certainly overwhelming and depressing events. But they were at least in part done away with and transcended by positive changes of fortune. Psalm 126:1 dreams of the turning point: 'When Yahweh restores the prisoners of Zion, then we shall be like those who dream. Then our mouth shall be filled with laughter and our tongue with praise.' The Deuteronomist indicates a first improvement in the situation: '. . . Evil-merodach, king of Babylon, in the year that he began to reign, graciously freed Jehoiachin king of Judah from prison; and he spoke kindly to him, and gave him a seat above the seats of the kings who were with him in Babylon' (2 Kings 5:27f.).

---

[53] Cf. Erhard S. Gerstenberger, *Leviticus* (ch. 4 n. 18), 369–98: id., '. . . zu lösen die Gebundenen', in *Kirchlicher Entwicklungsdienst der EKHN, Schulden erlassen*, Frankfurt 1999, 59–96.

With liberation by Cyrus firmly in view, Second Isaiah then proclaims the unprecedented mighty act of Yahweh, who sets world history in motion for his people and makes the return to Judah possible. In the books of Ezra and Nehemiah the Persian powers are again brought into service by Yahweh in the best interests of Israel. At some point the Persians gave permission for the people of Judah settled in Babylon to return (though this was taken up only by some of the exiles). Permission to rebuild the temple in Jerusalem will have been given around 520. In 515 BCE Judahites could consecrate the restored sanctuary. Messianic movements may have been connected with this; cf. Hag 2:23: 'On that day, says Yahweh Sabaoth, I will take you, Zerubbabel my servant, the son of Shealtiel, says Yahweh, and make you like a signet ring; for I have chosen you, says Yahweh Sabaoth.' In short, the communities in exile observed the developments in world history with great excitement, and – rightly or wrongly – discovered in them not only the punitive but also the liberating acts of their God. Therefore they were capable of experiencing the majestic power of their God in the midst of the hostile environment and terrifying defeats.

The just individual and the just community. The late writings of the Hebrew canon sometimes associate Yahweh very closely with the Torah as the comprehensive revelation of his will, or with the spirit of international wisdom. Both lines also occasionally fuse (cf. Ps 119). Torah piety makes Yahweh the great teacher of the people of Israel. Moses received from his hand the extremely compressed basic commandments for religious and civil life, the so-called Decalogue (Deut 5:6–21; Ex 20:2–17) and all further rules for life. There are sporadic reflections of the Ten Commandments in the Hebrew scriptures (cf. Hos 4:2; Jer 7:9; Micah 6:8). The custom of collecting fundamental norms for life or for particular spheres of life and impressing them on adolescents can also be read off many collections of ethical and cultic rules which take the form of a catalogue (cf. Lev 19; Ezek 18; Ex 23; 24, etc.). Claiming to originate from Moses and thus to have an authority hallowed by age, the Torah brings together all kinds of normative traditions from a variety of spheres of life. The members of the community are to follow this orientating tradition; not, however, in blind obedience of a militaristic kind but in accordance with the relatively democratic basic constitution of the early Jewish community. There respect for the authoritative word of God prevails, but at the same time a deeply-felt argument over its current meaning. With the collecting of holy scriptures the interpretation of scripture was also born. Writers, redactors and scribes 'read from the law of God, clearly; and they gave the sense, so that the people understood the reading' (Neh 8:8). The theological presupposition is that Yahweh has proclaimed his will, but that this will must constantly be reiterated. The Old Testament is the sole impressive testimony to the exciting work of interpretation in the early Jewish community, whether in worship or in the beginnings of the 'school'. Yahweh requires complete dedication to it, and this dedication is realized in its purest form in the constant study of the Torah (Ps 1:1; Deut 17:18f.). As in other religious communities, scribes and later rabbis became the relevant functionaries, freed for the representative study of the Torah (especially by the housework of their wives, who had a share in the earnings of the clergy for this). The ideal picture of the righteous man who takes his study of the Torah seriously, and the just community, which as a whole follows the way of the Torah, is the reflection of the teaching, holy God. In the wisdom tradition (cf. above all Proverbs; Koheleth; Job and some Psalms), *hokhmāh*, 'wisdom',[54] takes the place of the Torah. *Hokhmāh* also admonishes, calls for constant attention to herself and for full devotion:

> Wisdom has built her house, she has set up her seven pillars. She has slaughtered her beasts, she has mixed her wine, she has also set her table. She has sent out her maids to call from the highest places in the town, 'Whoever is simple, let him turn in here!' To him who is without sense she says, 'Come, eat of my bread and drink of the wine I have mixed. Leave simpleness and live, and walk in the way of insight' (Prov 9:1–6).

Those who follow the wise counsel of Lady Wisdom will gain life. Those who gladly and without being compelled entrust themselves to the norms of the Torah are righteous and thus blessed. Both modes of behaviour, although they are fed by different traditions, bring about the state of salvation: living in the sphere of Yahweh's will and activity.

World empire and belief in Yahweh. All in all, the early Jewish community's new belief in Yahweh makes an imposing impression. Many questions remain open, but it is clear that following the emergency of their defeat and deportation, the Judahites of the sixth and fifth centuries reacted in a very creative way with the formation of an exclusive doctrine of faith and life which embraced the individual, the community and world society. Where did people derive the strength for such a spiritual undertaking? There are many examples of how after catastrophes of the magnitude of the Babylonian defeat peoples and movements disappeared from the historical scene. That was true not least of the northern Israelites who were deported by the Assyrians in 722 BCE. Not a trace of them is to be found. There must be

---

[54] Cf. Gerlinde Baumann, *Die Weisheitsgestalt in Proverbien 1–9*, FAT 16, Tübingen 1996.

special reasons why this did not happen in the case of the defeated Judahites. The fact that the Babylonians allowed the closed, semi-autonomous settlement of the exiles in Mesopotamia; that in 562 (the year of the accession of Amel-Marduk) they pardoned the imprisoned King Jehoiachin and treated him as a friend of the great king (2 Kings 25:27–30); that Judahites played a role in the economic life of the victorious state and were given permission to return home and rebuild their temple, are indications of the strong will for survival in the Diaspora communities and a partial explanation of the creation of a world-embracing Yahweh theology. Favourable external conditions and a powerful faith came together and gave rise to the ongoing confession of the one God of Israel, the creator of heaven and earth, the ruler of the then known cosmos.

No one disputes that the theologians of Judah were very greatly influenced by the ideas and beliefs of Babylonia, later Persia, the country in which they were living. However, this dependence is rarely researched as a separate theme. Werner H. Schmidt goes into these relationships in his account of the faith of Israel.[55] Now as I have already mentioned, he persists in a 'fusion theory'. The faith community around Yahweh was able to master all alien influences and in this confluence of ideas about God to ensure that its own irreplaceable and authentic ideas were dominant. Rainer Albertz adopts the same approach in his history of Israelite religion.[56] For him, the establishment of a unitary Yahwistic opposition theology and the introduction of the Torah as a centre of reference for the newly-constituted community are the decisive moments in the exilic/post-exilic period. Here the experiences of Yahweh and the statements about his being remain the unchangeable constant. By contrast, I would take very seriously the normative reshaping of belief in Yahweh under the impact of the quite different political, economic and social conditions of the Babylonian empire. Yahweh became an essentially changed deity, who was no longer identical with the pre-exilic tribal and state God. Just as the former family deities did not correspond very closely to the God of the individualized community, so the new Yahweh did not correspond very closely to the pre-exilic Yahweh. Babylonian ideas about the creation of the world and the world empire, Persian views about the duality of the divine forces, and possibly Egyptian constructions of a rule which brought compensating justice took first place and transformed the faith of the Judahites. Their spiritual and theological achievement remains intact: it is absolutely amazing how the

---

[55] Werner H. Schmidt, *The Faith of the Old Testament*, Oxford 1983.

[56] Rainer Albertz, *History of Israelite Religion* 2 (ch. 3 n. 1), e.g. 375–98, 'The theological interpretation of the political catastrophe'; 464–92, 'The struggle over the identity of the community', i.e. in the post-exilic period.

little people made up of defeated prisoners appropriated central ideas from the victors for themselves. They offered resistance to the death against the domination of the rulers of the world and asserted themselves as a tiny marginal group in an empire of many peoples. But we cannot seriously claim that this process brought forth or encouraged a continuous, genuinely Israelite theology. The 'foreign' influences were too strong, and the changes from all the cults previously practised in Israel and the images of God that had been believed in and worshipped were too deep.

8.4 The cult: temple and synagogue

The cultic forms and rites were also reshaped in the exilic and post-exilic period. The temple was restored at great expense (cf. Hag 1 – 2; Zech 1 – 8) and consecrated. In this way the old central cult with its daily sacrifices again functioned as it had done before the deportations, but now without a state task. The temple now worked for the confessing community of Israel, and no longer for the Davidic dynasty and the preservation of the state, its military and officials. Must not new relations have formed between the temple and the early Jewish community? At any rate, precisely because the temple was also the one, central sanctuary, it no longer seems to have fulfilled its function completely; or rather, it fulfilled it in a different way. Alongside temple worship in the individual committees, and then also in regional schools, a form of worship of Yahweh came into being which was no longer exclusively orientated on the central temple and on bloody sacrifice.

> You have no delight in sacrifice; were I to give a burnt offering you
>   would not be pleased.
> The sacrifice acceptable to God is a broken spirit;
> a broken and contrite heart, O God, you will not despise (Ps 51:18f.;
> cf. 40:7; 50:8–13).

This and similar statements in the Psalms which are said to be critical of the cult may in fact show an inner change in favour of a more open, spiritual Torah – centred more on ethical and social life and thus on a liturgical practice focused on the individual in the community.

However, we learn positively of this shift only from the time of Nehemiah. Then Ezra the scribe[57] is said once to have held a great assembly

---

[57] Hans Heinrich Schaeder, *Esra der Schreiber*, Tübingen 1930; Wilhelm T. in der Smitten, *Esra. Quellen, Überlieferung und Geschichte*, Leiden 1973; Herbert Donner, *Geschichte* 2 (ch. 4 n. 24), 460–5 (Donner calls Ezra a 'state commissioner for the law of the God of heaven', ibid., 461).

of the people. In liturgical fashion (which still serves as a prototype today) it contained the reading of scripture and prayer (Neh 8). 'Ezra the scribe stood on a wooden pulpit' (even now the preacher stands elevated on a 'pulpit') and read from the book of books:

> And all the people gathered as one man into the square before the Water Gate; and they told Ezra the scribe to bring the book of the law of Moses which Yahweh had given to Israel. And Ezra the priest brought the law before the assembly, both men and women and all who could hear with understanding, on the first day of the seventh month. And he read from it facing the square before the Water Gate from early morning until mid-day, in the presence of the men and women, and those who could understand; and the ears of all the people were attentive to the book of the law. And Ezra the scribe stood on a wooden pulpit which they had made for the purpose; and beside him stood Mattithiah, Shema, Anaiah, Uriah, Hilkiah and Maaseiah on his right hand; and Pedaiah, Mishael, Malachiah, and Meshullam on his left hand. And Ezra opened the book in the sight of all the people, for he was above all the people; and when he opened it all the people stood. And Ezra blessed Yahweh the great God; and all the people answered, 'Amen, Amen', lifting up their hands; and they bowed their heads and worshipped Yahweh with their faces to the ground. Also Jeshua, Bani, Sherebiah, Hediah, Maaseiah, Kelita, Adraiah, Jozabad, Hanan, Pelaiah, the Levites, helped the people to understand the law, while the people remained in their place. And they read from the book, from the law of God, clearly; and they gave the sense, so that the people understood the reading (Neh 8:1–8).[58]

The scene is a stereotype. It describes the constitution of the people of Israel in the homeland. If we can trust the chronological sequence of the narrative in Ezra 3 – 6, the temple is functioning again. But the decisive commitment of the people to the law of Moses has not yet taken place. It takes place in this section, with the substantial, indeed fundamentally important collaboration of the whole community, the Jewish men, women and children. This is how Gunneweg sees the content of the pericope:

> . . . [The Chronicler] is at the same time also very concerned to show that the community of Israel as a whole is active and taking the initiative. It was not Ezra who had raised the question of the mixed marriages but the representatives of the people, and the scribe had used his office and taught what was to be done. It is the same even now. When the seventh

---

[58] Translation based on Antonius H. J. Gunneweg, *Nehemia*, KAT XIX.2, Gütersloh 1987, 108f. The following interpretation is largely according to Gunneweg.

month approaches, all Israel automatically knows what has to be done. The assembly of the people does not need to be called specially by Ezra; it assembles automatically, and on its own initiative and spontaneously asks Ezra to read out the law.[59]

Traces of this understanding of the people of God and worship based on the members of the community, the laity, have also been transferred to the Christian churches. Here and there remnants of this original awareness have been preserved in both Protestant and Catholic churches. And not only that. The basic outlines of community worship laid down then can still be recognized even now:

> The Chronicler is depicting an 'ideal scene' with aetiological content. By being anchored in the event of the restoration, a quite specific form of worship consisting of the Torah and the word of God is being established, and emphasis is placed on its constitutive significance, which is the basis of the community. The 'priest' Ezra brings the book of the Torah into the community; that is his priestly office, and the 'scribe' Ezra is asked to perform this service by the people. And it is the 'scribe' Ezra, mentioned here for the first time . . . who mounts the pulpit from which he performs his Torah office (v. 4). Here in an ideal scene we have the sketch of a morning synagogue service. With this celebration the festal month is opened and the constitution of the post-exilic community is introduced.[60]

As I have said, the pulpit from which the reading or the sermon is given still stands in our churches. The 'scribe' has the central position, but he is the community's official. The opening of the Torah scroll, the reading, the responses of the community (Amen, Amen), the attitude of prayer and the exposition of what has been read (here by 'levites', who are connected with Ezra [on an equal footing]) are also basic elements of the Christian liturgy of the Word of God. This sociological and ecclesiological background always needs to be noted in the discussion of Old Testament community theology. Reading and learning the Torah are the main activities, to which prayer and meditation are subordinated.[61]

---

[59] Ibid., 110.
[60] Ibid.
[61] The Chronicler is interested in 'a form of worship at the centre of which stands the law. The "whole people" is gathered to it, men, women and adults who have sufficient capacity for discernment, who understand the Torah appropriately or are led to such an understanding by instruction (V 3). The exalted significance of learning and teaching the Torah, studying the Torah, in Judaism has its biblical foundation here' (ibid., 111). For Jewish worship; cf. Ismar Elbogen, *Der jüdische Gottesdienst in seiner geschichtlichen Entwicklung* (1931), Hildesheim 1967; Simon P. de Vries, *Jüdische Riten und Symbole* (1932), Wiesbaden 1982; Jakob J. Petuchowski,

Of course in early Judaism there were other cultic institutions alongside the assembling of the whole community to hear and learn the Torah, though we know very little about them. But despite the increasing concentration on the pilgrimage to Jerusalem associated with it, the Passover festival was and remained a celebration which at heart was centred on the family and associated with a particular place (cf. Deut 16:2: 'Offer the Passover sacrifice . . . at the place which Yahweh will choose'; in Lev. 23 there is simply constant mention of the 'holy convocation', which apparently is to be held at the central sanctuary as opposed to the sabbath [Lev 23:3]).[62] Similarly, circumcision (cf. Gen 17) and rites of healing, which may have played a major role but are nowhere documented or specifically noted, were typically limited ceremonies which were not necessarily to be carried out by the whole community. And there were further cultic institutions about which we have virtually no contemporary information, i.e. from the sixth to fourth centuries, like the feast of Purim (Esther) or the 'Bewailing of Virginity' (Judg 11:37–40). Nor should the daily times of prayer be forgotten; they seem to have been introduced at least after the second century BCE (Dan 6:11: 'He went to his house where he had windows in his upper chamber open towards Jerusalem and he got down upon his knees three times a day and prayed and gave thanks before his God, as he had done previously'). A thanksgiving offered on such an occasion is quoted in Dan 2:

> Then Daniel blessed the God of heaven and said: 'Blessed be the name of God for ever and ever, to whom belong wisdom and might. He changes times and seasons; he removes kings and sets up kings; he gives wisdom to the wise and knowledge to those who have understanding; he reveals deep and mysterious things; he knows what is in the darkness, and the light dwells with him. To you, O God of my fathers, I give thanks and praise, for you have given me wisdom and strength, and have now made known to me what we asked of you; for you have made known to us the king's matter' (Dan 2:19–23).

Only the closing part (v. 23) relates to the concrete situation: the wise men of the city of Babylon are invited to rediscover and interpret for King

---

Beten im Judentum, Stuttgart 1976; Bernd-Jörg Diebner, 'Gottesdienst II', *TRE* 14, Berlin 1985, 5–28, surveys the Old Testament background and provides many literary references.

[62] For Lev 23; cf. Erhard S. Gerstenberger, *Leviticus* (ch. 4 n. 18), 334–54; in keeping with the fictitious situation, Ex 12 contains no references to a later central festival place, but merely instructions for the family feast. Verse 26, which points forward to life in the promised land, would have provided an opportunity to refer to the assembly in Jerusalem which became customary much later, say around the first century BCE; cf. Shmuel Safrai, *Die Wallfahrt im Zeitalter des Zweiten Tempels*, Neukirchen-Vluyn 1981.

Nebuchadnezzar a dream which troubles the king, but the content of which he has forgotten. By contrast, the first part of the prayer is a standard formula from the milieu of the wise or the school, or from the liturgy of household devotion: the subjects of the praise are the superior power of the God of heaven and his penetrating knowledge of all things.

If we compare the significance for the Judaism of the time of the temple cult and the synagogue assemblies which are just beginning, we easily arrive at the conclusion that the temple organizations (above all sacrifice, but possibly more and more community activities, e.g. services of praise, were shifted to the temple court) were forced into the background and that for the communities in Palestine, above all in the Diaspora, the liturgy of the word and prayer for the whole people, the prototype of which is described in Neh 8, had a far higher status. That is also the estimate of liberal Jewish scholars, whereas some Orthodox circles accord absolute priority to the temple.[63] For the manifold critical statements directed against the bloody sacrificial cult (e.g. Amos 5:21–24; Ps 40; 50; 51, etc.) and above all the strong emphasis on obedience to the Torah and ethical blamelessness[64] give a vivid picture of conditions in the early Jewish Torah community. In the worship of the exilic/post-exilic community, the book which embodied the presence of Yahweh in the word stood at the centre. It was brought near to the community by reading, meditation, praise, and sermon-like interpretation.[65] The Yahweh community seems to have been the first in the Near East to go over to a religion of the 'book'. At all events we have no report from the environment of Israel of a similar use of sacred writings, although collections of canonical texts in the hand of ritual experts are attested centuries earlier.

Despite all this, we should not ignore the sacrificial worship of the second temple. The sacrificial regulations of Lev 1 – 7 are the most comprehensive complex of texts to inform us about ritual practice in Jerusalem. Sacrifice is no longer completely shut off from community life.[66] As those offering the

---

[63] Cf. Menahem Haran, *Temple* (ch. 8 n. 50); on the other side Yehezkel Kaufmann, *The Religion of Israel*, Chicago 1960; Jacob Milgrom, *Leviticus 1–16*, AB 3, New York 1991. Israel Knohl, *Sanctuary* (ch. 8 n. 48), attributes interest in the temple only to a narrowly defined 'Priestly school' whose literary legacy is the 'Priestly Torah' (PT). He distinguishes from this the 'Holiness School', which is much more orientated on the community (ibid., 6, 8ff., etc.).

[64] Bernd-Jörg Diebner makes it clear from 1 Sam 15, the story of the rejection of Saul, that 'the practice of the sacrificial cult – however clear the motivation may be – is subordinate to hearing the voice of YHWH', *TRE* 14, 11. 'The opposition between true and false worship in "Israel" seems to be the basis for the composition of the canon of the Jewish Bible generally and also the tense juxtaposition of its partial complexes and the construction of the sections of the canon', ibid., 11. Even the paradise story is an example of this!

[65] Neh 8; Deut 29 – 30, etc. attest the practice of reading and address. The Holy Scriptures also served as a basis for prayer: Judith H. Newman, *Praying by the Book*, Atlanta 1999.

[66] Cf. Erhard S. Gerstenberger, *Leviticus* (ch. 4 n. 18), *passim*.

sacrifice, the laity are present near the altar of burnt offering: they slaughter and prepare the animal. The priest performs only the blood rite at the altar itself. The holocaust (the whole burnt offering) 'as a fragrant savour for Yahweh' seems to have become popular; at any rate the burnt offering occupies first place among the different type of offering (Lev 1). All in all, animal sacrifice was certainly important for the Jerusalem community, but the Judahites living abroad could at most take part in the ceremonies at pilgrimage festivals or through representatives.

8.5 Popular belief

Despite all the basic 'democratic' structures, we have to note that quite certainly the majority of the notions of God contained in the Hebrew and Aramaic writings derive from leading groups in the community. They need not indicate the actual state of community piety and the normal image of cultic behaviour. On the contrary, all kinds of polemic against a very diffuse popular religion, described in a stereotyped way, suggest that contrary to the sometimes very strict leadership of the community by the scribes and priests there was a variety of deviant behaviour. Deuteronomy already denounces whole catalogues of 'superstitious' practices:

> When you come into the land which the Lord your God gives you, you shall not learn to follow the abominable practices of those nations. There shall not be found among you any one who burns his son or his daughter as an offering, any one who practises divination, a soothsayer, or an augur, or a sorcerer, or a charmer, or a medium, or a wizard, or a necromancer (Deut 18:9–11).

The list contains mantic and magical activities which are abundantly attested from the environment of Israel and which were presumably also practised in Israel, contrary to all prohibitions by the leaders of the communities and the 'pious' or 'righteous' or, better, 'Yahweh-fearers'. The famous story of the witch of Endor (1 Sam 28) is an example of this. The late prophetic writings contain many accusations of constant idolatry, cf. e.g. Isa 57:3–13 ('But you, draw near hither, sons of the sorceress, offspring of the adulterer and the harlot . . .'), or Isa 65:2–5:

> I spread out my hands all the day to a rebellious people, who walk a way that is not good, following their own devices, a people who provoke me to my face, continually sacrificing in gardens and burning incense upon bricks, who sit in tombs and spend the night in secret places; who eat swine's flesh, and broth of abominable things is in their vessels, who say, 'Keep to yourself, do not come near me, for I am set apart from you.'

Such descriptions remain largely a closed book to us; we cannot make any connections with specific cults. But we must reckon that a variety of clichés are used in the polemic against 'alien' or 'deviant' cults; these are fantasies about what people cannot stand, which they transfer to other groups and thus suppress.[67] So there are numerous indications of a powerful and independent popular religion which does not coincide with the official faith of the scribes and the majorities in the communities. We cannot say much about the structure of this popular belief and its content, so we cannot make any rational judgment on it.[68] However, it is certain that the belief of the community in the early Jewish period was more colourful than we can establish by means of the canonical scriptures which have survived.

We can also conclude from this fact, which has often been noted but little evaluated, that the Hebrew canon offers only a tiny segment of the theology and piety of the communities from Judah. I said at the beginning that amazingly, according to the exilic/post-exilic evidence, the communities consisted not just of men but of women, men and 'understanding' children. However, the writings in the Hebrew canon were predominantly composed by men. Thus we have almost completely lost sight of an important part of religion, namely the feminine part – to the great detriment of the whole tradition and all that came afterwards. If we investigate the few texts in the scriptural canon which provide for the active involvement of women in worship and the formation of faith, we get a small insight into the tremendous loss of spirituality that has taken place in the Jewish–Christian tradition as a result of the exclusion of women's theology:

> Then [all the men . . . and] all the women who stood by, a great assembly, all the people who dwelt in Pathros in the land of Egypt, answered Jeremiah: 'As for the word which you have spoken to us in the name of Yahweh, we will not listen to you. But we will do everything that we have vowed, burn incense to the queen of heaven and pour libations to her, as we did, both we and our fathers, our kings and our princes, in the cities of Judah and in the streets of Jerusalem; for then we had plenty of food, and prospered, and saw no evil. But since we left off burning incense to the queen of heaven and pouring out libations to her, we have lacked everything and have been consumed by the sword and by

---

[67] Cf. Othmar Keel, *Feinde* (ch. 8 n. 39); Karel van den Toorn, *Dictionary* (ch. 7 n. 78); Erhard S. Gerstenberger, 'Sitten' (ch. 8 n. 25).

[68] The readiness often found among Christians in the ecumenical movement outside Germany to pay attention to popular belief, in principle first allowing it the right to exist (which is given with the existence of a group of believers), should make us think. The frontier between true and false belief does not run (particularly also according to Reformation views) along the traditional constitutional structure of the church, but right through the middle.

famine.' And the women said, 'When we burned incense to the queen of heaven and poured out libations to her, was it without our husbands' approval that we made cakes for her bearing her image and poured out libations for her?' (Jer 44:15–19).

Women, too, were active in the cult, but because of the male dominance which had come about in the cult of Israel they could only be active underground and contrary to the theology of the scribes.[69] In the pericope quoted they are mainly responsible for the worship, since the subject 'all men' (v. 15) is an insertion; the women are speaking independently and alone with the prophet (cf. v. 19). Their theological discourse is extensive and remarkably autonomous (vv. 16–19), and Jeremiah's answer is differentiated and remarkably restrained (vv. 20–30).[70]

As often in large societies, in Judah popular belief was officially either scorned or forbidden. We can hardly get to know it and judge it from the existing Hebrew writings. Above all, to dismiss it in a quite one-sided way as 'Canaanite' or 'idolatrous', etc. is impossible. Rather, as theologians we must also learn in particular from the 'popular belief' of ancient times and today in order to get to know people's real drives, fears and hopes and gain correctives to the intellectual approach of academic theology. Liberation theologians in Latin America can do this. They do not approach this religious subculture, which is indeed segregated from official religion, with the arrogant claim to have the sole truth for the academic sphere. They speak with people, take them seriously, and in their thought and speech encounter them as partners.[71] In connection with Old Testament popular religion we can only take up the hints contained in the canon and make them visibly present by analogies drawn from the ancient Near East and from modern anthropology and sociology. Here it becomes evident that, for example, the Mesopotamian manticism and art of conjuration, the Egyptian interpretation of dreams, the Hittite ritual taboos and certainly much that we

---

[69] E.g. Phyllis Bird, 'The Place of Women in the Israelite Cultus', in *Ancient Israelite Religion. FS Cross*, ed. Patrick D. Miller et al., Philadelphia 1987; Erhard S. Gerstenberger, *Yahweh the Patriarch* (ch. 2 n. 4), attempt to bring out the role of women in the cult. The recovery of women's theology is an urgent need for the whole church and for theology; cf. Elisabeth Gössmann et al. (eds), *Wörterbuch der feministischen Theologie*, Gütersloh 1991; Luise Schottroff et al. (eds), *Kompendium Feministische Bibelauslegung*, Gütersloh ²1999.

[70] Cf. Erhard S. Gerstenberger, *Yahweh the Patriarch* (ch. 2 n. 4); Renate Jost, *Frauen* (ch. 4 n. 81).

[71] Virtually no attention is paid to the relevant theological literature in Germany, and so virtually none of it has been translated into German. Cf. e.g. Carlos Mesters, *Sechs Tage in den Kellern der Menschheit*, Neukirchen-Vluyn 1982; B. Beni dos Santos et al. (eds), *A religião do povo*, São Paulo 1978; Carlos Rodrigues Brandão, *Os deuses do povo*, São Paulo 1980; id., *Memória do sagrado*, São Paulo 1985; Gustavo Gutiérrez, *We Drink from our own Wells*, Maryknoll and London 1984.

cannot demonstrate from the sources, had an effect on Israel or had always been practised there.[72] The official community theology in the early Jewish community certainly resolutely opposed anything 'alien' and allegedly idolatrous, but on the other hand it incorporated some popular practices and ideas into its own system. Thus e.g. Num 5:12–17 hands on a ritual involving cursed water which is to establish the infidelity of a wife. It could appear in a very similar form in any Babylonian incantation ceremony. Elisha raises a dead person by performing a magic rite (2 Kings 4:33–5). Psalm 91 contains formulae for warding off demons (cf. Ps 58:4–6; 59:7, 15, etc.). Or we might remember the sometimes incredibly archaic theological notions in the Priestly Writing: 'That is a burnt offering, a gift offering, a fragrant savour for Yahweh' (Lev 1:9, etc.). The direct feeding of the image of God, as attested in Egypt and elsewhere, is not presupposed. But by being burnt, this same food offering for the invisible God goes up in smoke and he can accept it with his sense of smell. The age-old taboo regulations about eating meat, sexual practices, striking skin diseases or mould on buildings or textiles, and the fear of deformed human beings and animals, which are certainly pre-Israelite, are quite incompatible with the strict belief in Yahweh inculcated by Deuteronomy or Deutero-Isaiah.[73] The tradition has also incorporated such magical miracle workers as Elisha and Elijah, who come from the popular milieu and with their healings, raisings of the dead and other miracles (the neutralization of poison; iron is made to float; a power of command over wild bears which tear forty-two children to pieces; authority over water and rain, etc.), do not belong in the category of the pure proclaimer of the word. That is good. All these traces indicate that the experts in scripture and theologians of that time, whose task it was to deal with the letters and collect the sacred tradition, had their feet on the ground. Seeing life as it is and accepting popular belief on a broad basis do not justify a fundamental exclusion of all popular theology.

[72] It is impossible to survey the literature on the theme from the ancient Near East. Cf. Werner R. Mayer, *Untersuchungen zur Formensprache der babylonischen Gebetsbeschwörungen*, Rome 1976; René Labat, *Traité akkadien de diagnostics et prognostics medicaux*, Paris 1951; A. Leo Oppenheim, *The Interpretation of Dreams in the Ancient Near East*, Philadelphia 1956; Walter Sommerfeld, *Traumdeutung* (unpublished manuscript); Erika Reiner, *Surpu: A Collection of Sumerian and Akkadian Incantations*, Archiv der Orientforschung, Beihefte 11, Graz 1958; Richard Caplice, 'Participants in the Namburbi Rituals', *CBQ* 29, 1967, 246–52; Erich Ebeling, *Aus dem Tagebuch eines assyrischen Zauberpriesters,* Osnabrück ²1972; *La Divination en Mesopotamie Ancienne. Referate vom Assyriologenkongress 1965*, Paris 1966. Stefan M. Maul, *Zukuftsbewältigung* (ch. 4 n. 25), is a particularly detailed and careful account of the nature of conjuration.

[73] Cf. Lev 11–15; 18; 20f., etc., and above all in Ezekiel. For the Leviticus passages; cf. Erhard S. Gerstenberger, *Leviticus* (ch. 4 n. 18). Little work has been done on popular belief in the underground of the Old Testament; cf. Oskar Loretz, *Vom kanaanäischen Totenkult zur jüdischen Patriarchen- und Elternehrung*, JARG 3, 1978 (appeared 1981), 149–204; Bernd Loretz, 'Bestattung und Totenkult im Alten Testament', *ZRGG* 42, 1990, 21–31.

The arrogance of the officials of a religious community was never based on fact, but rather always attests the effort of a particular group to defend its privileges, to keep the monopoly in the mediation of the divine presence and divine blessing. In short, the Old Testament scriptures reach into the depths of popular belief and from there derive their remarkable realism, which is striking even today.

8.6 The ethic of the Yahweh community

In the Old Testament, ethics are very important, and this importance extends down to our time.[74] There are hardly any fixed dogmas of the kind that we know from the history of Christianity. The early Jews were concerned more with orthopraxis than with orthodoxy. With a special kind of intensity they investigated, wrote down and discussed the rules of life which were to be valid in life before and with Yahweh. The Torah contains the authoritative collection of these norms, and since the canonization of the Torah Judaism has been solely concerned with the correct exegesis of the divine commandments from Sinai. That is easy to understand in the light of the beginning of the Jewish faith community in the sixth century BCE, when the communities formed in Palestine and the Diaspora. They had been robbed of the support of their own state and priestly sacrifice (the sacrificial practice of a wider community served as a means of binding the community together) and instead had to build up a cult of Yahweh without sacrifice and images; in the course of this new formation the question of the will of the one God who was responsible for Israel soon came to occupy a central place.

The ethical question which was put tenaciously and constantly was: what is the right life for the community of Yahweh? We should not fall into the common mistake of constantly investigating right and law in ancient Israel.[75] The false perspective which starts from the law (of the state) has

---

[74] However, there are relatively few general accounts of Old Testament ethics; cf. Johannes Hempel, *Das Ethos des Alten Testaments*, BZAW 67, Berlin 1938; Eckart Otto, *Ethik* (ch. 4 n. 96). There is a survey in Rudolf Smend, 'Ethik III', *TRE* 10, Berlin 1982, 423–35. Franz Segbers, *Die Hausordnung der Tora*, Luzern 1999, emphasizes the topicality of the Torah.

[75] Old Testament scholars often seem to be hypnotized by the legal dimension of the 'law texts'. Here they are unconsciously always thinking of formations of a state society. However, the early Jewish community was not a state but a faith community divided into parishes with many local characteristics and limited self-government and jurisdiction. Because of this, comparisons with the so-called legal corpora of the ancient Near East, like those of the imperial states of Mesopotamia, are possible only to a very limited degree. The legal standpoint predominates e.g. in Hans Jochim Boecker, *Recht und Gesetz im Alten Testament und im Alten Orient*, Neukirchen 1976; Frank Crüsemann, *Torah* (ch. 4 n. 108); Eckart Otto, *Ethik* (ch. 4 n. 96). Wolfgang Richter, *Recht und Ethos*, Munich 1966, and Erhard S. Gerstenberger, *Wesen*

also had bad theological consequences, since it does not bring out the liberating dimension of the ethical orientation.[76] But the question of the right way to live before Yahweh is a beneficial one because of the catechetical answers which are worked out from the tradition. The community needs the guideline of the Torah if it is to be able to identify itself, constitute itself and keep its head above water. The Torah is joy, life, redemption because it is the necessary strait-jacket for the Yahweh community.

How did the community get this strait-jacket? I have already remarked that the confession of the one God Yahweh and thus the demarcation from all other deities of the religiously pluralistic environment forms the indispensable foundation for the rules of life: 'Hear, Israel, Yahweh is our God, Yahweh alone' (Deut 6:4). The sense of belonging to this God is shown by participation in the Jewish assemblies and festivals, by observance of the sabbath and by the circumcision of male children. But the everyday rules are first given content from all the norms which have long applied in family, clan, village and local sanctuaries. When we investigate the origin of the rules for everyday and the sanctuary in the Old Testament, we are reminded of Paul's principle ('Test everything, hold fast to that which is good', 1 Thess 5:21). The 'catechisms' which are collected together in the Pentateuch[77] contain a mixture of ethical instructions and pieces of advice, threats and exclusions, which can only have come into being through a multiplicity of situations in life and social groups. Although the ethical orientation is put under the authority of Yahweh – compare Lev 19:2, 'You shall be holy, for I, Yahweh your God, am holy' – the individual precepts are very often completely neutral in religious terms and have been taken from the general norms of the societies of the ancient Near East.

We can roughly distinguish two large areas. This is a very old differentiation and one which at an early stage was used on the two 'tables

---

(ch. 4 n. 95), attempt to mediate between law and ethic from the ethical side; cf. id., '"Apodiktisches" – "Todesrecht"', in Peter Mommer et al. (eds), *Gottes Recht als Lebensraum*, Neukirchen-Vluyn 1993, 7–20.

[76] Frank Crüsemann has recognized that. He attempts by means of the Decalogue (why only there?) to formulate the ethic of liberation (*Die Bewahrung der Freiheit*, Munich 1983); Elga Sorge, *Religion und Frau*, Stuttgart, etc. 1985, also does that in her own way.

[77] In many collections the catechetical paraenetic tone seems to me to be so clear that the designation 'collection of laws' or 'law book' is inappropriate for the final redactional state. That applies above all to the Book of the Covenant in Ex 21–23 (thus also Ludger Schwienhorst-Schönberger, *Bundesbuch* [ch. 8 n. 15]). In the case of Deuteronomy, research has recognized more the parenetic (or homilectic) character (cf. Gerhard von Rad, *Deuteronomy*, OTL, London and Philadelphia 1966; Henning Graf Reventlow, *Gebot und Predigt im Dekalog*, Gütersloh 1962), whereas the so-called Holiness Code has been shifted more into the cultic sphere. However, this alleged 'legal corpus', too, is not such a thing, but consists of catechetical material for the community; cf. Erhard S. Gerstenberger, *Leviticus* (ch. 4 n. 18), 261ff.

of the law', or better, Torah tables – Ex 31:18; 32:19; 34:1. There are duties to God (the Holy One) and duties to fellow human beings in one's own community. No more than this is to be found in the Torah. There are no state laws and (in contrast to the wisdom literature) there are no international laws or human rights. In a community which claims to be confessing the one and universal God, that of course is a defect. But given the conditions, the limitation of ethics to one's own group is quite understandable in human and social terms; indeed it is necessary. No human being can give an ethic or religious orientation for other groups.

Dealing with the holy, in this specific instance with Yahweh the God of Israel, is addressed in the first half of the Decalogue.[78] The dominant features here are a command to be exclusive and a prohibition against depicting God. Both norms may once have had a completely identical significance: preventing people from turning away from the zealous or jealous God Yahweh. After the composition of the Decalogue, the second commandment took on the sense of preventing the depiction of Yahweh. In addition there is the prohibition against the misuse of the name and the sabbath commandments. That already exhausts the series of basic ethical rules specifically orientated on God, since while the fifth commandment, 'honour father and mother' (Ex 20:12), may still have in view the divine authority in upbringing mediated through the parents, and thus mention the parents as those commissioned by God, it already forms the transition to the social obligations of the so-called second table (see 4.4 above).

If we look at the norms orientated on God and keep in mind the situation of the early Jewish community, we cannot discover much that is special about these rules of life. They are not as unprecedented and unique as is often claimed. The misuse of the name is taboo throughout the ancient Near East, because people knew that black magic could be done with names. (At this point the commentaries usually refer to the fairy tale of Rumpelstiltskin.) The claim to exclusiveness by a god is latent in any relationship with God in antiquity, since every god has to care for his clientele, and any god or that god's mediator in the group sometimes attaches importance to being able to act without rivals.[79] The situation of conflict and demarcation in which the claim to exclusiveness is made always appears very clearly. Thus in Deut 4:

---

[78] For the Decalogue; cf. Frank-Lothar Hossfeldt, *Der Dekalog*, OBO 45, Göttingen 1982; Lothar Perlitt, 'Dekalog I', *TRE* 8, Berlin 1981, 408–13; Werner H. Schmidt, *Zehn Gebote* (ch. 2 n. 11).

[79] That follows from the debate on monotheism, which is apparently hesitant to drop the claims of all deities to sole representation or identifies them as claims of the priesthoods or groups of adherents concerned; cf. Bernhard Lang (ed.), *Der einzige Gott*, Munich 1981; Othmar Keel, *Monotheismus* (ch. 2 n. 21); Walter Dietrich and Martin Klopfenstein (eds), *Gott* (ch. 2 n. 21).

Yahweh will scatter you among the peoples and you will be left few in number among the nations where Yahweh will drive you. And there you will serve gods of wood and stone, the work of men's hands, that neither see, nor hear, nor eat, nor smell. But from there you will seek Yahweh your God, and you will find him, if you search after him with all your heart and with all your soul. When you are in tribulation, and all these things come upon you in the latter days, you will return to Yahweh your God and obey his voice, for Yahweh your God is a merciful God; he will not fail you or destroy you or forget the covenant with your fathers which he swore to them (Deut 4:27–31).

The situation of the exile is anticipated in retrospect. Israel is dispersed among the peoples and through exclusive loyalty to its ancestral God Yahweh has the possibility of giving a new foundation to its existence. The warnings against giving up this basis of survival permeate Deuteronomy and many other writings; cf. 1 Kings 18:37–9, the prayer of Elijah and its consequences:

'Answer me, Yahweh, answer me, that this people may know that you, Yahweh, are God, and that you have turned their hearts back.' Then the fire of Yahweh fell and consumed the burnt offering, and the wood, and the stones, and the dust, and licked up the water that was in the trench. And when all the people saw it, they fell on their faces; and they said, 'Yahweh, he is God; Yahweh, he is God.'

or, from the prophetic milieu of the exile:

But now hear, O Jacob my servant, Israel whom I have chosen. Thus says Yahweh who made you, who formed you from the womb and will help you: Fear not, O Jacob my servant, Jeshurun whom I have chosen. For I will pour water on the thirsty land and streams in the dry ground; I will pour my spirit upon your descendants, and my blessing on your offspring. They shall spring up like grass amid waters, like willows by flowing streams. This one will say, 'I am Yahweh's', another will call himself by the name of Jacob, and another will write on his hand, 'To Yahweh', and surname himself by the name Israel (Isa 44:1–5).

Thus says Yahweh, the king of Israel, and his redeemer, Yahweh Sabaoth: 'I am the first and I am the last; beside me there is no God. Who is like me? Let him proclaim it, let him declare and set it forth before me. Who has announced from of old the things to come? Let them tell us what is yet to be. Fear not, nor be afraid; have

I not told you from of old and declared it? And you are my witnesses! Is there a God beside me? There is no rock; I know not any' (Isa. 44:6–8).

These two controversy sayings are then followed in Isa 44:9–20 by a biting taunt song on the gods of the other peoples, which are as ineffective as the wood or metal from which their statues have been made.

All the demands for exclusiveness are purely pragmatic and relate to controversial theology. They reflect the vigorous argument between the exalted rulers of the world in Babylonia and the humiliated deportees who have to assert themselves in the face of the pride and the manifest contempt of the Babylonians. The demand of the Hebrew canon to the members of the community not to worship other gods is simply an appeal to remain true to their own tradition and identity. The sabbath commandment points in the same direction. It is meant to emphasize the uniqueness of the Jewish exile in a foreign land. Originally – though some scholars dispute this hypothesis – the sabbath goes back to a Babylonian day of the full moon (cf. the three earliest occurrences of 'sabbath + new moon' in Isa 1:13; Hos 2:13; Amos 8:5; are they really to be dated before the exile?), which within Israel was extended so that it became a taboo day occurring weekly (You shall do no work!) and was elaborated into a sign of Jewish faith.[80] So here too we cannot discover anything that is tremendously unique or merely Yahwistic. In fact all the demands in the first table of the Decalogue are quite compatible with the religious rules of the ancient Near East or analogous to them.[81] Nothing in the worship of Yahweh in ancient Israel and the early Jewish community falls out of the frame.

That is largely true of all the norms which follow Yahweh's claim to sole worship and which in detail regulate dealings with the sacred sphere and in the temple (cf. Lev 1 – 7; 11 – 15). At different levels, only full members of the community, ordinary priests and the high priests are admitted into the inner realm of the temple in which Yahweh himself dwells (i.e. the holy of holies, the temple and the forecourts). Those who visit the temple are to take precautionary measures and of course protect the deity (cf. as an

---

[80] Cf. Ernst Haag, *Vom Sabbath zum Sonntag. Eine bibeltheologische Studie*, TThSt Trier 1991; Abraham J. Heschel, *Sabbat*, Neukirchen-Vluyn 1990; Gnana Robinson, *The Origin and Development of the OT Sabbath*, Frankfurt am Main 1988.

[81] That even applies to the aniconic nature of Yahweh which is later interpreted into the second commandment, since aniconic worship of God is indicated, at least by many depictions in which the deity is thought of (not depicted) as standing on a pedestal, or also through symbols of God which evidently have the sense of avoiding an anthropomorphic depiction (cf. Othmar Keel and Christoph Uehliger, *Göttinnen* (ch. 4 n. 24), esp. 124ff.; 149ff.; Tryggve Mettinger, 'Aniconism – a West Semitic Context for the Israelite Phenomenon?', in Walter Dietrich and Martin Klopfenstein (eds), *Gott* (ch. 2 n. 21), 159–78.

example the annual ritual of atonement in the Holy of Holies, Lev 16:11–19). The regulations about food and uncleanness (Lev 11 – 15, etc.) extend far beyond the temple and priesthood; they concern the whole community. In these norms the concept of holiness is transferred to all members of the community (cf. Ex 19:5f.; Lev 19:2; Deut 7:6). They must not make themselves unclean, and they must preserve or restore the state of cultic perfection in their own bodies and in their dwellings with numerous precautionary measures or purification rituals. In the view of the professionals of the time, particular kinds of meat, sexual practices or bodily fluids, certain kinds of animals or moulds can damage the holiness of God. It is difficult to harmonize this notion with the saying at creation, 'Behold, it was very good' (Gen 1:31). So it looks as if information about whatever makes people unclean has come in from 'alien' theologies and views, or as if ancient traditions have been used which did not yet know of the one good creation of Yahweh. Be this as it may, in complete contradiction to the good creation, many animals are declared unclean, and contact with all the mass of lower worms and insects, what creeps and crawls on the earth and the sea, is forbidden in principle (Lev 11:41–5). Issues from the human body, especially from the sexual organs, and again specifically from the vagina (menstrual blood is so to speak hellishly dangerous!), fall under the same verdict (Lev 15). Primal taboos which are meant to prevent objects of two different genres being mixed are mentioned at other places:

> You shall not let your cattle breed with a different kind; you shall not sow your field with two kinds of seed; nor shall there come upon you a garment of cloth made of two kinds of stuff (Lev 19:19; cf. Deut 22:5, 9–11).

Manifestly, behind these prohibitions lies a great anxiety about anything like an uncontrolled mixing of substances.[82] This could spawn monstrosities from the underworld. We must imagine that for the people of antiquity nature was everywhere ensouled and animate. Things each had their own numen, and these numina might not be brought together by human hands contrary to their will. Such a mixture would inevitably have unforeseeable consequences, because the particular numina would both in a way lose their permanence, be thrown upon each other, and therefore could only react maliciously against the invader, possibly also taking vengeance on the person responsible. The violation of a divine being's home or sphere of influence was always a most dangerous affair for human beings. At these

---

[82] Cf. Mary Douglas, *Purity and Danger*, London 1966.

points of reverence for the holy in all its manifestations, no difference can be found between Israel and the surrounding peoples, even if some over-zealous scribes claimed at the time that their neighbours were sexually perverse and morally reprehensible, as in the story of Sodom and Gomorrah (Gen 19) or in the (later) introduction to the ancient catalogue of sexual taboos within the wider family (Lev 18:1–5, 24–9).[83] Given the state of our knowledge today we can say with some certainty that accusations of this kind against neighbouring groups or peoples always serve to express one's own self-imposed limits and one's own natural sense of superiority. Such external repudiations have nothing at all to do with the cultic or moral standards of neighbours. Psychologically they are more projections of what a people or group wants to reject as contemptible and thus imposes on the 'other'. That applies to all the derogatory verdicts of the Old Testament on the primal Canaanite population and the particular neighbouring peoples of the time.

The other great sphere of ethical norms is made up of the social obligations which now no longer applied to the family association, the clan or the village as such, but to the faith community. This of course remained organized in the existing small groups and community structures. Here brotherly (or sisterly) solidarity is the supreme commandment. 'You shall love your neighbour as yourself, I am Yahweh' (Lev 19:18). The main term for 'neighbour' is *rēaʿ*, originally fellow-member of the tribe and now fellow-believer or brother in the community. Like the commandment to love Yahweh (Deut 6:5: 'You shall love Yahweh, your God, with all your heart and all your soul and all your strength'), the commandment to love applies to the Yahweh-worshipper as the chief social commandment. Those who love Yahweh must also love others who, like them, are faithful to the God of Israel. The family concept – Yahweh the father of all believers – is at least in part a plausible metaphor ('You are our father', Isa 63:16; 64:7). Thus the two tables of the law are linked together. The content of this fundamental social norm, the way in which it is spelt out in everyday life in specific rules for behaviour, again takes place, with all that has already seemed right and good to the community. All the conventions which are largely also known from neighbouring cultures come into play: the threefold prohibition of killing, adultery and stealing (cf. Deut 5.17–19); the task of making just judgments at law (cf. Ex 23:1–9); the admonition to be honest in trading and exchanging goods (Deut 25:13–16); and above all the numerous precepts not to oppress or to exploit the poor and marginal groups (cf. Lev 19:9–16, etc.).

---

[83]   Erhard S. Gerstenberger, 'Sitten' (ch. 8 n. 25).

It is precisely this last feature which causes amazement. How is it that such a strong social feature comes into play in a secondary organization with a religious foundation? The situation of exile can itself explain a great deal. In the defeat and the exile, perhaps people came more closely together than within a secure state. The social development of the late monarchy and the exilic and post-exilic period was burdened with so many difficulties and social deteriorations that to a great degree Israel became impoverished (cf. e.g. Neh 5). The economic and social situation and the adoption of old traditions from family and clan which in fact made inter-personal solidarity in the kinship group the supreme value, combined with theological considerations, led to the development of an especially strong sense of community. The wider community circle of 'social kinship' is largely structured in norms of blood relationship. Talk of 'neighbour' coincides with the awareness of having to support one's 'brother' by blood when he is in need. The old family ethic was replaced by the new community ethic, by which even now Christian 'brotherhood' and 'sisterhood' lives.[84] The significance of the 'neighbour' or the 'other' is extremely great in the community ethos of early Judaism, so that on the basis of the Hebrew traditions one can rightly speak of an 'ethic of the other'[85] or assign the neighbour a central place in the Hebrew view of human beings and the world.[86]

Now in social ethics the norms of neutral civil laws, which serve in court to compensate for damages of all kinds (violation of the body, crimes against property, transgression of sexual norms, etc.), also stand within the framework of belief in Yahweh. However, we have no precise knowledge of how the early Jewish judicial system worked.[87] It was probably modelled on the pattern of the old judgment in the gate and had limited competence. The civil law contained in the Book of the Covenant is still least transformed into paraenesis and catechetical threat (cf. Ex 21:2 – 22:16, and in it more archaic formulations in Ex 21:15–17). It in fact largely corres-ponds with ancient Near Eastern law (cf. Ex 21:18 – 22:16). But Deuteronomy and the 'Holiness Code' have been heavily revised in the direction of catechesis. In these larger collections we get the impression that earlier legal material, too, still serves to dramatize situations of conflict and their solutions and to serve as admonition. One only has to compare the two 'legal' definitions of responsibility for the property of one's fellow human being:

---

[84] Cf. Max Weber, *Ancient Judaism* (ch. 6 n. 43); Christa Schäfer-Lichtenberger, *Stadt* (ch. 5 n. 13).

[85] Emmanuel Levinas, *La trace de l'autre* (ch. 8 n. 52); id., *Time and the Other*, Pittsburgh 1987.

[86] Cf. Martin Buber, *I and Thou*, Edinburgh 1958.

[87] Cf. Herbet Niehr, *Rechtsprechung in Israel*, Stuttgart 1987; Eckart Otto, *Ethik* (ch. 4 n. 96).

You shall not see your brother's ox or his sheep go astray, and withhold your help from them; you shall take them back to your brother. And if he is not near you, or if you do not know him, you shall bring it home to your house, and it shall be with you until your brother seeks it; then you shall restore it to him. And you shall do so with his ass; so you shall do with his garment; so you shall do with any lost thing of your brother's, which he loses and you find; you may not withhold your help.

You shall not see your brother's ass or his ox fallen down by the way, and withhold your help from them; you shall help him to lift them up again (Deut 22:1–4).

That is the purest, most unselfish ethic which is at the service of the community (cf. also the pastoral regulations about taking a pledge, Deut 24:6–13). However, as Max Weber notes,[88] its focus is purely inward, on one's own brotherhood. The form of address is direct; it woos and admonishes and appeals for 'brotherly feelings'. It is didactic and is meant to shape the community. Contrast the very sober, anonymous regulation about deposits in the old material in the Book of the Covenant, which is concerned with making good damage:

If a man delivers to his neighbour money or goods to keep, and it is stolen out of the man's house, then, if the thief is found, he shall pay double. If the thief is not found, the owner of the house shall come near to God, to show whether or not he has put his hand to his neighbour's goods (Ex 22:6; the matter is then taken further by discussing other modes of alienation and carelessness with the property of others, Ex 22:8–10).

Here a pure legal mind is now at work. The case is defined as clearly as possible; the matter, not the person, is in the foreground; and the legal consequences must be clear and aimed at recompense; in criminal transgressions the appropriate penalty (e.g. 'pay double') must be imposed. In unclear cases God is the ultimate arbiter – through a divine judgment which unmasks the guilty. The normal form of address in admonitions concerned with social ethics is urgent and personal. It allows us to infer a cultic *Sitz im Leben*, i.e. paraenetic addresses in worship in the exilic and post-exilic period. The old legal materials of the pre-exilic civil community

---

[88] Max Weber, *Ancient Judaism* (ch. 6 n. 43), speaks of an internal ethic which marks out the outsiders as the 'aliens'; cf. Deut 23:19f.: 'You shall not lend upon interest to your brother, interest on money, interest on victuals, interest on anything that is lent for interest. To a foreigner you may lend upon interest, but to your brother you shall not lend upon interest; that the Lord your God may bless you in all that you undertake in the land which you are entering to take possession of it.'

begin to be fused together into this sermonic admonishing of the community in the Book of the Covenant and are fully fused together in Deuteronomy and also in the book of Leviticus.

The first horizon of the communities of Judah was their life and survival in a world empire of many peoples. All reflections and practices involving faith and ethics served this immediate aim. The second and third horizons were their own ecumenical community under the one God Yahweh and the 'ends of the earth', which were claimed by the great political powers. Theologians of the early Jewish 'church' recognized the significance of the universal political and economic powers of their time. With amazing courage they asserted the universal rule of Yahweh over all peoples and all history, even contrary to what seemed immediately evident. In part they opposed the attack of the real world powers, not least by means of apocalyptic visions of the emptiness of political claims to rule (cf. Dan 2; 7). They did not develop ethical concepts of responsible action in the over-arching formations of society beyond their own little province and their settlements in a foreign land. They confidently left this work to subsequent generations, which would possibly one day take over political responsibility in wider societies.

8.7 What remains?

The theology and ethics, cult and morality, of the early Jewish community have proved extraordinarily effective. Through the canonical Hebrew writings many of the decisions and views of the time have made their way into Western culture and the church. Of course the whole heritage of the Old Testament has been revised, expanded and remodelled by the New Testament and Christianity, but frequently we can still discover basic features of the old precepts. One God, one world – there is no alternative to thinking and feeling in these categories. Cultic customs, rules, ethical values, views of the world order, personhood, society and many other things are prefigured in the Hebrew writings of the sixth to fourth centuries BCE. Seen from this perspective – as I have already remarked at other points – critical discussion of the old testimonies and what they have brought about in us through long tradition and interpretation is urgently necessary.

At the same time we have to realize that our present situations are basically different from all that our spiritual ancestors in the early Jewish community could experience. We need to reflect on these differences and make them fruitful for a theology and ethics with a responsibility of its own which can arise from dialogue with the ancient sources. Some essential differences in our world are: the abandonment of geocentricity in our view of the world (we are floating on an infinitely tiny planet on the periphery of a Milky

Way system and are not the centre of the universe); the alteration in the position of human beings *vis-à-vis* nature (we can no longer pretend that we are absolute rulers of the world with 'everything under our feet', i.e. there at our disposal); the modern definition of the roles of the sexes and the emancipation of the individual from society (patriarchalism is antiquated; new roles have to be defined on an equal basis; human dignity is unassailable and the supreme value in social ethics); the nations, groups, societies and continents of the earth have equal rights (there is no ruling race, nation, religion, etc.; which also means that resources must be divided equally over a range from the first to the fourth worlds), and so on. In the light of the changed presuppositions and conditions in life, of course theology and ethics have to be rediscovered in and for this world society, but they must take into account the sub-divisions down to the individual (or better, from below upwards). All that is said by the Old (and New) Testament is up for debate. There are no timeless statements of precepts of faith. Even the deepest insight in the Old Testament, 'There is only one God, and no others', is debatable as a statement of faith. We must know what this statement really means; we must understand it in terms of its genesis and original intention and ask whether it still corresponds to our faith. I personally think that monistic faith cannot be abandoned, because it is the best explanation of the present state of the world. Any dualism is pernicious because we cannot endure polarizations of the world (body – spirit; friend – foe; good – evil, etc.). The world is one and 'in need of redemption', but it is not corrupt beyond salvation. The patriarchalism, matriarchalism and monarchianism of the old world are outmoded and are unusable as models for our world. Human claims to domination are totally outmoded because they will cause catastrophe for our planet. Technology and science today show human beings their own limits, which they must learn to observe if they are not to perish. We must make a beginning by discussing a selection of these fundamental questions.

9

Polytheism, Syncretism and the One God

I must attempt to bring together my remarks about the many levels of testimony in the Old Testament. Here we can in no circumstances expect a unitary theology of the kind that would correspond to our ideas, namely a coherent thought structure about the being and action of God and God's claim on human beings. Any attempt of this kind to penetrate to the very being of God and so to speak explain the world from God's perspective, i.e. from the position of looking over the shoulders of the 'deity' and speaking as God's spokesmen and spokeswomen, is a priori doomed to failure. The visionaries of the ancient Near East who felt themselves transported to the presence of God and from there, like shamans, brought messages (cf. Micaiah ben Imlah, 1 Kings 22:19, 'I saw Yahweh sitting on his throne'; Amos 9:1, 'I saw Yahweh standing over the altar'), penetrated to the Most High in a rapture, a state of trance, or a dream. They too did not dare to describe God's being, but they brought specific messages from the divine sphere. No modern theologian makes comparable claims to have had a personal vision of God (perhaps that is a mistake?). All present-day talk of God is based on ancient texts, not on the experience of the presence of God. Thus also because of this self-imposed limitation, theology cannot be done from a transcendent sphere but only from belief, from the perspective of those concerned; consequently it is necessarily limited and conditioned truth. The phases of the history of faith and the different social formations in which the history of faith has run its course have convinced me that we must always and everywhere start from very different images of God. These are incompatible; each of them has its own justification, and we need to evaluate and investigate them separately.

9.1 Conceptual clarifications

A clarification of the main terms in this fundamental debate about the understanding of God is urgently necessary. For by 'polytheism' ordinary people probably understand an 'evil pagan' world in which a diversity of deities wait to be worshipped depending on whim and occasion. People commonly think of a divine brothel in which each may satisfy his desires. 'Syncretism' is imagined as a chemical laboratory in which the different religious ingredients have been boiled together into a poisonous brew and poured into unsuspecting victims. Visions of horrors have penetrated the human consciousness from the centuries of crude and very unimaginative polemic against all those deviating from the true dogma. In reality it is all quite different. The dispute over the one God takes place first at the level of practical life and the lived worship of God, not in theory. In the Old Testament almost everywhere the one God is the God who, according to the insight of the exilic/post-exilic theologians, has power and responsibility for Israel (cf. Deut 32:8). And people turn to him solely to safeguard their own identity. The central passage for Israel, Deut 6:4-6, shows that clearly. I shall quote it once again:

> Hear, O Israel: Yahweh is our God, Yahweh is one. And you shall love Yahweh your God with all your heart, and with all your soul, and with all your might. And these words which I command you shall be upon your heart . . .

Israel may concentrate on its God, who has made his will known – that is a commandment for self-preservation. It concerns the existence of the community of faith, not the existence of God. The exclusiveness of the worship of Yahweh asserted here is important in this moment of the Babylonian captivity and in the overwhelmingly powerful world of the gods of the rulers. We can also say that in certain situations everything depends on a community holding firm to a recognized goal, a decision that has been made, an important feature of life. Here there is no consideration of alternatives; the status of the confession must be preserved if one is not to be lost and the world is not to perish. There was such a situation in the Third Reich. There too we can lament that the laudable resistance against state religion and the establishing of a firm position were predominantly self-centred, largely leaving out the 'others' who needed to be protected, i.e. without complete identification with them and their needs. But that is the human/all-too-human situation in which we find ourselves time and again. Situations which call for a confession to be made are repeated time and again, and acts of resistance against murderous contemptuous power are then called for, even if in human terms they are inadequate. In such situations, too, mechanisms of exclusion are put in place, emphasis on the one thing that cannot be given up, which makes other possibilities impossible. That is the right application of the principle of exclusiveness; compare the 1934 Barmen Declaration: 'We condemn the false teaching . . .' or the excommunication by the Catholic bishop Dom Pedro Casaldaliga of the landowners in Mato Grosso who kept slaves.

Now if, as in Deutero-Isaiah, God's exclusiveness is heightened to the degree of becoming a uniqueness which is also asserted in the theoretical realm, in doctrine, the situation is still the same. In the context the quest for the possible ways in which the people of Yahweh can live can be recognized as a driving force:

> Turn to me and be saved, all the ends of the earth! For I am God, and there is no other. By myself I have sworn, from my mouth has gone forth in righteousness a word that shall not return: 'To me every knee shall bow, every tongue shall swear. Only in Yahweh, it shall be said of me, are righteousness and strength; to him shall come and be ashamed all who were incensed against him. In Yahweh all the offering of Israel shall triumph and glory' (Isa 45:22–25).

Thus fundamentally the whole monotheism of the early Jewish community is a great, impressively presented, monolatry which arose in a situation of confession and at a few points is theoretically supported by statements of uniqueness verging on an ontology. The oneness of Yahweh remains an appendix to the strict demand to hold firm in practice only to the one God, the God of Israel, for the sake of the existence of the community, i.e. to recognize his Torah as binding. At this point, with reference to the history which has taken place since Deut 6 and Deutero–Isaiah, we can add that so far no faith community and no academic theologian has succeeded in grasping the one, only exclusive God and realizing the consequences of this insight in life. Even the strongest advocates of theoretical monotheism necessarily recognize other forces than those of God in this world; they reckon with them and can neither calculate nor add up how the multiplicity of manifestations of power can be reconciled with the rule of the one God. We are and remain born polytheists, regardless of how much lip-service we pay to the one God. The history of the wars of the Christian nations of the West, the everyday experience of each individual, the doctrinal controversies in Christian church history, offer sufficient evidence for this assertion. The stratified structure of faith in the Old Testament period illustrates the notions and expectations, built up on different social interests, that we must take into account.

In more peaceful times, when its existence was less threatened, as we saw, the people of Israel presented quite a colourful religious spectrum in regions and places, family associations and prophetic communities. Are we to call it 'polytheistic'? That is possible. But in that case we must think in terms of a fixed, homogeneous religious community (the state?) which tolerates other cults alongside itself or even admits several deities to one and the same sanctuary. In reality there was no such uniform society in Israel. The functions of religious experience were distributed between different corporations and their members. But such different divine functions were also performed and celebrated in a single cult. Even if different names for God came to be used, this cannot really be called polytheism. Conversely, the theological claim that different activities, manifestations and effects derive from one God is not automatically to be regarded as monotheism. For the postulated unity of God is at most an intellectual construct. We cannot test whether the effects of God which we can recognize in our world of experience really lead up to a transcendent point of intersection. The claim that God is one makes sense as a way of interpreting our world, which is a unity, and which we do not want to hand over to the polarizing forces of two or more primal grounds. Dualistic systems do precisely that: they maintain the polarity and fundamental division of the world and the ultimate annihilation of the 'evil' or 'dark' part. Almost all the religions of the ancient Near East before the Persian period, including the 'polytheistic' ones, oppose this. A consistent monism prevails in the Old Testament (and in its Semitic environment) which admits dualism only at a late stage, in eschatology and apocalyptic. Here perhaps lies the decisive theological quest: we do not have to choose between Israel and Canaan – both cultural systems were built on the same foundation. What is more difficult is grappling with the dualism which came from Persia, and became partially established in Hellenism and in Gnostic Christianity.[1] But dualistic thought may not simply be represented as a product of hell. It is another attempt to approach the unconditional, though by giving up part of the world.

9.2 Changes: the accumulation and interdependence of images of God

If we look back at the history of Israelite religion from the beginnings in the twelfth to tenth centuries to the consolidation of the Yahweh community

---

[1] Hans Jonas has rightly recognized this basic religious question and made it the subject of an important investigation, *Gnosis und spätantiker Geist*, Göttingen 1934ff. E.g. Walter Dietrich, *Israel* (ch. 7 n. 28); Moshe Weinfeld, *Justice* (ch. 8 n. 39), and many others, argue for the opposition of two social systems in the environment of Israel.

in the Persian period and attempt to understand the changing theologies, we will inevitably get the impression that Yahweh (for once apart from the other deities known in the Old Testament) fundamentally changed, or better that the ideas of God in individual epochs and groups have to a great degree converged syncretistically and have also been driven apart syncretistically. Werner H. Schmidt has recognized that quite correctly.[2] There is no characteristic from the known religions of the environment which did not accrue to Yahweh. Or better, taking into account our principle of not wanting to argue deductively from the side of God, time and again there are only the opportunities of the particular time and the intellectual and linguistic means and models which are available from the situation and the environment. Our own tradition and experience is available, but it is already linked a thousandfold with the experiences and insights of all our neighbours, from whom we cannot completely shut ourselves off, even in the most acute case. The complete isolation of human groups from other hominids is an extreme exception – at least in the historical period – and therefore preoccupies the Robinson Crusoe fantasy of the literati. Moreover through communication with neighbours even the most recent religious currents always arrive at a given part of the population, though relatively limited. When, for example, the Indians from the tribe of the Desana (in the region of the Rio Negro) introduce into their creation story the white man with his flints alongside the priest with a book,[3] this is the indication of an actual momentous syncretism. For at some point in the twentieth century CE the world of the Desana came to include the whites, who wanted to rule others with force of arms. The unbelieving understanding of the Indians for the white mentality represents a syncretistic invasion of their own picture of the world.[4] Thus the existence of the invaders also has to be explained in the creation myth. Similarly, when the Zulu magician Madela retells the creation story of his tribe in a creative way he has to refer to the present changed circumstances of life, including white colonization.[5] Similar examples of rewriting and adaptation to new

---

[2] Werner H. Schmidt, *The Faith of the Old Testament*, Oxford 1983.

[3] Umúsin Panlon Kumu and Tolaman Kenhíri, *Antes o mundo não existia,* São Paulo 1980, 74, 213.

[4] In the Indian myth, the creator says to the seventh creature to leave the underworld: 'You are the last. I have given everything that I had to the first creatures. Now because you are the last, you must be a being without fear. You must be able to wage war in order to take their riches away from others. Then you will make money' (Umúsin Panlon Kumu and Tolaman Kenhíri, *Mundo* [ch. 9 n. 3], 74).

[5] Katesa Schlosser, *Die Bantubibel des Blitzzauberers Laduma Madela. Schöpfungsgeschichte der Zulu,* Kiel 1977; cf. e.g. 231–5: 'Has Matela created Sibi [the counterpart of Mvelinqangi] in parallel to Satan?,' under the chapter heading 'The Destruction of Mvelinqangi's Creation by his Brother Sibi'. The question is answered with a cautious affirmative (ibid., 235).

facts can be found in the Hebrew scriptures. When in Israel the question arose whether Yahweh was also responsible for growth and flourishing – in addition to warlike occasions – this theological problem was posed by a new agricultural way of life, but secondly also by an existing confrontation between Yahweh the god of the tribe and Baal the god of vegetation. We do not know precisely when both conditions were fulfilled; at any rate an important passage from Hosea seems to depict a later state of revision. (Lady) Jerusalem is presumably being addressed:

> Upon her children also I will have no pity, because they are children of harlotry. For their mother has played the harlot; she that conceived them has acted shamefully. For she said, 'I will go after my lovers, who give me my bread and my water, my wool and my flax, my oil and my drink.' Therefore I will hedge up her way with thorns, and I will build a wall against her, so that she cannot find her paths. She shall pursue her lovers, but not overtake them; and she shall seek them, but shall not find them. Then she shall say, 'I will go and return to my first husband, for it was better with me then than now.' For she did not know that it was I who gave her the grain, the wine, and the oil, and who lavished upon her silver and gold which they used for Baal (Hos 2:6-10).

So at least theoretically the text plays through the situation assumed – Israel has now settled in cultivated land – and asserts that Yahweh has a new responsibility for agriculture and fertility.[6] On this frontier between semi-nomadism and a sedentary life, if it ever really existed, an extraordinary great amount of syncretistic work was necessary to shape belief in God from and for the necessities of peasant and village life.

That applies equally to the transition from tribal religion to state religion. The new social structures which have been described (centralism; a system of taxation; imperial military service, etc.) call for new definitions of the image of God which are expressed most clearly in the use of court titles and court etiquette for the religious sphere. 'King', 'King of all Kings', 'Most High', etc. are designations of the monarch which were adopted in Israel (and above all in Jerusalem) in a necessary and completely legitimate way. But with them the earlier faith founded on a society which was not a state changed. It has to be said that in the time of the monarchy a new faith developed from the 'syncretisms' of the new social structures which was composed from tradition with the old name Yahweh; that is perhaps the only authentic, deliberately syncretistic

---

[6] That is the current interpretation; cf. Hans Walter Wolff, *Hosea,* Hermeneia Philadelphia, 1974; Wilhelm Rudolph, *Hosea,* KAT 13.1, Gütersloh 1966.

feature. So here I would prefer to begin from the human perspective and say that in the new circumstances, in the time of the monarchy in Israel, as a result of syncretism, a new type of religion came into being, primarily on the level of the state or the official level. The new ideas about God then certainly also made themselves felt in the traditional family and local cults. Therefore the term syncretism is not quite suitable for describing the phenomenon. It presupposes the attachment of some new features from outside to what is good, long known and homogeneous. Only with many qualifications is that the case. It is more important and more accurate to imagine creative processes at many levels on the basis of changing structures, goals and values. Every group and society works at shaping its faith and image of God with the traditions which come from the past (and therefore often also from different, outdated conditions), with influences from outside, and with the urgent questions and demands of the time and the particular interests of the group.

However, it is always the case that the last point, the challenge of the present, is least perceived in the conception of the substance of faith. People think that the prefabricated elements of the images of God can break completely with the past and be brought into our present. And that is an illusion. In reality, for example in the present day, however evangelical and true to the Bible one may be, one always gains the substance of an understanding of God from one's own present, from one's own environment or in deliberate segregation from it. What is present and seems important in the traditional material is fused with modern requirements, not vice versa. However, to reassure themselves – and here there is always also an element of self-deception – people want to present their theology and ethic as 'old', 'well-tried' and 'objective'; not as produced by themselves, but with the label 'revealed'. The longing for a fixed, irrevocable ground of faith drives us far into the remote past, where we want to give our own constructs of God safe anchorage. But in seeking to be responsible to the God of the present or the ground of being, it is our task to try to engage in constant, corrective dialogue with the old witnesses; we must look for the new form and formulation of faith which is valid today, appropriate to present conditions and human groupings, and 'right' for them.

A third example of a revolution in Old Testament belief in God is the rise of exclusive worship of Yahweh after the deportations at the beginning of the sixth century BCE. The new version of religion in Judaea and among the exiles in Babylon produced the holy scriptures and left a deep mark on them. This whole chapter has been about this reshaping which accompanies the reconstruction of the community of faith and so we need not go into details here.

9.3 Tensions between the theologies of ancient Israel

It should be said once again that because every situation and every human social grouping is mainly responsible for its faith, and because no human formation is completely homogeneous, but always carries around within itself its own internal contradictions, the statements of faith made in a particular era are contradictory, and each has to be taken seriously on its own terms. The question of true or false faith or images of God does not arise from assertions aimed at self-preservation along the lines of 'We are right and the others wrong.' Such claims to exclusiveness are usually coupled with the ideologies of power and rule and are therefore in themselves deserving of criticism. Those who claim to want to determine the true faith universally for all peoples of all times must arouse suspicion, because it is a basic human insight that our discourse is always limited and conditioned and cannot be universal. That also applies to central terms like 'God'. The mere history of the designations of God in the Old and New Testaments, not to mention further religious writings of humankind, shows with an unavoidable clarity how changeable and transitory the statements of faith are.[7] The transition from the personal name 'Yahweh' to the general Hellenistic term 'Kyrios', to the German 'Herr', the English 'Lord', the French 'Seigneur' and the Christian 'God Christ' is a striking demonstration of how attitudes of faith are conditioned by time and culture. Each term has to be investigated and understood in its own context, with the tensions and contradictions prevailing there. Then of course we have to raise the question of truth, which we do according to mixed criteria. Some criteria have to be developed from the time of the documents, as far as that is possible. We can and may ask whether the articulated theological statements of the situation of the time were appropriate to the knowledge and state of the problem. The other criteria derive from our own surroundings and the theological (political, social, etc.) questions and values of our time. They put the theology of the witnesses of the time to the test in terms of our day. And that opens up the theological discussion beyond times and cultural spheres.

In all societies, attitudes of faith and cultic practices exist quite peacefully side by side on different social levels, often even within the same organization. Thus despite some ostracism from the side of 'official' religion, family faith has never completely died out in the Jewish–Christian tradition. But in the Old Testament writings there are also signs of conflicts between

---

[7] Even such different studies as Tryggve N. D. Mettinger, *Search* (ch. 6 n. 70), and Mark S. Smith, *History* (ch. 6 n. 93), really prove only the same thing: there are no 'everlasting names'.

the currents of faith on a social basis. From a historical perspective, the family patriarchal religion is supplemented by local and tribal cults. The interests of the different groupings cannot always be harmonized (cf. Judg 6, Gideon). That becomes even clearer when the monarchy overlays and modifies all other formations of society (cf. Judg 9, Jotham). There will have been resistance from the tribal religions here and there. The more resolutely a social group or stratum puts forward its faith and claims to power, the more there is an internal clash over the toleration of parallel cults. That is the case in an extreme way in the exilic/post-exilic community. Under the pressure of conditions the community leaders (with the assent of the members?) decree the absolute incompatibility of any alien cult with Yahweh worship. Religious intolerance is born – as a means of self-assertion in a minority situation which seems hopeless. Down to the present day it has unleashed orgies of persecution and extermination from the side of the dominant majority and state religions, time and again, and with explicit reference to the religious sources of antiquity.

10

Effects and Controversies

We urgently need to reflect critically on our Old Testament heritage. If we fail to do so, we can only arrive at very curtailed statements of faith in our time. Those who preserved the Jewish and Christian traditions did well to take with them the baggage of the faith of millennia. In its unwieldiness and many-sidedness it is pre-eminently suitable for offering resistance to an I-faith, a solipsism which is related only to the present. If we are to be able to engage in dialogue with the old witnesses we must (a) get to know in broad outline the characteristics of our time and their demands on theological thought and construction and (b) relate the basic concepts of the Hebrew scriptures from the different social situations to these definitions in the present. Over the ages, what seem to be the urgent questions of the oneness and sameness of God dissolve into the quest for a functionally responsible image of God for our globalized world of the third millennium CE.

10.1 Christian perspectives?

The question of the Christian exegesis of the Old Testament is often pushed into the foreground out of a concern for self-preservation. In my view the problem is not very urgent: the Christian element in reading and under-standing the Hebrew scriptures lies in our tradition and not in the Old Testament texts. The first Christian communities took over the Jewish scriptures as testimonies to Jesus Christ, rightly recognizing that Jesus was a Jew. With the increasing distancing from Judaism and the formation of independent Hellenistic–Roman theologies, the interpretative distance from Jewish exegesis constantly increased. Today we live on the foundations of the Hebrew Bible, but with all kinds of superstructures and constructs from the Graeco-Roman world. That is how our Christian or post-Christian starting point has to be described. And it is from this standpoint that we approach the Hebrew theologies of the Old Testament. So we do not need first to incorporate a Christian filter into our reading of the Old Testament. It is already there in ourselves and in our tradition, in our perception and interpretation. Conversely, that means that the Hebrew scriptures also need our Christian or post-Christian positions as a corrective. Or, the Christian confessional basis of the New Testament in principle has the same dignity as the confessions of the Old Testament, with the difference that we Western Europeans stand in a more direct line of descent from the Greeks and Romans than from the cultures of the ancient Near East. Probably such regional involvements and ties are significant and important. However, Christians in the Middle East, of Syrian or Arabic descent, have different cultural parameters from ours. African, Asian or American Christians in turn have to take note of their cultural background.

At all events the Hebrew scriptures help us to understand the Jew Jesus, who among other things gave the impetus to our Western religion. For that reason alone they are indispensable for Christian existence. As I have already indicated often, through the continuous interpretation of the Old Testament in church history we also bear considerable parts of the Jewish tradition within us. They need constantly to be examined and corrected, and we urgently need the Jewish scriptures for this. For without the Old Testament the New Testament would be a torso which simply lacked essential elements of theology and ethics.

10.2 The ecumenicity of our theology

Today theology must focus globally on the whole of humankind and the whole planet earth without neglecting the subdivisions of the continents, cultural regions and social formations, extending to the family and individuals. That is a tremendous task which seems almost impossible. This time we begin 'from above'. The globality of existence is beyond question. All life and the whole of nature are incorporated into the network of human interdependencies. We know that indirectly when we make purchases in a supermarket and reflect on our economic interconnections. We see it every day in fragmentary fashion and superficially in the news broadcasts which bring us centres of conflict from around the globe. A deeper analysis would show us further unsuspected dimensions of the close links and mutual (often completely one-sided) dependence.[1] This global existence of creation (but

---

[1] Like burnt children, analysts in the Third World often perceive the demonic nature of this entangling of the world; cf. Hugo Assmann et al., *Die Götzen der Unterdrückung und der befreiende Gott,* Münster 1984; Hugo Assmann and Franz Hinkelammert, *Götze Markt,* Düsseldorf 1992; Jung Mo Sung, *Desejo, mercado e religião,* Petrópolis 1998.

for the moment limited to our solar system: I do not want to go too far and arrogantly introduce the other solar systems and galaxies)[2] is certainly glimpsed in the Hebrew scriptures, but today it has become a reality and a danger to a high degree. If it is impossible to think in terms of one world and to realize it in a form which is more conducive to human dignity and preserves nature, all efforts over human beings, the world and God are in vain. In this fact, from our present perspective, lies the justification of speaking of the one and only God: the one world stands under a destiny which is common to all beings, everything that exists.

But that certainly does not mean that the whole scale of smaller human associations must dance to the tune of global authorities (the United Nations, etc.). The hierarchical explanation of the world no longer applies, with all the theological consequences. Every human organization has its own right to exist, and that must be fought for – without warlike violence – and preserved. Such struggles between subordinate and superior entities are in process all over our planet. The strata, groups and interests are extraordinarily complex, indeed contradictory and antagonistic. Therefore compromises are necessary if we are to arrive at tolerable conditions. Insight into the nature of the other individual and the other group is the indispensable basis here. *De facto*, every stratum and group on this globe has its own deities. They represent its right to exist. According to our existing constitutions any discrimination against any group on religious grounds is forbidden. That does not exclude verdicts on what faiths are true and what false, what kind of community it is permissible to form and what not, since the laws of society must also be applied to religious communities. Slavery, rape, the exploitation of human beings, possibly even extending to the order to commit mass suicide,[3] are intolerable. But religious faith which does no one any harm must be protected and respected, even in all controversial discussions. In principle all confessions and religions have to listen to one another. They cannot go on vilifying one another. The modern situation in which all of humankind forms a single whole which can only either go on existing together or must perish together not only inspires the 'one world shops' but also compels the development of a world awareness and a world politics of justice, peace and the preservation of creation.

---

[2] The universe can be the background to boundless astonishment; cf. e.g. Ernesto Cardenal's poems *Psalm 19* or *Canto geral*. But it is no longer the playground for human self-assertion; cf. already Joseph Sittler, *The Ecology of Faith*, Philadelphia 1961.

[3] Cases of collective suicide have attracted world-wide attention in recent decades: the settings have been British Guyana, Switzerland, Texas, California, etc. They are probably a sign of an increasing loss of orientation and frustration in large societies.

10.3 The autonomous human being

Individuals are at the basis of human society, but in our time, at least in theory and in some legal practice, the individual has attained a unique status. Since the Renaissance, in our latitudes the individual has been at the centre of the world. This is the enlightened and autonomous individual, who by now can hardly go on bearing the burden of progressive dreams of omnipotence.[4] Freedom, autonomy and human dignity are the great slogans of modern times. We also have to adopt a theological attitude towards them, to take them seriously and attune our ideas of God to this basic concept of our time. Of course we need not be uncritical, but we must attune our ideas nevertheless. Many of our theological problems arise from the fact that despite all the beginnings of an individualizing of belief in the post-exilic period, the biblical texts largely do not yet know a modern autonomy of the individual. Rather (despite all the changes in the course of the long history of Israel), they constantly presuppose a patriarchal tribal consciousness,[5] which is completely unimaginable to us and above all to women who are fighting for emancipation. It is quite clear that the present-day foundation for our ideals and thoughts – following the human rights declarations of 1776 and 1789 – is unlimited personal responsibility and the self-determination of the individual. Among us (in theory) all social ties have to be negotiated between individuals with equal rights. It is equally difficult to arrive at lasting interpersonal relations.[6] Really an individual existence, which gives the greatest flexibility and autonomy, is the condition most worth striving for. In antiquity – and up to the dawn of the industrial age[7] – that was inconceivable, because (above all in the country, in farming economies, but also in the urban milieus of craftsmen) people worked together in the family, sharing the work. These two very different starting points in the Old Testament writings and in our time must be recognized and discussed.[8] Here – it should

---

[4] The analysis by Horst Eberhard Richter, *Der Gottescomplex*, Hamburg 1979, of the 'autistic' individual who is under pressure to produce and assert his whole autonomous world, is very interesting.

[5] Johannes Pedersen has emphasized this trait strongly in a somewhat romanticizing way, following Vilhelm Groenbech, *Israel. Its Life and Culture* (2 vols), London 1945.

[6] Cf. Elisabeth Badinter, *Ich bin Du* (ch. 4 n. 124).

[7] One asks oneself how far the industrial revolution and the transfer of production to machines played a part in the rise of modern atomistic individualism, since this picture of human beings cannot be derived solely from René Descartes' *cogito ergo sum* and other philosophical schemes (e.g. Leibniz's theory of monads).

[8] German feminist theology has still largely failed to perceive the different sociological models which then arise on the basis of an absolute individualism today and a patriarchal but collectivizing family consciousness, but cf. Carol Meyers, *Eve* (ch. 4 n. 10); Michelle Z. Rosaldo and Louise Lamphere (eds), *Women, Culture and Society*, Stanford 1974; Henriette Moore, *Mensch und Frau sein*, Gütersloh 1990.

be remembered – the biblical ideas of God which are orientated on the patriarchal model of the family are not directly available for our atomized society.

I should add that ironically the heightened sense of 'I' in modernity seems at least in part also to go back to Old Testament origins. For down to our own time the anthropological doctrine of 'being in the image of God' and the 'commission for human beings to rule the earth' (cf. Gen 1:26-8; Ps 8) has led to remarkably exaggerated views of human beings. Even the sensitive Gerhard von Rad in his commentary on Genesis still assigns the absolute peak position on this earth to human beings (all creatures see the image of God before them in the human being),[9] and the idea of the 'crown of creation' is time and again read into the Genesis passage. Carl Amery takes these interpretations very seriously and attributes today's exaggerated self-esteem of (Western, industrial) men and women and disregard of nature specifically to the biblical creation story.[10] In short, with the phenomenon of the autonomous human being we also see the consequences of the long history of the interpretation of an important (but by no means the dominant) statement of biblical anthropology. The distance between then and now is suddenly no longer so tremendously great:

> What is man that you are mindful of him?
> You have made him little less than God, and have crowned him with
>   glory and honour.
> You have given him dominion over the works of your hands; you
>   have put all things under his feet,
> all sheep and oxen, and also the beasts of the field,
> the birds of the air, and the fish of the sea,
> whatever passes along the paths of the sea.
> Yahweh, our Lord, how majestic you are in all the earth (Ps 8:5b–10).

Of course the individualism of modern times is a direct consequence of the freedom and human dignity which are the greatest priorities for us – and herein lies its incomparable significance. Only if one makes every human being, regardless of age, gender, race, faith, profession or status, autonomous or immediate to God, and allows no intermediate authorities to supervise or to require submission, can there be anything like equal rights and equal dignity for all. Thus individualism is a very striking aspect of the freedom of the individual: however, here responsibility for parts or the whole of the world is developed or reduced only in a rudimentary fashion.[11]

---

[9] Gerhard von Rad, *Genesis*, London and Philadelphia ²1972.
[10] Carl Amery, *Das Ende der Vorsehung*, Reinbek 1974.
[11] Cf. Ulrich Beck et al. (eds), *Freiheiten*; id. et al. (eds), *Individualisierung* (ch. 3 n. 7).

10.4 The unjust, unredeemed world

The (theoretically) strong position of the individual in modernity does not wholly correspond to our daily experience that the predominant majority of all men and women are helpless victims of the social, economic, political and indeed religious forces of society. The idea of the self-determining individual is a utopia, a beautiful dream, which is significant as the notion of a goal. However, raw reality is so devastatingly different that as a rule we can maintain the courage to live only by intensively repressing it. Almost all over this globe – and almost two-thirds of it is vegetating – people live in the stranglehold of social systems which enforce their tempo and manner of life as if by a spiritual hand. Here the one-third is probably excessively preoccupied with material concerns for all the necessities of life, but groans under the constant nervous pressure of a competitive society focussed on productivity. Such people can no longer compensate for the violation of their souls by planning leisure-time activities, by medical treatment and psychotherapy, or by family recreation. The two-thirds of humankind who are trapped in the lowest income levels or are unemployed (a growing minority also in the richest industrial countries)[12] also lack the material basis for life. They literally look for possibilities for life on the refuse heaps of prosperous society, as Manuel Bandeira says:

> Yesterday I saw an animal in the dirt of the courtyard.
> It was looking for something to eat among the refuse.
> When it had found something it did not investigate it,
> did not even smell it but greedily swallowed it all down.
> The animal was not a dog, or a cat;
> it was not a rat. The animal, my God,
> was a human being.[13]

---

[12] Cf. the discussion paper of the Evangelical Church in Germany and the Catholic conference of bishops which was also a semester theme for the Marburg faculty, on the economic and social situation in Germany, *Zur wirtschaftlichen und sozialen Lage in Deutschland*, Hanover and Bonn 1994. After giving an account of the changes and aporias in the overall situation the study concludes: 'To see once again in a new light the indissoluble connection between faith and ethical action is for Christians the appropriate answer to the situations of upheaval which we are currently experiencing' (ibid., 52). The leitmotif is the 'reform and consolidation of the welfare state' (ibid., 30ff.). By contrast, advocates of the pure, competitive market economy in the USA and Europe quite clearly want the demolition of the welfare state and the reduction of democratic rights. After two years of very wide discussion this social study was published in a provisional final version in 1997: *Für ein Zukunft in Solidarität und Gerechtigkeit*, Hanover and Bonn 1997.

[13] According to Hermann Brandt, *ZThK* 78, 1981, 370. Cf. Rudolf H. Strahm, *Warum sie so arm sind*, Wuppertal 1985.

Hunger, poverty, sickness, exploitation – theoretically we know the deadly cycle in which millions upon millions of people are caught, without any hope for a change in their situation. For the structures of the world which have come into being, built up by the dominant rich nations, especially the economic structures, seem unchangeable, and hold the poor nations and regions in the stranglehold of exploitation. In the face of these dangerous pressures it is ridiculous to want to speak at all of a freedom of the individual or of freedom generally for the majority of people. There is no such thing.

The pioneer thinkers of the new age were not so stupid as to overlook the problem of injustice completely. It was posed to them in the form of political inequality and the end of capricious monarchical rule down to the nineteenth and twentieth centuries. They countered this form of the limitation of freedom, especially after the French and American Revolutions, with their concept of universal political co-determination, democracy and control of the government.[14] Only in the course of the last two centuries did some scholars then discover that freedom can also be dangerously impaired by economic or ideological strait-jackets.[15] Thus democratic institutions and procedures can serve to limit the worst caprices and give place to the majority will of the people, the citizens. But the people of the Bible did not know the modern understanding of democracy, and consequently democracy could not play any role, even for the relation to God and the image of God at the time. We have seen how instead – at the level of the larger societies – after the looser tribal structures had been overlaid only monarchical notions flourished. Down to our day, antiquated, monarchical rules of submission play a major role in human religious behaviour. They derive from the hierarchical state structures of antiquity and have therefore been superseded in an order the theory and constitution of which is obligated to democracy. So a discussion of the right notions of authority is urgently necessary.

In addition, our democratic society has been fundamentally secularized in the light of the civic constitution and mentality. Religion – and this too was recognized in the wake of the revolutions mentioned above, which ushered in modernity or the philosophical Enlightenment – is a purely private matter, which does not concern the state and the legislator in the least. Certainly we know that this assertion too does not correspond to real

---

[14] The history of the political freedom movements is a rich one and has many levels; cf. Hans Werner Bartsch et al., 'Freiheit', *TRE* 11, Berlin 1983, 497–549.

[15] Cf. above all Karl Marx, *Early Writings*, Harmondsworth 1992, and e.g. the efforts in Germany after the war at 'prosperity for all' (e.g. Ludwig Erhard and Alfred Müller-Armack, *Sozial Marktwirtschaft*, Frankfurt 1972), or the social commitment of the liberation theologians.

life, but we accept its intention. The separation of state and church[16] is synonymous with allowing freedom to all confessions and religions, in so far as they respect the constitution and human rights, in other words synonymous with an almost unimaginable diversity of faith communities in our environment. However, the great churches are far from having internalized this state of affairs. They continue to live in the tradition of state-sanctioned monopolies, of the kind that they thought they could already recognize from the biblical writings. The ambivalent term 'Israel' is present everywhere, especially in the Hebrew canon. It suggests a homogeneity which to my knowledge was never a reality. But modern interpreters fail to note the many social strata in ancient Israel and read their daydreams into scripture. Then an accord between the faith community and society is read out of the Bible. Israel knew only one God or allowed only one God. We are today's Israel. So we prescribe faith in the one God, namely our own. That is still the secret attitude of many Christians in our latitudes (the situation is quite different where Christianity is in a minority situation, as often in Africa and the Asian countries). Here too and today we shall have to adapt our exegesis and theology to the religious pluralism of a wider society. It is in some respects comparable with the organization of the empire in antiquity (religious pluralism; unitary political structuring; aggression), but in other respects qualitatively different. Ideally there is no hierarchical structure; the dimensions of our modern global society have expanded tremendously, thanks to an increase in the population, in science, technology and communication. Thus the inequalities of class, race and nation are becoming more acute.

10.5 God: personal or impersonal?

The natural sciences have decisively changed our world-view by comparison with that of our ancestors. Whereas in antiquity in principle all events in nature and society were understood in personal terms, for us in broad areas of life a mechanistic, causal, physical and chemical explanation has become more plausible. But how are we to think of 'God' when we imagine the course of the laws of nature from the microbiological to the astrophysical sphere? Or, looking at it from another perspective: personal relations still shape our life in small groups. So at the 'lower' levels of society we can also

---

[16] In principle many states preserve an ideological neutrality. After the 'change' in reunified Germany there has again been a constitutional discussion as to whether a reference to 'God' and the Christian tradition may appear in the preamble to the Basic Law. The traditionally 'Christian' parties and convictions have once again won through; cf. the relevant documentation and, on the Basic Law in general, Peter Römer, *Im Namen des Grundgesetzes*, Hamburg 1989.

understand the old world-view, according to which the personal will is decisive in events. From this standpoint of course we can also quite naturally use the personal concept of God – as long we do so in connection with interpersonal activities. The scientific interpretation also already extends down to this level, for example if we contract an infectious disease or if we are dealing with electricity, motors, communication equipment, etc. Be this as it may, we know important areas of life in which religious behaviour, too, can be expressed only in personal categories. But what means of imagination and expression are at our disposal in those other worlds in which we all commonly think in terms of impersonal causal connections? Can we not introduce into our causal thinking which is related to the wider society and science a personal deity who intervenes according to his own assessment and reverses the causal connections? That will be possible only in exceptional cases, perhaps in an unexpected healing or a puzzling accident. As a rule our normal scientific explanation of the world cannot be reconciled with the ancient ideas of the personal direction of the world by divine powers. So we are challenged to develop new ideas of God for the anonymous spheres, perhaps in dialogue with Jewish and Christian (and Muslim) mysticism and with the Far Eastern religions, for which the category of person has quite a different status.

10.6 The liberating God

Apart from a few late witnesses, the Old Testament scriptures have a purely this-worldly stamp; in other words they expect the help and coming of God on this earth and in the framework of existing societies and empires or in connection with them. The New Testament community came into being after an apocalyptic interval, at a time when the religious environment was more and more attuned to another world, completely renewed and utterly spotless. Therefore resurrection and the transcendent kingdom of God are also the great content of Christian preaching. Today, by contrast, the expectation of the transcendent world has declined markedly in northern Europe. With the disappearance of the idealist philosophy which was able to give convincing form to belief in the beyond and the decline in traditional Christian convictions, there has been a heightened tendency to see faith as valid – if at all – first or only for this earthly life. Does that amount to abandoning the substance of Christianity? Compare 1 Cor 15:14: 'But if Christ is not risen, then our preaching is vain and your faith is in vain.' Since according to our basic principle there are no eternally unchanging statements of faith, we must also regard Paul's words from this perspective. The people around us do so to a considerable degree. They say: 'Resurrection? Eternal life? I don't know. It doesn't interest me.'[17] People's feelings about life are predominantly this-worldly, even in the best Christian opinions and activities. It is a matter of perceiving God's will for endangered humankind and creation here and now. What comes afterwards is not up to us and need not concern us. Gustavo Gutiérrez, Leonardo Boff and others time and again count among the characteristics of liberation theology an urgent responsibility for the world which exists now.[18] Bishop Pedro Casaldaliga expresses it like this in a popular song of the Brazilians who have no land:

Somos um povo de gente,	We too are human,
somos o povo de desu.	we are God's people.
Queremos terra na terra,	We want land on earth,
já temos terra nos ceus.	we already have it in heaven.

These few lines contain more theology than some academic monographs. The certainty of the world to come which becomes the basis for self-assertion in this world is precious. Thus we really get back to Old Testament categories: the justice of God and human justice is important in this connection. A sense of the beyond underlies other laws which we cannot grasp. Therefore we do better to keep quiet, rather than wanting to set heaven and hell in motion.

This also relativizes preliminary decisions for the world to come, i.e. the ideas of judgment (cf. Matt 25). How could we predict here and now, for ourselves and even for others, what will happen at the 'final reckoning'? Ideas of the end of the world are equally impossible, though they are often expressed in tense apocalyptic times. A minority of our contemporaries belong to groups or churches which believe that the end is so near that they can identify and define the end time. On a bus journey of more than six hundred miles to São Paulo I had a Pentecostalist and a Baptist sitting behind me and they began to open the seven seals of the Apocalypse and explain the relevant events. It was exciting, but in sober Europe such an interpretation of the Bible would hardly interest many people. In general one can assume that specific social conditions and religious conditioning are a presupposition for the apocalyptic view. Millennial expectation has also remained within bounds and has long since given place to the everyday quest for meaning and profit.

---

[17] Cf. the various demographic surveys of the last decades under the general question 'What do Germans believe?'.

[18] Gustavo Gutiérrez, *Theology of Liberation*, Maryknoll and London ²1988; Leonardo Boff, *Do lugar do pobre*, Petrópolis 1984.

10.7 An ethic of responsibility

Modern ethics – in keeping with the predominant theoretical individualism – is stamped by the individual's quest for happiness. In the American tradition this was called 'the pursuit of happiness'. And in keeping with the Puritan way of thinking predominant there, in the USA both among Christians and in society generally it was noted that this personal quest for happiness went by Old Testament rules. Those who wanted to be happy had to be morally impeccable (even today the Puritan morality plays a very great role, for example in presidential election campaigns). In some regions of Europe, some of the custom and morality provided by the church has been preserved. But in the cities and largely elsewhere ethical norms are fluid. People speak of a universal change of values, but there are also strong conservative currents which form an opposition. The good is largely what is useful for me, or what furthers my quest for happiness. For the majority, traditional values and norms play an ever more minor role. The acceptance of behaviour which was formerly ruled out is becoming greater, and tolerance even of phenomena which are disapproved of is getting wider.

Here it is highly remarkable that the link between ethical precepts and the singular 'I' is practised and proclaimed almost everywhere, in complete contrast to the link to the plural 'we' in the Hebrew scriptures. Where a basis is given in those scriptures for ethical norms or ethical behaviour, we find sentences like 'That sort of thing is not done in Israel', or 'Root out the evil from Israel', or 'That is an atrocity', or 'that it may be well with you in the land which Yahweh your God will give'. In other words, in the ancient texts references to social entities, the family, clan, people or community, stand in the foreground. For the simple terms 'atrocity', 'shame', 'evil', 'despicable' and so on[19] also have a specific social background.

In conversations surrounding these lectures I have stressed time and again that temporary social conditions must not in any way be made norms or idealized. Such idealization hinders responsible exegesis in our time. But it is a legitimate task to develop ideas on the basis of the ancient witnesses. In particular two Jewish scholars in our day have attempted to investigate the question under debate. I quote them as examples of ethical thought which consistently tackles the conditions of our time. Hans Jonas' last great work was a sketch of ethics, *The Imperative of Responsibility*. And Emmanuel Levinas has undertaken in several articles and studies to sketch an 'ethic of

---

[19] This involves a series of Hebrew terms, the significance of which has been investigated above all by Martin A. Klopfenstein; cf. e.g. id., *Scham und Schande nach dem Alten Testament*, Zurich 1972.

the other'.[20] Whereas Hans Jonas wants to take the old starting point, the 'I' in question, as a basis, bringing out the new dimensions of responsibility for the world which have arisen through an enormous increase in human power, Emanuel Levinas begins, not from the 'I' but from the neighbour. But first Hans Jonas: through the progress in science and the technological revolutions, the foundations of life and the human capacity for action have changed by comparison with the pre-industrial period. Thus the ethical responsibility of human beings has also shifted.

> Nature as a whole has become vulnerable to human action. This discovery . . . changes our whole idea of ourselves as a causal factor in the broader system of things. Through its effects it brings out the fact that the nature of human action has changed *de facto*, and that an object of a completely new order, no less than the whole biosphere of the planet, has been added to our responsibilities, because we have power over it.[21]

However, a little later he dwells on the human monopoly in perceiving this responsibility; this human being is always the human being 'who says "I"':

> In so far as the last pole of reference which makes the preservation of nature a moral interest is the fate of human beings in their dependence on the state of nature, here too the anthropocentric orientation of all classical ethics has been preserved. Even then the difference is great [because the quality of the action transcends the old dimensions of spatial and temporal nearness].[22]

In fact, Hans Jonas sees the new dimensions of action and ethics better than most people before him. Emanuel Levinas goes further, in that he puts in question the way in which ethical guidance is rooted in the 'I'. Consequently he regards the claims of the other on me as being really constitutive and primary, even in the formation of the 'I', but also in its responsible activities.

> The absolute other is not reflected in the consciousness. It is so resistant to the consciousness that not even its resistance changes in the content of the consciousness. The temptation is even to overthrow the I-relatedness of the I; the countenance disarms the intentionality aimed at it.

---

[20] Cf. Hans Jonas, *Das Prinzip Verantwortung* (1979), Frankfurt 1984; Emmanuel Levinas, *Trace* (ch. 8 n. 52).

[21] Hans Jonas, *Prinzip* (ch. 10 n. 20), 26f.

[22] Ibid., 27.

This is a matter of putting the consciousness in question and not one of becoming conscious of the questioning. The I loses the unlimited coincidence with itself, its identification by which the consciousness victoriously returns to itself in order to rest in itself. In the face of the demand of the other, the consciousness is driven out of this repose and is not the already victorious consciousness of this expulsion. Any proneness to the self would destroy the directness of the ethical movement. But the way in which this wild and exuberant freedom, intrinsically certain of its refuge, puts these things in question is not reduced to this negative movement. The putting in question of the self is none other than the receiving of the absolute other. The epiphany of the absolute other is a countenance in which the other addresses me and shows me an ordering by his nakedness, by his need. His presence is an invitation to give an answer. The 'I' becomes aware not only of the need to answer, as if it were a matter of guilt or indebtedness about which it had to make a decision. In its position it is responsibility or diaconia through and through, of the kind that we find in chapter 53 of the book of Isaiah.

Hence 'I-ness' means not being able to evade responsibility. This excrescence of being, this exaggeration that one calls 'I-ness', this outbreak of selfhood in the being, takes place as a growth in responsibility. The fact that my self is put into question by the other puts me in solidarity with the other in an incomparable and unique way. Not in solidarity in the way in which the material is in solidarity with the block of which it forms a part, or an organ is in solidarity with the organism in which it performs a function. Here the solidarity is responsibility, as though the whole edifice of creation rested on my shoulders. The oneness of the I lies in the fact that no one can respond in my place. The responsibility which drives out the imperialism and egotism from the I, even if it is an egotism of salvation, does not turn into a moment of universal order. It confirms it in its selfhood, in its function as a bearer of the universe.[23]

By contrast, its seems to me that schemes of Christian ethics have to grapple far more with the formal problem of revelation, the dogmatized individualism of salvation, a one-sided imprisonment within the parameters of a wider society, with traditional notions of law and gospel, the two kingdoms and the coming world. Consequently they find it difficult to go into the interests of our world.[24]

---

[23] Emmanuel Levinas, *Trace* (ch. 8 n. 52), 223–5.

[24] Cf. only Eckart Otto, *Ethik* (ch. 4 n. 96); Wolfgang Schrage, *Ethics of the New Testament*, Philadelphia and Edinburgh 1988; Ethel L. Behrendt, *Christologie der Gerechtigkeit. Eine gesamtbiblische Theologie für rechtsstaatliche Ordnung*, 3 vols, Munich ⁵1992; Ulrich Duchrow, *Alternativen zur kapitalistischen Weltwirtschaft*, Mainz und Gütersloh 1994; Hans G. Ulrich (ed.),

10.8 Images of God today

The modern world-view and images of God cannot be repeated mechanically. I can refer only to a very few important points. The unity of the world and the unity of God which are recognized in the Old Testament scriptures have persisted so fundamentally in our cultural circles that one can only note this with amazement. We all live together on this basic assumption and even the most resolute atheists share it unquestioningly, without suspecting that this monistic principle is a primal religious datum from the sphere of the ancient Near East and the biblical proclamation. As I have already said, the Persians put forward a consistently dualistic system. Any element of a world-view which goes beyond monism has fundamentally changed in the course of the millennia. Geocentrism has become heliocentrism and has completely dissolved: our universe has no centre (or does it?).[25] Not only has space fundamentally changed but also time: the biblical 5700 years which are said to have passed since God's first action have become ten billion years. The stars on the fixed firmament have become (fixed) stars, galaxies and shining and black cosmic clouds. But despite all the cosmic shifts, the essential prejudices and states in (Jewish–Christian) humanity really remain unchanged, like the naïve faith that human beings stand at the centre of the world as the darlings of providence or nature. No one really takes seriously the possible decentralization of the divine attention to millions of planets which bear life in the universe.

So all along the line most people unconcernedly keep to old ideas of God or the origin and destiny of the world which derive from theologies of family, people or community. It may also be that there is little readiness to change anything here. People naïvely suppose that a personal God resides somewhere in space who can intervene in events for his cause and ours (justice? peace? goodness?). Or they think of a God spiritually present in all things and events who guides life in broad outline, not in individual actions. The divine in human beings and in the loftiness of nature are such images of God which have relatively no contours. All in all, except in extreme situations, our contemporaries seem to prefer to rely on human power and brilliance (e.g. in cases of sickness). The far-reaching knowledge and skills

---

Evangelische Ethik, Gütersloh 1990; Christofer Frey, De Ethik des Protestantismus von der Reformation bis zur Gegenwart, Gütersloh ²1994; Hans-Günter Gruber, Familie und christliche Ethik, Darmstadt 1995; Anselm Hertz et al. (eds), Handbuch christlicher Ethik (3 vols), Freiburg 1993; Martin Honecker, Grundriss der Sozialethik, Berlin 1997; Siegfried Keil, Lebensphasen, Lebensformen, Lebensmöglichkeiten, Bochum 1992; Franz Segbers, Hausordnung (ch. 8 n. 74).

25 Cf. the modern theories about the origin of the world, Stephen W. Hawking, A Brief History of Time, London 1988, etc.

in the spheres of science and medicine make such trust possible, but they also evoke a degree of scepticism, since everywhere today, far more than twenty years ago, the boundlessness and also the limits of human art and power are becoming evident, not least in the threats to nature and through nature.

It has become clear that the discussions with our spiritual forebears who have left us the Old Testament do not take place simply in a confrontation between 'old' and 'new', 'antiquated' and 'modern'. Our relationship to the biblical texts is on too many levels. On the one hand our social structures are different from those from which the Hebrew scriptures were formulated. On the other hand there are clear questions and insights which have persisted since the exilic/post-exilic period of Israel. And yet a third problem is not only conceivable but can actually be demonstrated at some points: the old witnesses sometimes went much further than us in their thought and confession because they had a 'more correct' view of human beings, God and the world for their time and shaped the future better. In that case we must possibly attempt to catch up with them in our analogous development. We are walking behind them and not marching proudly ahead on some path of human progress. In any discussion we should always be aware of the way in which all theological statements are conditioned by time and society. I can only hint at some points at which discussion with the Old Testament is rewarding.

10.9 Parallel theologies (pluralism)?

The way in which the social levels on which theology is done are stacked is important. Family theology is not identical with community theology; tribal theology does not correspond completely with national theology; and none of the four levels mentioned already produces universal or global theology of itself. All levels have their relative justification. It will never be possible to harmonize these theological levels completely, but it is urgently necessary to attune them to one another as far as possible. Every theology must remain capable of criticism, of itself and of the other levels. In our time the primary issue will be the theology of the individual (which is not yet fully developed in the Old Testament) and global theology, which similarly has never before been fundamentally conceived of in the history of humankind. At both extreme ends of the scale the Old Testament can give only qualified advice. Because of the overall development of humankind we face authentically new theological tasks. How can we articulate theology for the individual and for the whole of humankind adequately and self-critically?

Here it should be clear from the start that according to our basic convictions human life has that core which makes it worth living in interpersonal
relations, not in the macro-sphere of society (as the New Testament puts it,
'What would it help a man if he gained the whole world and harmed his
soul?'). If that is correct, it follows that the micro-social sphere is paramount;
all the larger systems which are built up on it are to be subjected to it in
theology and ethics. The latter have ancillary functions. Larger societies
should make a humane life possible, not hinder it, as largely happens. It is
true that the theology and ethic of the larger groups have to advocate the
interests of regions, nations and the planet. But they should do so with
relation to the reality in which human beings live, in order to protect and
further people and not out of self-interest. It cannot be the supreme principle
'of the market' that share prices rise when at the same time more and more
people are put out of work.[26] Larger societies must create a framework
within which people everywhere can live in a humane way, and in which
peace prevails and nature is preserved.

10.10 Relativity, absoluteness, globalization

Just to take up the question of global strategies (in any case individual
ethics will continue to be treated in church circles): in no way can global
theology be thought of and then ordered from a centre, whether this is
determined in personal, institutional or global terms. The time when German
or European theologies were normative is long past. For the knowledge of
truth is always limited. We may not stylize any theological part-truths as
absolute truths. But the opportunity on offer is a description of divine truth
from different perspectives, shaped by the context. That applies within
Christianity: theological truth must display an ecumenical breadth and
colour. A European or American domination in Christian theology is illegitimate, even if it still prevails because of the concentrated power of finance
and publication in these regions. It also applies in inter-faith terms. In the
light of our claim, grounded in the Old Testament, to confess the one God,
we cannot in principle exclude any other religion. Any human attempt to
talk of God, the 'ground of being', the 'future of the world', 'the absolute
claim on us', is suspicious. Some tricks which certainly are played constantly
and in all religious circles judge themselves and do not need our constant
condemnations. Where human beings are harmed by other human beings
with some name of God on their lips, we must offer resistance, unmask and

---

[26] Some business managers also recognize ethical responsibilities; cf. Daniel Goeudevert, *Mit
Träumen beginnt die Realität*, Berlin 1999.

condemn, whether in our own ranks or in other confessions and religions. Sometimes the courts have to intervene to protect the victims. But in the broad spectrum of innocuous religious practice which is well disposed to human beings, dialogue – inter-confessional and inter-religious – must take place. It may be that it first succeeds at the level of practical theology and church practice, because (fortunately?) in our latitudes practice does not have so marked a function in constituting communities. In our tradition the determining factors for communities lie more in the sphere of the intellect and theology, in confession and church order. Thus dialogue will not begin at the centre of a particular self-understanding. But it must thoroughly relativize the sense of identity, so that it does not make itself absolute and exclude others in principle.

10.11 Monism and dualism

So far I have said that Old Testament faith rests on the acceptance of a strict monism: the one world is conceivable only as the world of one deity, one source of life. This principle applies quite consistently in all the canonical Hebrew writings, but also in the Jewish–Greek and to a great degree the Christian tradition. It applies to the oldest strata of the canon, even when other deities come into play and when the supreme God is not called Yahweh but e.g. El (Deut 32). In other words, in the religions of the Semitic peoples a ground of all things is assumed: there is no duality of a creator and a destroyer of the world. To be more precise: in the struggle with chaos the baneful powers which are opposed to any order and shape are destroyed. Only then can creation begin (cf. Ps 104). Nevertheless, later schemes of the world even in Christianity have toyed with the notion of a fundamental schism in the divine world and thus also in the world in which we live. (Satan is God's adversary.) All dualistic systems can refer to the underivable power of evil which is present in the world. Must one not then cut evil off at the roots and hand it over to destruction? And what then stands in the way of identifying the physical and material with evil along the lines of the Platonic and Neo-Platonic history of the world and splitting it off theologically?

It will be difficult to come to an unprejudiced decision about this basic philosophical and theological question of the West. Today in our thought we are still very strongly attached to monistic models of explanation and take this into account when the existence and efficacy of evil cannot be sufficiently explained. For the concentration of the two qualities and powers in one deity does not lead to a harmonious notion of God. By contrast, dualistic models explain fundamental and actual evil as an independent power, but cannot give full expression to the unity of the world. They have to solve the problem by the radical overcoming of evil, usually on a distant day of judgment. The conversation between monists and dualists can perhaps be helped on by not making the two systems of interpretation absolute, but seeing them as human expedients; the important thing at present is to develop shared strategies for the survival of humankind.

10.12 Anthropology

I have already remarked that our anthropology and ethics are strongly stamped by the models and norms of the Old Testament and today need to be changed or developed. We can no longer simply and (I would say) blindly accept the pattern valid in Old Testament antiquity (in the sense of a one-sided history of its interpretation and influence). Our time calls rigorously and with the despair of those who fear for their survival for new criteria of being and action.

We know that human beings have been created 'male and female' (Gen 1:27). But because there is nothing remotely like today's demand for the equality of the sexes in this Priestly version of creation or in the Yahwistic version (Gen 2:22; 3:16), we cannot make the model of humankind at that time binding on us, transfer it to our situation or even introduce our ideas into it.[27] The patriarchal order of the history of ancient Israel was certainly not identical with the modern patriarchate of the industrial age: we have no evidence of a marked, one-sided arbitrary male rule (even the horror stories of Judg 19 or Judg 11 speak of specific extreme situations, not of a general and absolute power of man over woman). So we must leave the pictures of women and men at that era as they are, and at the same time seek responsible parameters which are valid today for the roles of women, men, children, grandparents and relations. Much though we may regret it, the old role pictures do not fit our time and cannot be an obligation on us. That can be demonstrated quite clearly not only by the stereotypes for woman and man but also by the whole structure of the family, profiles of occupations, human dignity, principles of equality, etc.

I shall limit myself to a central observation: in antiquity in general and in ancient Israel the individual was not worth as much as in our days. 'The person' really counted only in the couple or the family bond, or as a collective. As an isolated individual the person was lost. A later text describes the situation like this.

---

[27] The priestly authors of Gen. 1:27 were hardly thinking of the equality of the sexes in our current sense, but of the specific patriarchally defined roles of the 'male' and the 'female' in society; cf. Erhard S. Gerstenberger, *Yahweh the Patriarch* (ch. 2 n. 4).

Again, I saw vanity under the sun: a person who has no one, either son or brother, yet there is no end to all his toil, and his eyes are never satisfied with riches, so that he never asks, 'For whom am I toiling and depriving myself of pleasure?' This is also vanity and an unhappy business. Two are better than one, because they have a good reward for their toil. For if they fall, one will lift up his fellow; but woe to him who is alone when he falls and has not another to lift him up. Again, if two lie together, they are warm; but how can one be warm alone? And though a man might prevail against one who is alone, two will withstand him. A threefold cord is not quickly broken (Eccles 4:7–12; cf. Gen 18 – 25; Prov 1:10–31, etc.).

The united strength of a family is also expressed in Ps 127:3–5:

Lo, sons are a heritage from the Lord, the fruit of the womb a reward, like arrows in the hand of a warrior are the sons of one's youth.
Happy is the man who has his quiver full of them!
He shall not be put to shame when he speaks with his enemies in the gate.

In antiquity, the purely physical necessity of sharing work in order to sustain life forged families together. The opposite pressure, to be employed as flexibly as possible in an industrial, mobile occupation orientated on production, drives people apart and into solitude. So the basic anthropological conditions are now quite different from those at the time of the Hebrew scriptures. I have already remarked that the pure individualism of our time, the sheer effort to achieve autonomy, may seem to us in need of improvement – first of all we must recognize and accept its existence and shape our picture of human beings accordingly. Above all, we cannot censure those who now call for their own rights and spheres of freedom on the basis of the individualistic foundations of our culture. Anyone who has such freedom cannot refuse it to others with the remark that the autonomy of the individual is such a harmful thing that as far as possible it should not be given to the rising generation. However, in that case we must seek possibilities of forming community on the basis of freedom and dignity. Understandably they are difficult to find and can be realized only through contracts between those with completely equal status.[28] 'Single' existence is more and more becoming the norm (as is very consistent and logical), partnerships are shorter term, and priority is given to professional careers. In so far as the rights and freedom of the individual must be protected, one

---

[28] The idea is not new; cf. already Jean-Jacques Rousseau, *Contrat social* (1762).

can only be in favour of all this. But in so far as the basic human needs for fellowship, for face-to-face exchanges, for security and inter-relationship, suffer under the modern autonomies and ultimately also do serious damage to individuals in their solitude (cf. especially the children whose development is stunted by sitting too much in front of the television), we have the obligation to seek ways out of or modifications to the ideals and pressures of autonomy. The biblical texts cannot give us precise models for our social formation. But they can be striking challenges, and from a distance show us possibilities of shaping life together which we can then reflect on and work on under our changed conditions.

If the social structure has so fundamentally changed on the innermost front, it follows that the norms of behaviour for the interpersonal sphere too do not take on the same shape as they did in Israel. If there the supreme basic principle was, 'You shall show solidarity with the members of your group,' today it is, 'You must constantly seek your own way and advantage in the face of all rivals.' When it comes to one's fellow human beings, similarly the starting point is entirely one's own interests and condition: 'What you would not want others to do to you, do not do to them!' So instead of unconditional solidarity there is the slogan that as far as possible the other should not be needlessly harmed; in other words, there should be a certain compassion. In all fairness it must be pointed out that similar tones were also known in antiquity: 'You shall love your neighbour as yourself.' But in our time these tones of concern for self have become so much stronger that we can confidently say that they are characteristic.

Of course the other norms in ethics and social ethics are to a large degree influenced by the basic constellation of 'the individual and his property' (to use Max Stirner's phrase). Questions of social ethics, the ethics of possessions and business, civil and criminal law, etc. are treated quite differently if they have to be solved on the basis of the autonomy of the individual. We see that even the ethical norms of the Decalogue or other paraenetic texts in the Old Testament need examination. But here too they are so deeply and firmly rooted in us by our tradition that time and again we must attack our old prejudices, and not just the givens of antiquity.

10.13 History and eschaton

Time, history and the eschaton are treated in a highly differentiated and contradictory way in the Hebrew scriptures. Earlier exegesis got from the texts ideas about history, salvation history, cosmology and the end of the world which were pleasing to it, and occasionally also first read them in, in order then to have delight in discovering them. This also led to the legend of a unilinear Hebrew thought, always directed towards the future, and the so-called cyclical thought of the Greeks, which thus advanced to a diametrically opposed understanding of history.[29]

By contrast, we have to note soberly that the different strata and periods of the Hebrew Bible also produce different pictures of history. A 'cyclical' understanding of the course of the year prevails in the cultic festal calendars. In the historical narratives there is past, present and future, as there is with us. Poetry has its own basic aesthetic laws, and the prophetic writings tend towards an eschatological view which in the end transforms itself into an apocalyptic view. Thus we are simply left with the task of carrying on conversations with the different conceptions which can be got out of the Hebrew Bible.

That will perhaps be the case most intensively with the eschatological or apocalyptic expectation. Under the pressure of economic and political conditions, there were expectations of the end-time in Israel during the exilic/post-exilic period, perhaps on occasion even earlier. The present became intolerable; trust in God's loyalty called for a fundamental change in conditions. Thus – if the state of the world could no longer be improved from within – there remained only a radical punitive judgment and a new beginning guided and inspired by God.

> Therefore wait for me, says the Lord, for the day when I arise as a witness. For my desire is to gather nations, to assemble kingdoms, to pour out upon them my indignation, all the heat of my anger; for in the fire of my jealous wrath all the earth shall be consumed (Zeph. 3:8).

In the book of Zephaniah this message of the annihilation of the peoples apparently replaces more original threats of the punishment of his own people Israel. In the exile, eschatological faith increasingly turned to the annihilation of enemies and the deliverance, rehabilitation and exaltation of the people of Israel:

> Then Yahweh will go forth and fight against the nations as when he fights on a day of battle . . .
> On that day living waters shall flow out from Jerusalem, half of them to the eastern sea and half of them to the western sea; it shall continue in summer and in winter. And Yahweh will become king over all the earth; on that day Yahweh will be one and his name one . . . (Zech 14:3, 8f.).

---

[29] Cf. Thorlief Boman, *Hebrew Thought Compared with Greek*, London 1960; Gerhard von Rad, *Old Testament Theology* (2 vols), Edinburgh 1962, 1965; against them already James Barr, *The Semantics of Biblical Language*, Oxford 1961.

Today the expectations of the end time come from quite different contexts and angles, and the big question is whether we have the right – like the ancient Israelites – to rely on the intervention of Yahweh, who in sovereign manner brings this history to an end and gives a new form to the world. The fact that humankind today is bundled together for better or worse, that it is sharing in the destruction of the environment – though in very different proportions in individual countries – should make us sceptical about an eschatology and apocalyptic concentrated on God. Humankind (organized industrially) is guilty of an end-time mood and an end-time conditioning. Therefore today the judgment of the world is evidently taking the form of a creeping death for the ecosystem of planet earth. Thousands of species of animals and plants are already dying out without any dramatic sounds of the last trumpet. The eschaton has already been going on for decades, and this fact should move us to use different pictures of the end of history from those of eschatology and apocalyptic.

10.14 Our God today

The image, or rather the images, of God corresponding to our time have in part still to be found. Our religious imagination is impoverished; it has constantly fixated itself only on what is there in the Bible and has regarded these images as the only possible metaphors. Children are sometimes theologically more productive[30] than highly-educated theologians, because they have a living and actual relationship to the divine. A learned insistence on the remote revelations of God has stunted our capacity to perceive the God who is present.[31] Otherwise we would not be so dumb and anxious about God's cause. I can refer here only to a few basic requirements.

At any rate in Europe and North America, our theological ideas can no longer presuppose monarchical or imperialistic conditions. We live under democratic constitutions, in which electors and citizens have certain possibilities of action and co-determination. God is not therefore the king of all kings but perhaps the president or presidential adviser. God cannot exercise the patriarchal authority of a former time or even be imagined as masculine in a sexist way. He/she is neutral to gender and race. God cannot be thought of in a particularistic nationalist way; he/she is a global God for all peoples and groups.

My view is that on the personal level our God today remains a God who can be addressed personally. How can we imagine he/she/it in a direct

---

[30] See the various collections of children's letters to God.

[31] The biblical theologies could be investigated from the perspective of theological creativity; cf. also Hermann Spieckermann, *Heilsgegenwart* (ch. 4 n. 139).

relationship in other than personal terms? And if for some children it is impossible to imagine God as father, a comparison with a friend may open up new dimensions of the divine. But in the higher formations of society, science, technology and international politics we will be able to indicate God more in forms of regularities, abstract forces and overarching metaphors. Believers and seekers in their own situations will decide how far 'love', 'power', 'justice', 'peace', 'retribution' can be appropriate attributes of the divine. It is part of the impossibility of knowing and calculating the deity that we cannot harmonize the different contextual notions of it.

God is not – or is not constantly – the transcendent, majestic, wholly other, who rules and commands far above the world. According to our experience, which not least goes back to Isaiah's servant of God, the suffering just person of all times, Jesus of Nazareth, God is also the one who has compassion, who is immersed in time and the human world, who collaborates both actively and passively. On the other hand we human beings have a share in God's activity; we are above all collectively responsible for the fate of the world. This share of responsibility brings about a new relationship with God.

10.15 God for all

All in all, in the old canonical scriptures God played the role of the supreme ruler and judge of the world, who intervened in events along human lines and directed them as he wanted. Alongside and below this a personal God acted as the protector of his particular clientele. There are also the beginnings of talk of universal divine powers in the wisdom literature. Today 'God' has been involved far more in the business of the world and is inseparably bound up with human creative forces. That has lead to completely new perspective on an appropriate and 'correct' theology. We must recognize that our views of God are not in themselves so tremendously important. What is decisively important is the dynamic developed by faith, the way it has an effect on world history. A belief in God which was 'contemporary' would have to be orientated on Christian and human goals, on justice, peace and the preservation of creation:

> For thus says Yahweh, who created the heavens (he is God), who formed the earth and made it (he established it; he did not create it a chaos – he formed it to be inhabited), I am Yahweh, and there is no other (Isa 45:18).

In responsibility to the tradition and the present world Christian belief can only aim at a comprehensive commitment to the one undivided world.

Christian belief in God is conscious of its serving, reconciling, peacemaking functions. In the good world into which we have been born, lies and violence largely prevail. Christian faith holds firm to the basic orientation of the world, our planet, which is favourable to life and the programme that is implanted in it: to offer the whole of nature possibilities of existing for millennia. It holds fast to the equality of all human beings, regardless of gender, age, race, nationality, profession, state of health, religion or confession. It engages critically with other faiths and ideologies, economic and political theories and practices which make self-interest the supreme value and exploit other human beings. Christian faith lives in the hope of a future improvement of the fate of all human beings whose human dignity is infringed, and of a conversion or humanization of those who rob others of the possibilities of life. Given all these aims, we must take account of the social conditions under which faith is articulated and practised, for we live in restricted conditions which are contextually different and yet may have the whole totality in view.

Appendix:
God in Our Time

Farewell Lecture in the Old University at Marburg, 23 July 1997

You surround me on all sides
and hold your hand over me.
This knowledge is too wonderful and too high for me,
I cannot grasp it.

1 Universality and contextuality

The little word GOD is a very precious treasure of our cultural history. It bears within it the experiences of our ancestors, thousands of years old, in dealing with what shapes and sustains human beings and the world. At the same time this little word is a stumbling block, indeed a millstone, and the embodiment of human confusion, arrogance and obstinacy. We often think that we know its content, we like to dwell on traditional definitions, feel personally disturbed by contradictory statements. When it comes to grasping the ultimate and the absolute in words, we want to use the potential power that we suspect in it for ourselves and behave like children who know everything. Above all, theologians, women and men, the former perhaps more gently than the latter, are obsessed with the idea that God can be fixed in texts. We exegetes want to be God's private secretaries. We confuse our earthly temporal standpoint with the divine and eternal standpoint, peer over the shoulders of the one who decrees the fate of the world, or have no inhibitions about interpreting his plans for the world from eternity to eternity. We arrogate to ourselves what shamans and prophets really experience, but is no longer given to us in our studies: they were caught up into the heavenly council and could bring back reliable news from there (thus Micaiah ben Imlah in 1 Kings 22:19–22). On the other hand the tormented Job already shows up his comforters as mere theorists and reproaches them to their faces: 'Will you speak falsely for God, and speak deceitfully for him? Will you show partiality towards him, will you plead the case for God?' (Job 13:7f.). 'Have you sat in his council . . . ?' And contrary to the highly educated theologians, he is right. God himself declares at the end that they have not spoken 'what is right' of him, as has Job (Job 42:7–9).

So those of us who are supposed to be experts must be self-critical, and together with you, who acknowledge yourselves to be theological 'laity', must approach the task of looking out in our time for what is reliable, what gives meaning to our life and world, what gives us grounds for hope despite all moods of catastrophe. We are aware that despite all our preoccupation with the eternal our thoughts and speech remain temporally conditioned, our insights partial and our noblest concerns and actions fragmentary. No amount of eloquence can conceal the fact that we cannot succeed in finding long-term or finally valid formulae for the absolute. The statements that we make in preaching and teaching and which have God as subject ('God says, thinks, acts') are misleading. They always have quite limited validity. They are not to be understood literally, but subjectively: someone assumes, experiences, thinks it correct that God does this or that. The pure reality of the all-embracing and supra-temporal cannot either be imagined or put into words. Is that only a heritage of the Reformation (cf. Calvin's basic principle: *finitum non capax infiniti*)?

The essential limitations of time, space and society which govern our talk of God apply equally to the biblical evidence. It is to be read con-textually, as statements in a particular situation. Even the loftiest and most effective discourses, even those uttered by the deity in the first person, have become word and scripture only through human mediation. 'I am Yahweh, your God, who has brought you up out of Egypt, out of slavery' (Ex 20:2; Deut 5:6) is a theological insight of particular people in a given historical and social situation. The lofty words are introduced by the quotation formulae of the mediators, scribes, theologians: 'God spoke all these words' (Ex 20:1); 'he said' (Deut 5:5). This is synonymous with a statement which clearly comes from a teacher: 'Hear, Israel, Yahweh is our God, Yahweh alone' (Deut 6:5).

Today I want to describe to you how I, as an Old Testament scholar, approach my task historically in dialogue with the biblical witnesses. Stimulated by problems of the present, during this semester we investigated the manifold experiences in faith of the men and women of the Old Testament. We attempted to have an open conversation among ourselves and with the old insights about God which can give us orientation, but do not provide any stereotypes for our present-day experience of God. The aim was to find limited statements about what is needed in our time.

2 Experiences of God in the past

The biblical witnesses each need to be understood in terms of their environment and special situation. They do not offer a coherent dogmatic structure, but answers to the pressures of life and the terror of death in the world appropriate to the contemporary state of knowledge and the particular practice of the time. The statements that people make about God and the attitudes that they adapt towards the deity to a large degree depend on the social structures into which life is organized. People do not react to the question of meaning in small intimate groups in the same way as they do in anonymous mass societies. What can we know about belief in God in ancient Israel? How are the statements of faith made by the individual groups to be distinguished from one another, and how do they relate to one another?

Faith as family faith

Narratives about the era of the patriarchs, of instability, of a lack of land are governed by the awareness that the ancestors, i.e. Abraham and his clan, had worshipped 'other gods' than Yahweh beyond the Euphrates (cf. Josh. 24:2; Ex 6:3). Comparative studies in the sphere of the ancient Near East indicate that kinship groups each worshipped its own guardian deity. This 'personal' or family deity looked after the elementary interests of those under its protection: food, descendants, health, clothing, dwelling-place, harmony among members of the group, i.e. also a certain hierarchy of authority in the network of relationships. The divine name hardly played any role; one could even name the deity after the head of the family ('God of Abraham', etc.). Formally the deity belongs to the family alliance, as some personal names indicate (e.g. Abram = father is exalted: is this the indication of an ancestor cult?). He was worshipped in or by the house (Ex 21:6; Judg 17:3–5). Presumably the housewives were primarily responsible for family religion; this can be inferred from the very loose way in which Rachel and Michal deal with the 'teraphim', the little household gods whose images have been found by the hundred in Israelite cities (Gen 31:19–35; 1 Sam 19:13–17).

Domestic worship of God had presumably been customary since prehistoric times. It was *the* original form of religious activity, because for millennia human beings lived in small kinship groups and by shared work, whether gathering or hunting, or later by agriculture and cattle-breeding in a sedentary situation. The common life of the small group (or large family) of perhaps ten to fifteen people required an attitude towards super-human forces which was binding on its members. The great discovery in this very long phase of human history which precedes all the larger forms of society was doubtless that the powers that dominated the outside world (who could be experienced in fearful outbreaks of violence and in concomitant activities of blessing) could be addressed personally. They could be understood as a friendly 'you' and drawn into the family circle, or as a hostile opponent whom one had to avoid and from whom one had to protect oneself. Even today we live by this discovery of early humankind when we dare to address the deity directly, like a human counterpart. Family religion was the starting point of all belief in God and has remained its foundation.

Faith in the settled alliance

From as early as the tenth millennium on, settlements can be demonstrated in the Near East (or more precisely in Upper Mesopotamia) which attest that human beings had gone over to sedentary ways of life based on agriculture and cattle-breeding. This was a real cultural revolution which had far-reaching consequences for behaviour and all spheres of life. Even belief in God was directly affected, since now a number of families with a patrilinear structure lived together with their particular guardian deities. The inhabitants of such a settlement combined common interests in the yield of the fields and pastures, the use of water, and protection against enemies. Every place in Israel had a simple open-air sanctuary at which people celebrated sacrificial festivals (1 Sam 9:12–14; 20:6).

The shared worship of all the inhabitants of the village was devoted to a deity who is still visible in old place names (e.g. Anathoth – the plural of the name of the goddess Anat; Jerusalem – perhaps 'Shalim has founded'. Strangely there is no evidence of place names compounded with Yahweh!). Communal occasions were celebrated; at an early stage these probably also included certain transitional rites like the initiation of young men and women (Judg 21:19–21: the plunder of women at the feast in Shiloh) or fertility ceremonies for field and cattle.

Domestic worship of God had not become superfluous as a result of the shared cultic practice of the village. Both forms of religion continued to stand side by side (as they still do today). The great breakthrough in the history of the faith of humankind is that now people living side by side who were not related by blood discovered what they had in common in society and in religion (social relationship!). They learned to show solidarity to one another, even where the obligation on the family to extract blood vengeance no longer applied. They developed a first legal system which was to regulate conflicts. The civil law that we find in the Old Testament has in principle been developed from the world of the village community and presupposes this (cf. Ex 21:12 – 22:16, the 'casuistic law' of the Book of the Covenant). Thus with the community in the settled alliance the horizons of belief in God extended further. The village deity gives blessing to a mixed community, imposes on it obligations to be peaceful and to care for one another, creates respect for the elders, and offers solutions to conflicts in cases of dispute (e.g. over property). In short, the deity takes on ethical and legal contours.

Tribal and state religion

When we come to the tribe and state we are looking at numerically stronger formations of society which arose in the Near East in the course of the intensification of population after the fourth millennium. If the family community can operate with around ten persons and the village community with around a hundred, at the tribal level a thousand and more may be appropriate, and at the level of the state, ten thousand. The tribe is a loose alliance of autonomous family groups which forms mainly as an alliance for self-defence or waging war. The tribal leaders are possibly men, sometimes women, endowed with the spirit, who exercise limited authority and merely occupy the chief seat in the tribal council. In no case may the office be hereditary. The desire for hereditary succession marks the transition to the monarchy (cf. Judg 8:22f.; 11:5–11).

As far as we know, belief in Yahweh first arose at the tribal level. The earliest texts deal with great victories which Yahweh had won with tribal warriors (Judg 5; 11; Ps 68). Consequently in the pre-state phase Yahweh must have been a god of war who dwelt on a remote holy mountain (Sinai? The mountains of Seir? Paran?) and who hastened down to help his oppressed followers. Possibly during the warlike campaigns Yahweh dwelt in a portable tent, or he was enthroned invisible above the sacred ark. An old war cry runs, 'Arise, Yahweh, and let your enemies be scattered, and let those who hate you flee before you' (Num 10:35). Thus the language and thought world of the earliest Yahweh tradition are completely dominated by warlike events. The tribal battles were apparently fought with extreme brutality, frequently, it seems, in a berserk intoxication. Yahweh's demand to the warriors was unconditional commitment to the common cause. In the sphere of tribal religion a heroic male ethic was dominant. Women were involved with this religion at most when they greeted the men with drumming and song as they returned home victorious (Ex 15:21; 1 Sam 18:7).

In a way the urban and rural states of the ancient Near East continued the socialization of larger populations, but applied different principles from the segmentary tribal order, which reckoned with clans with equal rights. The state had a centralist and hierarchical structure, i.e. as a rule it had at its head a monarch appointed by God, who ruled with full authority: he raised taxes and levies to maintain the court, a standing army and building activity; conscripted citizens for forced labour; and all in all behaved in a very arbitrary and absolutist way.

It is quite clear that such a monarchical social order needed a strong state god to legitimate the monarchy. David made Yahweh the chief god of Jerusalem in order to demonstrate continuity with the time of the tribes. The temple was built as an imperial temple and entrusted to priests who directly supported the royal administration. The ambivalent consequences can be foreseen: on the one hand a strong and successful royal rule possibly brought the whole people economic gain and both political and legal security. On the other hand people were often exposed to caprice and exploitation on the part of the court. There were also both positive and negative consequences for the people's understanding of God; they certainly continued their well-tried minor cults as long as these did not conflict with the interests of the state. By contrast the greater official cult concentrated on the interests of the larger organization.

It is extremely significant that during the monarchy a political and religious opposition (we call it the prophets) can be heard. It appeals to the more democratic basic values of the clans and also to the monarchical duty of care laid down in the royal ideologies of the ancient Near East, in the name of Yahweh calling for solidarity with the weak and the poor. Moreover it occasionally rejects the worship of the élite strata, who engage the state god for their activities of exploitation (Amos).

For our purposes, the conclusion to be drawn from two such different larger organizations can only be that the progressive socialization of an increasing number of human beings was unstoppable. In the structures which came into being, new basic problems appeared which also had to be solved theologically, i.e. within the structure of meaning of the whole. For example, with the increasing concentration of power in the hand of the leaders the misuse of constitutional violence became more probable and dangerous. Law and order, protection and prosperity are to some degree goals which are also theologically legitimate. By contrast, arbitrary rule, corruption, imperialism, abuse of religious authority, contradict the spirit of justice which in the ancient Near East was from the beginning associated with the will of the state deity.

The satirical fable of Jotham, which is probably ancient, is significant for the cutting criticism of the monarchy. Jotham, the sole survivor of a political massacre, proclaims it to the inhabitants of Shechem. There is a desire to appoint a king: 'The trees once went forth to anoint a king over them; and they said to the olive tree, "Reign over us." But the olive tree said to them, "Shall I leave my fatness, by which gods and men are honoured, and go to sway over the trees?"' The fig tree and the vine answer to the same effect. After three refusals from the noblest species, the trees turn to the most inferior shrub. 'They said to the bramble, "Come you and reign over us." And the bramble said to the trees, "If in good faith you are anointing me king over you, then come and take refuge in my shade; but if not, let fire come out of the bramble and devour the cedars of Lebanon"' (Judg 9:8–15).

The criticism of the monarchy, which is so easily and so inevitably corrupted by human arrogance, also applies to majestic notions of God which support such forms of rule. In this way theological ideas of universal justice, cultic honesty and the need for permanent religious criticism as a way of controlling power are born.

The Jewish confessional community

The really decisive period of the Old Testament theologies begins with the Babylonian exile at the beginning of the sixth century BCE. Most of the writings contained in the Hebrew canon were brought together only in this relatively late period (between the sixth and second centuries BCE). In almost all the books of the Old Testament they reflect the circumstances of the new Jewish confessional community which was coming into being, which had lost its independence as a state and was exposed to the favour or disfavour of alien, imperial systems of rule. At home and in Babylon the people of Judah were left with a degree of religious and civil self-administration. They made use of the scope offered them, and under the leadership of priests and scribes, community teachers and preachers, set down on parchment the traditions that could be remembered. They organized meetings, festivals and services (cf. Neh 8) and even succeeded in rebuilding the Jerusalem temple (which was consecrated in 515 BCE). The restored building was not so much the symbol of an independent state and the Davidic dynasty as a sign of worldwide religious recognition and union, the religious centre of the dispersed community.

The successes of the conquered and humiliated Judahites are remarkable. Their theological insights have been influential for millennia and still cast a spell on us today. According to one leading thought, Yahweh has assumed an imperial role. Contrary to all appearances, he becomes the universal

God of heaven, who has created the world, holds the people in his hand and leads them secretly, and who – as is said increasingly clearly under the growing pressure from outside – will guide world history to a catastrophic conclusion, so that he can found his new kingdom of peace and justice.

The universal theology which came into being after the exile is quite clearly an answer to the conditions of the time; it is an emergency defence against the supremacy of the Babylonian and Persian empires. The thought-patterns used – the unity of the world, the unity of God's rule and the unity of humankind – have been taken over from the ruling cultures. Fusing these with their own Israelite, Judahite and Canaanite traditions (e.g. of the bringing up of ancestors from Egypt, the election of mount Zion and the Davidic dynasty) the theological paradigms are shaped into a tense complex of universality and particularity.

The people of Israel or the new community of Judah stand closer to the universal Yahweh than do the other peoples. The Jewish community which is coming into being has so to speak the right of the firstborn in the face of all the claims of the world empires, which for their part appeal to divine origin and divine commissioning. This spiritual and theological militancy is also the emergency measure of a small and insignificant people which had been forced right to the periphery by the world empires of the time. But what courageous faith underlies such theologies, which stand the political realities of the time on their head!

Inwardly, the reorganization of the community was along much more traditional lines, although here too theological innovations are to be noted. The theologians of the exilic and post-exilic community drew on many sources for their revision of old traditions. They introduced belief in Yahweh from the state and tribal constitutions, and under the pressure of circum-stances made it absolutely binding on all members of the community. Household and special cults, the worship of any other deities than Yahweh, were strictly forbidden (Ex 20:2–6; but cf. the documents from Elephantine which clearly indicate the worship of deities with and alongside Yahweh in a Jewish military colony under Persian rule, around 450 BCE). Sole allegiance to Yahweh and the revelation of his will, the Torah, was the basic commandment for all Judahites in so far as they wanted to submit to this norm. The structure of a confessional community which in principle was accessible to people who were not Judahites and made it possible for born members to leave meant that the decision of the individual had priority in matters of faith. Here was the beginnings of a confessional individualism (cf. also the ethical individualization in Ezek 18). The religious concern of the family was now seen to lie in the community bond; family faith and village community ethics fed the new community structures. Memories of the monarchy and the current involvement in the imperial politics of the Babylonians and Persians ensured that the interests of wider society, indeed world society, did not completely disappear from view. But all in all the internal ethic of the community had the character that we know from the level of the village community. The leadership of the community lay with the scribes and priests. Yahweh was transformed into a universal God of heaven, above the world, who is also present in a caring fatherly way in every community through the Torah.

3 GOD in our time

Interpretations of the Bible cannot stop at bringing out theological or religious features. Because in the Bible we have a foundation document of our faith and our culture, we are directly involved with the biblical testimonies They are 'bone of our bone, flesh of our flesh', and of course one does not deal with one's ancestors as one deals with strangers. In the biblical past we recognize ourselves, our blessing and our curse, but at the same time we have the task of recreating this spiritual heritage in our present in accordance with the parameters of our times and societies. Here we need to understand the changed social structures and basic insights before engaging in dialogue with the ancient texts. We are looking for the most important characteristic of the time for faith today, or for its main structures and main problems.

Here the presupposition is that the attempt to react to life, the world, the unconditional, cannot be made only through ancient texts. Latin American theologians like Carlos Mesters speak openly of a long quest by the exegete. The path goes 'from life to the Bible' and 'from the Bible to life'. That means that biblical interpreters expose themselves to reality, recognize life-creating power in structures and events today, and suffer under the influences of death. They enter into dialogue with the biblical witnesses and their insights and return to present-day life. In traditional language, if God is really God, then he/she/it is also active in and with present-day circumstances. The experiences of antiquity are valuable beacons. But we must find the course of the ship of faith today in unknown, new waters.

The individual in the business of society

What then are the present-day conditions in which we encounter the claim of the other, the oppressive life, the inexplicable suffering and the question of the meaning of it all? The stratification of human society is still a reality, though significant restructurings have been achieved. At the beginning there is no longer the family unit but the autonomous, almost autistic (to use Horst Eberhard Richter's term) individual. This is a world of its own, and everything else is allegedly made for its sake. Even the global market, the opposite end of the spectrum, is still meant to serve the individual: is this a modern delusion which in the present state of affairs hands over the mass of the world's population to misery and disaster?

Between the two poles, the individual and world society, there are those social forms of the classes of tens, hundreds, thousands, hundreds of thousands and millions which we already know from antiquity. Industrial society has fundamentally remodelled them in accordance with its demands. Above all the individual has to be mobile, ready to become involved as a tiny cog in a great business. The family still exists in a markedly reduced form. It still brings up children, worse rather than better. It offers a bit of security which is often so precious to the autonomous individual, and the exchange of ideas between married couples is said on average still to claim five or six minutes a day. Numerous other groups in the sphere of the tens and hundreds in human socialization have supplemented or replaced the family alliance. From the kindergarten to the seniors' club, from work, leisure and cultural associations, from help and self-help circles to political and religious groups, countless little social formations ensure the necessary web of relationship which can only be experienced face-to-face. For a long time similar structures of dependence and dominance, shared cultural achievement and self-destructive conflict, have dominated in the numerically larger forms of society. The heaven-storming increase in human power brought about by mechanical and electronic equipment (from the craftsman's tool to the thinker's tool) and the excessive dimensions of economic systems certainly have both good and bad effects on wider societies, but both in antiquity and in modernity the contours of these anonymous, bureaucratic forms of society, which are difficult to make democratic, resemble one another.

Our main problems are obvious: the role of the individual in the ever-greater business of society, the flourishing interaction of individual formations in society, a democratic structuring of authority, a far-reaching way of dealing with natural resources, a life worth living for everyone, a just global order for the economy and for society.

The one world under the one God

It is not only the social changes that today play a role for theological discourse. There are also the revolutions in science and technology and the new relation to nature which arises from them; this must influence our thought-patterns hallowed by tradition. From the depth of the universe and time, from the genome structures and the miraculous world of the atom, the great mystery confronts us and requires us to adopt an attitude towards it. How and why do we find ourselves on this planet on the edge of a galaxy, somewhere on the periphery of the universe? Our ancient forebears perhaps saw much very differently in their geocentric, or at best heliocentric, anthropomorphic and patriarchal world, which they were able to survey. Theology, the church and all rational beings can no longer avoid the fundamental questions which are put to their own position.

The urgency of the essentially religious question is heightened by the fact that according to forecasts for humanity and life on this planet which need to be taken seriously we have very little time. The apocalyptic nightmares nurtured by humankind for millennia (cf. Dan 2; 7; Rev 20f.) now seem close to realization. The main problems are the threat to the biosphere of the planet and the failure to control scientific and technological, not to say economic and political, development.

Every segment of our society needs to be taken seriously and will develop its own theological parameters in accordance with the results of biblical interpretation. These parameters cannot immediately be harmonized. But it is our task to relate the stratified models to one another, not to let any of them get the upper hand and to orientate them all as far as possible on the goal of the one world under the one God. Here the cultural and religious shapes which have been acquired through history offer help. For since biblical antiquity, which soon (from Hellenistic times: Alexander the Great) allied itself with Greek thought, we have become accustomed to think and construct the world e.g. monistically and not dualistically, more rationalistically than mystically, increasingly individualistically instead of collectively, transcendentally with strong injections of immanence, often hierarchically with important elements of democratic tradition, but in a way which is unfortunately far more patriarchal than seeking equal rights for all. This list shows that not all the traditional thought-patterns are good for us. But we have to grapple with them. They are in our blood and in our cultural and religious baggage.

Changes in talking about God in the individual sphere

Since that first capacity to make choices about religion (Ezekiel!), in the Western tradition the individual has increasingly become the centre of all thought (the Renaissance, the Enlightenment, the Industrial Revolution). Thus the individual has become theologically significant, far beyond the old pattern of family faith in the Old Testament and the ancient Near East. We can no longer construct the world from the family unit, the patriarchal 'we-group', as conservative Christians have occasionally attempted to do. Moreover the ancient bi-polarity of the sexes which divided the world into two sexually different spheres of life has no significance for the way in which we lead our lives, nor – on the basis of the existing principles of law – should it. In principle our world is unisex and homogeneous.

For theological anthropology today that means that the individual has a dignity which is unassailable because it is willed and protected by God. The sexes are absolutely equal, and every human being must be accorded the same rights, regardless of land of birth, social status, race, gender or confession. The privileges include the human rights which have often already been formulated, but today we need to think again and in view of the grandiose success of human research and technology and the unimaginably high level of production by comparison with antiquity accept fundamental rights to life like those to work, education, abode, health, etc.

The recognition of the individual as the fundamental point of reference is theologically necessary. But that does not mean that the individual in his or her autonomy must be the only and last point of reference. The world contains many individuals. They are forced to co-exist and co-operate, because *de facto* no one can exist completely without other people and without the natural environment. We are all interwoven into wider contexts in which deity manifests itself in a different way, i.e. *other* rules apply.

Individuals in an atomized society often feel betrayed and abandoned. They experience their environment, themselves, God, as hostile and oppressive. Christian community should stand beside the oppressed in a pastoral way, helping them. Then perhaps a new confidence could grow, even in the unfathomable God. In childlike naïvety we could say 'You' to that which oppresses us yet bears us up. A psalm puts it like this: 'Yahweh, my heart is not lifted up, my eyes are not raised too high. I do not occupy myself with things too great and too marvellous for me. But I have calmed and quieted my soul, like a child quieted at its mother's breast' (Ps 131:1f.). The transition to the small group is clear.

Changes in the sphere of primary groups

In the two and a half millennia since the Old Testament period, hardly any social formation has been subjected to such a marked change as the family and the clan. From being a self-sufficient and comprehensive unit for living, working and believing, the primal association of human society has degenerated into a limited place of reproduction and – if it keeps its head above water – a repair shop for burdened solitary fighters. The losses of function in the natural intimate community are enormous. One is amazed that the number of single-person homes is not far greater than it already is. The way in which some church statements still regard the family as the only valid norm for human social life is pure wishful thinking. A diversity of other forms of community have come into being alongside the family. Alongside those living alone who have already been mentioned, there are single parents, communities of very varied kinds, same-sex couples, teams of workers, technicians and artists, and many kinds of purposive and leisure groups. As was sporadically also the case in antiquity, people live intensively together temporarily or for a longer term and find that a considerable part of the meaning in their lives derives from such associations outside the family.[1]

So the ancient kinship group has competitors. Today small societies have become very important, and we cannot avoid seeking the ethically right behaviour for them and with them. The essential thing is that God can be seen as the fellow human beings, as a 'you', in an intimate atmosphere. Love, security, personal acceptance can be experienced almost exclusively in the realm of small groups. Thus the opposite can also be said: these small groups are not uninterested in the divine or the world as a whole. The intimate groups have a responsibility for individuals and for more highly organized society. In analogy to the ancient families and clans they form their own ideas of what is right and worth striving for, and therefore frame norms which are aimed at an overall context of meaning. That is where their theological significance lies.

Changes in the secondary and tertiary sphere

The numerically stronger social groupings, from the village and city level to that of the people, the state, the alliance of states, the religious and cultic communities, in turn follow their own laws. Theologically they are especially interesting, because in them the most important economic and military, scientific and cultural forces are at work. Finally, all these 'higher' developments of the human capacity for invention and creativity depend on the shared work of many individuals – and especially, today, on the corresponding capital expenditure of larger associations. As the ancient narrators who reported the building of the tower of Babel already knew, achievements of any kind require a shared effort and much money. These narrators rated the human achievement so high that even God had to be afraid of it (Gen 11:1–9).

It should be clear from human history that increasing power in these forms of socialization leads to an extraordinarily great need for religion.

---

[1] In my view the churches attach far too much importance to the sexual components of social life on the basis of antiquated ideas of taboo. Sexuality is only one of the forces which aims at social ties. It should not be emphasized in isolation, but apart from possible criminal actions should simply be left to personal responsibility. Cf. my report on homosexuality in the Old Testament in Klaus Bartl (ed.), *Schwule, Lesben . . . -Kirche*, EKHN-Dokumentation 2, Frankfurt 1996, 124–58, and my commentary *Leviticus* (ch. 4 n. 18), on Lev. 18 and 20.

Power seeks to give itself divine legitimation; it therefore urgently needs to be corrected by a totality which transcends it. Modern nation states with their developed systems of symbols offer the best example of secularized forms of religion. But economic enterprises sometimes attempt to surround themselves with an aura and construct hagiographies to safeguard their own existence. Religious communities work predominantly in wider societies, but almost always with local base groups. Theology has the task of illuminating the structures which have come into being and are changing; of making a critical examination of their ideas of God; and of countering the misuse of developments of power. From the perspective of biblical traditions and according to some critical investigation by sober contemporaries, the larger societies clearly have subordinate functions. They should serve men and women and not absolutize them.

The outlines of an image of God at the intermediate level of the great organizations could be described with biblical terms: peace, justice, the preservation of creation – those points of orientation for the 'conciliar process' which some years ago drew the attention of the church and the public to the need for a shared new reflection. At all events, the time of anxious demarcations is past. The planet can no longer support intolerance and claims to exclusiveness. The one unknowable deity guarantees all creatures the right to live and imposes co-existence on them all. In the particular and ancient language of a psalm:

> He will lighten our land with his presence
> steadfast love and faithfulness will meet; righteousness and peace will
>   kiss each other (Ps 85:10b–11).

Theology must become contextual and ecumenical

Our pluralistic global society requires a new scheme of theology. Our present-day reality is so complex that no individual can survey it fully any longer. We are becoming more and more dependent on electronic data systems and the experts who go with them. In the end they alone can prepare decision-making processes for wider areas.

Despite the immense difficulties, theologians will have to insist that a global theology comes into being, precisely within the framework of the globalization of living conditions on this planet. This cannot be the mission theology of former centuries, constructed on imperial models. But in the experience of our world as a unity which is endangered by humankind the question of God comes through to us. What is the significance of this speck of earth in the solar system? (I shall not pursue the question further, for we can guess at the existence of millions of world bodies which have produced life.) The limited answer, based on our traditional attitudes, could be that the earth with its forms of life is an experiment the viability of which is being tested. We are taking part in this test.

But there is one thing that global theology cannot mean, and that is a compact, coherent doctrinal system. With its complex content, which differs on many social levels, the little word GOD points to the unfathomable mystery of the world and human existence. Many difficulties that we have with contradictory concepts of God arise from the fact that we constantly attempt to bring the most different statements about God logically under one heading. These attempts must come to grief on reality.

But if in a deeply pluralistic world we renounce calculating unification; if in the knowledge of our theological limitations we look with wonder at the diversity of the world behind which the unity of God is indefinably but (in our view) really hidden; if in our questions about the survival of humankind we seek common answers and fight through to shared decisions, we are best living in harmony with the presence of God in this world. The question of God is a problem for humankind. Like all religious action and contemplation it is a question of being or not-being. If we want to preserve civilization on this planet, we shall have to change the way we think about God. But the possibility of being able to say something pointing towards the unconditional that holds our world together 'in the innermost depths' may prove the opportunity (perhaps the only opportunity) to recognize the world as a whole and to come to terms with it in the long run. But if that is to happen, we must be prepared to open up our narrow thoughts and claims. In other words, theology must be contextual and ecumenical.

> *Everything is shaped by mystery, for everything comes from your hands,*
> *or from the hands of human beings, your co-creators:*
> *the paper on which I write, the ball-point which I use,*
> *the table at which I sit,*
> *the books which surround me,*
> *the clothes which cover me, the air which I breathe,*
> *the light which I see, the ground which supports me.*
> *My heart leaps for joy. The shining impact of an all-embracing totality.*

HELDER CAMARA

Abbreviations

AASF	Annales Academiæ Scientiarum Fennicae
AASOR	Annual of the American Schools of Oriental Research
AB	Anchor Bible
ABD	*Anchor Bible Dictionary*
ANET	*Ancient Near Eastern Texts Relating to the Old Testament*
AOAT	Alter Orient und Altes Testament
AOS	American Oriental Series
ATANT	Abhandlungen zur Theologie des Alten und Neuen Testaments
ATD	Das Alte Testament Deutsch
BA	*Biblical Archaeologist*
BAB	Becks archäologische Bibliothek
BagFor	Baghdader Forschungen
BASOR	*Bulletin of the American Schools of Oriental Research*
BE	*Biblische Enzyklopädie*
BES	Biblical Encounter Series
BHH	*Biblisch-Historisches Handwörterbuch*
BiBe	Biblische Beiträge
BiE	*Bulletin de l'institut égyptien*
BiKi	*Bibel und Kirche*
BJSt	Brown Judaic Studies
BKAT	Biblischer Kommentar, Altes Testament
BWANT	Beiträge zur Wissenschaft vom Alten und Neuen Testament
BZAW	Beihefte zur ZAW

CBOT	Coniectanea biblica: Old Testament Series
CBQ	*Catholic Biblical Quarterly*
CDOG	Colloquium der deutschen Orient-Gesellschaft
CTM	Calwer theologische Monographien
DBAT	*Deilheimer Blätter zum Alten Testament und seiner Rezeption in der Hen Kirche*
EdF	Erträge der Forschung
EncRel	*Encyclopedia of Religion*
EvTh	*Evangelische Theologie*
ExuZ	Exegese in unserer Zeit
FAOS	Freiburger altorientalische Studien
FAT	Forschungen zum Alten Testament
FJCD	Forschungen zum jüdisch-christlichen Dialog
FOTL	The Forms of the Old Testament Literature
FRLANT	Forschungen zur Religion und Literatur des Alten und Neuen Testaments
GAT	Grundrisse zum Alten Testament
HAL	*Hebräisches und aramäisches Lexikon zum Alten Testament*
HAT	Handbuch zum Alten Testament
HSM	Harvard Semitic Monographs
HSS	Harvard Semitic Studies
HThKAT	Herders theologischer Kommentar zum Alten Testament
HTKAT	Herders theologischer Kommentar zum Alten Testament
JAAR	*Journal of the American Academy of Religion*
JBL	*Journal of Biblical Literature*
JPES	*Journal of the Palestine Exploration Society*
JSOT	*Journal for the Study of the Old Testament*
JSOTSup	JSOT Supplement Series
KAT	Kommentar zum Alten Testament
KS	*Kleine Schriften*
LAI	Library of Ancient Israel
MAES	Monographs of the American Ethnological Society
MDOG	Mitteilungen der deutschen Orient-Gesellschaft
NBL	*Neues Bibel-Lexikon*
NEB	Neue Echter Bibel
NSB	Neukirchener Studienbücher
NTDH	Neukirchener theologische Dissertationen und

	Habiltationen
OBO	Orbis biblicus et Orientalis
OBT	Overtures to Biblical Theology
OTL	Old Testament Library
OTS	*Oudtestamentische Studiën*
PJ	*Palästina-Jahrbuch*
PTH	Praktische Theologie Heute
RAC	*Reallexikon für Antike und Christentum*
RLA	*Reallexikon der Assyriologie*
SAOC	Studies in Ancient Oriental Civilizations
SBS	Stuttgarter Bibelstudien
SHCANE	Studies in the History and Culture of the Ancient Near East
TEH	Theologische Existenz heute
THAT	*Theologisches Handwörterbuch zum Alten Testament*
ThQ	*Theologische Quartalschrift*
ThR	*Theologische Rundschau*
ThSt	Theologische Studien
ThW	Theologische Wissenschaft
ThWAT	*Theologisches Wörterbuch zum Alten Testament*
TRE	*Theologische Realenzyklopädie*
TThSt	Trierer theologische Studien
TUAT	*Texte aus der Umwelt des Alten Testaments*
UF	*Ugarit Forschungen*
UTB	Uni-Taschenbücher
VF	*Verkundigung und Forschung*
VT	*Vetus Testamentum*
VTSup	VT Supplements
WdF	Wege der Forschung
WMANT	Wissenschaftliche Monographien zum Alten und Neuen Testament
WZLGS	*Wissenschaftliche Zeitschrift der Karl-Marx-Universität Leipzig; Gesellschafts- und sprachwissenschaftliche Reihe*
ZA	*Zeitschrift für Assyriologie*
ZAW	*Zeitschrift für die alttestamentliche Wissenschaft*
ZdZ	*Zeichen der Zeit*
ZRGG	*Zeitschrift für Religions und Geistesgeschichte*
ZThK	*Zeitschrift für Theologie und Kirche*

Bibliography

Ackroyd, Peter R. *Exile and Restoration: A Study of Hebrew Thought of the Sixth Century B.C.* OTL. Philadelphia: Westminster, 1968.

Ahlström, Gösta W. *The History of Ancient Palestine from the Palaeolithic Period to Alexander's Conquest.* Minneapolis: Fortress Press, 1993.

Albertz, Rainer. *Persönliche Frömmigkeit und offizielle Religion: Religionsinterner Pluralismus in Israel und Babylon.* CTM A/9. Stuttgart: Calwer, 1978.

———. *A History of Israelite Religion in the Old Testament Period.* 2 vols. Translated by J. Bowden. OTL. Louisville: Westminster John Knox, 1994. (German ed. 1992.)

Alt, Albrecht. *Kleine Schriften zur Geschichte des Volkes Israel.* 3 vols. Munich: Beck, 1953–59; partial translation in *Essays on Old Testament History and Religion.* Translated by R. A. Wilson. Oxford: Blackwell, 1966.

Amery, Carl. *Das Ende der Vorsehung: Die gnadenlosen Folgen der Christentums.* Reinbek: Rowohlt, 1972.

Anderson, Bernhard W. *The Contours of Old Testament Theology.* Minneapolis: Fortress Press, 1999.

Assmann, Hugo, *Crítica à logica da exclusão.* São Paulo: Paulus, 1994.

———, and Franz Hinkelammert. *Götze Markt.* Düsseldorf: Patmos, 1992.

Assmann, Jan. *Moses the Egyptian: The Memory of Egypt in Western Monotheism.* Cambridge: Harvard Univ. Press, 1997.

Bach, Alice, editor. *Women in the Hebrew Bible: A Reader.* London: Routledge, 1999.

Badinter, Elisabeth. *The Unopposite Sex: The End of the Gender Battle.* Translated by B. Wright. New York: Harper & Row, 1989. (French ed. 1986.)

Balentine, Samuel E. *The Torah's Vision of Worship.* OBT. Minneapolis: Fortress Press, 1999.

Barr, James. *Biblical Faith and Natural Theology.* Gifford Lectures in Natural Theology. Rev. ed. Oxford: Oxford Univ. Press, 1994.

————. *The Concept of Biblical Theology: An Old Testament Perspective.* Minneapolis: Fortress Press, 1999.

Bartelmus, Rüdiger. *Heroentum in Israel und seiner Umwelt: Eine traditionsgeschichtliche Untersuchung zu Gen. 6, 1-4 und verwandten Texten im Alten Testament und der altorientalischen Literatur.* ATANT 65. Zurich: Theologischer Verlag, 1979.

Beck, Martin. *Elia und die Monolatrie: Ein Beitrag zur religionsgeschichtlichen Rückfrage nach dem vorschriftprophetischen Jahwe-Glauben.* BZAW 281. Berlin: de Gruyter, 1999.

Beck, Ulrich, and Elisabeth Beck-Gernsheim, editors. *Riskante Freiheiten: Individualisierung in modernen Gesellschaften.* Frankfurt: Suhrkamp, 1994.

Bellis, Alice Ogden, and Joel S. Kaminsky, editors. *Jews, Christians, and the Theology of the Hebrew Bible.* SBL Symposium Series. Atlanta: Society of Biblical Literature, 2000.

Bernhardt, Reinhold. *Zwischen Grössenwahn, Fanatismus und Bekennermut: Für ein Christentum ohne Absolutheitsanspruch.* Stuttgart: Kreuz, 1994.

Bird, Phyllis A. *Missing Persons and Mistaken Identities: Women and Gender in Ancient Israel.* OBT. Minneapolis: Fortress Press, 1997.

Blenkinsopp, Joseph. *A History of Prophecy in Israel.* Rev. ed. Louisville: Westminster John Knox, 1998.

Bloch, Ernst. *Atheism in Christianity: The Religion of the Exodus and the Kingdom.* Translated by J. T. Swann. New York: Herder & Herder, 1972. (German ed. 1969.)

Blum, Erhard. *Die Komposition der Vätergeschichte.* WMANT 57. Neukirchen-Vluyn: Neukirchener, 1984.

Böcher, Otto. *Dämonenfurcht und Dämonenabwehr: Ein Beitrag zur Vorgeschichte der christlichen Taufe.* BWANT 90. Stuttgart: Kohlhammer, 1970.

Boecker, Hans Joachim. *Law and the Administration of Justice in the Old Testament and Ancient East.* Translated by J. Moiser. Minneapolis: Augsburg, 1980. (2nd German ed. 1984.)

Boff, Clodovis. *Theology and Praxis: Epistemological Foundations.* Translated by R. R. Barr. Maryknoll, Orbis, 1987. (Portugese ed. 1978.)

Brueggemann, Walter. *David's Truth in Israel's Imagination and Memory.* 2nd ed. Minneapolis: Fortress Press, 2002.

———. *The Land: Place as Gift, Promise, and Challenge in Biblical Faith.* 2nd ed. OBT. Minneapolis: Fortress Press, 2002.

———. *Old Testament Theology: Essays on Structure, Theme, and Text.* Edited by P. D. Miller. Minneapolis: Fortress Press, 1992.

———. *The Prophetic Imagination.* 2nd ed. Minneapolis: Fortress Press, 2001.

———. *Theology of the Old Testament: Testimony, Dispute, Advocacy.* Minneapolis: Fortress Press, 1997.

Brunner-Traut, Emma. *Die alten Ägypter: Verborgenes Leben unter Pharaonen.* Stuttgart: Kohlhammer, 1974.

Buchkremer, Hansjosef. *Familie im Spannungsfeld globaler Mobilität: Zur Konstruktion ethnischer Minderheiten im Kontext der Familie.* Interkulturelle Studien 2. Opladen: Leske & Budrich, 2000.

Childs, Brevard S. *Biblical Theology of the Old and New Testaments: Theological Reflection on the Christian Bible.* Minneapolis: Fortress Press, 1999.

———. *Introduction to the Old Testament as Scripture.* Philadelphia: Fortress Press, 1979.

Cohen, Mark E. *The Canonical Lamentations of Ancient Mesopotamia.* 2 vols. Potomac, Md.: Capital Decisions, 1988.

Coogan, Michael D. "Life in the Diaspora: Jews at Nippur in the Fifth Century B.C." *Biblical Archaeologist* 37 (1974) 6–12.

Cox, Harvey. *The Secular City: Secularization and Urbanization in Theological Perspective.* New York: Macmillan, 1965.

Croatto, J. Severino. *Exodus: A Hermeneutics of Freedom.* Translated by S. Attanasio. Maryknoll, N.Y.: Orbis, 1981. (Spanish ed. 1978.)

Cross, Frank Moore. *Canaanite Myth and Hebrew Epic: Essays in the History of the Religion of Israel.* Cambridge: Harvard Univ. Press, 1973.

Crüsemann, Frank. *Der Widerstand gegen das Königtum: Die antiköniglichen Texte des Alten Testamentes und der Kampf um den frühen israelitischen Staat.* WMANT 49. Neukirchen-Vluyn: Neukirchener, 1978.

———. *The Torah: Theology and Social History of Old Testament Law.* Translated by A. Mahnke. Minneapolis: Fortress Press, 1996. (German ed. 1992.)

Davies, Philip R. *Scribes and Schools: The Canonization of the Hebrew Scriptures.* LAI. Louisville: Westminster John Knox, 1998.

Deschner, Karlheinz. *Kriminalgeschichte des Christentum.* 5 vols. Reinbek: Rowohlt, 1986–.

Dever, William G. *Recent Archaeological Discoveries and Biblical Research.* Seattle: Univ. of Washington Press, 1990.

Dietrich, Walter. *Israel und Kanaan: Vom Ringen zweier Gesellschaftssyteme.* SBS 94. Stuttgart: Katholisches Bibelwerk, 1979.

———, and Martin A. Klopfenstein, editors. *Ein Gott allein? JHWH-Verehrung und biblischer Monotheismus im Kontext der israelitischen und altorientalischen Religionsgeschichte.* OBO 139. Göttingen: Vandenhoeck & Ruprecht, 1994.

Donner, Herbert. *Geschichte des Volkes Israel und seiner Nachbarn in Grundzüge.* 2 vols. GAT 4. Göttingen: Vandenhoeck & Ruprecht, 1995.

Duchrow, Ulrich. *Alternatives to Global Capitalism Drawn from Biblical History, Designed for Political Action.* Utrecht: International Books, 1995. (German ed. 1994.)

Elbogen, Ismar. *Der jüdische Gottesdienst in seiner geschichtlichen Entwicklung.* 3rd ed. Frankfurt: Kaufman, 1931; reprinted Hildesheim: Ohlms, 1962.

Finkelstein, Israel. *The Archaeology of the Israelite Settlement.* Jerusalem: Israel Exploration Society, 1988.

Fischer, Irmtraud. *Die Erzeltern Israels: Feministisch-theologische Studien zu Genesis 12–36.* BZAW 222. Berlin: de Gruyter, 1994.

Fohrer, Georg. *Glaube und Leben im Judentum.* UTB 885. Heidelberg: Quelle & Meyer, 1979.

Fowler, Jeaneane D. *Theophoric Personal Names in Ancient Hebrew: A Comparative Study.* JSOTSup 49. Sheffield: JSOT Press, 1988.

Fritz, Volkmar. *Die Stadt im alten Israel.* BAB. Munich: Beck, 1990.

———. *Die Entstehung Israels im 12. und 11. Jh v.Chr.* BE 1. Stuttgart: Kohlhammer, 1996.

Galilea, Segundo. *Religiosidade Popular e Pastoral.* São Paulo: Paulus, 1978.

Gerstenberger, Erhard S. *Der Bittende Mensch.* WMANT 51. Neukirchen-Vluyn: Neukirchener, 1980.

———. *Yahweh The Patriarch: Ancient Images of God and Feminist Theology.* Translated by F. J. Gaiser. Minneapolis: Fortress Press, 1996. (German ed. 1988.)

———, and Wolfgang Schrage. *Woman and Man.* Translated by D. W. Stott. BES. Nashville: Abingdon, 1981. (German ed. 1980.)

Gleis, Matthias. *Die Bamah.* BZAW 251. Berlin: de Gruyter, 1997.

Goeudevert, Daniel. *Mit Träumen Beginnt die Realität*. Berlin: Rowohlt, 1999.

Gottwald, Norman K. *The Tribes Of Yahweh: A Sociology of the Religion of Liberated Israel, 1250–1050 B.C.E.* Maryknoll, N.Y.: Orbis, 1979.

Gutiérrez, Gustavo. *A Theology Of Liberation: History, Politics, and Salvation.* Translated by C. Inda and J. Eagleson. Rev. ed. Maryknoll, N.Y.: Orbis, 1988. (Spanish ed. 1972.)

Haag, Ernst, *Vom Sabbat zum Sonntag: Eine bibeltheologische Studie.* TThSt 52. Trier: Paulinus, 1991.

Hanson, Paul D. *The People Called: The Growth of Community in the Bible, with a New Introduction.* Louisville: Westminster John Knox, 2001.

Haran, Menahem. *Temple and Temple-Service in Ancient Israel: An Inquiry into Biblical Cult Phenomena and the Historical Setting of the Priestly School.* Oxford: Clarendon, 1978. Reprinted Winona Lake, Ind.: Eisenbrauns, 1985.

Hasel, Gerhard F., *Old Testament Theology: Basic Issues in the Current Debate.* 4th ed. Grand Rapids: Eerdmans, 1991.

Hawking, Stephen W. *A Brief History of Time.* Rev. ed. New York: Bantam, 1998.

Hayes, John H., editor. *Dictionary of Biblical Interpretation.* 2 vols. Nashville: Abingdon, 1999.

Hoffmann, Hans-Detlef, *Reform und Reformen: Untersuchungen zu einem Grundthema der deuteronomistischen Geschichtsschreibung.* ATANT 66. Zurich: Theologischer Verlag, 1980.

Honecker, Martin. *Grundriss der Sozialethik.* Berlin: de Gruyter, 1995.

Hossfeld, Frank-Lothar, *Der Dekalog: Seine späten Fassungen, die originale Komposition und seine Vorstufen.* OBO 45. Göttingen: Vandenhoeck & Ruprecht, 1982.

———, and Erich Zenger. *Psalmen 51–100.* HTKAT. Freiburg: Herder, 2000. (*Psalms 51–100.* Translated by L. M. Maloney. Hermeneia. Minneapolis: Fortress Press, forthcoming.)

Jacobsen, Thorkild. *Treasures of Darkness: A History of Mesopotamian Religion.* New Haven: Yale Univ. Press, 1976.

Jahnow, Hedwig, et al. *Feministische Hermeneutik und Erstes Testament: Analysen und Interpretationen.* Stuttgart: Kohlhammer, 1994.

Janowski, Bernd, *Sühne als Heilsgeschehen: Studien zur Sühnetheologie der Priesterschrift und zur Wurzel KPR im Alten Orient und im Alten Testament.* WMANT 55. Neukirchen-Vluyn: Neukirchener, 1982.

Jeremias, Jörg. *Theophanie.* 2nd ed. WMANT 10. Neukirchen-Vluyn:

Neukirchener, 1977.

Jonas, Hans. *The Imperative of Responsibility: In Search of an Ethics for a Technological Age.* Translated by H. Jonas and D. Herr. Chicago: Univ. of Chicago Press, 1984. (German ed. 1979.)

———. *Der Gottesbegriff nach Auschwitz: Eine jüdische Stimme.* Frankfurt: Suhrkamp, 1987.

Kaiser, Otto, *Der Gott des Alten Testaments: Theologie des Alten Testaments.* 2 vols. UTB. Göttingen: Vandenhoeck & Ruprecht, 1993–98.

Kaminsky, Joel S. *Corporate Responsibility in the Hebrew Bible.* JSOTSup 196. Sheffield: Sheffield Academic, 1995

Keel, Othmar, *The Symbolism of the Biblical World: Ancient Near Eastern Iconography and the Book of Psalms.* Translated by T. J. Hallett. Winona Lake, Ind.: Eisenbrauns, 1997. (German ed. 1972.)

———, and Christoph Uehlinger. *Gods, Goddesses, and Images of God in Ancient Israel.* Translated by T. H. Trapp. Minneapolis: Fortress Press, 1997. (German ed. 1992.)

Keil, Siegfried. *Lebensphasen, Lebensformen, Lebensmöglichkeiten: Sozialethische Überlegungen zu den Sozialisationsbedingungen in Familie, Kirche und Gesellschaft.* Bochum: SWI, 1992.

Kessler, Rainer. *Staat und Gesellschaft im vorexilischen Juda: Vom 8. Jahrhundert bis zum Exil.* VTSup 47. Leiden: Brill, 1992.

Knierim, Rolf P. *The Task of Old Testament Theology: Substance, Methods, and Cases.* Grand Rapids: Eerdmans, 1995.

Knohl, Israel. *The Sanctuary of Silence: The Priestly Torah and the Holiness School.* Minneapolis: Fortress Press, 1995.

Köckert, Matthias. *Vätergott und Väterverheissungen: Eine Auseinandersetzung mit Albrecht Alt und seinen Erben.* FRLANT 142. Göttingen: Vandenhoeck & Ruprecht, 1988.

König, René. *Grundformen der Gesellschaft: Die Gemeinde.* Rowohlts deutsche Enzyklopadie 79. Hamburg: Rowohlt, 1958.

Lang, Bernhard, editor. *Der einzige Gott: Die Geburt die biblischen Monotheismus.* Munich: Kösel, 1981.

Lemche, Niels Peter, *Prelude to Israel's Past: Background and Beginnings of Israelite History and Identity.* Translated by E. F. Maniscalco. Peabody, Mass.: Hendrickson, 1998. (German ed. 1996.)

Levenson, Jon D. *Sinai and Zion: An Entry into the Jewish Bible.* Minneapolis: Winston, 1985.

Lévi-Strauss, Claude. *The Elementary Structures of Kinship.* Rev. ed. Translated by J. H. Bell et al. Boston: Beacon, 1969. (French ed. 1967.)

Levinas, Emmanuel. *Humanisme de l'autre homme.* Livre de poche: Biblio essays. Montpellier: Fata Morgana, 1972.

Lewis, I. M. *Ecstatic Religion: An Anthropological Study of Spirit Possession and Shamanism.* Pelican Anthropology Library. Harmondsworth: Penguin, 1971.

Lewis, Theodore J. *Cults of the Dead in Ancient Israel and Ugarit.* HSM 39. Atlanta: Scholars, 1989.

Linafelt, Tod, and Timothy K. Beal, editors. *God in the Fray: A Tribute to Walter Brueggemann.* Minneapolis: Fortress Press, 1998.

Long, Burke O. *Planting and Reaping Albright: Politics, Ideology, and Interpreting the Bible.* University Park: Pennsylvania State Press, 1997.

Loretz, Oswald. *Habiru—Hebräer: Eine sozio-linguistische Studie über die Herkunft des Gentiliziums ibrî vom Appelativum habiru.* BZAW 160. Berlin: de Gruyter, 1984.

Maul, Stefan M. *Zukunftsbewältigung: Eine Untersuchung altorientalischen Denkens anhand der babylonisch-assyrischen Löserituale (Namburbi).* BagFor 18. Mainz: von Zaubern, 1994.

Mesters, Carlos. *Vom Leben zur Bibel, von der Bibel zum Leben.* 2 vols. Mainz: Grünewald, 1983.

Mettinger, Tryggve N. D. *In Search of God: The Meaning and Message of the Everlasting.* Translated by F. H. Cryer. Philadelphia: Fortress Press, 1988. (Swedish ed. 1987.)

Meyers, Carol, *Discovering Eve: Ancient Israelite Women in Context.* New York: Oxford Univ. Press, 1988.

———, editor. *Women in Scripture: A Dictionary of Named and Unnamed Women in the Hebrew Bible, the Apocryphal/Deuterocanonical Books, and the New Testament.* Boston: Houghton Mifflin, 2000.

Miller, Patrick D., Jr. *The Divine Warrior in Early Israel.* HSM 5. Cambridge: Harvard Univ. Press, 1973.

———. *Israelite Religion and Biblical Theology: Collected Essays.* JSOTSup 267. Sheffield: Sheffield Academic, 2000.

———. *The Religion of Ancient Israel.* LAI. Louisville: Westminster John Knox, 2000.

Miller, Patrick D., Jr., Paul D. Hanson, and S. Dean McBride, editors. *Ancient Israelite Religion: Essays in Honor of Frank Moore Cross.* Philadelphia: Fortress Press, 1987.

Niditch, Susan, *War in the Hebrew Bible: A Study in the Ethics of Violence.* New York: Oxford Univ. Press, 1993.

Niehr, Herbert. *Der höchste Gott: Alttestamentlicher JHWH-Glaube im Kon-*

text syrisch-kanaanäischer Religion des 1. Jahrtausends v. Chr. BZAW 190. Berlin: de Gruyter, 1990.

———. *Rechtsprechung in Israel: Untersuchungen zur Geschichte der Gerichtsorganisation im Alten Testament.* SBS 130. Stuttgart: Katholisches Bibelwerk, 1987.

———. *Religionen in Israels Umwelt: Einführung in die nordwestsemitischen Religionen Syrien-Palastinas.* NEB. Wurzburg: Echter, 1998

Niemann, Hermann M. *Herrschaft, Königtum und Staat: Skizzen zur soziokulturellen Entwicklung im monarchischen Israel.* FAT 6. Tübingen: Mohr/Siebeck, 1993.

Noth, Martin. *Das System der zwölf Stämme Israels.* BWANT 52. Stuttgart: Kohlhammer, 1930.

Oeming, Manfred. *Das wahre Israel: Die "genealogische Vorhalle" 1 Chronik 1–9.* BWANT 128. Stuttgart: Kohlhammer, 1990.

Otto, Eckart. *Theologische Ethik des Alten Testaments.* ThW 3,2. Stuttgart: Kohlhammer, 1994.

Perdue, Leo G. *The Collapse of History: Reconstructing Old Testament Theology.* OBT. Minneapolis: Fortress Press, 1994.

Perlitt, Lothar. *Bundestheologie im Alten Testament.* WMANT 36. Neukirchen-Vluyn: Neukirchener, 1969.

Preuss, Horst Dietrich. *Old Testament Theology.* OTL. Louisville: Westminster John Knox, 1995–96. (German ed. 1991–92.)

Rad, Gerhard von. *Old Testament Theology.* Translated by D. M. G. Stalker. 2 vols. New York: Harper & Row, 1962–65. Reprinted in OTL. Louisville: Westminster John Knox, 2001. (German ed. 1957–61.)

———. *Wisdom in Israel.* Translated by J. D. Martin. Nashville: Abingdon, 1972.

Rendtorff, Rolf. *Canon and Theology: Overtures to an Old Testament Theology.* Translated by M. Kohl. OBT. Minneapolis: Fortress Press, 1993. (German ed. 1991.)

———. *Theologie des Alten Testaments: Ein kanonischer Entwurf.* 2 vols. Neukirchen-Vluyn: Neukirchener, 1999–2001.

Ribeiro, Darcy. *The Civilization Process.* Translated by B. J. Meggers. Washington, D.C.: Smithsonian Institution Press, 1968.

Richter, Horst-Eberhard. *Patient Familie: Entstehung, Struktur und Therapie von Konflikten in Ehe und Familie.* Reinbek: Rowolt, 1970.

———. *All Mighty: A Study of the God Complex in Western Man.* Translated by J. van Heurck. San Bernadino, Calif.: Borgo, 1984 (German ed. 1979.)

Römheld, Diethard. *Die Weisheitslehre im Alten Orient.* Munich: M.Goerg, 1989.

Rose, Martin. *Der Ausschliesslichkeitsanspruch Jahwes: Deuteronomische Schultheologie und die Volksfrömmigkeit in der späten Königszeit.* BWANT 106. Stuttgart: Kohlhammer, 1975.

Rüterswörden, Udo. *Die Beamten der israelitischen Königszeit: Eine Studie zu sr und vergleichbaren Begriffen.* BWANT 117. Stuttgart: Kohlhammer, 1985.

Safrai, Shmuel. *Die Wallfahrt im Zeitalter des Zweiten Tempel.* FJCD 3. Neukirchen-Vluyn: Neukirchener, 1981.

Schäfer-Lichtenberger, Christa. *Stadt und Eidgenossenschaft im Alten Testament: Eine Auseinandersetzung mit Max Webers Studie "Das antike Judentum."* BZAW 156. Berlin: de Gruyter, 1986.

Schmidt, Werner H. *The Faith of the Old Testament: A History.* Philadelphia: Westminster, 1983. (5th German ed. 1987.)

———. *Die Zehn Gebote im Rahmen christlicher Ethik.* EdF 281. Darmstadt: Wissenschaftliche Buchgesellschaft, 1993.

Schoenborn, Ulrich. *Gekreuzigt im Leiden der Armen.* Mettingen: Brasilienkunde, 1985.

Schottroff, Luise, Sylvia Schroer, and Marie-Theres Wacker. *Feminist Interpretation: The Bible in Women's Perspective.* Translated by M. Rumscheidt and B. Rumscheidt. Minneapolis: Fortresss Press, 1998. (German ed. 1995.)

Schroer, Silvia. *In Israel gab es Bilder: Nachrichten von darstellender Kunst im Alten Testament.* OBO 74. Göttingen: Vandenhoeck & Ruprecht, 1987.

Schüngel-Straumann, Helen. *Die Frau am Anfang: Eva und die Folgen.* Frauenforum. 2nd ed. Freiburg: Herder, 1997.

Schulz, Hermann. *Stammesreligionen: Zur Kreativität des kulturellen Bewusstseins.* Stuttgart: Kohlhammer, 1993.

Schwab, Ulrich. *Familienreligiosität: Religiöse Traditionen im Prozess der Generationen.* PTH 23. Stuttgart: Kohlhammer, 1995.

Schwantes, Milton. *Sofrimento e Esperança no Exilio.* São Leopoldo: Sinodal, 1987.

Segbers, Franz. *Die Hausordnung der Tora.* Lucerne: Exodus, 1999.

Seifert, Elke. *Tochter und Vater im Alten Testament: Eine ideologiekritische Untersuchung zur Verfügungsgewalt von Vätern über ihre Töchter.* NTDH 9. Neukirchen-Vluyn: Neukirchener, 1997.

Sigrist, Christian. *Regulierte Anarchie: Untersuchung zum Fehlen und zur Entstehung politische Herrschaft in segmentären Gesellschaften Afrikas.* 2nd ed. Frankfurt: Syndikat, 1979.

Shostak, Marjorie. *Nisa: The Life and Words of a !Kung Woman.* Cambridge: Harvard Univ. Press, 1981.

Smith-Christopher, Daniel L. *A Biblical Theology of Exile.* OBT. Minneapolis: Fortress, 2002.

——. *Religion of the Landless: A Sociology of the Babylonian Exile.* Bloomington, Ind.: Meyer-Stone, 1989.

Smith, Mark S. *The Early History of God: Yahweh and the Other Deities in Ancient Israel.* 2nd ed. Grand Rapids: Eerdmans, 2002.

——. *The Origins of Biblical Monotheism: Israel's Polytheistic Background and the Ugaritic Texts.* New York: Oxford Univ. Press, 2001.

Spieckermann, Hermann. *Heilsgegenwart: Eine Theologie der Psalmen.* FRLANT 148. Göttingen: Vandenhoeck & Ruprecht, 1989.

Spronk, Klaas. *Beatific Afterlife in Ancient Israel and in the Ancient Near East.* AOAT 219. Neukirchen-Vluyn: Neukirchener, 1986.

Steck, Odil Hannes. *Friedensvorstellungen im alten Jerusalem: Psalmen, Jesaja, Deuterojesaja.* ThSt 111. Zurich: Theologischer Verlag, 1972.

Stolz, Fritz. *Strukturen und Figuren im Kult von Jerusalem: Studien zur altorientalischen, vor- und frühisraelitischen Religion.* BZAW 118. Berlin: de Gruyter, 1970.

Sung, Jung Mo. *Desejo, mereado e religião.* Petropolis: Vozes, 1998.

Thiel, Winfried. *Die soziale Entwicklung Israels in vorstaatlicher Zeit.* 2nd ed. Neukirchen-Vluyn: Neukirchener, 1985.

Tigay, Jeffrey H. *You Shall Have No Other Gods: Israelite Religion in the Light of Hebrew Inscriptions.* HSS 31. Atlanta: Scholars, 1986.

Toorn, Karel van der. *Family Religion in Babylonia, Syria and Israel: Continuity and Changes in the Forms of Religious Life.* SHCANE 7. Leiden: Brill, 1996.

Trible, Phyllis. *God and the Rhetoric of Sexuality.* OBT. Philadelphia: Fortress Press, 1978.

Uehlinger, Christoph. *Weltreich und "eine Rede": Eine neue Deutung der sogenannten Turmbauerzählung (Gen 11, 1-9).* OBO 101. Göttingen: Vandenhoeck & Ruprecht, 1991.

Underhill, Ruth M. *Red Man's Religion: Beliefs and Practices of the Indians*

North of Mexico. Chicago: Univ. of Chicago Press, 1965.

Veijola, Timo. *Verheissung in der Krise: Studien zur Literatur und Theologie der Exilszeit anhand des 89. Psalms.* AASF B/220. Helsinki: Suomalainen Tiedeakatemia, 1982.

Wacker, Marie-Theres, editor. *Der Gott der Männer und die Frauen.* Theologie zur Zeit 2. Düsseldorf: Patomos, 1987.

Weber, Max. *Ancient Judaism.* Translated by H. H. Gerth and D. Martindale. Glencoe, Ill.: Free Press, 1952. (6th German ed. 1976.)

Weinfeld, Moshe. *Social Justice in Ancient Israel and in the Ancient Near East.* Minneapolis: Fortress Press, 1995.

Weippert, Helga. *Palästina in vorhellenistischer Zeit.* Handbüch der Archäologie 2/1. Munich: Beck, 1988.

Wilhelm, Gernot, editor. *Die orientalische Stadt: Kontinuität, Wandel, Bruch. 1. Internationales Colloquium der Deutschen Orient-Gesellschaft, 9.-10. Mai 1996 in Halle/Saale.* Colloquien der Deutschen Orient-Gesellschaft 1. Saarbrücken: SDV, 1997.

Wilson, Robert R. *Prophecy and Society in Ancient Israel.* Philadelphia: Fortress Press, 1980.

Zadok, Ran, *The Jews in Babylonia during the Chaldean and Achaemenian Periods according to the Babylonian Sources.* Studies in the History of the Jewish People and the Land of Israel Monograph Series 3. Haifa: Univ. of Haifa Press, 1979.

Zevit, Ziony. *The Religions of Ancient Israel: A Synthesis of Parallactic Approaches.* New York: Continuum, 2001.

Zwickel, Wolfgang. *Räucherkult und Räuchergeräte: Exegetische und archäologische Studien zum Räucheropfer im Alten Testament.* OBO 97. Göttingen: Vandenhoeck & Ruprecht, 1990.

Index of Biblical References

Index of Modern Authors